"In
give
dist

ltensky
ople in
kinds."

"Th
latic
and
proj

nd re-
ctical,
g, and

"Th
and
Opt
selo
clie

earch,
Risks,
coun-
ng for

"Pr
too
holi
get
wha

s, and
uitably
ch to-
t that

stralia

"W , this book provides a
framework and some easily understood tools that will allow you to bring the power of
their approach to the challenges of your work."

— Judge Andy Shookhoff
Associate Director
Vanderbilt Child and Family Policy Center

"Isaac and Ora Prillentensky have written an astonishingly creative, timely, and important book about the determinants of well-being and about ways to promote and protect

it. All of us in the health field struggle to transcend our disciplinary silos and we all know how difficult it is to succeed. Isaac and Ora help us to see the interconnectedness of our personal, community, and organizational lives; and they demonstrate in refreshingly clear and practical ways how we can integrate these dimensions of our lives. This book could not have come at a better time."

—S. Leonard Syme, PhD
Professor of Epidemiology and Community Health (Emeritus),
School of Public Health
University of California, Berkeley

"Whether you are a psychologist, social worker, policy maker, physician, organizational consultant, philanthropist, government official, or community organizer, this book will help you understand well-being in new and important ways. The unique integration of the personal, organizational, and collective in promoting well-being is the way of the future, and the Prilleltenskys are leading the way."

—Dr David Morawetz
Clinical and Counselling Psychologist
Founder and Director, Morawetz Social Justice Fund
Melbourne, Australia

"The approach taken by the Drs. Prilleltensky is to invite the reader into a rich, stimulating conversation, conveying a level of warmth and intimacy that is unique and highly engaging."

—Ellen Hawley McWhirter, PhD
Associate Professor
Director of Training, Counseling Psychology Program
College of Education
University of Oregon

"Thoughtful attention is paid to inequality, corruption, and resulting poor health. Most interesting to me were the successes of the Nordic cooperative societies that focused on education and social equality and the failures of competitive corporate consumer societies. While the issues are complicated, the tone is informal, conversational, and easy to read. The book is an original and creative effort to tie together a broad range of forces relevant to well-being."

—George W. Albee, PhD
Emeritus Professor, University of Vermont
Former President, American Psychological Association

"The United Way system is committed to broadening its mission to change community conditions leading to suffering, in addition to addressing the human service needs of individuals. The work of the Prilleltenskys, as presented in *Promoting Well-Being*, has come to life in our transformation and has been a significant part of the success we have had to date and expect to continue to have."

—Mark H. Desmond
President and CEO
United Way of Metropolitan Nashville

"This book introduces ideas and strategies for wellness: personal, organisational, and community, to a wider and needy public."

—Dale Guy
Area Service Director
Child Guidance Clinic of Winnipeg, Canada

"This is an eloquent book, broad in scope and ambition, that moves deftly between individual, organizational, and community perspectives to help us understand and promote all dimensions of well-being. Refusing to work with simple explanations and prescriptions, the Prilleltenskys draw on current events, scholarship, and wonderful real-life anecdotes to provide a sweeping and comprehensive picture of what it would take to achieve well-being in our lives, our institutions, and our social systems. This is a 'must read.' It is a blueprint for action for counselors, consultants, community organizers, and human service providers interested in individual and social change."

—Lisa Goodman
Associate Professor of Counseling,
Department of Counseling and Developmental Psychology,
School of Educations
Boston College

"Isaac and Ora Prilleltensky have written a necessary book. A book wanted not only in academic libraries but in the workrooms of practitioners, students, and people interested in introducing in their lives, not the concept of 'well-being,' but its practice."

—Maritza Montero
Coordinator, Doctorate Studies in Psychology
Universidad Central de Venezuela
Caracas, Venezuela

"From the micro to the macro levels, there is something in this book for students, practitioners, and the general public interested in pursuing well-being in families, clinics, workplaces, communities, and government. This book succeeds in bringing together fields that for too long have remained separate."

—Amiram Raviv, PhD
Professor and former Department Chair, Psychology Department
Tel-Aviv University
Former Chief Psychologist at the Israeli Ministry of Education

"This is an optimistic book that is clearly and persuasively written, using a wealth of psychological knowledge. The Prilleltenskys use humour and real life examples to demonstrate their points. The argument is grounded in serious psychological research and includes practical exercises for moving ahead."

—Jenny Sharples, PhD
Director, Wellness Promotion Unit
Victoria University, Melbourne, Australia

"*Promoting Well-Being* is the right book on a neglected topic. This book is outstanding on several counts: not only considers personal origins and effects of well-being, but also the relational and social; balances analysis and action, scientific causes and moral reasons. It also makes great efforts to integrate the different aspects and levels of wellness in a meaningful, amenable to practice way, trying to make compatible a wide-scoped multifactorial analysis with a practical, action-oriented focus."

—Alipio Sanchez Vidal
Professor of Ethics and Community Psychology
Universidad de Barcelona

"This book provides a refreshing perspective on well-being—moving away from individualistic and deficit-oriented positions, toward a comprehensive understanding of how organizations and communities affect our sense of well-being. The book reflects a world-view that emphasizes interdependence and optimism about our capacity and duty to care and support one another. I agree with the authors that critical awareness has to become a central component of any efforts to overcome oppression and exploitation, and such awareness can lead people to take steps to transform their own social reality. This book has many practical lessons and applications that students and practitioners would enjoy."

—Fabricio E. Balcazar, PhD
Professor, Department of Disability and Human Development
University of Illinois at Chicago

"The Prilleltenskys' bold and wise work make it clear that our efforts to nourish personal psychological well-being in the 21st century have to consider the health of our relationships within the groups and communities we are a part. This book is both theoretically astute and eminently practical, inviting the reader through exercises to put into practice the models for working on personal, organization, and community well being that are discussed. A clear, concise work, replete with moving examples, *Promoting Well-Being* brings us into the heart of a more interdependent paradigm of healing."

—Mary Watkins, PhD
Pacifica Graduate Institute

Promoting Well-Being

Linking Personal, Organizational, and Community Change

Isaac Prilleltensky

and

Ora Prilleltensky

WILEY

John Wiley & Sons, Inc.

To our son, Matan, the gift of our life.

Contents

Preface

Who are we? If you bought this book (thank you), you deserve to know who wrote it. If you are considering buying it, you need to know why you should spend some of your money on our work. Ora is a licensed counselor with a doctorate in counseling psychology. She is also a wheelchair user, who has lived for most of her adult life with a physical disability. Isaac is a community psychologist. Prior to that, he was a clinician working with children, youth, and families. Each of us has over 20 years of experience in the helping professions, working with children, youth, and adults in schools, clinics, rehabilitation settings, and universities. We have consulted with numerous government and nongovernment agencies in several countries. We have worked with individuals, families, organizations, communities, and governments in four countries: Israel, Canada, Australia, and the United States, in chronological order. We have also published quite extensively in the field. Now we are both academics at Peabody College of Vanderbilt University. Ora teaches in the Master's of Counseling Program and Isaac directs the PhD Program in Community Research and Action. Our son, Matan, who has taught us much about everything we know, is a student at Clark University. If you really want to know more about us (though we really don't see why), just Google us or go to www.vanderbilt.edu. But enough about us. Now about you.

For whom did we write this book? This is a book for helping professionals in the health and human services, for organizational and community practitioners, counselors, therapists, educators, consultants, managers, psychologists, nurses, social workers, and just about anyone who is concerned with the promotion of well-being in individuals, groups, organizations, and communities. We immodestly think we have something to say about that.

Why did we write this book? Because we have chutzpah (well, at least Isaac does). Beyond that, we saw a need to integrate individual, organizational, and community approaches to the promotion of well-being. For too long, counselors, organizational consultants, and community practitioners have been working in isolation, depriving themselves of insights and opportunities to be more effective and holistic in their work. We felt the need to offer a conceptual framework that would transcend parochial understandings of well-being and dogmatic solutions to complex problems.

What can you expect in this book? A user-friendly treatment of how personal well-being is intimately connected to the well-being of organizations and communities, and some guidelines to pursue communal, organizational, and individual well-being at the same time. You can also find many stories, examples, and exercises designed to bring theory and research as close to your life experience as possible (or so we hope). We strove to write an accessible book that would illustrate the power of thinking and acting on several levels at the same time. We hope this book can help students and professionals integrate values with science in their pursuit of well-being.

What was it like writing this book together? It seemed like a good idea at the time . . . but we still love each other.

ISAAC and ORA PRILLELTENSKY

Nashville (How did we get here?)
February 2006

By the time this book is out, we will have moved to the University of Miami in Florida. Ora will be working in the Department of Educational and Psychological Studies, and Isaac will be the dean of the School of Education.

July 2006

Acknowledgments

Many of the stories and examples we use in the book derive from individuals and organizations that shall remain nameless due to confidentiality. In some cases, we name a few organizations who have given us permission to do so. We are very grateful to all the individuals and groups who have allowed us to be a part of their lives, even if for a short period of time. We have been privileged to work with extraordinary people in various countries. We have learned a great deal from our colleagues and partners in the pursuit of well-being.

We want to thank especially our son, who provided so much material for this book. He is truly a mensch, a compassionate, generous, vivacious, spirited, smart, one-of-a-kind kid who doesn't call his parents often enough.

We have learned a great deal from our students. Graduate students at Vanderbilt University in the New SPECs project in particular have been a source of inspiration and learning. Kimberly Bess and Scot Evans have enriched Isaac's understanding of organizational well-being in many ways. Leslie Collins, Patricia Conway, Carrie Hanlin, Diana McCown, and Courte Voorhees have contributed greatly to the success of the New SPECs project, as have scores of undergraduate and other graduate students interning with us. Their commitment and dedication are second to none. It has also been a privilege working with my esteemed colleagues Bob Newbrough and Doug Perkins on this project.

Since coming to Nashville, we have struck up many friendships with colleagues in the health and human services field. In particular, we have been inspired by the work of Jane Fleishman, Judy Freudenthal, and Hal Cato from Oasis Youth Center, Inc. Isaac has also benefited from his collaboration with Mark Desmond, president and CEO of the United Way of Metropolitan Nashville. Marsha Edwards and Christine Jackson of the Martha O'Bryan Center have also been wonderful collaborators. They have all supported our work and encouraged us to pursue, in partnership, a new paradigm for community health and human services in the pursuit of well-being.

Sherrie Lane, our graduate secretary in the Department of Human and Organizational Development at Vanderbilt University, has helped Isaac in many big and small ways. Thank you, Sherrie.

Our editors at Wiley were very professional and helpful in their handling of our book. We want to thank Katherine Willert, editorial assistant, and Lisa Gebo, senior editor.

We also want to thank the publishers listed below for allowing us to re-produce a few tables and figures from our earlier publications:

- Lawrence Erlbaum for Tables 9.1 and 9.2 (original source: "Value-Based Leadership in Organizations," by I. Prilleltensky, 2000, *Ethics and Behavior*, *10*(2), p. 139)
- Palgrave Macmillan for Tables 13.1 and 13.3 (original source: *Community Psychology: In Pursuit of Liberation and Well-Being*, by G. Nelson and I. Prilleltensky (Eds.), 2005, New York: Palgrave)
- Taylor and Francis for Figures 2.1, 2.2, and 2.3 (original source: "Promoting Well-Being: Time for a Paradigm Shift in Health and Human Services," by I. Prilleltensky, 2005, *Scandinavian Journal of Public Health*, 33, pp. 53–60)

I

Mapping Well-Being

The four chapters in this part answer, respectively, *where*, *what*, *why*, and *how* questions about well-being. Chapter 1 suggests that well-being is situated in individuals, organizations, and communities. To promote one, you need to promote the others. To understand one, you need to understand all of them. Our basic premise is that individual well-being cannot be fostered in isolation from the organizations that affect our lives and the communities where we live. Promoting personal well-being in isolation is inefficient. Personal, organizational, and community well-being exist in a tight web of reciprocal influences. The first chapter situates well-being in individuals, organizations, and communities and in the links that tie them together.

The opening chapter frames well-being in terms of five **S**s: **S**ite, **S**ign, **S**ource, **S**trategy, and **S**ynergy. Sites refer to the location of well-being, whereas signs refer to the expressions of it. Sources are the determinants of well-being, and strategies are simply ways to enhance it. Synergy is the confluence of sites, signs, sources, and strategies. Synergy pertains to our synergic understanding and our synergic actions.

Chapter 2 deals with a *what* question: What is it that we're specifically trying to promote? What is the paradigm that we want to advance? The answer lies in the acronym SPEC: Strengths, Prevention, Empowerment, and Changing Conditions. We formulate a new paradigm for health and human services based on these four principles. Our prescription is an antidote for deficit-oriented, reactive, alienating, and ecologically insensitive approaches that hope to promote community or organizational well-being one person at a time.

The third chapter answers a *why* question: Why promote personal, organizational, and community well-being? This is a values issue. We postulate values for personal, organizational, and community well-being and discuss their interdependence. Our approach to well-being is firmly grounded in a value-based perspective.

Where, what, why, and now *how*. In Chapter 4 we suggest promoting well-being through I VALUE IT roles. The letters stand for **I**nclusive host, **V**isionary, **A**sset seeker, **L**istener, **U**nique solution finder, **E**valuator, **I**mplementer, and **T**rendsetter. By enacting these eight roles, professionals and helpers of any kind can make a difference in the lives of individuals, organizations, and communities. We use this model throughout the book and attach to the roles specific strategies and techniques for change in various contexts.

We think of each chapter as a web: webs of wellness, growth, values, and strategies. Together, these four chapters lay the foundation for the promotion of well-being.

1

Webs of Wellness: The Sites of Well-Being

Sister Margaret was a 72-year-old nun who was suffering from persisting back pain. She was accepted at an outpatient pain management program where I, Ora, was providing psychological consultation. Due to my hectic schedule, I was unable to see Margaret until she was well into her physiotherapy and occupational therapy program. In fact, I was told that she had made significant physical gains and would be discharged from the program in the coming weeks. It was unlikely that I would need to see her beyond the initial screening.

As it turned out, Margaret and I met for some eight counseling sessions. I took an immediate liking to her and appreciated her openness and willingness to share her life story. Margaret, who had never been to a psychologist before, confirmed that her physical pain had significantly subsided. Nonetheless, she had some issues in her life that were weighing her down and causing significant distress. She welcomed the opportunity to explore them.

Over the next 8 weeks, I was privileged to hear about Margaret's life in a Catholic mission. With four other nuns, she was sharing a small house owned by the parish. They were all assigned to live there by a central committee in charge of housing. According to the custom in that congregation, the cooking, cleaning, and other household tasks were shared among the housemates. Meals were eaten together, and weekly meetings were held to discuss the budget, plan the week ahead, and make joint decisions. Most of the day was dedicated to different aspects of community work and social action.

I am sharing this with you as it provides the backdrop for Margaret's struggle for personal, organizational, and community well-being. Margaret committed her life to serving God and the community. Working as a public health nurse until her retirement, she was highly committed to serving underprivileged members of the community. In addition to her nursing job, she volunteered her time for various social justice initiatives. Margaret certainly gave to her community.

Yet, Margaret was unhappy and frustrated when she came to see me. She told me about the deaths of her brother and a close friend in the past year. She told me about how she now spends most of her time in the house as she is no longer working and is unsure what contribution she can make. Most important, Margaret told me about the distress associated with her current living arrangement.

Of the four women she was house-sharing with, Margaret was close to one, on agreeable terms with two others, and at great odds with the fourth. The more she talked about this conflictive relationship and the distress that it was causing, the more apparent it became that these issues were never properly addressed. These women, who were assigned to live together by an organizational committee, had no tools to address their differences and resolve conflict.

Ironically, the high value attributed to harmony and the greater good stood in the way of personal and organizational well-being. Margaret told me that in the weekly meetings, nothing of substance was discussed, no feelings were shared, and feedback was never offered. In fact, Margaret reasoned that the congregation had totally neglected members' need for control over their lives, for emotional connectedness, and for personal validation.

Throughout our work together, Margaret and I searched for ways to enhance psychological wellness at the personal, organizational, and community levels. She decided that it was time to make some changes in the overall philosophy of the congregation, placing greater emphasis on personal empowerment, agency, and control. We planned how she could approach those at the top of the organizational hierarchy with her suggestions. On the interpersonal front, Margaret was determined to instigate some in-house changes.

Things had gotten so bad that she was uncomfortable making references to her back problems and was doing chores that were clearly counterindicated for her condition. We discussed the irony of living with people who are committed to equality and justice on the outside and who are oblivious to the needs of those on the inside.

Margaret took great interest in some of the resources I lent her on interpersonal communication and problem solving. We discussed the possibility that part of each weekly house meeting would be dedicated to sharing feelings and giving constructive feedback. She thought that this might work, especially if strengths were acknowledged and positive feedback was also provided.

What about community well-being? Margaret had been finding some of her house chores exhausting and often had back pain as a result. We reasoned that a redistribution of tasks was called for. Some of the younger housemates would take on the more physically demanding chores, affording

Margaret more time and energy to pursue community work. Margaret thought that this would work, as the problems were never really about chores but about poor interpersonal and organizational communication.

We began to discuss Margaret's reinvolvement in the community work that she so valued and missed. I have to say that I was of relatively little help to her in this domain. Margaret could teach me, and I suspect many others, about ways to contribute to one's community.

Sister Margaret's story says a great deal about the three main topics of this book: personal, organizational, and community change for well-being. Her story shows the interdependence of these three facets of life. Her personal well-being was being diminished by the lack of organizational wellness in her living arrangements. Community well-being, a big part of her life, was also being affected by her health and emotional state. The more she contributed to community well-being, the better she felt.

WHY THIS BOOK?

Personal, organizational, and community change influence each other in multiple ways. If we want to promote one, we need to know about the others. If we want to understand one, we need to understand how they all interact. This is the mission of this book: to understand how personal, organizational, and community well-being are part of a web, a web of wellness. A change in one affects the others; an improvement in one increases the chances of betterment in others. Building on knowledge about networks and interactions, we want to show how personal, organizational, and community change can work in unison to enhance the well-being of individuals and the community alike.

The lessons we want to share can be helpful to those working with people in multiple contexts and settings: health and human services, schools, community agencies, businesses, universities, government and nongovernment organizations, grassroots movements, and in general all people who have an interest in promoting their own well-being and the health and prosperity of others.

If you're in the helping business, we hope you will find here strategies that go beyond the dogmatic application of theories and practices that concentrate on single sources of well-being. Wellness is a complicated issue that defies simplistic explanations and magic solutions. Yet, we believe a methodical and comprehensive approach to wellness can help us get unstuck, individually, organizationally, and collectively.

Missed Opportunities

Many problems have biological, social, and economic roots. People suffer because of lack of resources and power inequality, but also because of psychological put-downs, verbal and emotional abuse, and plain disrespect.

There is good reason to make health and the economy social priorities; people require these resources to meet basic needs. But it would be a mistake to neglect the importance of psychological wellness, for the lack of it is costing us millions of dollars in health care and lost productivity, not to mention immeasurable psychological pain.

There is much to be gained from educating ourselves about the benefits of empathy, effective communication, and social skills. We teach children all kinds of things, but we neglect psychological wellness: how to deal with personal feelings like anger, frustration, and aggression; how to listen to others without judging; how to cry without feeling guilty.

No, we're not suggesting that psychological wellness is a panacea for our social ills, nor that it should be our single focus of attention. But the fact is that we have a great deal of knowledge about how to improve human relationships that we don't use. There is a tremendous body of research that informs the development of psychological wellness, but it is largely wasted. As a society, we don't have a plan for systematically developing interpersonal and psychological health. There is a huge gap between what we know and what we do in families, schools, and the workplace.

Many problems could be prevented if we methodically fostered psychological wellness in families, schools, and jobs. Families are ideal places for the promotion of emotional wellness. Unfortunately, many parents are not equipped to teach it to their children because they lack it themselves. We know that a secure attachment is crucial for psychological development, that consistent rules with emotional support are highly beneficial, and that family cohesion protects children against adversity. However, secure attachments, effective parenting, and family harmony are not easy to come by.

Although parenting courses are offered to the public, not all parents realize how crucial it is to learn from others and to obtain support in this lifelong endeavor. In Sweden, there is a major national campaign to teach parenting throughout the life cycle. In Ontario, Canada, there is currently a push to make parenting courses mandatory in schools.

Schools are another ideal site for the development of psychological wellness. We have no doubt that many teachers foster in children interpersonal respect, sensitivity to others, and the desire for conflict resolution. Their excellent efforts notwithstanding, this type of instruction is rarely systematic or an integral part of the regular curriculum. Social and emotional learning improves school climate and tolerance, reduces bullying, and helps children to resist pressure to smoke, drink, and engage in premature sex. Yet, we're still waiting for these findings to be implemented and institutionalized.

Interpersonal conflict at work is a major source of stress for millions of people. Insensitive bosses, inflexible rules, and weak leadership are major causes of aggravation. People stay home because of conflict, go to incredible lengths to avoid certain people at work, endure put-downs, and suffer from negative working environments. Many people in positions of authority don't have a clue how to treat others. Workplaces should do much more than they currently do to train managers and workers in psychological wellness.

Interpersonal harm cannot be completely prevented, but much can be done to curtail it. Both of us have seen firsthand the pain that interpersonal harm can cause and the benefits that prevention can bring. To improve personal well-being, we need to intervene at the organizational and community levels. It is not enough to undertake one-on-one therapy, however helpful that might be. As we shall see in this book, community changes can lead to more equality, more justice, and more respect for diversity.

Sins of Omission, Sins of Commission

Each of us, Ora and Isaac, has more than 20 years of experience working as psychologists, counselors, teachers in schools and universities, and consultants in organizations and government. We have worked in clinics, counseling centers, rehabilitation hospitals, schools, and universities in four countries: Israel, Canada, Australia, and the United States. Wherever we have worked, we have witnessed sins of omission and sins of commission.

We have felt these sins not only in our professional lives, but in our personal lives as well. How often do we fail to attend to a child's need for attention? How often do we neglect to inquire about a peer's well-being? People close to us make affectionate gestures that we ignore because we're too busy or preoccupied. These are sins of omission.

What about sins of commission? Are you sick of people telling you how to live your life? For us, a sin of commission is when others try to shape or control your life in ways that don't make sense or don't feel right for you. How many people have given you unsolicited advice or tried to impose on you a point of view that didn't respect who you are or didn't appreciate your emotional state? In Isaac's case, the worst unsolicited advice he ever got was to "be a man" and not to cry.

We are very concerned with one-size-fits-all therapies and types of advice that don't respect your unique situation. Have you ever shared a problem with a friend or professional helper, only to find out that this person was so eager to give you advice that he or she didn't even listen to the whole story? Details are important. General advice that doesn't seriously consider your unique personality or family situation doesn't work. We've seen this time and time again in our professional and personal lives.

Some of our counseling students are so eager to give advice that they sometimes jump to conclusions before the client has had a chance to share the whole story. Yet, they wholeheartedly admit that what they value most is for others to listen to them without interruptions. Our friends sometimes respond judgmentally to some of our decisions because of their personal issues, not because our decision is necessarily wrong. Some of them hasten to offer advice that is based not on our needs but on theirs. Not only that, some of the advice we get is based on others' insecurities, unfinished business, or projections or other defense mechanisms that reflect their own unresolved issues and not ours.

We're also very concerned about prefabricated advice. A cookie-cutter type of help is not suitable for human beings. We're not as malleable as dough, nor are we like the previous cookie. And one-line mantras don't fit into our lives because our lives can't be reduced to one line.

We doubt we're beyond reproach ourselves, though. Both of us have offered plenty of unsolicited advice to our son. We're sure that Matan, our 19-year-old son, has had to endure more than his fair share of parental sins, which probably accounts for his occasional parental deafness.

To overcome sins of commission we need an antidote for arrogance. To overcome sins of omission we need antidotes for blindness and passivity. Both of us have developed some antidotes. For the sin of arrogance, we try not to make assumptions about people before we know them well. We don't presume to know more than we do, and we refrain from giving advice that doesn't suit the person or the occasion. Although sometimes we think a particular opinion may help somebody, we know that the timing may not be right. If the timing is not right, the person won't be in the right frame of mind to hear or assimilate the advice. Finally, we try not to commit character assassinations by telling clients or colleagues that they are "defensive," "immature," or "fixated" on certain issues.

To avoid the sins of blindness and passivity we try to see beyond the obvious, and we try to act beyond the comfortable. As a psychologist, a counselor, consultant, friend, or a parent, it's very easy to ascribe emotional problems to the person in front of you. After all, she is the person seeking advice or making your life miserable. But the person in front of you may be reacting to family or social circumstances that are bringing her down, not to some deep-seated psychological trauma we should cure. Furthermore, she may be reacting to the fact that *you* are making her life miserable!

We have to see people in context. No matter how strong our tendency to blame people for their misfortune, we should see the personal, interpersonal, organizational, and social components of their problems.

In fact, it's always comfortable to think of problems in terms of other people's psychological issues because they don't require us to change something about ourselves, our family, or our society. Our friends and relatives are uncomfortable when our behavior doesn't suit their expectations. Does that mean we have to change our behavior, or that they have to change their expectations? When Isaac became a vegetarian, his Argentinian meat-eating family had a hard time accepting his new habit.

To overcome the threat of passivity, we have to think about helping people on their own terms. Furthermore, we have to think about help that addresses the psychological, the interpersonal, and the social as well, even if it goes against the received wisdom that "it's all in your head."

A little bit of knowledge is a dangerous thing. If all we have is a hammer, all our problems are going to look like nails. If we know how to use only a psychological hammer, all our sources of suffering will look like psychological nails. We favor a holistic approach that incorporates a range of theories and techniques and that tries to match the solution to the problem, not the other way around: trying to make everything look like nails because all we've got is a hammer. To move beyond our comfort zone we have to contemplate various sources of suffering and multiple ways of addressing them.

How, you ask, is our toolbox different? We believe in your own expertise and in your ability to create a path of wellness for yourself and others. We think we all need help in seeing things more clearly, in avoiding arrogance, in illuminating blind spots, and in moving beyond our comfort zones. Our approach to wellness builds on personal, organizational, and community change to promote personal, organizational, and community well-being at the same time. It's not one or the other: It's the collective synergy that makes for holistic wellness.

It's not enough to be free of anxieties, fears, and obsessions to experience psychological wellness. We need to experience satisfaction in relationships, and we need to live in thriving communities. Many approaches to emotional health fail to grasp the importance of social settings.

Psychological changes often need to be accompanied by changes in families, relationships, organizations, and communities. We often blame victims and expect them to change something within themselves when in fact something external, oppressing them, needs to be changed. When we struggle to change the social context we help ourselves by feeling empowered and in control of our lives. In this book, we go beyond the personal, the interpersonal, and the social. We integrate the three perspectives to offer a holistic view of wellness. Throughout the book we search for psychological wellness in unlikely places that combine the personal, the organizational, and the collective. What we invariably find is that psychological wellness is always better promoted and better preserved when personal, organizational, and community needs come together at once.

THE FIVE Ss OF WELL-BEING: SITE, SIGN, SOURCE, STRATEGY, AND SYNERGY

We can talk about the well-being of a person, an organization, or a community. These are different *sites* where well-being takes place. We can tell by certain signs if each one of these sites or places is experiencing well-being. A sign of personal well-being is a sense of control over your life, something that Sister Margaret had in short supply. Many decisions about her life were being made by the organization, without a lot of input from her. Physical health is another sign of personal well-being. Sister Margaret was suffering from physical pain that also diminished her well-being.

Worker participation in decision making is a sign of organizational well-being. Good communication among workers and colleagues is another. Clear roles and productivity are also important signs of organizational well-being. Sister Margaret's organization was definitely not showing some of these signs. Communication among housemates and with the church was poor.

A clean environment, freedom from discrimination, safe neighborhoods, good schools, and employment opportunities are signs of community well-being. These are communal goods that benefit everyone. Sister Margaret worked with the poor, a group that is often deprived of these resources.

The next S stands for *sources*. Personal, organizational, and community well-being derive from a variety of sources. Experiences of mastery and success contribute to self-esteem and personal well-being, and participatory structures, clear roles, and efficient practices bring about organizational wellness. Community well-being, in turn, derives from multiple sources, such as a sense of cohesion, belonging, equality, universal access to health care, and democratic traditions.

The fourth S is for *strategies*. To promote well-being in each of the sites of interest—persons, organizations, and communities—we need a plan of action. Sister Margaret chose to discuss the division of labor in the house and made a decision to communicate better her concerns. She also worked on her physical ailments and had some ideas about promoting community well-being among the poor and disadvantaged.

Synergy, the fifth S, comes about when we combine an understanding of sources and strategies. In accord with the concept of webs, the best results for any one site of wellness come about when we work on all fronts at the same time. Sister Margaret could not improve her back unless she addressed the organizational communication problems, nor could she improve her mood while feeling isolated. Personal solutions often include organizational solutions. Organizational solutions, in turn, are supported by collective norms of respect for the well-being of workers and by communal expectations of ethical practice. When collective norms weaken, corporations and public institutions cease to be responsive to community needs. Personal, organizational, and community solutions are closely linked. We create synergy among various solutions when we address a problem on multiple fronts at the same time.

If you work in human services, you know the experience of working with clients on a strategy, only to see it diminished by overwhelming social forces. How far can you go in helping a teenager feel safer when he goes back to a crime-infested neighborhood? How effectively can we curb violence against women when the media and the culture are full of it? Collective problems require collective solutions.

Although there are things we can do to help people individually, such as making fitness plans, offering assertiveness training, and teaching communication skills, many of these problems are organizational and communal, and as a result they demand organizational and communal solutions. This book is about ways to tackle personal, organizational, and communal issues at the same time. We have tried doing one at a time, and it hasn't worked very well. It surely hasn't worked for many of the problems that health and human service workers face, problems such as child abuse, addictions, poverty, diabetes, crime, teenage pregnancy, gang violence, poor parenting, educational underachievement, obesity, and unemployment. The time has come to address problems comprehensively and synergistically. Research has shown that the mere act of working with others on collective problems can improve self-esteem, self-efficacy, social support, and empowerment. It is not only the outcome that matters, but the process itself (Nelson, Lord, & Ochocka, 2001). Of course we wish to be successful in our efforts to eliminate child abuse and violence against women, but even if results are not readily apparent, we, and all the people who struggle against these issues, derive personal benefits from the struggle itself. This is in part how the helper-therapy principle operates: I help myself by helping others—in my family, my circle of friends, and the community (Reissman, 1965).

To promote well-being we need an understanding of its main constituents. To recap: Well-being consists of sites, signs, sources, strategies, and synergy. There are three primary sites of well-being (personal, organizational, and collective), each of which has specific signs or manifestations, sources or determinants, and strategies. Once we understand what well-being is all about, we can identify the most promising approaches to its maximization.

Various traditions within the health and social sciences have concentrated on either personal or collective correlates as manifestations of well-being. Whereas psychology has focused on subjective reports of happiness, well-being, and psychological wellness (Seligman, 2002), sociology and public health have focused on collective and objective measures, such as longevity and infant mortality (Marmot & Wilkinson, 1999). A group of medical sociologists and investigators has also concentrated on the importance of relationships, an important part of personal and organizational well-being (Berkman, 1995). Our claim is that well-being is not one or the other, but rather the combination of personal, organizational, and collective sites, signs, sources, and strategies of well-being (Nelson & Prilleltensky, 2005). In other words, well-being is not either personal, organizational, or collective, but the integration of them all. For any one of these spheres—personal, organizational, or collective—to experience well-being, the other two need to be in equally good shape.

In our view, well-being is a positive state of affairs, brought about by the synergistic satisfaction of personal, organizational, and collective needs of individuals, organizations, and communities alike. There cannot be well-being but in the combined presence of personal, organizational, and collective wellness (I. Prilleltensky & Nelson, 2002). We use well-being and wellness interchangeably in this book, and we refer to psychological well-ness as a state of affairs in which the person feels that his or her personal, organizational, and collective needs are fulfilled. Of course, these definitions beg the question "What are the needs of well-being at each one of the personal, organizational, and collective levels?" Table 1.1 shows the main needs that we have to fulfill to experience personal, organizational, and community well-being. In addition, Table 1.1 displays the values associated with each one of these needs. Needs require actions, and actions require values to guide them. We uphold these values to promote, morally and re-sponsibly, actions that meet the needs for well-being. Without them we could not know what the most ethical way to behave is.

Sites of Well-Being

As noted earlier, sites refer to the location of well-being. Here we concern ourselves with *where* well-being is situated. We maintain that there are three primary sites of well-being: individual persons, organizations, and communities or collectives. Although we can distinguish among the well-being of a person, an organization, and a community, they are highly interdependent. Each of these entities is unique and dependent on the others at the same time. None can be subsumed under the others, nor can they exist in isolation. They are distinguishable sites, but inseparable entities all the same. Figure 1.1 makes it clear that the three sites of well-being are separate but interconnected at the same time. Well-being is like a three-legged stool: Take any one of the legs, and the stool collapses.

There is empirical evidence to suggest that the well-being of relation-ships in informal and formal organizations such as families and work has beneficial effects on individuals (Ornish, 1998). Likewise, there is a wealth of research documenting the deleterious consequences for individuals of de-prived communities and the advantageous consequences of prosperous communities (Hofrichter, 2003).

Communities as sites of well-being embody such characteristics as af-fordable housing, clean air, accessible transportation, and high-quality health care and education. All these factors take place in the physical space of communities. Organizations, in turn, are sites where exchanges of mate-rial (money, physical help) and psychological (affection, caring, nurturance) resources and goods occur. People work for money, but not only for money. Exchanges of affirmation and appreciation, in both informal and formal or-ganizations, are a vital part of participation in organizations. Persons,

Table 1.1 Basic Needs and Values for Personal, Organizational, and Community Well-Being

Basic Considerations	Sites of Well-Being					
	Personal Well-Being		Organizational Well-Being		Community Well-Being	
Needs	Mastery, control, self-efficacy, voice and choice, skills, growth, spirituality	Emotional and physical well-being	Effectiveness, sustainability, productivity, clear roles	Participation, involvement, dignity, and respect for identity	Sense of community, cohesion, formal support	Economic security, shelter, clothing, nutrition, access to vital health and social services
Values	Self-determination, freedom, and personal growth	Health, caring, and compassion	Accountability and responsiveness to common good, transparency	Collaboration and democratic participation, respect for human diversity	Support for community structures	Social justice
Definition of values	Promotion of ability of children and adults to pursue chosen goals in life	Protection of physical and emotional health, expression of caring and support	Promotion of transparent ethical behavior and procedures to protect and uphold the well-being of all stakeholders affected by an organization's activities	Promotion of fair processes whereby children and adults can have meaningful input into decisions affecting their lives, respect for diverse social identities	Promotion of vital community structures that facilitate the pursuit of personal and communal goals	Promotion of fair and equitable allocation of bargaining powers, obligations, and resources in society

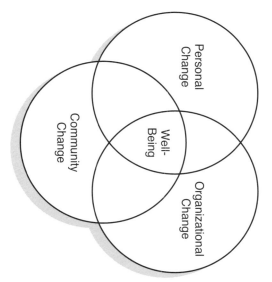

Figure 1.1   The Synergy of Well-Being.

finally, are sites where feelings, cognitions, and phenomenological experiences of well-being reside. In this book we sometimes also refer to interpersonal wellness, which is not a site of wellness per se, but an important aspect of relationships in families, organizations, and communities. Interpersonal wellness can be a sign of personal well-being, as in feelings of caring and compassion that we experience in close relationships, and also a sign of organizational well-being, as in respect for diversity and participatory structures. It can also be an expression of community well-being, representing signs of belonging, solidarity, and cohesion. Interpersonal or relational wellness is the glue that connects personal, organizational, and community wellness.

We have to be able to honor the uniqueness of the three sites of well-being and their interdependence at the same time. We can have a community endowed with excellent jobs, schools, parks, and hospitals where many people feel miserable because relationships in the community are acrimonious or alienating. If we thought of well-being only in terms of community, we would miss the experiential component of personal well-being and the influential role of organizations and relationships in advancing personal satisfaction. Conversely, we can have a select group of people who, despite poor community conditions, experience high levels of well-being because of privilege. In this case, exclusive focus on the well-being of these people might miss the need to heal, repair, and transform the community conditions (poverty, discrimination, epidemics) that are diminishing the well-being of those who cannot protect themselves.

From this general level of geographical and physical location of well-being, we can proceed to ask more specific questions about signs of well-being in each of the three sites. Although they are interconnected, we will see that each site has distinct signs of well-being.

Signs of Well-Being

By signs, we refer to manifestations or expressions of well-being at the different sites we explored earlier. Signs answer the question "How do I know that this site is experiencing well-being?" At the personal level, signs of well-being are identified by looking at correlates, by asking people to share what they feel and think when they are happy, satisfied, or experience a high quality of life. A variety of research methods have been used to look at personal signs of well-being, including surveys, interviews, observations, and comparative analyses (Snyder & Lopez, 2002). Similarly, multiple approaches have been used to find out the signs, characteristics, or correlates of well or healthy communities and organizations (Eckersley, Dixon, & Douglas, 2002).

Based on multiple sources of evidence, a few signs of personal well-being come to the fore: self-determination and a sense of control, self-efficacy, physical and mental health, optimism, meaning, and spirituality. Signs of organizational well-being include respect for diversity, democratic participation, collaborative relationships, clarity of roles, and learning opportunities. Expressions of collective well-being include a fair and equitable allocation of bargaining powers, resources, and obligations in society; gender, ability, and race equality; universal access to high-quality educational, health, and recreational facilities; affordable housing; employment opportunities; access to nutritious foods at reasonable prices; safety; public transportation; a clean environment; and peace. Though not exhaustive by any means, these lists are fairly representative of the research on well-being at the three levels (Goleman, 1998; Maton & Salem, 1995; Totikidis & Prilleltensky, 2006).

Each of these signs is intrinsically beneficial to the well-being of a particular site and extrinsically beneficial to the well-being of the other two sites. Supportive organizations foster self-determination of their members, and just communities contribute to personal growth through a fair allocation of opportunities in society.

Sources of Well-Being

Each one of the sites of well-being and their corresponding signs has particular sources or groups of determinants. Self-determination, for example, derives from prior opportunities to exercise control, voice, and choice. In the organizational domain, participation and collaboration derive from traditions of inclusion, learning, and horizontal structures. Signs of collective well-being, such as high-quality public education, depend on policies that promote social justice, which, in turn, distribute resources fairly.

Personal wellness is based on a number of sources. We all require a sense of control over our lives, a sense of mastery and a measure of stability. We need to be nurtured, cared for, and appreciated. Our needs for health, control, optimism, empathy, and emotional nourishment are a precondition for psychological wellness.

But it wasn't until Sir Michael Marmot (1999; Marmot & Feeney, 1996) published the Whitehall studies that health and social scientists could really appreciate the impact of control on personal wellness. The British scientist, who was knighted for his groundbreaking research in England, studied the lives of thousands of British civil servants for more than 25 years. After he eliminated all other possible sources of health and illness, he realized that workers who experienced little control over their jobs were two, three, and even four times more likely to die than those who experienced a lot of control over their jobs.

Marmot divided the civil servants into four groups: manager, professional, clerical, and other. Managers had the most amount of control over their jobs, whereas the group called "other" had the least. Professionals were second and clerical staff third. As can be seen in the graph in Figure 1.2, compared to managers, professionals were twice as likely to die, clerical staff three times as likely, and the group called other, which included people with few skills, were four times as likely to die. If anyone had doubts about the role of control in personal wellness, Marmot erased them.

Although specific sources refer to particular signs, we have to remember that each sign has multiple sources and that the different determinants always interact. Thus, access to high-quality public education, a collective

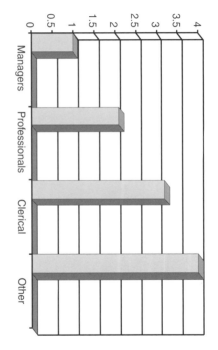

Figure 1.2   Risk of Death by Employment and Level of Control.

sign of well-being, enhances opportunities for control and self-efficacy of students, which are signs of personal well-being. As noted earlier, sites, signs, and sources of well-being are interdependent, as are the strategies to promote them.

Strategies for Well-Being

The key to successful strategies is that they must be specific enough to address each one of the sites, signs, and respective sources of well-being at the same time. Interventions that concentrate strictly on personal sites neglect the many resources that organizations and communities contribute to personal well-being. Paradoxically, strategies that concentrate exclusively on personal well-being actually undermine well-being because they do not support the infrastructure that enhances well-being itself. This has been a major gap in previous efforts to sustain individual well-being through strictly psychological means such as cognitive reframing, positive thinking, information sharing, and skill building. Individuals cannot significantly alter their level of well-being in the absence of concordant environmental changes (Smedley & Syme, 2000). Conversely, any strategy that promotes well-being by environmental changes alone is bound to be limited. There is ample evidence to suggest that the most promising approaches combine strategies for personal, organizational, and collective change (Stokols, 2000). It is not one or the other, but the combination of them all that is the best avenue to seek higher levels of well-being in the three sites of our interest.

Take, for example, the powerful influence of social support on health. Support for the soul can increase or restore health and wellness in two ways. First, social support can enhance wellness through bonding, attachment, appreciation, and affirming messages. The more support I have, the better I feel, and the better I feel, the more likely I am to withstand adversity and develop resilience. According to our model, interpersonal wellness leads to personal wellness.

The second mechanism through which social support enhances wellness is by providing emotional and instrumental support in times of crises. The stressful reactions associated with divorce, moves, transitions, and loss may be buffered by the presence of helpful and supportive others.

Compared with people with lower levels of supports, those who enjoy more support from relatives or friends live longer, recover faster from illnesses, report better health, and cope better with adversities (S. Cohen, 2004). Studies have shown that women with advanced breast cancer have better chances of survival when they participate in support groups. For example, after a follow-up of 48 months, Spiegel and colleagues (Spiegel, Bloom, & Kraemer, 1989) reported that all the women in their control group, who did not participate in a support group, had died, whereas a third of those who received group support were still alive. The average survival for the women in the support group was 36 months, compared to 19 months in the control sample. This study, reported in the prestigious British journal *Lancet*, made medical history.

One year later, Richardson and colleagues (Richardson, Sheldon, Krailo, & Levine, 1990) made similar claims on a sample of patients with blood malignancies. Their study, published in the *Journal of Clinical Oncology*, claimed that "the use of special educational and supportive programs . . . [is] associated with significant prolongation of patient survival" (p. 356). Finally, Fawzy and colleagues reported in 1993 that patients with malignant melanoma were more likely to die or experience recurrence of the disease if they did not receive the group intervention that the experimental group received. Out of 34 patients in each group, only 7 of those who received group support had experienced recurrence and 3 had died at the 5-year follow-up, compared with 13 who experienced recurrence and 10 who had died in the control group. Altogether, these three teams of researchers found that social support can enhance health and longevity in the face of deadly diseases.

One way to make sure that we maximize the benefits of social support is by enhancing our sense of community and the availability of support throughout the life cycle, and not just in times of need. There is a role here for the community at large and for public institutions in promoting belonging, affection, and mutual help. We need to think of public institutions as promoters of well-being and not only as restorers of well-being when our physical or emotional integrity is compromised by illness or crisis.

Synergy of Sites, Signs, Sources, and Strategies

We can integrate sites, signs, sources, and strategies in the following formulation: The well-being of a *site* is reflected in a particular *sign*, which derives from a particular *source* and is promoted by a certain *strategy*. To wit, personal well-being is reflected in control, which derives from opportunities to exercise voice and choice, and is promoted by empowerment. In this case, the site is personal wellness, the sign is control, the source is opportunities to experience voice and choice, and the strategy is empowerment.

In the organizational domain, we can integrate the four Ss as follows: Organizational well-being is reflected in the presence of supportive relationships among workers, which derive from a culture of trust and reciprocity, and is promoted by empathy and opportunities to give and receive caring, compassion, and constructive feedback. In the collective domain, we can claim that collective well-being is reflected in universal access to health care, which derives from policies of social justice, and is promoted by social movements that strive to create, maintain, and improve institutions that deliver services to all citizens, irrespective of means.

In synthesis, then, the well-being of site q is reflected in sign x, which derives from source y, and is promoted by strategy z. By using this simple formulation, we can integrate a vast amount of research in operational and actionable terms. Table 1.2 shows examples of signs, sources, and strategies for different sites of well-being.

An example of synergy is the beneficial effects that accrue from community cohesion. Individuals, organizations, and communities all gain when high participation and reciprocity are the social norm.

Wellness always takes place in a context. Contexts of discrimination create resentment, and contexts of crime and violence breed disharmony. Conversely, cultures of acceptance foster harmony and cohesion. Our personal, interpersonal, and collective lives are intertwined, and so should be the

Table 1.2   Synergy: Examples of Signs, Sources, and Strategies of Different Sites of Well-Being

		Sites of Well-Being		
		Personal	Organizational	Community
Signs	Personal	Control	Worker satisfaction	Sense of community
	Organizational	Satisfying peer relationships	Participatory structures	Community supports institutions
	Community	Community health	Institutions responsive to community needs	Support for the poor and for universal health care
Sources	Personal	Experiences of self-efficacy	Workers skilled in team work	Personal contribution to common good
	Organizational	Peer support	Culture of respect and affirmation	Agencies that work at multiple levels
	Community	High quality health and education	Norms that promote collaboration	Culture that understands and fosters interdependence
Strategies	Personal	Empowerment	Development of empathy and social skills	Collective and political intelligence
	Organizational	Voice and choice in teams	Conflict resolution and growth orientation	Social support and rewards for participation in social change
	Community	Participation in political process	Norms that affirm mutuality and oppose competition	Social movements that fight injustice

means of wellness promotion. Personal and interpersonal wellness began to attract attention in psychology in the past few years, and *community cohesion* and *social capital* started gaining currency in sociology and political science not long ago (Blakeley, 2002; Putnam, 2001). These terms speak about the potential of communities to improve the well-being of their members through the synergy of associations, mutual trust, sense of community, and collective action. We all have community needs. They are the need to live in a safe, friendly, and cohesive community with good schools and employment opportunities for everyone. We need access to health care, transportation, and recreation. We require places with a wealth of social capital.

In his widely popular book *Bowling Alone: The Collapse and Revival of American Community*, Robert Putnam (2000) distinguished among physical, human, and social capital: "Whereas physical capital refers to physical objects and human capital refers to properties of individuals, social capital refers to connections among individuals—social networks and the norms of reciprocity and trustworthiness that arise from them" (p. 19).

In our view, social capital refers to collective resources consisting of civic participation, norms of reciprocity, and organizations that foster trust and improve the community. Social capital, in the form of connections of trust and participation, enhances community capacity to create structures of cohesion and support. Research indicates that cohesive communities and civic participation in public affairs enhance quality of life for everybody. Communities with higher participation in volunteer organizations and local and professional associations perform much better in terms of health, education, crime, and welfare than communities with low rates of participation. This finding has been replicated at different times across various states, provinces, and countries.

Putnam (2000), a political scientist from Harvard, studied community participation and volunteerism in the United States during the past century. Armed with data from surveys going back decades, he discovered that communities where people volunteer and participate more in social affairs have better educational achievements, less crime, less child abuse, and better health outcomes overall than communities with low rates of volunteerism.

When people associate with others for the benefit of the community, there are tangible outcomes. Putnam (2000) calls the networks of trust and reciprocity *social capital*. The more social capital there is in communities, the more personal wellness for their residents. In the United States, Minnesota, Vermont, and the Dakotas are some of the states with higher levels of social capital and better outcomes in terms of health, education, welfare, and crime. The more social capital there is in various states, the higher the levels of health, welfare, education, and tolerance. The only pattern that works in reverse is crime: The lower the social capital in a state, the higher the level of crime.

In addition to community participation, economic equality is another predictor of personal and interpersonal wellness. Richard Wilkinson (1996) compared levels of inequality and health among the wealthy nations of Japan, Sweden, and the United States. In his book *Unhealthy Societies: The Afflictions of Inequality*, he reported that in countries like Sweden and Japan, where the gap between rich and poor is relatively small, people live longer than in other rich countries like the United States and England, where the gap between rich and poor is much wider. Researchers claim that economic equality is a central feature of community wellness that is reflected in how long people live. Inequality breeds jealousy and envy that, in turn, increase stress to achieve more and more. How exactly inequality and envy are translated into longevity is not clear, but the consequences are clear enough: The smaller the gap between rich and poor, the longer people live.

Because of more egalitarian income distribution, the life expectancy of Japanese people increased by 7.5 years for men and 8 years for women in 21 years. This dramatic increase took place between 1965 and 1986. Japanese people experience the highest life expectancy in the world, near 80 years, in large part because in that period of time they became the advanced society with the narrowest income differences. Communities with higher levels of social cohesion and narrow gaps between rich and poor produce better health outcomes than wealthier societies with higher levels of social disintegration.

In summary, social capital, community participation, and inequality play a big role in personal and community wellness. We search for wellness not only in the depths of our mind, but also in community and economic exchanges.

ROWS FOR WELLNESS

Exercise 1: Your Personal Situation

All of us experience risks, opportunities, weaknesses, and strengths (ROWS). They all influence our psychological wellness. Risks and opportunities refer to external factors affecting our life, whereas strengths and weaknesses refer to internal factors. You can think of risks and opportunities in terms of organizational and community wellness. Strengths and weaknesses, in turn, refer to personal wellness.

A risk to wellness may be related to acrimonious relationships with your partner. Poor relationships are a risk to your interpersonal and psychological wellness.

Moving to a cohesive community with good schools may be a definite opportunity for wellness, for yourself and for your kids. Applying to a new job with better pay and better working hours may be another great opportunity for wellness.

Good interpersonal skills and a caring attitude may be strengths of yours. A good sense of humor may be another. You may be good with your hands or with kids, or you may know a lot about certain topics, such as history, music, sports, or pottery. Perhaps you have good leadership and organizational skills, or you're an expert in gardening or cooking. We all have strengths that we need to nourish and polish.

Personal weaknesses may relate to lack of confidence, anxieties, obsessions, a tendency to overwork, and pleasing others at a personal cost. Each of us is very different, and it's important to know our own personal ROWS.

In this and following chapters of the book, you will have a chance to consider the ROWS affecting your life. Each chapter deals with a different aspect of wellness. Hence, in each of the following chapters you will consider different ROWS affecting your life. After you do the ROWS exercise, you will have a chance to assess your readiness for wellness. To see how it works, we provide a case study from our work. After you see how it works for the people in the case study, you can do your own exercise and measure your own readiness. Consider first the case of Jane.

Jane's Dilemmas

She turns off the alarm clock and snuggles beneath her blankets. It's 5:45 A.M. She has 15 minutes of peaceful reflections before the hustle and bustle of the morning routine sets in. There are children to wake up and get ready for school, lunches to make, and a house to put in order. At least this is the 1 day a week when she doesn't have to get ready for work herself.

Jane is a 38-year-old mother of two. She has been married to Michael for 13 years and has a 9-year-old girl and a 7-year-old boy. Jane is a speech therapist and works 4 days a week at a child guidance clinic. She loves her family, enjoys her work, and derives satisfaction from her volunteer work as a phone counselor. However, Jane can no longer ignore the high level of stress in her life. She feels like she is on a fast-moving train that never stops and rarely slows down.

Jane knows that something has to change. She is simply too busy for her own good. Michael leaves the house at 7:00 A.M. to begin his long commute to work. He is rarely home before 7:00 P.M. After getting up and making the children's lunch, Jane runs around getting herself, her children, and her home ready for an 8:00 departure. She then drives the children to school and rushes off to work. Some days she goes to the clinic for meetings or report writing. On other days she goes to one of the four schools she services. Her days are spent on individual therapy sessions, assessments, and meetings. She often eats her lunch on the go as she commutes from one school to the next.

Wednesday is her only day off. However, despite her intentions to take some time out for herself, the day just whizzes by. It's not that she doesn't know where the time has gone. By the time she picks up the kids at 3:30, she would have done the weekly grocery shopping, put in a couple of hours of volunteer work, and paid a visit to her mother-in-law. This is a new addition to her day "off." Her mother-in-law has recently moved to a senior citizen home and is having troubling adjusting. Jane's visits mean a lot to her.

Jane knows that she is not doing very well. She hasn't been sleeping well lately and often feels tired and irritable. She hasn't had time to exercise properly or to read for more than a few minutes at night. Reading and exercising are two activities that she loves, that she knows she needs for her own sense of well-being.

But how to change it all? What to give up? And at what price? Jane knows that Michael is working very hard. She appreciates the patience he has for the kids at the end of the day and on weekends. However, he does most of the fun stuff, like story reading and soccer coaching, while she runs the ship. Shopping, cooking, laundry—it never seems to end. At least they have help with cleaning once a week, otherwise she is sure she would collapse altogether.

Give up her job? Never. They need the money, and besides, she finds it satisfying and rewarding. If she could only protect her time better, rather than try to meet every request that comes her way. She knows that she is a competent clinician and is highly respected at the schools she services. However, she tends to be a pleaser and is not good at turning down requests. So, when they asked her to assess one more student, she gave up her precious time for report writing and said yes. The report will be written at night, once the kids are in bed.

What about asking Michael to do more at home? Seeing how exhausted he is at the end of the day prevents her from bringing it up. On weekends, Michael plays basketball between children's activities and family commitments. How can she ask him to give up basketball? But can't he see how tired she is? Is he even aware that she barely has time to exercise? That she falls asleep after 5 minutes of reading? She knows that he appreciates the fact that she visits his mother. She also knows that it is the right thing to do. But at what price to herself?

Finally, her volunteer work is taking up 5 hours a week—2 hours on Wednesday and 3 on Saturday. But give that up? After all the training she has been through? Giving back to her community is consistent with Jane's values. She has always taught her children that life is not just about meeting your own needs. She also enjoys phone counseling, despite its hectic nature. At times, it can be emotionally draining.

And is she spending enough time with the kids? As much as she loves them and enjoys their company, it seems that most of her time is spent on "child-servicing" tasks: cooking, driving, supervising homework. Only yesterday, 9-year-old Natalie complained that it has been ages since Jane has played a game with her. Her 7-year-old brother seems to get more of

Mom's time. He has just started school this year and is having some difficulty with reading. Although his teacher said not to worry, Jane doesn't want him to fall behind. She has been spending a lot of time with him on reading games and activities that he seems to enjoy. But is she short-changing Natalie just because she is doing so well?

Form 1.1 shows how Jane would complete the ROWS exercise. Jane knows that these are some of her ROWS related to wellness. Ideally, she would try to do something to maximize her opportunities and strengths and to minimize the risks and weaknesses.

Now, what are your own personal ROWS? Using Form 1.2, think about your life and write down your own ROWS. In doing the exercise, think about factors related to personal, organizational, and community wellness. Remember that wellness emerges at the intersection of these three spheres. Remember also that interpersonal wellness is a big part of personal, organizational, and community wellness. Don't limit yourself to your work or family situation; consider community factors as well.

What can you do about your ROWS? You can reinforce strengths, or you can fight risks and weaknesses. Ideally, you would do both. Each person is at a different stage in his or her development of wellness. To help you assess where you are with respect to your own development, we have created a wellness readiness scale that is completely personalized to fit your profile and not somebody else's. Before we ask you to do this, however, let's see how this would work in Jane's case.

Wellness Readiness Check 1: Synergy in Jane's Case

We saw in the ROWS exercise some of the factors affecting Jane's life and your own life. The question now is what can be done about them. To help you create a plan, we have devised a series of wellness readiness scales. The first one is called synergy because this is the main message emerging from this chapter. Wellness is about the synergy or coming together of personal, organizational, and community wellness.

Next to each one of the ROWS, we ask you to put a checkmark under one of the following options:

1. I never thought about doing something about it.
2. I'm thinking about doing something about it.
3. I'm prepared to do something about it.
4. I'm doing something about it.
5. I've been doing something about it for some time.

These five options parallel a well-known theory of personal change developed by psychologists Prochaska, Norcross, and DiClemente (1994). By assessing your own situation along these five options, you will create your own wellness map. Let's see how this would work in Jane's case. What we do is quite simple: We take the ROWS that Jane described and we insert them in the table. Next to each one of them we ask Jane to check what she's doing about her ROWS. In some cases, she is doing something about them, in others she is only thinking about them. We would encourage Jane to try to do something to reinforce her strengths and maximize her opportunities. Similarly, we would encourage her to do something to minimize risks and address weaknesses. Form 1.3 shows how we think Jane would have completed this wellness readiness check.

Now that you've seen a complete example, it can be pretty easy to complete your own wellness readiness check. Simply transfer the ROWS from the previous exercise into Form 1.4 and put a checkmark below the option that suits your situation best. When you finish, think about what can be done to maximize opportunities and strengths and how you may minimize risks and weaknesses. In chapters to come, you can check your wellness readiness for various aspects of your life.

Form 1.1   ROWS Exercise 1: Jane's Case

Risks	Michael's long working day
	My own hectic schedule
	Insufficient help at home
	Daniel and my mother-in-law needing a lot of my time
Opportunities	Michael's easy-going nature and willingness to engage in dialogue
	My parents' willingness to help with the kids
	A new volunteer who may be able to share some of my shifts
	Raise possibility of hiring another speech therapist at work
Weaknesses	Tendency to please others at work—without thinking of outcome
	Feeling like I have to be perfect at everything I do
	Too readily giving up favored activities
	Not fully sharing my frustrations with Michael
Strengths	Commitment to family
	Commitment to community
	Hard-working
	Ability to juggle many tasks and responsibilities

Form 1.2   ROWS Exercise 1: Your Personal Situation

Risks				
Opportunities				
Weaknesses				
Strengths				

Form 1.3 Wellness Readiness Check 1: Synergy in Jane's Case

ROWS	1 I never thought about doing something about it.	2 I'm thinking about doing something about it.	3 I'm prepared to do something about it.	4 I'm doing something about it.	5 I've been doing something about it for some time.
Risks					
Michael's long working day	X				
Insufficient help at home					
Daniel and my mother-in-law needing a lot of my time		X			
My own hectic schedule			X		
Opportunities					
Michael's easy-going nature and willingness to engage in dialogue			X		
My parents' willingness to help with the kids		X			
A new volunteer who may be able to share some of my shifts			X		
Raise possibility of hiring another speech therapist at work	X				

Form 1.3   (Continued)

ROWS	1 I never thought about doing something about it.	2 I'm thinking about doing something about it.	3 I'm prepared to do something about it.	4 I'm doing something about it.	5 I've been doing something about it for some time.
Weaknesses					
Tendency to please others at work without thinking of outcome			X		
Feeling like I have to be perfect at everything I do	X				
Too readily giving up favored activities			X		
Not fully sharing my frustrations with Michael			X		
Strengths					
Commitment to family					X
Commitment to community					X
Hardworking					X
Ability to juggle many tasks and responsibilities					X

Form 1.4   Wellness Readiness Check 1: Your Personal Situation

ROWS	1 I never thought about doing something about it.	2 I'm thinking about doing something about it.	3 I'm prepared to do something about it.	4 I'm doing something about it.	5 I've been doing something about it for some time.
Opportunities					
Weaknesses					
Strengths					
Risks					

2

Webs of Growth: The SPEC of Well-Being

I saac, you'll be coming to live with us now."

Everyone was making an effort to conceal the truth, but I knew that something was horribly wrong. My whole being knew it. My cousin's words only confirmed what I had suspected for the past 2 days. On that day, November 11, 1967, my life would change forever.

I had asked for the newspaper the day before. I wanted to see the obituaries. Their refusal to give me the papers only fueled my suspicion. I still can't understand what led me to the obituaries section—I never used to read the papers at that age; I was only 8 years old. But I needed to know, and nobody would talk to me.

I had been waiting for my parents to return from their business trip. They were unusually late, 2 days late. I had been sitting on the porch of our friend's house for most of the day, waiting for my dad's car to turn from Avenida La Patria in Córdoba, Argentina. That was the routine when my parents traveled to their hotel near Iguazu Falls, a natural wonder near the border between Argentina and Brazil. My siblings and I would stay with our friends for the duration of our parents' short trip. This time, the routine was broken.

When I saw Oscar's car instead of my dad's, I knew what my cousin was going to say. "It can't be true, it can't be true!" I shouted. He didn't have to say much. Although he meant well, the part about my parents being in heaven felt insulting. A car accident had taken my parents' lives.

Losing my parents was bad enough. Witnessing the grown-ups discuss the future of the orphans was sheer agony. Would we be together? Would we be apart? I had just lost my parents and there was talk of separating me from my brother and sister. My aunt stepped in and put an end to the discussion; a widow and quite ill, Aunt Eusebia took us.

My two siblings and I went to live with my aunt and her three children. Mario, my older brother, was 16, my sister, Myriam, was 12. Oscar and

Daniel, my older cousins, were already in medical school, and their sister, Sissi, was finishing high school. My three cousins became our siblings; my Aunt Eusebia became our mother.

Sissi tried to comfort me with her attempts to convert tears to laughter. I don't remember exactly how I learned it, but I knew that tears would sadden my aunt. For years, I had to halt my tears. I had to be strong. People didn't know what to do with a little boy who lost his parents. The best intentions were not enough. Caring was not enough. People had to know something about grieving and emotional wellness, but nobody did. Not even in school. I knew I wasn't allowed to cry, but at times I just couldn't stop it. Mother's Day and Father's Day were the worst. School celebrations were next. Reminders of my loss made me want to hide. I was different; I was a *pobrecito*, Spanish for someone you pity.

A bit of psychological awareness, no doubt, would have gone a long way in alleviating my grieving. There was caring and empathy, but there wasn't an understanding of what it takes to promote wellness in adversity. There was a fear that if they let me cry they wouldn't know what to do with my pain. I didn't want them to do anything, just to let me cry. Eventually, I learned to censor myself, sometimes better than others. Either way, I was in agony: If I cried I felt guilty, if I didn't I felt a perpetual lump in my throat. Occasionally Myriam and I would cry under the dining room table.

There was nothing wrong with my body, and my aunt took very good care of my health. From the outside, I looked in good shape. But inside I was hurting, and few people noticed. People are afraid to touch pain and discomfort. In most cases, however, pain and discomfort must be confronted, not denied. Ironically, a great deal of psychological pain is caused by denying the existence of a previous psychological pain. Now we're dealing not only with grief and loss, as in my case, but also with repression and inhibition. I would have liked to cry openly and unrepentantly. It took me 37 years to return to the porch of the house where the news was shared.

Perfecting the body and neglecting the soul is a dangerous thing. Many people have a body that works very well, but their emotional life is a disaster. People who lack awareness about psychological wellness are usually reminded of it when it's too late. People who lack psychological wellness suffer and can cause enormous suffering as well. Violent husbands, abusive parents, despotic bosses: They may all have bodies that work very well but psychological problems that ruin other people's lives. My life was not ruined by the premature death of my parents (they were in their early 40s), but a good deal of suffering could have been prevented by using some of the principles of SPEC. The acronym SPEC stands for strengths, prevention, empowerment, and changing conditions. These four principles capture much of what is needed to promote webs of growth. Letting me cry would have prevented the guilt associated with feeling like crying; asking me what I needed would have given me some voice and choice; and celebrating my strengths instead of concentrating on what I lacked would have restored dignity. Nobody could have returned my parents, but better conditions could have been created for dealing with the loss. When linked together, the principles of strengths, prevention, empowerment, and changing conditions can be a powerful prescription for growth and human, organizational, and community development.

THE SPEC OF WELL-BEING: INVESTING IN STRENGTHS, PREVENTION, EMPOWERMENT, AND CONDITIONS

To advance well-being at the three sites of interest—personal, organizational, and community—it is necessary to devise strategies that cover the entire range of domains and that attend to the variety of signs and sources of well-being. Hitherto, most approaches to well-being have concentrated on single sites and on small groups of signs and sources (Nelson & Prilleltensky, 2005; I. Prilleltensky, Nelson, & Peirson, 2001). The literature is full of approaches to promote personal well-being or policies to advance community development, but very few authors try to attach personal, organizational, and community well-being to the natural web to which they belong (Capra, 1996, 2003).

We claim that a comprehensive and efficacious pathway for the promotion of well-being must attend to four complementary domains: time, ecology, participation, and capabilities. These four domains belong in two fields. The contextual field consists of intersecting continua of temporal and ecological domains, creating four contextual quadrants. The affirmation field reflects the interaction of the participation and capabilities domains. In the following, we elaborate on the two different fields and their corresponding quadrants.

The Contextual Field

A contextual approach to well-being must account for the role of temporal and ecological variables. The temporal domain spans the continuum of reactive to proactive or preventive services and approaches. The ecological domain, in turn, covers the full range of interventions, from individual change to change in collective conditions, affecting quality of life for entire groups of people. The temporal domain accounts for the P in SPEC, and the ecological domain accounts for the C: P stands for prevention and C stands for changing conditions. When the two domains intersect, as may be seen in Figure 2.1, a contextual field with four quadrants is formed. Given the history of exclusive focus on individual and reactive interventions, we need to balance them with a big P for prevention and a big C for changing conditions. Let's see why.

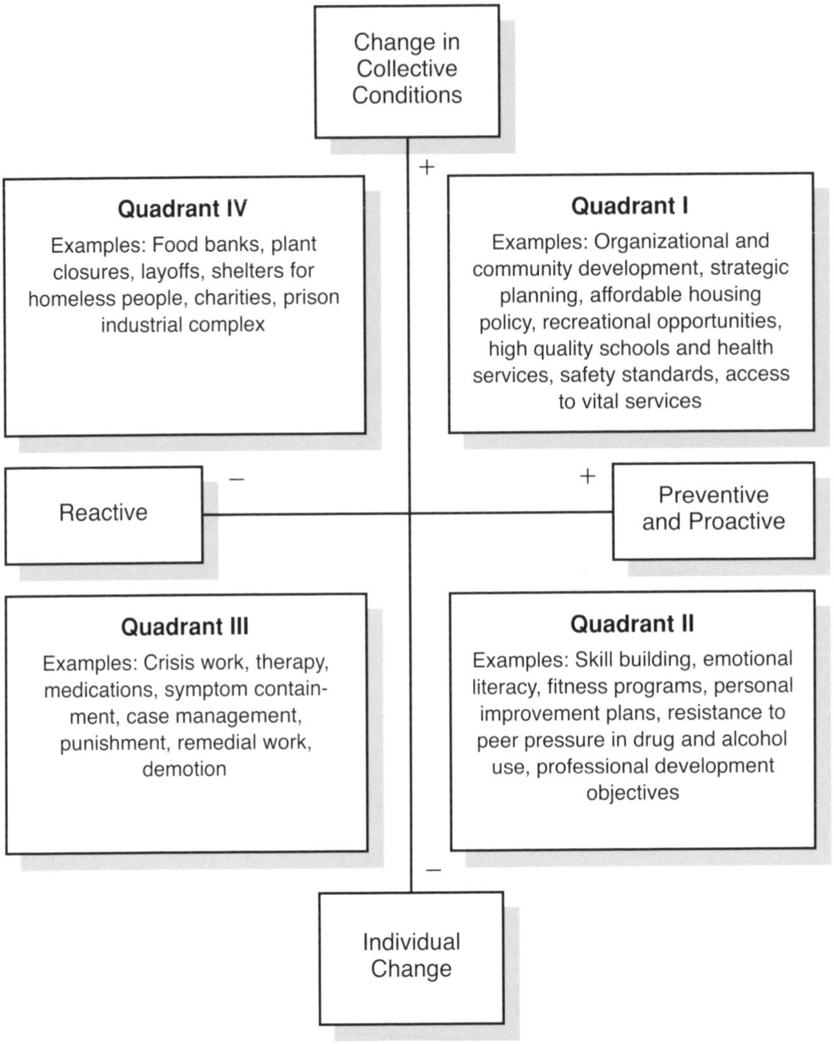

Figure 2.1   The Contextual Field of Well-Being: Efforts at the Intersection of Temporal (Reactive-Proactive) and Ecological (Individual-Collective Conditions) Domains.

The Temporal Domain   This domain has to do with the timing of interventions. There is evidence to suggest that in Canada and the United States only a small amount of resources is allocated to prevention (Goldston, 1991; Nelson, Prilleltensky, Laurendeau, & Powell, 1996). The vast majority of resources are assigned to rehabilitative costs, such as hospital beds, expensive treatments, and therapeutic interventions. This is so despite the fact that high-quality preventive interventions have proven efficacious, cost-effective, and enormously more humane than waiting for citizens to develop maladies that medicine and psychology can treat only at very high financial and human costs. The reactive approach, a vestige of the still dominant medical model, obstructs the imperative to devote more resources to prevention. For as long as local governments, states, provinces, nations, and international bodies neglect prevention, not much will change in the health and well-being of the population. The status quo will only continue to deprive the poor and underserved of vital services and resources (I. Prilleltensky, 1994).

It is crucial to pay more attention to exemplary models of prevention. The tremendous imbalance between reactive and preventive approaches in favor of the former must be challenged, repaired, and healed, and with great urgency. Otherwise, the endless treadmill of new cases will never cease. Health and human services must understand that no mass disorder afflicting humankind has ever been eliminated or brought under control by treating the affected individual (Albee, 1990). Similarly, they must realize that there will never be enough workers to attend to the people afflicted with psychological and physical ailments. The only way to make a dent in the incidence and prevalence of suffering is through prevention.

An ounce of prevention is worth a pound of cure. Pay now or pay later. A stitch in time saves nine. We all know the logic of prevention, but few industries and few sectors take it seriously enough to invest in them the required resources. We all know that prevention is better than cure, but provincial ministries of health in Canada and parallel departments in the United States devote less than 1% of their budgets to prevention of mental health problems. Most of the money goes toward treatment (Goldston, 1991; Nelson et al., 1996). We want teenagers unprepared for parenthood to stop having children, but we are unwilling to invest in them family planning or educational and preventive services. We know that about 26% of children in North America experience behavioral, learning, emotional, or social problems, but nobody seems to panic. We understand that brain malleability is greatest during the 1st years of life, but we spend most of our economic and social resources on adults and seniors. We require a license to fish, but have no standards to ensure that parents know how to treat their children (Nelson, Prilleltensky, & Peters, 1999).

In the United States, every day three children die from abuse and neglect. Of these children, 77% die before their 5th birthday. Most recent statistics indicate close to 3 million reports of suspected abuse per year, with about 1 million of these cases confirmed. Nearly 60% of the children suffered neglect, and close to 20% were physically abused. Ten percent were sexually abused. Many kids also suffered emotional abuse, medical neglect, and other forms of maltreatment. The National Child Abuse and Neglect Data System reported an estimated 1,300 child fatalities in 2001. In Tennessee, where we live now, more than 100 children are reported abused or neglected every day. The Department of Children's Services in the state responds to more than 37,000 reports of child abuse and neglect annually. Recent statistics indicate that reports of abuse and neglect increased 6.9%

from 1998 to 1999, for a total of 33,629 reports. Nationally, crime and delinquency, which cost approximately $25 billion annually, have been linked to histories of abuse. The enormous price of punitive and rehabilitative services drains our social wealth to the point that little is left for preventing abuse from occurring in the first place (I. Prilleltensky, 2003).

In Canada, a child is reported missing about every 8 minutes, for a total of 67,809 cases in 2003. Many of these children leave their home to escape abuse. Over a million, or 15.6%, of children in Canada live in poverty, more than in 1989, when the entire House of Commons voted to end child poverty by the year 2000 (Campaign 2000, 2004).

In Australia, the federal health minister stated:

The burden of mental health problems and mental disorders is rising in our community. . . . And it is also becoming increasingly clear that treatment interventions alone cannot significantly reduce the enormous personal, social and financial burden associated with mental health problems and mental disorders. It is also clear that interventions earlier in the development of these conditions will be beneficial. ("An Important Direction for Mental Health Promotion, Prevention, and Early Intervention," 2000)

"Crime costs the Australian community approximately $18 billion per year; that is, 4% of Gross Domestic Product" (Chisholm, 2000, p. 1). "The institutional and noninstitutional costs of mental disorders in Australia have been estimated at $2.58 billion in 1993–94 alone" (Australian Institute of Health and Welfare, 1998, p. 31). Mental health

constitutes 8.3% of the total health system costs. . . . Intentional self-inflicted injuries cost a further $69 million. . . . Hospitals and nursing homes account for almost 64% of all mental disorder treatment costs. It should be noted that the burden of mental disorders to the Australian community is much more than these costs, as costs relating to absenteeism, lost productivity, the burden of careers and family, legal costs, and lost quality and years of life are not included. (p. 31)

The principle of prevention applies also to organizational well-being. Changes in demographic trends, technology, and the economy require that businesses, government, and nonprofit organizations try to foresee preventable problems (Elsdon, 2003). The everyday operations of a business require a great deal of prevention. In mining and construction, for instance, the prevention of accidents is a primary concern. Having accurate maps of mines and enforcing high standards of safety are essential to preserve the health and well-being of miners.

On July 24, 2002, nine coal miners in Pennsylvania were the victims of poor prevention. The Quecreek flood, which trapped the miners for 72 hours inside a small hole, might have been prevented with more accurate information and safety standards. An environmental attorney in the county said, "It's well-known in the industry that the old deep mine maps are inaccurate, so a prudent mining company would drill to determine where the coal barriers are. This [accident] could have been prevented if the Department of Environmental Protection permit staff was more diligent" (Hopey, McFeatters, & Bull, 2002). It turns out that two other floods, similar to the one at Quecreek, had taken place in other mines operated by the same company, Black Wolf Mining (J. Bakan, 2004).

Joel Bakan (2004, p. 97), who studied corporate operations and government regulation in depth, noted that enforcement of safety standards by government agencies is vital in the mining industry: "It is reasonable to presume that an appropriately staffed and well-functioning agency might have ensured that the Quecreek miners had accurate maps and thus prevented their horrible ordeal."

These are the problems. What's the answer? Address the root causes of the problem and interrupt the vicious cycle. The barrier? Cynicism about the ability of corporations, governments, and communities to stop abuse, to prevent industrial accidents, to promote mental health, and to eradicate child poverty. The evidence? Many emotional, cognitive, behavioral, and social problems, including child maltreatment, can be significantly prevented. Research shows that some prevention programs are effective and save governments up to $7 for each dollar invested (Nelson et al., 1999).

We know a great deal from research about how to prevent mental health problems and how to promote well-being (Durlak, 1997; I. Prilleltensky, Nelson, et al., 2001), but we do not use that scientific knowledge in policy and practice (Keating & Hertzman, 1999; McCain & Mustard, 1999). We know from research that the best time to invest money in human development is very early in life, but most governments spend relatively little in the early years and large amounts in the late years of life (McCain & Mustard, 1999; Shonkoff & Phillips, 2000).

The Australian case is typical of many developed nations. Following an audit of child abuse prevention projects in New South Wales, Tomison (1997) reported that these programs are far from implementing what is known about prevention, both in terms of breadth and depth. There are not enough programs, and those that exist lack scientific rigor. In a comprehensive review of early intervention programs in Australia, Davis, Martin, Kosky, and O'Hanlon (2000, p. 46) concluded that many programs "were pilot programs or received funding for only one or two years."

Longitudinal, experimental, and controlled studies of high-quality preventive interventions indicate their success in reducing and even eliminating risks for children and adults. Universal and targeted interventions, when properly implemented, theoretically grounded, and empirically supported, can be quite effective (Olds, Kitzman, et al., 2004; Olds, Robinson, et al., 2004). Conditions that have been dramatically reduced by successful preventive programs include child maltreatment, delinquency, drug abuse, and learning, emotional, behavioral, and social problems. These positive outcomes have been documented in meta-analytic studies (Durlak, 1997; MacLeod & Nelson, 2000; Nelson, Westhues, & MacLeod, 2003) and in independent investigations (Albee & Gullotta, 2000; Davis et al., 2000; Commonwealth Department of Health and Aged Care, 2000; Kaplan, 2000). This body of knowledge demonstrates that high-quality prevention programs can be quite effective. The time has come to give more attention, and more resources, to prevention efforts; hence the P in SPEC.

The Ecological Domain   This continuum is concerned with sites of well-being and their corresponding strategies. Paradoxically, an approach that focuses exclusively on individuals diminishes the chances of personal well-being, for personal well-being depends heavily on relational, organizational, and collective well-being. Efforts to enhance personal wellness in the absence of corresponding improvements in the social conditions of living are limited at best and injurious at worst (Smedley & Syme, 2000). Working with single individuals may be more convenient than trying to change community conditions and social policies, yet one must be aware of the long-term repercussions of continuing to focus on a single source of suffering, the person, to the exclusion of sometimes overwhelming environmental factors.

Take the cholera epidemic that threatened London in 1854. On the night of August 31, 56 people died of cholera; 143 died on the night of September 1, and 116 the following night. Medical personnel had been treating patients afflicted by the disease, but no amount of caring for each sick patient did anything to stop the epidemic. John Snow, a physician, began a systematic investigation of the water quality consumed by the patients. A few years earlier, Snow had published a pamphlet postulating that cholera was a water-borne disease. His theories, which were politely ignored at a few medical conferences, were proven beyond doubt in 1854.

His investigation led him to conclude that the Broad Street pump was the main source of cholera. Most people who drank from it became ill and died soon after. (Parenthetically, Snow nearly gave up his theory when he realized that about 70 workers in the brewery next to the pump were unaffected by the poor quality of the water. It turns out that workers in the brewery didn't trust the water and drank only beer!) Snow ordered officials to remove the handle on September 7, 1854, stopping a major epidemic.

Snow didn't know how to save people one at a time. Instead, he searched for the root cause. He understood that such massive outbreak of disease had to be related to an environmental problem and not to an individual problem. By removing the handle from the Broad Street pump, he was able to prevent hundreds, if not thousands, of deaths (Summers, 1989).

Meet Len Syme, world-renowned public health expert. For more than 40 years, he has been trying to promote population health. Isaac met Professor Syme in Melbourne in 2002, when we were still living in Australia. Based at the University of California in Berkeley, he travels often to consult with organizations around the world. Syme shared with me some valuable lessons about public health. After investing massive amounts of money and effort to change individuals' behaviors, he concluded that this is definitely not the best way to invest money or promote health. Instead, Syme told me, we should invest in changing the social environment. He recounted the results of one of his major public health initiatives, the MRFIT (Multiple Risk Factors Interventions Trial) project. Syme and colleagues screened thousands of men at high risk for heart disease. After 6 years of training 6,000 highly motivated participants with the best available techniques in better health habits, the results were rather disappointing: "62% of these men continued to smoke after 6 years of effort, 50% still had hypertension, and very few men had changed their eating patterns" (Smedley & Syme, 2000, p. 4). Not only did the participants fail to change; the societal factors influencing disease remain unaffected. This is what Syme had to say in 1996 (p. 22):

Even when people do successfully change their high risk behaviors, new people continue to enter the at-risk population to take their place. For example, every time we finally helped a man in the MRFIT project to stop smoking, it is probable that, on that day, one or two children in a schoolyard somewhere were for the first time taking their first tentative puffs on a cigarette. So, even when we do help high risk people to lower their risk, we do nothing to change the distribution of disease in the population because . . . we have done nothing to influence those forces in the society that caused the problem in the first place.

Syme's conclusions are very much in line with our model of well-being: You cannot help individual people unless you do something about the causes of the problems. And even when you manage to help some individuals, others continue to be affected by the same untreated causes. Treating symptoms alone won't do. How easy can it be to improve eating habits when all around you eat junk food? How likely is it that you'll exercise when all around you are couch potatoes? How can we prevent smoking in youth when cigarettes are available everywhere?

As Syme showed, the cost of doing nothing about the social forces that intoxicate us is enormous. The healthiest people are found in the healthiest communities, and the unhealthiest people in the unhealthiest parts of town.

Across the Atlantic, Richard Wilkinson (1996) conducted comparative studies on health, inequality, and longevity. His conclusions support the views expressed by Syme. Unless we change the social environment in which people live, our chances of improving health and well-being are minimal (G. Evans & Kantrowitz, 2002). Wilkinson regrets the current state of affairs in the health and helping professions:

Sometimes it is a matter of providing screening and early treatment, other times of trying to change some aspect of lifestyle, but always it is a matter of providing some service or intervention. This applies not just to health, but also to studies of a wide range of social, psychological, developmental and educational problems. What happens is that the original source of the problem in society is left unchanged (and probably unknown) while expensive new services are proposed to cater for the individuals most affected. Each new problem leads to a demand for additional resources for services to try to put right the damage which continues to be done. Because the underlying flaw in the system is not put right, it gives rise to a continuous flow, both of people who have suffered as a result, and of demands for special services to meet their needs. (p. 21)

These are not radical voices any more. In a recent study by the Institute of Medicine in the United States, the committee recommends the endorsement of a "social environmental" approach to health and health intervention" (Smedley & Syme, 2000, p. 3). The committee, which Syme cochaired, reported that

societal-level phenomena are critical determinants of health. . . . Stress, insufficient financial and social supports, poor diet, environmental exposures, community factors and characteristics, and many other health risks may be addressed by one-to-one intervention efforts, but such efforts do little to address the broader social and economic forces that influence these risks. (p. 3)

Their point is that "fixing individuals" without "fixing societies" is obviously not enough. But there is a second strong point to be made: "One-to-one interventions do little to alter the distribution of disease and injury in populations because new people continue to be afflicted even as sick and injured people are cured" (p. 3).

So far, we have been talking about community conditions affecting well-being, but organizational conditions also have enormous impacts on quality of life for workers. Organizational conditions affect productivity, retention, creativity, stress, and overall climate.

Elsdon (2003) recounts the story of Sam, a successful manager who left his company when a new management team instituted a culture of control and intimidation. As Elsdon writes, "It was no surprise when Sam left three months later, for a competitor that was building its business model on co-operation, integrity and commitment. It was also no surprise when Sam's former operation went into steep decline, losing market position and employees" (p. 34). Cultural and objective conditions affect the morale, motivation, attitude, and well-being of workers, not to mention organizational effectiveness and service to the community.

The Broad Street pump, the MRFIT project, Wilkinson's research, and Sam's story show that conditions matter. It is noble but not enough to change individual habits one person at a time. We have to look at the underlying conditions that create dissatisfaction in a workplace and suffering in the community. For all these reasons, we shouldn't neglect the C in SPEC.

Contextual Quadrants   As may be seen in Figure 2.1, four quadrants are formed by the intersection of the temporal and ecological domains. Clockwise, Quadrant I is formed by the intersection of the positive ends of the x and y axes. Examples of collective and preventive approaches include organizational development, affordable housing policies, provision of high-quality health care, incentives to achieve high educational standards, investments in education, family planning, and mental health, as well as policies that distribute wealth among the population.

Quadrant II represents interventions that are proactive but person-centered. Examples include skill building, emotional literacy, and education for proper eating and exercise to prevent physical illness. Many drug prevention programs that teach youth resistance skills and knowledge about the effects of alcohol, smoking, and illicit drugs fit into this quadrant.

Quadrant III reflects the medical model tradition whereby the intervention is aimed at containing symptoms and managing crises. Medications, therapy, and crisis intervention are the prototypical approaches in this quadrant. Practitioners wait until patients, clients, or community members complain of an ailment to intervene, usually in a medical, clinic, or community agency setting. Similarly, managers wait until there are organizational crises to put out fires.

The last quadrant, IV, is created by the intersection of collective and reactive approaches. Like many charity efforts, food banks, plant closures, layoffs, and shelters for homeless people are aimed at alleviating the ill effects of injustice or the unpredictable outcomes of economic downturns.

The Affirmation Field

To experience well-being, human beings have to experience affirmation first. Affirmation comes from, among other things, an acknowledgment of a person's strengths, voice, and choice. Health and human services have been, and many still are, notorious for concentrating on deficits and for creating clienthood and patienthood instead of citizenship (Mullaly, 2002). The focus on weaknesses and the insistence that patients passively acquiesce to professional dictates run against affirmation of strengths, voice, and choice (see Figure 2.2). When empowerment and strengths are promoted, the experience of affirmation grows.

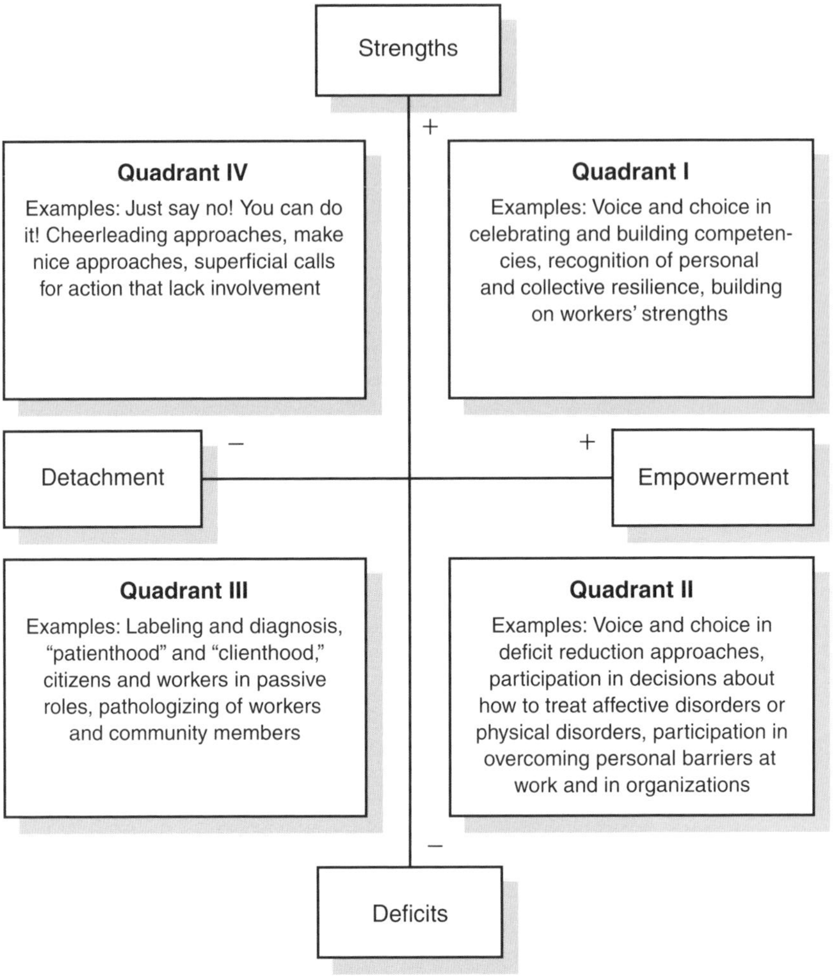

Quadrant IV
Examples: Just say no! You can do it! Cheerleading approaches, make nice approaches, superficial calls for action that lack involvement

Detachment

Quadrant III
Examples: Labeling and diagnosis, "patienthood" and "clienthood," citizens and workers in passive roles, pathologizing of workers and community members

Strengths

Deficits

Quadrant I
Examples: Voice and choice in celebrating and building competencies, recognition of personal and collective resilience, building on workers' strengths

Quadrant II
Examples: Voice and choice in deficit reduction approaches, participation in decisions about how to treat affective disorders or physical disorders, participation in overcoming personal barriers at work and in organizations

Empowerment

Figure 2.2 The Affirmation Field of Well-Being: Efforts at the Intersection of Participation (Detachment-Empowerment) and Capabilities (Strengths-Deficits) Domains.

The affirmation field consists of two intersecting continua: the participation and the capabilities domains. Together, they create four distinct approaches to helping and healing.

The Participation Domain Citizens are variably involved in services, programs, and policies promoting health and well-being. For the most part, however, they tend to be detached from decision-making processes directly affecting their own health or the health and well-being of the entire community. Usually, citizens are at the receiving end of decisions made by professionals or politicians, decisions that place citizens in the role of clients, patients, or customers, but rarely in the role of partner (I. Prillel-tensky, 1997).

As a result of this culture of patienthood and clienthood, many community residents feel completely detached from the professional, communal, and political processes affecting their lives. This is reflected on the lefthand side of the x axis of Figure 2.2. At the other extreme, we have feelings and actual experiences of empowerment whereby citizens feel and are in control of helping, healing, and community-building processes.

"Why should we trust you? How do we know that you're any different from other researchers who have come and gone and given us nothing?" That was a rocky start. These were the words of a community member at the first meeting of an agency to introduce the SPEC model. Together with colleagues, students, and the United Way of Metropolitan Nashville, Isaac's action research team is involved in helping local organizations in Nashville to change. We are working with health and human services to implement the SPEC philosophy. One of our partner organizations is the Martha O'Bryan Community Center affiliated with the Presbyterian Church.

In each organization, we have a transformation team, or T-team. The aim of the T-teams is to apply the SPEC model to each partner agency. At Martha O'Bryan, we created a T-team with several staff, community partners, and community members. At our very first T-team meeting, the vocal community member just quoted told us in no uncertain terms that he is suspicious of another university coming and "doing research on us" and then "leaving the community without contributing anything." This community advocate was very clear about his mistrust. He wanted the community concerns to be heard, and he wanted us, the Vanderbilt team, to be accountable to him and to the community he represents. We humbly acknowledged and validated his mistrust. After all, research teams had come and gone and behaved pretty much the way he described.

It is very important for us to have community members as part of the transformation process at Martha O'Bryan. They actively contribute to the change work and make sure community issues are addressed. Several members of the neighborhood served by Martha O'Bryan exercise voice and choice in the T-team and are closely involved in the group. They are given opportunities to influence how the center will serve the community, and they feel heard. Albeit in a small way, this core group of community members is fighting the detachment that often exists between helpers and communities. Our T-team listens carefully to community members and involves them in all the working groups navigating the change process. I would lie if I said that their input is always welcome and validated around the table, but we struggle to make it work for all stakeholders. Perhaps the best sign that they feel welcome is the fact that they have rarely missed a weekly meeting since the project began. Empowerment is not easy to actualize, but the research and our experience support its merits.

In another T-team, this one with Oasis Youth Center, also in Nashville, staff have been empowered to voice their opinions about the direction of the organization as a whole. This T-team, which is now in its 3rd year of operations, has been a very open and inclusive process. Workers in this 45-person organization have participated extensively in the creation of a new philosophy statement, in strategic planning, and in the translation of the SPEC philosophy into operational guidelines for all its programs. The T-team consulted widely with the workforce and youth served by the agency in developing the philosophy statement in Figure 2.3. Counselors at Oasis

OASIS
C E N T E R

Our Philosophy

*In every act, in every interaction, in every social action,
we hold each other accountable to promote*

People's dignity, safety, hope and growth
Relationships based on caring, compassion and respect
Societies based on justice, communion and equality

We are all better when these values are in balance.

To put these values into action, we will:

Share our power
Be proactive and not just reactive
Transform the conditions that create problems for youth
Encourage youth and families to promote a caring community
Nurture visions that make the impossible, possible

We commit to uphold these values with

Youth and their Families
Our Employees
Our Organization
Our Community

This is a living document. We invite you to discuss it, to critique it, to live it.

Figure 2.3   Philosophy Statement.

feel empowered to participate in the process of change. They are energized by this work and feel committed to the actualization of the philosophy statement. Unlike organizations in which philosophy and mission statements merely adorn the walls, at Oasis workers feel passionate about their mission and engage in the painstaking job of specifying what the philosophy statement means for them, every day, in all they do. Probably not all workers feel similarly passionate about it, but there is a sizable majority who do (S. Evans, Hanlin, & Prilleltensky, in press).

For the community members at Martha O'Bryan and for the counselors at Oasis, empowerment means being active participants in decision-making processes affecting their lives. They lend strong support to the E in SPEC.

The Capabilities Domain   The y axis of Figure 2.2 depicts the deficit-strength continuum. Few are the professionals who start a relationship with clients based on what the latter actually do well. Typically, the opening line of questioning is, explicitly or implicitly, "What is wrong with you?" or "What have you done wrong?" On account of limited time, physicians and psychologists eager to "get to the bottom of it," refrain from exploring sources and manifestations of resilience. Opportunities to build on strengths, or to promote affirmation, are often missed in the search for pathology.

In the medical field, research suggests that communication between practitioners and patients is often faulty and aimed at pathology. A study by Beckman and Frankl (1984) confirms this claim. In a sample of 74 office visits, only 23% of the patients had a chance to finish their explanations of concerns. Doctors were found to interrupt patients in 69% of the visits. On average, doctors interrupted patients after they had spoken for only 18 seconds. In another study, West (1983) reported that patient-initiated questions were discouraged. Out of a total of 773 questions asked in 21 medical encounters, only 9% of the questions were initiated by patients. The use of jargon, patronizing attitudes, and patient anxiety contribute to miscommunication between doctors and patients.

Although we advocate for patient assertiveness and communication training, we should be cautious about the potential of such interventions to make lasting changes. The origins of the patriarchal mentality in medical settings are profound and may not be undone by workshops on communication. Lupton (1994, p. 59) warns:

To assume that the majority of patients, given appropriate training in communication competencies, will have equal authority in the doctor-patient relationship is to ignore the structural and symbolic dimensions of this relationship. Although there is limited opportunity for patients to assert their agency, the whole nature of the doctor-patient relationship and the healing process rests on the unequal power balance and asymmetry of knowledge between patient and doctor.

It is clear that fundamental changes in the medical establishment will have to occur to improve communication and the search for strengths instead of the quick search for pathology.

A welcome development in the helping professions is the emergence of the positive psychology movement, which builds on people's capacities, creativity, strengths, resilience, and coping skills (Seligman, 2002). Contrary to many schools of thought that characterize the professional-client relationship as a pursuit of pathology, positive psychology, like solution-focused and narrative therapies, promotes the pursuit of strengths. We call this *asset seeking*. Many of our community partners in Martha O'Bryan know how to cope with random violence, poverty, and underfunded schools for their children. They have been stigmatized, pathologized, and minimized. Our project, like many others, is about recovery and validation of their strengths, dignity, and life-affirming struggles.

People with disabilities have been particularly victimized due to stigma. Community members with psychiatric diagnoses have been marginalized and stereotyped. Fortunately, in the past 2 decades there has been growth in self-help groups that build on the very strengths of people with psychiatric problems. Psychiatric consumer survivors, as many of these groups prefer to call themselves, have built businesses, provided support to each other, lobbied for improved housing, and become contributing members of society, fighting negative stereotypes that denigrate their potential and dignity (Nelson, Lord, et al., 2001; Nelson, Ochocka, Janzen, & Trainor, in press).

The death of my (Isaac's) parents had become, in people's eyes, a deficit in my life. Instead of focusing on my strengths, many acquaintances, teachers, and relatives used to focus on my tragedy. Pity was not exactly what I needed, but nobody had the psychological insight to reinforce my strengths. After all, I was doing pretty well, except for holding in a flood of tears that were never allowed to come out. Needless, prolonged suffering might have been averted, had my caregivers known how to deal with loss and grief. I felt diminished by the aura of tragedy and pity that surrounded my encounters with adults in particular. My closest friends, I'm happy to say, were a tremendous source of support. These 8-year-olds knew intuitively what many adults didn't: to give me time, space, and an opportunity to use my strengths, in soccer, in friendships, in coping. They knew when to talk about "it" and when to normalize things. They let me be, in sadness, in confusion. With adults, on the contrary, I was not allowed to be. I still remember the contrived gestures by some distant relatives who would take me out on Sunday or to the movies because I was an orphan.

The box of pity is incredibly constraining, for an 8-year-old who lost his parents and for a mature woman with a physical disability, who was once introduced as "the victim of muscular dystrophy," as in Ora's case. Life challenges are not your greeting card: "Hi, I'm Isaac, I lost my parents when I was 8." There is more to orphans and people with disabilities than their tragedies. There is more to psychiatric patients than their condition. A focus on strengths is imperative for anyone who is seeking help or struggling with a challenge.

Affirmation Quadrants Quadrant I in Figure 2.2 represents interventions that promote voice and choice in celebrating and building competencies. People have an opportunity to exercise control over decisions affecting their lives, while building on former experiences of success.

Quadrant II affords community members voice and choice in methods of deficit reduction. Citizens are made partners in the struggle against depression, stress, obesity, or infectious diseases. Quadrant III is the epitome of clienthood and patienthood. Not only are people deprived of an opportunity to participate in helping and healing, but most of the focus is on diagnosis of pathology and labeling of maladaptive behavior.

Quadrant IV represents the unique combination of approaches that strive to be positive while keeping the person detached from the change process. Popular yet ineffective campaigns such as "Just say no to drugs" and cheerleading efforts such as "You can do it if you want" represent empty promises of better health. Though positive and effusive, such strategies fail to connect with the real-life experience of youth growing up in drug-infested communities or with the struggle of many people to lower their weight despite lack of access to affordable and nutritious food.

The SPEC Field

By combining into one plane the contextual domains with the affirmation domains, we can portray the SPEC field in Figure 2.4. The positive ends of the two contextual continua create the positive end of axis x in Figure 2.4: proactive and collective interventions. Similarly, the positive ends of the affirmation continua form the positive end of the y axis in Figure 2.4: strength-based and empowering approaches. The negative end of the former continuum comprises reactive and individual interventions, and the negative extreme of the latter contains detached and deficit-oriented practices.

Quadrant I in Figure 2.4 fosters voice and choice in community development, policy making, and wellness promotion. Quadrant II, in turn, addresses communitywide issues proactively, but from a deficit orientation. Efforts in Canada and Australia to educate aboriginal children in Western traditions were proactive and collective strategies employed by government and church officials. Colonizers removed aboriginal children from their families to educate them in Western traditions; they regarded aboriginal culture as deficient and inferior. Native families didn't have a say in the matter, nor did the children, who were often later subjected to abuse and neglect.

Quadrant III in Figure 2.4 is about the prototypical medical model, whereby help seekers become patients in an elaborate system of labeling,

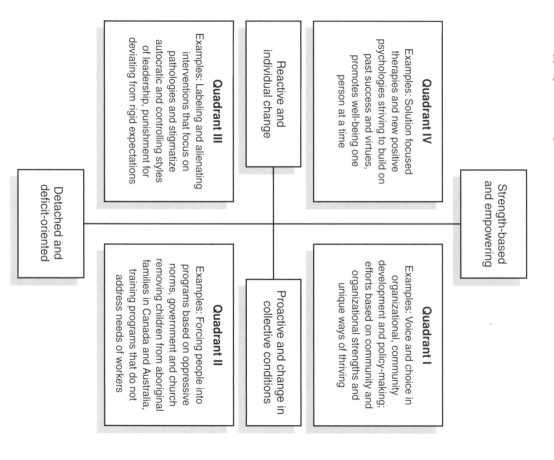

Strength-based and empowering

Reactive and individual change

Detached and deficit-oriented

Proactive and change in collective conditions

Quadrant IV
Examples: Solution focused therapies and new positive psychologies striving to build on past success and virtues, promotes well-being one person at a time

Quadrant I
Examples: Voice and choice in organizational, community development and policy-making; efforts based on community and organizational strengths and unique ways of thriving

Quadrant III
Examples: Labeling and alienating interventions that focus on pathologies and stigmatize autocratic and controlling styles of leadership, punishment for deviating from rigid expectations

Quadrant II
Examples: Forcing people into programs based on oppressive norms, government and church removing children from aboriginal families in Canada and Australia, training programs that do not address needs of workers

Figure 2.4   The Strength, Prevention, Empowerment, Change in Condition (SPEC) Field of Well-Being: Efforts Combining the Contextual and Affirmation Fields.

diagnosis, and alienation. Quadrant IV embodies strength-based and empowering interventions that are reactive and person-centered.

Solution-focused therapy and certain aspects of the new positive psychology represent this modality of helping. Oriented toward resilience and past successes, this approach is predicated on individuals knocking on professional doors for help after a physical or psychosocial problem has set in.

In summary, reactive, individual, alienating, and deficit-based approaches that foster patienthood instead of health, citizenship, and democracy have dominated the field of health and human services for decades (I. Prilleltensky & Nelson, 2002). It is time to shift paradigms and give strength-based, preventive, empowering, and community-oriented approaches a chance to promote personal, organizational, and collective well-being. SPEC-based approaches have proven cost-effective and more humane than the predominant and disempowering medical model (Nelson, Lord, et al., 2001).

ROWS FOR WELLNESS

Exercise 2: Organizational SPEC

Toward the end of Chapter 1, we introduced the idea of ROWS. This is a tool to help you devise a plan of action on your own terms. In the previous chapter, we concentrated on a personal situation that you may have experienced. In this chapter, we concentrate on changes that may need to take place at the organizational level. The exercise will help you reflect on an organization that influences your life. This may be your place of employment, your school (if you are student), or a service agency that you come into contact with. If you work for a helping organization, we recommend you use it for the exercise.

Keeping SPEC in mind, assess to what extent the organization implements a philosophy based on strengths, prevention, empowerment, and changing conditions. Using Form 2.1, list some of the risks, opportunities, weaknesses, and strengths of the organization when it comes to following SPEC. Try to identify ROWS for each one of the letters of SPEC. For example, try to come up with an opportunity for a strength-based approach for prevention, empowerment, and changing conditions. Do the same for risks, weaknesses, and strengths.

The next step, as in Chapter 1, is to devise a plan of action. To do that, we transfer the various items under ROWS into Form 2.2, which we call the Wellness Readiness Check.

Now that you've identified ROWS for SPEC, you're ready to begin work on the process of organizational change. How exactly to do that is the topic of Part III of the book.

Form 2.1   ROWS Exercise 2: Organizational SPEC

Risks *Example from human service organization:* My organization would like to engage in more preventive activities, but the community expects us to do charity work with individuals, instead of community work that changes conditions for many people.			
Opportunities *Example from human service organization:* Despite the fact that some staff and board members expect us to help one person at a time, they realize that this approach is not effective because there will never be enough staff to meet the demand of people in need. This may be an opportunity for us to promote the SPEC agenda.			
Weaknesses *Example from human service organization:* Many staff members have been trained in reactive therapeutic approaches and they lack skills in prevention and community-based interventions. Some of them have seriously embraced an expert approach that minimizes voice and choice of consumers.			
Strengths *Example from human service organization:* Staff members are very caring toward residents who come for help, and would be willing to undergo training in community development to get to the root causes of the problems.			

Form 2.2   Wellness Readiness Check 2:   Organizational SPEC

ROWS	1 I never thought about doing something about it.	2 I'm thinking about doing something about it.	3 I'm prepared to do something about it.	4 I'm doing something about it.	5 I've been doing something about it for some time.
Risks					
Opportunities					
Weaknesses					
Strengths					

3

Webs of Values: The Morals of Well-Being

Values have been vulgarized and debate has been debased. Why? Because of polarization. Polarization attracts viewers to television programs such as *Crossfire* and *Hardball*, where the left and the right engage in moral pugilism. Proponents of the culture wars adamantly defend their right to put each other down, in a downward spiral of communication breakdown (Baker, 2005; Lakoff, 1996; Wolfe, 1998). For commercial reasons, the media treat values as spectator sports. Fanatics inflame debate about welfare, gay rights, abortion, health care, inequality, and social justice. For these and other reasons, values ignorance reigns supreme.

Instead of engaging in reasoned exploration of values, the mass media and demagogues count the punches that sides inflict on each other. Venomous sound bites are cheered like goals in a soccer stadium. For the citizen willing to turn off the television set and look elsewhere for enlightened discussion of values, a few options remain. Some resort to established institutions, such as religion, whereas others seek secular study. These are well-respected traditions that provide people with a moral compass. However, the transmission of values in these settings is often through indoctrination, not exploration, resulting in dogmatism, one-sidedness, and even denial of wrongdoing (Dokecki, 2004).

Every time the word *values* is invoked, people react viscerally in either defensive or attacking postures, especially in the United States, where the word has been associated with abortion, the death penalty, guns, and euthanasia. We hope that much of what has been polarized in this country can be bridged with reasoned dialogue.

We delve here and later into the topic of polarization because it's at the core of much of the confusion about values. Popular discourse relishes opposites: the right of the individual versus the right of the community, the right of the mother versus the right of the fetus, the well-being of a parent versus the well-being of the child, the motivation of the achieving student versus the laziness of the dropout, the intelligence of the wealthy versus the incompetence of the poor. Americans love categories and ranking people. And the media prey on that (Baker, 2005; Lakoff, 1996).

We argue here that dichotomizing issues, people, and values into good/bad, meritorious/undeserving, and right/wrong simplifies to the extreme complicated matters—matters that require more consideration than time between commercials permits. Here we take the time to explore, not dichotomies, but rather webs of values and webs of wellness.

Contrary to popular opinion that positions the state against the individual, we claim that the individual cannot flourish without the state. No issue elicits more passions in Tennessee, our adopted state, than taxes. Taxes are seen as evil. It is the state robbing you of your hard-earned money. It is you or the state, nothing in between, or nothing that connects your taxes to your well-being (Lakoff, 1996).

Kekes (1993, p. 44) defines values as "humanly caused benefits that human beings provide to others. . . . By way of illustration, we may say that love and justice are moral goods." Kekes provides an abstract concept of values as well as concrete illustrations. This is a useful point of departure for thinking about values. Values guide the process of working toward a desired state of affairs. They are precepts that inform our personal, professional, and political behavior. But values are beneficial not only because they guide behavior toward a future outcome, for they also have intrinsic merit (Carson, 2000). We espouse such values as self-determination, caring, and solidarity, not just because they lead toward a good or better society, but also because they have merit of their own accord (Hill Collins, 1993, 1998; Kane, 1994; Kekes, 1993; H. Lewis, 1990). Indeed, according to Mayton, Ball-Rokeach, and Loges (1994, p. 3), "Values may be defined as enduring prescriptive or proscriptive beliefs that a specific mode of conduct (instrumental value) or end state of existence (terminal value) is preferred to another mode of conduct or end state." S. H. Schwartz (1994, p. 21) points out that values "serve as guiding principles in the life of a person or other social entity." Values, then, are the principles that guide our actions toward the "good and the just" (H. Lewis, 1990, p. 7).

Liberty and freedom, these much-loved American values, cannot prosper in the absence of safe and healthy communities. Healthy communities, in turn, cannot prosper in the absence of capable individuals who can contribute to the common good, through taxes, work, volunteer efforts, and compassion.

The right in this country has traditionally defended a libertarian approach, the rights of the individual above all, whereas the left has adopted a more interventionist approach, asking government to influence the course of events in the community (Lakoff, 1996). Well, this is not a dichotomy, as it has been traditionally presented, but rather a dialectic situation. Liberty cannot thrive without common resources, and communal goods cannot exist without the efforts of organized individuals. We propose, therefore, a set of complementary values that strive to promote personal and communal well-being at the same time (D. Bakan, 1966; Loewy, 1993). But these two desired states can be achieved only by the work of organizations. Hence, we also introduce into the mix organizational values.

Organizations are the mediating structures between individuals and communities. Organizations are the places where individuals pursue their goals, where governments enact policies, and where human service workers try to ameliorate suffering and promote wellness for all.

The metaphor of a web symbolizes the interdependence of components (Capra, 1996, 2003). Personal values such as self-determination, health, and development rely extensively on access to resources such as education, health care, and employment. These resources require the organized effort of governments at the local, state, and federal levels. The more we explore separate values such as freedom and liberty, the more we see how linked they are to other values, such as a sense of community and social justice (Clark, 2002; Nussbaum, 1999; Sen, 1999b). We have to replace the idea of a zero-sum game with the notion of synergy (Kohn, 1986).

No matter how fervently we believe that individuals can lift themselves up by their bootstraps, the facts tell us otherwise. If you don't have any boots, there are no bootstraps. So-called exemplars of independence always rely on others who help them get ahead: their mothers, their mentors, their privilege, their education, and their connections.

As we shall see in this chapter and throughout this book, the facts are that motivation, drive, and determination come from somewhere. They come from exposure to opportunities, from a culture that extols achievement, and from the heritage of privilege. This is not to say that people without privilege cannot have drive, but that it is hard to find people with motivation and determination who did not have strong influences on them to become who they are. It is all a matter of how hard you look into the antecedents of behavior. There is a long tradition in this country of ascribing success and failure to the individual, but when you look deeper into the causes of behavior, you always find an external cause that plays a big factor: access to good schools, networks, education, opportunity, and the like (I. Prilleltensky, 1994). And when you ask who has access to good private schools, networks, and the like, you find that those with privilege are usually the ones benefiting from opportunities the most. When you ask further why some people have privilege and others don't, you realize that privilege usually comes in generations. And the more you look back into behaviors and ask what are the reasons for educational achievement or socioeconomic status, you realize that communal, economic, and political conditions have a lot to do with them (Hook, 2004; Layard, 2005). Therefore, we have to pay attention to collective values and organizational values that afford opportunities to individuals to fulfill their private aspirations (Eckersley et al., 2002; Hofrichter, 2003; Nussbaum, 1999).

We segment, dichotomize, and polarize values at our own peril (Baker, 2005). We want to believe that if clients of human services wanted it hard enough, they could get to college, stop dependency on welfare, and become healthy and independent (Ife, 2001, 2002). We really want to believe that it all starts with the person. But persons live in contexts, and contexts need to be improved for all to take advantage of them (Shinn & Toohey, 2003). Organizations play a role in that. It is the aim of this chapter to explore how personal, organizational, and collective values intersect and sustain each other.

VALUES FOR WELL-BEING

Before we present our conception of values for the good life and the good society, we want to share with you where these values come from. You should never accept any set of values at, you guessed it, face value. Our proposal derives from biological, psychological, sociological, historical, economic, and philosophical sources (Layard, 2005; H. Lewis, 1990). From biology and psychology, we learn the basic needs that human beings require to sustain life, grow, and achieve their goals. From sociology, economics, and history we appreciate the conditions that enable individuals and communities to cooperate or to fight. From philosophy, we learn how to discern what is fair and how to allocate resources in society (Clark, 2002; Layard, 2005).

Philosophical scrutiny is indispensable because certain groups may have internalized and expressed needs that reinforce their privilege at the expense of others. Unless we scrutinize needs and wants, we face the risk of granting to some groups wishes that perpetuate oppression and injustice. This is why values cannot derive exclusively from opinion polls. Surveys reflect what people want and need, but not necessarily what is just or moral. People's opinions are subject to the same simplifying and polarizing effects that our values are subjected to (Mustakova-Possardt, 2003). Giving people a voice is a necessary but insufficient condition for the establishment of values and the promotion of the good society (Nussbaum, 1999).

By relying on diverse sources, we are able to create a realistic yet morally sound conception of values. In every instance in which one of these considerations is neglected, we witness unsatisfactory value systems (Kane, 1994; Kerruish, 1995; Ralston Saul, 2001). When the sociology of values is ignored, we end up with theories that begin and end in people's heads, as if the circumstances of their growing up did not matter. When psychology and biology are not taken into account, we create theories that expect human beings to behave like superhumans, which they are not. And finally, every time philosophy is ignored, we devise systems that lack a vision of a just society. It's important to know what people need and want, under what conditions their needs can be met, and what principles we need to use to distribute resources and opportunities fairly. It is from an integration of these sources that we derive the following principles.

Values for Personal Well-Being

In the following sections we provide brief descriptions of central values for individual well-being. We organize them in several clusters.

Self-Determination, Freedom, and Personal Growth   Ask people in any society about their conception of the good life, and freedom, choice, and human development spring immediately to mind (Clark, 2002; Kahneman, Diener, & Schwarz, 1999; Layard, 2005). People have personal projects to pursue, dreams to fulfill, and goals to achieve.

However, it is not only about the outcome, but also very much about the journey. Having the ability to exercise self-determination and to be in control of one's life are primordial values. Having the right to make wrong decisions is a very significant part of self-determination. These are the pillars of empowerment: voice and choice (Nelson, Lord, et al., 2001).

Empowerment sits right in between underempowerment and overempowerment. Whereas the former is an expression of oppression and silencing, the latter is a manifestation of domination. In any domain of our lives, we can recognize instances of the three forms of empowerment: too little, too much, or just about the right amount.

Community members who feel disempowered yearn for the opportunity to feel more control over their lives. This is why the E of SPEC is so vital. As we saw in the previous chapter, empowerment is an essential ingredient of any helping approach. Helpers need to understand that empowerment is not just an outcome, but also a journey. It is fairly disempowering to be told what to do "because in the end you will have more control over your life." The art of helping lies in coconstructing with community members empowering paths for sustainable, empowering outcomes (Ife, 2001; McWhirter, 1994).

The interdependence of self-determination with external circumstances is nicely captured in Erich Fromm's (1965) dual conception of freedom: *freedom from* and *freedom to*. The removal of barriers is very much a part of empowerment. This is freedom from—freedom from psychological, economic, social, cultural, and political barriers. Our ability to pursue goals in life is eminently determined by the social and physical landscape around us (Sen, 1999b). Freedom from hunger, from discrimination, from fear, from ignorance, from illness: We have witnessed them all in our community projects.

Only after *freedom from* is achieved we can meaningfully talk about *freedom to*. To reach the stage of *freedom to* we have to attend to the collective values of social justice and support for community structures. Once the main barriers to self-determination are out of the way, humans face the question of freedom *for what*. What is one to do with her or his freedom? This is, many philosophers claim, a matter of personal choice, and we agree. But we have to keep in mind that somebody's *freedom to* can become somebody else's *freedom from*. In other words, a person's pursuit of happiness must take into account how her or his actions may become, however innocently, barriers to somebody else's well-being.

This dictum looks simple enough: My freedom ends where somebody else's begins. But people fail to see how their actions or lack thereof affect others. We are not talking here about armed robbery or domestic abuse, where the actions of one explicitly and undoubtedly diminish the freedom of the other. There are multiple ways in which subtle and even imperceptible actions perpetuate oppression (I. Prilleltensky & Gonick, 1996). Refusing to pay more taxes to fund health care for all is a civic action with dire consequences for thousands of people. Ignoring the plight of hungry children is another. These are sins of omission, wherein my lack of action impinges substantially on the well-being of others.

Like all other values we explore in this chapter, self-determination has intrinsic and extrinsic value. Intrinsic merits relate to the feeling of being in control, whereas extrinsic merits refer to the pursuit of goals in the future. In short, freedom and self-determination are good for their own sake and for the sake of other goods, such as desirable ends.

Self-determination, freedom, and growth relate to all the letters of the SPEC model. By recognizing people's strengths, we reinforce their self-determination; by supporting their freedom, we prevent stress; and by giving them voice and choice, we create opportunities to exercise decision-making power. The C of SPEC reminds us that without changing community conditions, some people will be forever limited in their ability to pursue goals. The values of *freedom from* and *freedom to* are conditioned by situational and environmental factors, such as access to resources, safety, economic disadvantage, discrimination, and educational opportunities (Frey & Stutzer, 2002; Layard, 2005).

Health, Caring, and Compassion   Along with self-determination and human development, physical health and psychological well-being are primordial values. Without them, we cannot pursue *freedom to*, as we are limited by illness or preoccupation. Like self-determination, health also has intrinsic and extrinsic properties; it has intrinsic value in that it results in feeling good in the here and now, and it has extrinsic value in that it sustains the achievement of other goals in the near and distant future. Illness and psychological problems interfere with daily functions in varying degrees (Clark, 2002; Farmer, 2003; Nussbaum, 1999; Sen, 1999b).

Our vulnerability to poor health invokes the second set of values in this category: caring and compassion. As noted in Chapter 1, social support has beneficial effects on both the provider and the receiver. Caring and compassion are sine qua non conditions for a moral community. Not only are they psychologically and physically beneficial, but they represent the highest form of ethical behavior (Loewy, 1993; Mustakova-Possardt, 2003). Caring for the sick and the poor is a high value in many religions. And judging by the importance given to these values, we would expect more of it in our society.

Why is it that almost everyone is in favor of caring and compassion and yet our society continues to neglect the disadvantaged? As we write this chapter, 323,000 people are going to be dropped off our state medical insurance program. The public at large seems resigned to the fact that it is the right thing to do to balance the budget.

The two of us have lived in other countries in which everyone is covered, regardless of ability to pay insurance. In Israel, Canada, and Australia, everyone is covered by the system. We lived for 15 years in Canada in two provinces and we never, ever received a bill for the excellent care we received. We don't mean to romanticize these medical systems, for problems exist, but at least there was a national consensus that health care was a right, and not a privilege (Hofrichter, 2003). We are frankly astounded by the lack of public outcry regarding the 45 million people who lack health care in the United States.

People rationalize this state of affairs by invoking proximal caring at the expense of distal caring. Proximal caring is the attention and compassion afforded people close to us through chance, birth, or association. We express proximal caring to our children, parents, peers, and the people we serve through our volunteer work in schools, hospitals, and community centers. We feel good about what we do and think that we have fulfilled our caring obligations toward society. But this perception is inaccurate, for caring consists not only of proximal, but also of distal caring. Distal caring is compassion for those whom we don't personally know, but who nevertheless deserve our compassion. Sometimes people who live two blocks away from us are lacking in basic necessities, and for some reason we don't regard them as falling within the realm of our caring obligations. This is because people concentrate on proximal caring and neglect distal caring. Both components of caring, distal and proximal, are equally valid. Yet, by focusing only on the proximal aspect, people feel they have dutifully discharged their caring obligations, leaving social issues to politicians and government officials. Big mistake! Dropping hundreds of thousands of people from the state medical system is a caring issue, and not just a policy issue to be delegated to state officials.

Proximal and distal duties must be discharged for the value of caring to be fulfilled. If more people embraced this dual conception of caring and compassion, more people would be on the streets protesting the lack of health care and nutrition for many in their community. Distal caring matters as much as proximal caring; both are essential values.

The value of health is especially noteworthy in the United States. The United States is the industrialized country that spends the most on health care and covers the fewest people (Reinhardt, Hussey, & Anderson, 2004). Many of the clients of health and human services lack basic health care and suffer the consequences of illness, lack of preventive care, and neglect of routine checkups.

The value of health is underpinned by all the letters of SPEC. When we think of assets and strengths, we need to think of personal and communal health. Similarly, when we think of prevention we have to address known risk and protective factors, such as nutrition, exercise, and alcohol consumption. As noted in Chapter 1, a sense of control and empowerment contributes to good health. Finally, the C in SPEC, for conditions, is essential for good health. Conditions of pollution and exposure to carcinogens lead to reduction in health and quality of life. Lead in the paint of housing projects causes brain damage and developmental delays. Likewise, exposure to psychological conditions of abuse and neglect result in psychological trauma, depression, isolation, and poor self-esteem (G. Evans & Kantrowitz, 2002). To enjoy health, we need to pay simultaneous attention to all the components of SPEC.

Values for Organizational Well-Being

In the following sections we nominate key values for organizational health.

Accountability, Transparency, and Responsiveness to the Common Good

This set of values refers to the relationships between the organization and the community it serves and between managers and the workforce. Let's explore the relationship between agencies and the community first.

Health and human services exist to serve the community (Ife, 2001). This is their ultimate goal: to improve community well-being. To do that, they must respond to community needs and aspirations. But to make sure that their services and programs do just that, they have to be transparent and accountable to the people they serve.

Typically, human services have a measure of community representation on their boards. For the most part, however, these are influential people, whose voices do not represent the most disempowered. That's a problem. Concerted efforts need to be directed at recruiting community members who represent the interests of the grassroots.

To be responsive to the common good, agencies conduct periodic needs assessments and strategic planning. This is desirable practice. Nevertheless, needs assessments often concentrate on the needs of individuals and don't capture the community conditions that require transformation.

There are multiple challenges to the enactment of accountability, transparency, and responsiveness to the common good. At present, many social services do not have mechanisms for ongoing dialogue with clients or community members about their programs. Most agencies have some sort of feedback form or program evaluation that clients fill out, but these efforts fall short of establishing continuous dialogue with the community.

Partners in one of the agencies with whom we cooperate decided to canvass the community following the SPEC model. Their goal was to obtain accurate and representative views of community residents about how to assist them. It is taking some time to achieve this goal because the agency has never undertaken such a project before in a systematic way that embraces SPEC principles.

Adopting the principles of accountability, transparency, and responsiveness is a tall order. Although these principles should be routine, the expertdriven approach has created a distance between service recipients and service providers. So much so that it seems unusual to ask people what they need and how services may be improved (Mullaly, 2002; I. Prilleltensky & Nelson, 2002). Today it may seem difficult, but with time, this may become part of the regular business of being responsive to the community.

The SPEC approach and the values under consideration have a reciprocal relationship. By sharing with the community the inner workings of the organization, we are creating capacity in the community and we are helping service providers to be more in tune with the needs of residents. Furthermore, we are empowering the community to be more involved in the life of the organization. By being responsive to the needs of the community we can prevent foreseeable problems that the community knows about and the experts don't. We can achieve this by listening closely and carefully to the problems and solutions from the perspective of residents (Ife, 2001, 2002).

John McKnight (1987), a seasoned community organizer in Chicago, tells the story of dog bites and traffic accidents in a community. Public health officials didn't know how to solve these problems, but community members were quick to point out solutions. They had information about traffic accidents that city council didn't. They knew from experience where most accidents took place, and they knew how to organize kids in the neighborhood to catch stray dogs. Within a few days, the neighborhood was free of stray dogs, and traffic accidents went down considerably. These outcomes could not have been achieved without the help of the community. Residents identified conditions that led to problems. There are certain things that professionals cannot see from their offices. In the following chapters, we detail strategies for building on community assets and for putting into effect the values of accountability, transparency, and responsiveness.

The values of transparency, accountability, and responsiveness to the common good, however, are not directed exclusively at the community. The workforce deserves the same entitlements. It is vital to have an open climate where dilemmas are shared with employees, where people are accountable for follow-up on decisions, and where the common good of workers and managers alike is nurtured (Burke, 2002). Many agencies we know go to great length to engage staff in decision-making processes affecting their jobs, whereas others fail to do so. The result of failure is predictable disengagement. Token accountability and cloudy transparency are sometimes worse than no accountability at all because they reflect hypocrisy. The SPEC approach guiding our work calls on organizations to develop mechanisms for enhancing responsiveness to workers and clients alike. The external work of the organization cannot be carried out without embracing internally what we wish for the community externally.

Collaboration, Democratic Participation, and Respect for Human Diversity
Much of what is needed to achieve accountability, responsiveness, and transparency relies on collaboration, democratic participation, and respect for human diversity. Without these, self-determination cannot prosper. Creating spaces for people to participate in decision-making processes affords them an opportunity to exercise their voice and choice. Collaboration and democratic participation are values that should be enjoyed by workers and community members alike (Nelson, Prilleltensky, & MacGillivary, 2001).

Community members bring an important voice to the table. They need to have an opportunity to share their experiences in a nonthreatening setting. For the most part, recipients of services interact with providers around problems and challenges; they are defined by the situation as the needy ones. This routine places them in a position of habitual inferiority. Opportunities to interact with providers in another capacity, as a voice of the community, bring forth voice and choice. Self-determination needs to be practiced, and there is no better way than structured collaborations to do so.

Just as self-determination needs to be practiced, so does democratic participation. Either in individual sessions or group situations, we cannot take for granted that community members feel secure enough to express their opinion, let alone dissent. Democratic participation needs to be nurtured with skills, opportunities, and training. It's not good enough to hold a community forum and expect that residents will feel empowered to voice their concerns. Democracy is not a show but a tradition; it cannot be accomplished in a one-shot deal.

Much has been said in this country about diversity, but not enough has been done about it. Respect for diversity flows from the recognition we afford every individual by virtue of her or his humanity (Taylor, 1992). This value recognizes the uniqueness of every human being. Furthermore, it grants all persons the right to define themselves as they see fit. It is a fundamental human right. That much we know. What we don't know enough about is how to put it into practice beyond multicultural festivals, food, songs, and dance. This value can be enacted in either tokenistic or profound ways.

Here we are interested in deep and meaningful ways of having people from diverse classes, races, abilities, languages, ages, and gender orientations included in the life of organizations and communities. Collaboration, democratic participation, and respect for diversity begin at home. Organizations vary in their degree of commitment to these values, and every worker knows how much or how little her or his voice is heard. Building a tradition of collaboration and participation requires intentional effort and prolonged commitment. The E of SPEC addresses this value directly. How much voice and choice do workers and community members have in the organization? Do they feel respected, heard, appreciated? Do they exercise any control? Without collaboration, there is no empowerment, and without empowerment, there is no chance of practicing self-determination.

Values for Community Well-Being

Now we address a series of values that support the health and well-being of communities.

Support for Community Structures   The evidence is clear that human beings cannot flourish in isolation, nor can they develop without access to communal goods such as health care, housing, high-quality education, and a clean environment. These communal goods, particularly a clean environment, are good on their own accord, but are also good for the satisfaction of essential human needs (Clark, 2002; Sen, 1999b). In short, they have intrinsic and extrinsic properties. To support these communal goods, we require community structures. Civic society creates institutions to preserve the common good, such as the Sierra Club and Amnesty International to protect the environment and human rights, respectively. Unfortunately, volunteer organizations can go only so far in meeting basic needs. This is why we rely on government to serve the educational, safety, and health needs of the community. Some governments provide more services than others, but all governments cover some minimal services that are essential for running cities and municipalities.

The state does have a role in promoting citizen well-being. When we lived in Canada, Ora was able to obtain through a government program a very expensive electric wheelchair. In addition, our son enjoyed many years of excellent public schools. In Melbourne, Australia, we enjoyed an excellent transportation system. Here in Nashville, we were able to obtain another excellent electric wheelchair, but only through private insurance. Our son goes to a private school, and the transportation system leaves much to be desired. We can appreciate in our own family the benefits of access to public goods.

In the United States, support from the state for the poor is being aggressively withdrawn. In Tennessee, as we mentioned, 323,000 people are about to be dropped completely from the state medical insurance program, and thousands of others are about to have their medication and other health benefits severely cut. For some reason, most people seem to accept the verdict without much opposition. We, in our family, will not be affected by the cuts, but we work with people who will. Let's not forget that every year about 18,000 people die because of lack of health insurance (Institute of Medicine, 2002).

Access to health services is but one example of the need to support civic and government institutions that perform essential services. Education, housing, welfare, employment, and transportation are others.

Proponents of less government support are quick to point out that consumers should have more money in their pockets and be able to choose what medical insurance they get. This works for the people who have stable jobs. What about those with jobs without benefits? There are 45 million people in this country without any medical insurance. For them, the system is not working. We can blame them, call them lazy, and feel self-righteous, or we can look at the structural sources of the problem (Lakoff, 1996).

At a time when government support for vital services is diminishing, it is more important than ever to appreciate the role that community structures play in well-being. This value resembles the C of SPEC: conditions. Community conditions are improved or impoverished by the presence or absence of enabling structures like schools, clinics, parks, and public housing, as much as volunteer organizations like community centers, sport associations, and self-help groups (Nelson & Prilleltensky, 2005).

Social Justice   "To each his or her due," states a traditional definition of justice. To wit, justice is the fair and equitable allocation of power, resources, and obligations in society (D. Miller, 1999). This is a useful beginning, but it begs the questions of what's fair and what's equitable. How do we decide that some people deserve more or less pay, or welfare, or medical coverage? According to Sidgwick (1922, p. 274), the cardinal question of justice is whether there are "any clear principles from which we may work out an ideally just distribution of rights and privileges, burdens and pains, among human beings as such."

Our point of departure is that common resources are limited. If they weren't, we wouldn't have a big problem. Everyone could have access to medical services, excellent schools, and affordable housing. That is not the case. Day in and day out, we struggle to allocate limited services, resources, and obligations in a fair way. Some philosophers have offered a useful way of thinking about distribution. They argue that it all depends on the situation, which makes sense, because it's hard to come up with principles out of context (Facione, Scherer, & Attig, 1978; D. Miller, 1999). We all agree that fairness is a good principle, but it is an abstract one. What is fair in one situation may be unfair in another. Hence, we have to know the specific circumstances affecting people and society to determine the just way to act.

Facione et al. (1978) propose two useful criteria for distributing resources in society: work and need. Depending on the circumstances, they claim, it may be fair to use one criterion but not the other. Let's examine the two criteria. First, need. By virtue of our humanity, we all deserve to have our basic needs met: shelter, food, clothing, education, emotional nurturance, and the like. We are all born equal, and we are all equally deserving of a basic standard of living (Clark, 2002). It follows from this premise that if I have a limited resource, and I have several people claiming it, I will distribute it first among those whose basic needs have not been met yet. If I still have some of it left after I fulfilled the basic needs of a person or a group, I can proceed to distribute it on another basis, such as work or merit.

The second criterion for distributing resources is work. This criterion refers to the time, ability, effort, and talent invested in a job. Work and merit reflect the fact that someone deserves something due to effort, intelligence, diligence, or a combination thereof. Assume for a moment that you and your coworker have been asked to perform a job, but you work many more hours than your peer does and you end up doing a far superior job. Your partner, in turn, does very little and spends a lot of work time playing video games on the computer. Should the two of you receive the same compensation? Should your partner be equally rewarded? Assuming that the two of you have your basic needs met, it would make sense to reward the one who works so much harder. In this case, we're not worrying about basic needs, because both of you are above subsistence level. Rather, we're concerned with rewarding hard work or talent in a fair manner. It makes sense in this situation to reward the one who worked harder and delivered a better product.

Concerning the need criterion, Facione and colleagues (1978, p. 186) argue that it is "reasonable to suggest that persons are strictly equal as persons. This means they all have some very basic human needs. . . . On this criterion people are equally deserving of having these needs met," a position endorsed by Singer (1993). In essence, the criterion for distribution would be determined by the reigning social circumstances. Consider the following scenario:

(a) There is sufficient work so that there are jobs for all who need them, (b) the jobs available to each person include jobs that the person has the abilities to perform, and (c) the jobs pay well enough so that whenever a person takes one, it will enable him or her to earn enough so that his or her needs are met. (Facione et al., 1978, p. 190)

Under such circumstances, the winning criterion is clearly *work*. But consider now the following set of circumstances:

(a) It may be that there are fewer jobs than there are people who need them.
(b) Persons may be unable to perform the jobs that are available owing to simple lack of ability. . . . The lack of ability may be socially dependent in the sense that skills that people do have can become outmoded and no longer needed in a rapidly changing and technologically progressive society. Or it may be that in a nation as a whole there are sufficient jobs to match the abilities of the people, but the people with the abilities are not located where the jobs are. . . . It could also be that some are denied opportunities to do the

work for which they are qualified owing to various forms of job discrimination. (c) It may be that the jobs for which some people qualify, or that they are able to handle given their other responsibilities, simply do not pay well enough to meet their needs. The wages may be extremely low, or the work may be part-time or seasonal. (pp. 190–191)

If any of these conditions obtain, the criterion of need must take precedence over the criterion of work. At Vanderbilt University, where we work, there have been heated debates about a living wage for some employees. Some of our workers in janitorial positions earn a minimum wage that is insufficient to cover their family needs. The scenario depicted by Facione and colleagues is very real indeed.

We have millions of people in this country and around the world whose basic needs are not met. If we all agreed that we're going to distribute common goods according to need, there would not be hungry children or homeless people in this country. The grim reality is that we're not distributing sufficient food to the hungry or adequate housing to the homeless. Why? Some people argue that there just aren't enough food, houses or appropriate resources to afford health insurance to the uninsured. Others argue that there is enough food and there are enough resources to provide health insurance, but that these resources are not distributed fairly. That is to say, some get a disproportionate amount of food or pay, and others get a minuscule amount. The problem is not the amount of resources, for they exist, but rather the way they are distributed.

Take health expenditures, for instance. As noted, the United States spends more on health per capita than any other country in the Organization of Economic Cooperation and Development. Why is that? The huge bureaucracy that exists in many private insurance companies is a serious cause of inflated prices: They all need to make a profit. As a result, they are eager to charge as much as possible; they are in business to make money. In countries where health care is nationalized and provided by the government, bureaucracies are smaller and the profit motive does not exist. As a result, the costs are lower and the countries can afford health care for everyone. In short, the argument that there aren't enough resources to provide health care for all can and has been challenged (Hofrichter, 2003; Navarro, 2000, 2004; Navarro & Muntaner, 2004).

Governments make decisions about how to invest public money. Legislators decide whether to expand the military or cut welfare payments. They decide whether to cut taxes for the rich or invest in failing schools. The argument that there are not enough resources is not very solid at all. The question is what the priorities are and how the money is allocated.

Proponents of the merit argument, that people should receive resources based on their effort and/or talent alone, apply the principle of work indiscriminately, that is, without regard for context. They assume that all people have equal opportunities to advance, get jobs, get a degree, and make good choices for themselves and their children. In fact, people do not have the same opportunities in life. As a result, it would be unfair to distribute resources only according to merit or work. We agree that if we all had the same opportunities it would be fair to reward the ones who work harder, but we're very far from achieving that situation of equality. The starting point of a child born to a single mother living on welfare is very different from the starting point of a child born to two parents who send him to private schools, feed him nutritious foods, and take him to regular checkups. The former does not have a computer; the latter may have two or three. The former does not participate in extracurricular activities; the latter does sports and is on the debate team. By the time they finish high school, if the former finishes at all, the latter would have accumulated a huge advantage over the years. Should we punish the child who grew up on welfare? Should we deprive him of medical insurance because his mother could not get a job? Is it justified to apply the principle of merit in this case? We're not talking about giving the former a Cadillac and a vacation in the Bahamas; we're talking about the basic human right of health care and nutritious foods in home and at school (Ife, 2001).

We, too, would be happy to apply the principle of reward for effort, but only after basic needs have been met. In many cases, recognition is well deserved, and we agree that dangerous and demanding jobs, for instance, require good remuneration. Firefighters, teachers, day care providers, they all deserve so much more than they currently receive. However, recognition for a job well done, or for effort, cannot become the only criterion for the distribution of basic resources. There are people who have not had opportunities to develop their skills or apply them. Recognition of effort is a solid argument for rewarding people, but only after basic needs have been met (D. Miller, 1999). Otherwise, we are punishing those kids who grow up without opportunities. And unless you have never driven through a public housing project, or visited a school in one of them, or read the papers, you would know that opportunities are not distributed equally in this country. Therefore, in talking about social justice, it's essential to talk not only about the fair distribution of rewards and services, but also about a fair distribution of opportunities, for without opportunities there are no available means of achieving recognition or practicing one's talents. We develop the concept of social justice further in Chapter 15.

THE INTERDEPENDENCE OF VALUES

The temptation is great to concentrate on a single value at the expense of others: It makes life easy, it offers simple solutions, and it follows well-established traditions (Baker, 2005; Lakoff, 1996). Reality, however, points us in the opposite direction. The empirical evidence indicates that values are interdependent (Capra, 1996, 2003; Clark, 2002). We cannot pursue self-determination in the absence of opportunities, nor can we attain collaboration and democratic participation without chances to express voice and choice (Ralston Saul, 2001).

The reciprocal nature of people's abilities and opportunities determines the weblike nature of values. Needs are most efficiently and humanely met when all values act in concert. Anytime one of the values is singled out as most important, others are bound to suffer. Take the prevalence of individualism in the United States. No wonder there is so much competition and lack of solidarity in the country. Looking out for Number One is a national obsession, reinforced by the media and popular culture (Kohn, 1986).

Take now the opposite case of the former Soviet Union. People had to sacrifice for the state, and there was no room for self-determination. The support for the state expected from Soviet citizens overshadowed the need for self-expression and freedom—*freedom from* and *freedom to*.

The interdependence of freedom and community requires that we place limits on both of them. To begin, certain limits on freedom are required to protect the common good (Loewy, 1993). We punish people who drive while intoxicated because they risk killing themselves and others. Similarly, we put limits on what communities can do to individuals so that we may protect their privacy. Parts of the community may wish to regulate sexual behavior, but laws prevent the state from entering the bedroom. Respect for diversity comes to the rescue of *freedom to* (freedom to choose a sexual identity), while social justice comes to the rescue of *freedom from* (freedom from hunger and preventable diseases).

There cannot be a *single* value to promote personal, organizational, and collective wellness at the same time (Kane, 1994). Rather, we need a *set* of values that is internally consistent, that avoids dogmatism and relativism, and that promotes congruence between means and ends. Whereas some values may advocate personal more than collective wellness, such as the principle of self-determination, others may balance it by fostering caring and compassion for others. This reasoning calls for a search of values that can balance the promotion of personal wellness with the affirmation of collective and organizational wellness at the same time. If we did not have rules against smoking in public spaces, more children would be affected by secondhand smoke. We need collective norms to protect citizens against potential abuses of power and excesses of individual rights.

Although it is clear that helpers pay attention to personal, organizational, and community wellness, it is important to determine just how much attention, and what type of attention, we are talking about. Is our level of interest in social justice high or low? Is our interest in such a value at the level of discourse or also at the level of action? The distinction between discourse and action is a crucial one because we often talk about values but we do not always act on them.

Concerning personal wellness, we place heavy emphasis on personal well-being, and there is significant congruence between discourse and action. Many community-based and prevention programs are designed to enhance the level of skills and knowledge of individuals on a particular topic, such as parenting, drug abuse, social skills, and assertiveness. In fact, it has been argued that most prevention programs tend to be person-centered, striving to change the person and not the environment that affects the individual (Albee, 1996; Albee & Perry, 1995; Levine, 1998).

We develop techniques for collaboration and democratic participation in research and community programs (Nelson, Prilleltensky, et al., 2001), yet we are not as attentive to social and political processes of conflict. We concern ourselves with dispute resolution in small circles such as steering committees and community programs, but neglect to address class and racial differences in the political arena.

In comparison to personal wellness, collective wellness occupies a background position in many helping professions. When it comes to promoting social justice and a fair distribution of resources, we look to others to fulfill the job. I. Prilleltensky and Nelson (2002; Nelson & Prilleltensky, 2005) maintain that most of our efforts in the helping professions are ameliorative, as opposed to transformative, in nature. Unfortunately, community interventions strive to alleviate suffering and minimize the impact of unjust policies, not to change society to prevent problems in the first place. More focused attention on collective wellness and social justice, in both discourse and action, will bring us closer to personal, organizational, and community well-being.

EITHER/OR THINKING

The interdependence of values is imperiled by dogmatism and relativism. The antidote to these extreme beliefs is contextualism.

Dogmatism and Relativism

Dogmatism leads to the coercive enforcement and application of single sets of beliefs, an approach that undermines human diversity (Taylor, 1992). Relativism, in turn, grants equal merit to any set of values, thereby paralyzing us because we have no criteria by which to praise or condemn competing orientations (Hill Collins, 1998; Kane, 1994). Dogmatism and relativism are common traps in discussions about values because they promote either/or thinking, as opposed to both/and reasoning (Kane, 1994, 1998; Kekes, 1993; Lerner, 1996).

Contextualism

Values are guidelines for helping others (Kekes, 1993; H. Lewis, 1990). We are especially, but not exclusively, interested in values that promote the well-being of disadvantaged people. Given that people's needs vary according to their particular circumstances, it is nearly impossible to formulate a universal list of values (Giddens, 1994; Kane, 1994, 1998; Kekes, 1993). Hence, we must remember that any proposed set of values contains contextual limitations. Therefore, we should avoid the dogmatic application of values regardless of the context.

Some groups may require, because of their context, certain values more than others. Whereas people with low income may need financial support more than signs of compassion, wealthy people with a disability may need emotional support more than material help.

We should also keep in mind that the meaning of values varies according to people's experiences. The value of independence may have a completely different meaning for an able-bodied person than for a person with a physical disability. In cases like this, interdependence may be more valued than independence. Keeping in mind that the context determines the set of values that is required is a good antidote against the dogmatic application of beliefs. Asking people themselves what they need goes a long way to ensure that we do not impose on them inappropriate values.

Within a given social context, some values appear at the foreground of our consciousness, and others remain in the background. To attain the necessary balance, we must shift the neglected values to the foreground. In the present social context, this means shifting the value of social justice from the background to the foreground and pushing the obsession with personal advancement from the foreground to the background. If we keep neglecting social justice and our collective duties, we will merely reinforce the same unjust state of affairs that perpetuates oppression, and if we keep exalting self-determination, we will undermine any possible sense of community.

It is also crucial to distinguish between ameliorating living conditions within the present social structure and transforming the conditions that create and perpetuate oppression in the first place. Caring should not be limited to meeting people's basic needs on a charitable basis. Caring should entail a commitment to changing negative social conditions so that charity becomes obsolete; that's the C in SPEC.

Perhaps the most obvious application of value-based practice is in programs and policies. If we agree that our interventions should produce equilibrium among personal, organizational, and collective wellness, we should develop guidelines that prevent excessive emphasis on one kind of wellness at the expense of another. Table 3.1 provides a summary of such

Table 3.1 Application of Values in Policies and Programs

Values	Policies	Programs
Self-determination, freedom, and personal growth	Devise policies in consultation with community stakeholders. Establish policies for teaching employment skills and for accessible recreational and educational opportunities.	Promote voice and choice of community members in selection and administration of programs. Build into programs competency enhancing components for personal, educational, and occupational growth.
Health, caring, and compassion	Facilitate access to health care services through universal and outreach programs.	Establish networks of support and create self-help groups.
Respect for diversity, collaboration, and democratic participation	Promote inclusive work and social policies that do not discriminate on basis of marital status, gender, class, culture, or any other source of social power. Promote educational policies that teach importance of civic duties and skills required for meaningful participation in democracy.	Consult with diverse groups of stakeholders and develop inclusive and culturally sensitive programs based on partnerships with the community. Foster climate of respect and develop skills for meaningful and democratic participation in programs.
Accountability and responsiveness to common good	Set up policies that require ongoing dialogue with most disempowered members of the community about their needs and views on services.	Make sure boards of directors have 51% representation from clients of services. Create mechanisms to reflect on how programs address personal, organizational, and community wellness at the same time.
Support for community structures	Promote policies that strengthen high quality basic community services such as education, health, and income security.	Produce awareness and assistance for creation and preservation of effective formal and informal supports.
Social justice	Implement equitable policies and taxation laws that provide adequate resources to the poor.	Offer comprehensive supports that meet the needs for housing and economic security of disadvantaged families.

guidelines. This table can be used as a template for devising value-based interventions in multiple settings (e.g., community centers, schools, workplace, hospitals) with a variety of foci (e.g., health promotion, drug abuse prevention, teen pregnancy, formal and informal support, minority rights, child abuse).

ROWS FOR WELLNESS

Exercise 3: Putting Values into Action in Your Life, Your Organization, and Your Community

In Chapters 1 and 2, we used ROWS to assess your personal and organizational situation, respectively. Now we want to see to what extent the six values presented in this chapter figure in your personal, work, and community life. You can choose to concentrate on private, organizational, or community matters.

You will find in Form 3.1 the six values discussed in this chapter under each one of the ROWS letters. Try to identify the risks, opportunities, weaknesses, and strengths involved in living up to each one of the six values. Try to answer the question: What are the ROWS of putting these values into action in (a) my life, (b) my organization, and (c) my community? After you do this, we move forward to the wellness readiness check.

The next step, as in previous chapters, is to devise a plan of action. To do that, we transfer the various items under ROWS into Form 3.2.

Use Form 3.2 to plan an action to advance the opportunities and strengths and to deal with risks and weaknesses. You can use this exercise in your organization and ask others to complete the ROWS and wellness readiness check. You can all compare notes and identify the ROWS, and decide what you can do about them as a group.

Form 3.1   ROWS Exercise 3: Putting Values into Action in Your Life, Your Organization, and Your Community

Risks
Self-determination, freedom, and personal growth
Health, caring, and compassion
Respect for diversity, collaboration, and democratic participation
Accountability and responsiveness to common good
Support for community structures
Social justice
Opportunities
Self-determination, freedom, and personal growth
Health, caring, and compassion
Respect for diversity, collaboration, and democratic participation
Accountability and responsiveness to common good
Support for community structures
Social justice
Weaknesses
Self-determination, freedom, and personal growth
Health, caring, and compassion
Respect for diversity, collaboration, and democratic participation
Accountability and responsiveness to common good
Support for community structures
Social justice
Strengths
Self-determination, freedom, and personal growth
Health, caring, and compassion
Respect for diversity, collaboration, and democratic participation
Accountability and responsiveness to common good
Social justice

Form 3.2   Wellness Readiness Check 3: Putting Values into Action in Your Life, Your Organization, and Your Community

ROWS	1 I never thought about doing something about it.	2 I'm thinking about doing something about it.	3 I'm prepared to do something about it.	4 I'm doing something about it.	5 I've been doing something about it for some time.
Risks					
Opportunities					
Weaknesses					
Strengths					

4

Webs of Strategies:
The Practice of Well-Being

What do I do now? It's a question practitioners ask themselves all the time. For every corner you turn in a helping relationship, a group process, or a community project, you have to make new choices. Do I confront my client on the inconsistency between his values and his actions? Do I do it now or later? Do I share with the group that I noticed some people feel silenced while others dominate the discussion? And if so, how do I handle the fallout? Do I challenge the organizational leader on her authoritarian style? And if so, how do I do that? When do I let go of the agenda so that community members can feel empowered and take over the project? What do I risk by doing that? Will they bungle the project? You can't have preconceived answers to these questions because every situation involves different constellations of factors. What worked before may not work now. What we need is a road map and not a cookbook. We need strategies that will help us see each context in its own light. Each context requires its unique prescription and its unique answer to the question *What do I do now?*

Every summer I (Isaac) teach on the West Coast a course on participatory action research. This is an intense, 3-day course. The groups vary in size from 10 to 18 students. The participants are for the most part mature students who have returned to graduate school to pursue a degree in psychology. At a recent class, I noticed that some students were particularly quiet. I was picking up signals that certain group dynamics might have been interfering with some people's learning. A foreign student in class was particularly quiet. During one of the breaks, I mentioned her being so quiet. Her reply was, "It's not fun feeling like a fish out of water." After the break, an animated discussion took place over a presentation. Several students raised their hands to participate. I noticed that a couple of students were politely waiting for their turn, while others were speaking out of turn. I acknowledged a student who was waiting quietly for her turn while another student jumped the queue to make a comment out of turn. The student who had been waiting whispered to me, "It happens all the time." She was referring to the fact that some students dominate the discussion. This incident, together with the comment by the foreign student, told me that I had to do something. If I didn't do anything, some students would continue to feel marginalized and silenced. At the end of the session, I told the class that I noticed some students were particularly quiet. As that was the last session of the day, I suggested that we talk about it first thing the next day. Students agreed.

Upon arrival the next morning, a couple of students approached me before class with some anxiety and trepidation. One of the vocal ones told me that she thought "we were doing well for our group" and that she was surprised that I thought some students were quiet. Was she feeling defensive? Another student asked me if I had some "hidden agenda" and if I wanted just to "illustrate a technique." I told him and the entire class that I had no hidden agenda and that if my perceptions were wrong, we wouldn't have to spend time discussing the issue.

The first thing I did was to obtain permission from the group to approach the topic. This group of students spends 4 years together in a degree program. I teach them only once during their graduate school career, and it wasn't my intention to disrupt group dynamics and then leave. After the group gave me permission to approach the subject, I suggested that we come up with certain ground rules for discussing a delicate issue. After all, sensitive material might come up. Some people might be accused of being domineering and others might be told they come across as aloof and distant. We generated a list of ground rules that included being respectful, taking turns, having the right to pass and not participate, limiting the discussion to 45 minutes with an option to extend it another 15 minutes, checking in with all students at the end of the session to see how they felt, and ensuring that there would be follow-up. We agreed ahead of time that students would meet again without me to continue the discussion.

After the ground rules were in place, I opened the discussion by simply checking my perceptions and asking the group if indeed some people talked more than others and if we needed to do something about it. Students confirmed my perceptions and agreed that something had to be done. They proceeded to share their views. During the discussion, students clarified their perceptions of each other and talked openly about their feelings in class. The foreign student explained that in her country people are much more polite and don't talk out of turn. Another student confessed to being introverted but leading an extroverted life outside graduate school as a school vice principal; she enjoyed being able to be quiet and reflective in graduate school. Another student confronted a peer who usually dominates the discussion and called that situation "the elephant in the room." At the end of the session, students felt that it was a healthy process, and they came up with some ideas for enabling more open communication among peers, inside and outside of class.

Why do I tell you this story? Because it illustrates some of the strategies and skills required for promoting well-being, in this case, the well-being of a group and its participants. Managing a group of 17 graduate students, most of them with degrees already and many years of experience in the workforce, is not simple. I had to rely on a variety of complementary roles and skills.

One of the first things I did was to behave as an *inclusive host*. I wanted everyone to feel welcome and comfortable. We talked about being respectful of each other and acknowledged that people had the right to pass; nobody felt forced to talk. At the same time, we agreed that at the end of class each person would have a chance to say how he or she felt during the discussion. The process gave people a chance to express their views and feel empowered. They could talk in a safe environment. The group told me it was the first time there was an opportunity to talk about something several of them had been feeling for a long time.

While the group was talking I noticed that they were being very respectful of each other and that they were handling a sensitive situation with great care. I acknowledged the *assets* of the group and complimented them on their own skills. I wanted the group to have a *vision* of what it would be like to enable wider participation and a more inclusive experience for everybody. They resonated with that vision. I *listened* carefully to what each one was saying, and I *listened* also to the signals that triggered the discussion in the first place. Together with the group, we devised a *unique solution* that suited their unique situation. We came up with ways to resolve the situation with further dialogue. We also *evaluated* the process and ensured that there was *follow-up*. Instead of having this discussion once, the group wanted it to be a *trend and make it sustainable*. By *implementing* the solution, we made sure we had a productive process. This incident had all the elements of I VALUE IT roles and skills that we deem essential for the promotion of well-being. I VALUE IT is an acronym that stands for the following roles:

- Inclusive host
- Visionary
- Asset seeker
- Listener and sense maker
- Unique solution finder
- Evaluator
- Implementer
- Trendsetter

ROLES FOR PROMOTING WELL-BEING: WHAT, WHY, WHEN, WHERE, AND HOW

The I VALUE IT roles can be used in promoting well-being, preventing the loss of well-being, and restoring well-being. Furthermore, they can be used in promoting personal, interpersonal, organizational, and community well-being. In this section, we preview briefly the roles, discuss why they are important, and mention where and when they can be applied. The next section elaborates on the How question. That's where we elaborate on the strategies that go along with the different roles.

What Roles?

To answer the question, *What do I do now?* it's helpful to think in terms of the different roles we adopt during a helping or change process. We identified eight generic roles summarized in the acronym I VALUE IT: Being an **I**nclusive host, **V**isionary, **A**sset seeker, **L**istener, **U**nique solution finder, **E**valuator, **I**mplementer, and **T**rendsetter at the same time is challenging. To unpack what each role means, we need to discuss the set of skills that go along with each.

Why Are These Roles Important?

These roles are important for a variety of reasons. First, they are based on the values we introduced in Chapter 3. To enable self-determination, we need to behave as inclusive hosts and make people feel accepted. To respect diversity, we need to find unique solutions to problems afflicting individuals and communities. Second, these roles are based on research. Studies demonstrate the need for each one of the I VALUE IT roles for change to be effective and sustainable (Beutler, 2000; Hayes, 2002; Ivey & Ivey, 2003; Nelson & Prilleltensky, 2005; Prochaska et al., 1994; Prochaska & Norcross, 1998). Finally, practice and experience support the complementary nature of the eight roles. To do some but not all compromises the quality and durability of the interventions (Conyne & Cook, 2004).

When Do I Practice These Roles?

These roles can be practiced in any one of the following situations: when we wish to promote well-being, when we wish to prevent the loss of well-being, and when we wish to restore well-being. The roles apply equally well to each.

Where Do I Practice These Roles?

We practice these roles in the different sites of well-being. In this book, we are particularly concerned with personal, organizational, and community well-being, but these roles apply equally well to family and interpersonal well-being. In essence, the roles serve the function of facilitating well-being wherever human beings are concerned. You will find them useful working with individual clients, families, groups, organizations, and communities.

How Do I Practice These Roles?

This is the question requiring the most elaboration. Each role requires a different but complementary set of skills. We discuss each role and its associated skills in the next section.

STRATEGIES FOR PROMOTING WELL-BEING: I VALUE IT

Following a description of roles and strategies for each of the letters, we describe common pitfalls and offer a checklist. Together, these four elements will help you internalize each one of the eight roles.

Inclusive Host

Next we explore the different facets of being an inclusive host.

Role   The role of an inclusive host is to make sure everyone feels welcome, including you. If people are to explore changes in their lives, organizations, or communities, they have to feel safe and appreciated. When you go somewhere for the first time, you want to be acknowledged, seen, listened to, and respected. People have to see you as a safe container of their anxieties. People have to feel safe to explore delicate aspects of their lives, avenues for empowerment, vulnerabilities, and strengths (Menzies Lyth, 1988, 1989).

Strategies   If you think back and reflect on a situation in which someone made you feel welcome, you will probably deduce the best strategies for being an inclusive host yourself. We can think of *verbal* and *nonverbal* strategies. Nonverbal strategies include making eye contact, shaking hands if appropriate, calling people by their first name if appropriate, and adopting an attentive posture when they talk to you (Goleman, 1998; Hayes, 2002). This may be leaning forward when they speak, or looking at them. Some aboriginal cultures consider looking people in the eye disrespectful, so you will do well to learn about the customs of your partners.

One verbal strategy is showing interest in the people you work with. This may be in the form of asking questions about their kids, their hobbies, their job if they have one, or anything they want to talk about. If you're working with an individual, you want to make sure the person knows that what is discussed between you two is *confidential*. If you're working with a group, you need to establish rules for making sure that what is said in the group stays in the group, unless otherwise agreed. This is sometimes called *Las Vegas rules*: What happens in Vegas stays in Vegas.

Of course, people want to make sure that there are no negative repercussions from their participation or lack thereof in any organizational process.

Creating a climate of *safety* requires that participants feel absolutely free to be there or not to be there, to speak or not to speak. Ideally, we want everyone involved in a change process to participate actively in it, but at first, people have to have space and time to feel comfortable with the idea of being in a change process (Dimock, 1992).

Building trust is part and parcel of being an inclusive host. Trust is gained over time. You should be prepared to stick with people for a while before they fully trust you. Why should they trust somebody they have only just met? Being completely honest will facilitate trust. *Transparency* about the aims and methods of whatever processes you are about to embark on will serve you well, even if you don't know with full certainty how the process will unfold. If you don't know, say you don't know. Share what you know and what you don't know (Prochaska & Norcross, 1998).

An inclusive host strives to make all members of the group as accepting of each other as possible. This requires reading where people are during the conversation. Skillful facilitators take the pulse of the group at all times. This is quite a sophisticated ability, as it requires identification of people's moods as individuals and as a group (Goleman, 1998; Hayes, 2002). In my interaction with the class in the example I gave earlier, I took the pulse of the group and realized that some people were not feeling totally comfortable; they were quiet and somewhat marginalized. After we processed the group dynamics, the quiet members thanked me for helping them feel more welcome. They felt acknowledged and valued; they appreciated the fact that I paid attention to their silence.

Common Pitfalls   Most pitfalls have to do with overdoing or underdoing a role. Overdoing the inclusive host means being so solicitous that people feel invaded. There is an optimal space, physical and psychological, that people wish to protect. Another way of overdoing the inclusive host is artificial demonstrations of interest or exaggerations. Some of these behaviors come across as disingenuous; examples include telling your partner that he or she is the most interesting person in the world, or that you never met somebody so smart or handsome. You get the point. The prototype of the phony inclusive host is the waiter or waitress who wants to be so nice to you that he or she can't stop smiling at you.

Part of overdoing it is overidentifying with the person. If a person has experienced illness or death in the family, the overidentifier can't stop saying "It must be terrible for you."

What about underdoing it? It's easy to identify the noninclusive host. We all have had experiences of feeling ignored. If you haven't, you're lucky. I have been in situations where people have so dominated the conversation that they didn't care to ask me what I do, where I come from, nothing. It has happened to me in my family, in work situations, and at cocktail parties.

It may take some time for you to realize how much attention people feel comfortable with, especially as everyone is different. It takes some time to read people's level of comfort in social situations. In our community and clinical work, we have encountered many people who want to be part of a process or a conversation but are too afraid to say the wrong thing. These people require some cajoling and support. We should not automatically assume they don't want to speak. In our experience, most people do want to participate, be acknowledged, and be heard (Nelson, Lord, et al., 2001).

Checklist   This is a partial list of questions you can ask yourself about being an inclusive host:

- Is everyone feeling comfortable?
- Is someone dominating the discussion in the group?
- Are there some people who feel afraid to speak?
- Have I made an effort to hear from all people in the group?
- Are people leaving the meeting enthusiastic or disappointed?

Visionary

The roll of visionary is crucial. We explore several aspects of it next.

Role   In our role as visionaries, we do two things: We help to envision a better future, and we help to envision a respectful and efficient process. We fulfill the dual task of aspiring toward a better state of affairs and creating norms that will help us work together at the same time. In short, we envision the ends (outcome) and the means to achieve it (process). In individual work, there are only two people making decisions about personal growth or coping strategies. In group situations, the process of developing a vision and choosing values can be fairly involved.

Let's talk about the role of creating a vision first. Some people have a rather limited view of the world of possibilities. Some grew up in conditions of abuse or family repression, and that's all they know. Others grew up in families where nobody went to college, and that's all they know: Go to school, perhaps finish high school, perhaps not, and try to get a job. Some people are accustomed to pain and suffering and cannot imagine a world without it. Our parents' generation grew up thinking that divorce is the end of the world and that women put up with abusive men because ending the marriage was not an option. Oppressed communities often need a prophet who can envision with them a future of freedom. We can never underestimate the importance of presenting alternatives to the status quo, to the personal, organizational, or collective status quo. A vision of a better future, or even examples of what it might be like living without oppression, without abuse, without hunger, can be empowering and energizing (Nelson & Prilleltensky, 2005).

The second role of the visionary is to formulate, with clients and partners, values and ground rules for the work together. What values should guide the collaboration? If we're working in a group, do we choose to make decisions by consensus? Do we establish ground rules, as I did with my class? What ground rules do we follow? It is best to decide together; setting the parameters and expectations together builds ownership and commitment.

Strategies   To craft a vision of a better future we need to stimulate people's imagination. *Provocative questions* can help. We can try to answer together questions such as these: What would it be like if our children finished college? What would it be like if we lived without fear of crime in our community? What would it be like if we lived without fear? What would it be like if everyone had health insurance, or housing? *Brainstorming* answers can be stimulating.

Examples from other communities or other lives where people enjoy safety, housing, health care, jobs, and racial harmony can also be energizing. Martin Luther King empowered the Black community to fight for racial equality. Gandhi inspired India to live without British rule.

To envision a better future is to think outside the box. I, Isaac, have learned to think outside the box by comparing how different countries help families and children. Some, such as France, provide child care; others do not. Some, such as Canada, provide universal health insurance; the United States does not. It's important to ask not only why we have such a state of affairs, but also why we do not have services and policies like other countries.

Action research is another avenue for developing a vision. As we saw earlier in the book, Oasis Youth Center generated a vision by asking staff and community members what they would like the Center to be. By interviewing each other about their respective visions, staff and clients formulated a new vision statement. Provocative questions, brainstorming, exemplars, outside-the-box-thinking, and action research can all help.

What about values for the process of working together? For some people this is a surprising exercise. Nobody asked them before how we should solve a problem, let alone how we should work together as a team. In many instances, this will be the first time they are asked their opinion about how to resolve an issue or how to approach a problem. We recommend asking about what an ideal process would look like in their minds. We can reassure partners that there are no wrong answers. We can write on a board or flip chart their answers and decide by consensus the ground rules.

In addition, we can write a *list of values* for well-being (see Chapter 3) and ask the group to apply them to their work. For example, we can ask the group what it would mean to promote self-determination, caring and compassion, or respect for diversity in the process. Some might say that sky breeds disillusion more than action. In addition, a vision has to be owned by the community, organization, or individual. It cannot be your vision imposed on somebody else. We have to be cautious not to come to the scene with a cooked version of our vision. Similarly, we have to let people struggle to come up with their own vision without too much help from us. We needn't rescue them. Visions have to be realistic and participatory.

Common Pitfalls   To be inspiring, a vision has to be realistic. Pie in the everyone needs to be heard, that there should be rotating leadership, or that people should share the load. Once the group generates a vision for how they want to work together, you can revisit it before every meeting.

The same applies to the process of working together. The group needs to own its ground rules. In working with a community organization, my colleagues and I felt that the process was not going well. We had discussed sharing the leadership, but no one from the organization had stepped forward. By default, my team was running the meetings, until one day I provoked a mini-crisis and asked the partner organization if they were really committed to the process. The question created some discomfort around the room, but it revealed important information. It turns out that they didn't like our approach. They didn't like the way we were leading the process and were somewhat passive-aggressive about it all. Once I asked the simple question, "What's wrong?" they told us that they were frustrated by the way we "university people" were conducting the meetings. It was all too abstract for them. They wanted more action; they wanted to get out to the community and start "doing something." We were "too much into planning." I challenged them to articulate their vision for the process and they did. Until that point, they had felt that they couldn't challenge us "university people." Once permission was granted to discuss the process, they expressed their misgivings and decided to take matters into their own hands. I was only too happy to see that they took ownership of the process. I had assumed that we had discussed how to run the project. But the discussion had taken place a long time ago and we hadn't revisited it. Our mistake was not to check with our partners whether our original ground rules still applied or needed to be changed. They wanted us to set the agenda at the outset of the project, but they wanted to change it later on. We were still under the (wrong) impression that they wanted us to be in charge.

Another potential pitfall in creating visions for the future or for the process is the pursuit of perfection. Some people want to have a perfect vision or a perfect process laid out before they proceed to action. Others, like our partners in the previous example, want to get out there and "do something." It is important for the vision not to block action, if that is what people want. At the same time, it is important to realize that without a vision, or some planning, actions can too easily reproduce the status quo we are trying so hard to change. Too much vision at the expense of action is just as risky as too much action without a vision. It's a tough balancing act.

Checklist   Some questions a visionary can ask include:

- Have all people expressed their aspirations?
- Are we able to think of alternative ways of being?
- Have we established a process that is democratic and inclusive?
- Have we had time to think about the norms that we all want to follow?
- Is there collective ownership for the values and vision we have created?

Asset Seeker

Searching for strengths and competencies is a crucial step.

Role   As an asset seeker, we look for sources of resilience, strength, and ingenuity in the people we work with (Ivey & Ivey, 2003). In individual encounters, it is important to validate what the person in front of us is already doing well to cope with a problem or to fight injustice. Marginalized community members are used to hearing about their deficits, when in fact many of them have remarkable talent in coping with adverse circumstances. In group work, we should be careful not to leave anyone behind in our search for assets and strengths. People have experiential knowledge they want recognized.

For a number of reasons, we must not underestimate the value of acknowledging strengths. First, it is part of what makes up our dignity. Second, community members have grounded knowledge, insights, and intuitions that can be vital in any change process. And third, the mere act of validating strengths is therapeutic and empowering (McWhirter, 1994; Nelson, Lord, et al., 2001).

Strategies   *Asking good questions* can help us identify strengths in the community. In a canvassing project we are currently conducting we are asking residents of a poor neighborhood what gifts they have: gifts of the head (speaking, reading) heart (caring for children, looking after pets), or hands (gardening, cooking). Most people can see themselves in one or more of these three categories.

Another line of questioning is: What has worked for you before? Tell me of a time when you did not have this problem? What was happening then? (S. Miller, Hubble, & Duncan, 1996). *Asset mapping* is another strategy that involves identifying people, places, and resources that can be helpful in fostering a vision and generating change.

Common Pitfalls   Ignoring people's assets and concentrating instead on deficits is an all too frequent practice. When people enter a therapeutic service, one of the first questions they are asked is what their problem is. Then they are asked to fill out questionnaires replete with problem statements.

We often neglect natural sources of help in the community and concentrate instead on professional resources. Relatives and neighbors can be mobilized to great effect.

Checklist   To make sure we are effective in our search for assets we can ask the following questions:

- Have I asked people how they cope with this difficult situation?
- Have we discussed what each of us can contribute to the process?
- Are we able to combine our strengths in a synergistic way?
- Have I offered my input as an equal member of the group?
- Have we explored different types of knowledge and wisdom that can help us in our collaborative work?

Listener and Sense Maker

Listening and interpreting are vital roles for the change agent. We offer some guidance in the next few sections.

Role   As a listener and sense maker, the first job is to attend carefully to what people are telling us about their lives, challenges, struggles, and aspirations. We cannot emphasize enough the importance of letting people speak and explain on their own terms what they are experiencing, hoping, and feeling. It is not uncommon for eager helpers to rush in and give advice before they have listened carefully. Each of us brings to the table multiple assumptions that can lead to unwarranted conclusions about people's lives. It is best not to assume anything until we have an opportunity to corroborate our impressions with them (S. James & Prilleltensky, 2002).

Once we have a good grasp of the issues and challenges ahead, we begin to conceptualize the problem and isolate the main factors causing and perpetuating suffering, injustice, and oppression in personal, organizational, and community life. We always have our antenna up for signals of oppression, exclusion, and silence. Power differentials and inequality figure prominently in the lives of people we work with (Community Mental Health Project, 1998; J. A. Lewis, Lewis, Daniels, & D'Andrea, 2003).

The role of sense maker demands that we interpret challenges and opportunities in light of all the evidence. We need to put together all the pieces of the puzzle. This is an analytical job: trying to understand relationships among factors, people, and dynamics in people's lives. We make sense of problems and opportunities by connecting the personal with the interpersonal, organizational, and social. What is happening in the organization or the community that is affecting worker morale? What family dynamics are impacting the well-being of my client? What personality characteristics interfere with healthy relationships? Under what circumstances does the group work best and worst? Posing and answering these questions is the job of the sense maker. First, we listen and examine all the information available, and then we try to make sense of it.

As we make sense of the case, we have to keep in mind that our hypotheses may differ from those of the group or the client (S. James & Prillel-tensky, 2002). We have to consider the possibility that our conceptualization may be wrong. It is better to be tentative rather than conclusive when we share perceptions with our partners.

Strategies We live in a culture of quick fixes. For every complex problem, there must be a ready-made solution. We also live in a culture that doesn't tolerate ambiguity or anxiety (Menzies Lyth, 1988). Therefore, deep or prolonged explorations of issues are greatly unpopular. Beginning helpers operate from the same vantage point most people in our culture do: They want to offer quick solutions, and they want to run away from uncertainty. Our culture values outcomes and results but not processes. If it cannot be shown on a graph, it must not be useful. We warn helpers to avoid the quick-fix mentality.

Some strategies include *taking time to listen*. The right amount of time is, of course, a subjective judgment. Seasoned clinicians may be comfortable with a few minutes of silence, whereas neophytes may experience a few seconds as eternity. *Role-playing* the listener is most useful. Time and again our students have been surprised at how quickly they jump to rescue others, and how uncomfortable they are with other people's anxieties. We don't mean to listen forever, or for its own sake, but to make sure we get the picture before we say anything. To get the picture means attending to all elements of the story. To elicit the full story, we have to ask open-ended questions:

- Can you tell me more about it?
- What was your experience like in that situation?
- How did you feel?

Practicing open-ended questions is a worthwhile exercise for anybody. *Getting feedback* on our listening style is very useful. The best way to maximize a role-play is by videotaping it, reviewing it, and asking your peers for feedback. After you role-play listening, ask your interviewee how she felt about your listening. Would she have needed more time, more probing questions? Were your open-ended questions sufficiently inviting?

Being an inclusive host complements the listener role very well. Whatever you can do to make the person or group comfortable will help. *Attentive posture* will also help: You are showing interest in your interviewee, group, or community.

An essential skill is *nonjudgmental listening*. People are ultrasensitive to judgment. If we feel that we are being judged, we will tend to distort the story in a way that pleases the interviewer. As interviewer, we can easily send signals of approval or disapproval. Those signals will be picked up by the interviewees and incorporated into their narratives. Remember, we don't want to hear what will please us or confirm our biases, but rather the subjective experience of the person in front of us. This brief overview of listening cannot do justice to the intricacies of this art. We recommend the excellent work of Ivey and Ivey (2003) as a very useful starting point for refining your listening skills.

Strategies for sense making include getting as much information as possible, making diagrams of all the potential ways different factors interact (family relationships, cultural norms, individual perceptions, organizational climate, community problems, etc.), understanding what needs are being met or neglected in a particular situation, figuring out power relations among players in the drama, considering various interests at stake, and taking into account hopes, fantasies, and aspirations. Of course, the more you study, the more capable you are of making connections among psychological, social, cultural, economic, and political factors. The more you know about human, organizational, and community development, the more connections you'll see and the better sense maker you'll become.

Common Pitfalls   The rush to solve problems before people have had sufficient time to relate their story is a common ailment in the helping professions. We easily fall prey to the cultural demand for quick fixes. We cut people off before they have had a chance to finish.

Most human and social problems are fairly complicated and require thoughtful consideration. Jumping to conclusions is dangerous. Not only can we get it wrong, but we can also prevent the person from discovering his own solutions. The best solutions are arrived at by a process of self-discovery.

Sense making has its own pitfalls. A little bit of knowledge is a dangerous thing. If all you know is psychoanalysis, or cognitive therapy, or behavior modification, you may be quick to apply it regardless of the unique circumstances of the case. If all you know is sensitivity training, you may want to solve every organizational problem with T-groups. This can easily lead to the one-size-fits-all syndrome: No matter what the problem is, you always apply the same framework. The antidote for this risk is to learn as much as possible and to research as many approaches as possible. Human beings and organizations are complex, and we usually require more than one lens to get the full picture (Bolman & Deal, 2003).

Checklist   To remind ourselves of the various tasks involved in being a good listener and a good sense maker, we can use the following prompts:

- Have I listened without interruptions to what people have to say about their issues?
- Have I thought about it in ecological terms of personal, organizational, and community factors?
- Have I expressed disagreement or alternative conceptualizations in a respectful way?
- Have I thought about the influence of power inequality in this person's life?
- Has the group agreed on the definition of the problem and possible solutions?

Unique Solution Finder

Applying prefabricated solutions is a common risk. We discuss ways to avoid this pitfall next.

Role   Problem definition is crucial, but action is what gets changes under way. When the group or the individual is ready to take action, we have to contribute our academic, professional, and personal knowledge to the process of change. If a group wishes to use a confrontational technique with a school board and you know that this strategy will alienate potential allies, you should discuss the merits of other options. If a victim of spousal abuse wishes to return to the marriage and you know from her past experience and other research that this will likely not work out, as a unique solution finder you should raise the possibility that this may not be the best way to proceed. In either case, our alternatives have to suit the unique circumstances of the situation.

As a unique solution finder, your job is to listen, conceptualize, formulate actions, and collaborate with your partners in ways that match their special needs, expectations, and context. This is an essential part of our job in working with individuals, small groups, organizations, and communities: our ability to identify transformational actions that are uniquely suited to the people and the context. It is all too easy to apply canned solutions. It is harder to figure out in collaboration with our partners what will make the most sense in this particular situation, at this point in time.

Learning is truly a lifelong journey. This is not just a cliché. Although we are able to extrapolate from one situation to another, more often than not new situations require a new lesson in how to solve problems. We have to be open to challenges and unexpected turns in our work. We have to rely on our knowledge, experience, research, and enlightened intuitions as much as on our ability to discover with our partners the best solution for them.

Strategies   To arrive at the unique solution for a particular challenge requires two sets of strategies. The first set consists of the *application of previous knowledge, research, and experience to the issue at hand*. This is a cognitive exercise requiring a methodical review of the literature and making comparisons between other situations and the one we are currently facing. By comparing and contrasting, we *eliminate unlikely options* and reduce the world of possibilities to a manageable size.

The second set of strategies involves the engagement of our partners in a process of *discovery and ownership* of the solution. It is not only *what* we will do, but *how* we will do it. As participants in the process, we can recommend avenues for promoting well-being. However, ultimately, our clients and partners will enact the changes and recommendations. Therefore, we have to brainstorm with them solutions, review their chances of success, analyze risks and threats, and gauge ownership and buy-in. This process complements the asset seeker role. Whatever we end up doing, we have to make sure we build on strengths, resources, and opportunities available.

People need a great deal of support to experiment with new ways of being and relating to the world. These include person-centered changes, such as enhanced self-esteem, and environmental modifications. Action must take into account research on resilience, for it elucidates naturally occurring mechanisms that can be incorporated into helping processes (Ungar, 2005).

Groups can act as powerful resources in introducing new behaviors in their members or getting rid of undesirable ones (D. Johnson & Johnson, 2000). The literature on mutual help and organizing confirms that empowerment often grows out of social support and solidarity (Levy, 2000; Speer & Hughey, 1995; Speer, Hughey, Gensheimer, & Adams-Leavitt, 1995).

Common Pitfalls   The risk of dogmatism—the application of prefabricated solutions that may have worked in other settings but don't transfer to this one—is ubiquitous. This is not to discount previous efforts. On the contrary, we want to learn from previous experiences and we definitely don't want to reinvent the wheel. But we want to find the right wheel and not just any wheel.

Another pitfall is rescuing the person, group, or community. If we see them struggling, we may rush to their rescue and offer alternatives that we believe in. Due to their state of desperation, our clients may embrace our solution, only to find out later that it really doesn't work for them. In such cases, we have not only wasted time, but we have also been blamed for the solution not working. This is not to say that we are forbidden from offering advice, recommendations, or ideas. Rather, our sage advice, if we have any, has to be owned and internalized by the group.

Checklist   Questions that sharpen our skills as unique solution finders include:

- Have I considered with the group the risks and benefits of every course of action?
- Have I consulted colleagues and the literature on the merits of various alternatives?

- Is our work balancing attention to process with attention to outcomes?
- Does the proposed solution tap into individuals' strengths and past successful attempts at problem solving?
- Does the solution take into account the unique needs and circumstances of the partner?

Evaluator

The role of evaluator adds rigor to the process of change.

Role In this role, we explore how we're doing, what's working well, how people are feeling, what we are doing wrong, and what results, if any, we're achieving. Many of us are used to getting the job done. This quality may be a great asset, but we have to be careful that in our rush to accomplish things we don't forget how we're accomplishing them. Evaluation is not a solitary activity but a collaborative one. Our partners in change have to be able to express their views on the process and outcomes of our work together.

There are two types of evaluation we wish to pursue in our work. The first is a *process* evaluation. Our role is to create opportunities for partners and us to consider whether the process is working. Is the process sufficiently participatory? Are the jobs to be done clear? Are tasks being accomplished? Is leadership effective? These are the kinds of questions an evaluator wants to pursue.

The second kind of evaluation concerns *outcomes*. Are we achieving what we set out to do? Are we satisfied with the results of our work together? Are there noticeable changes in the organization or community? Have rates of child abuse dropped? Are there fewer traffic accidents in the neighborhood? Are children eating more fruits and vegetables? These are outcome questions worth pursuing (S. M. Pancer, 1997).

Strategies The key in evaluation is to *ask the right questions* using the *right methods*. At the outset of any process of change it is important to ask process and outcome questions. An outcome question asks: How would we know if we achieved our goals? A process question asks: What factors enabled or inhibited our work together? Outcome evaluations are usually done at the end, once the intervention has taken place; process evaluations are done throughout the project. The advantage of doing so is that we can feed back the information gathered and improve the way we're going about change. Once the data are collected, we provide feedback to participants and make adjustments accordingly.

Quantitative and qualitative methods can be used to address process and outcome questions. Quantitative methods include surveys, questionnaires, and behavioral observations, such as the number of times a child engages in aggressive behavior during a specified period of time. Qualitative methods include interviews, focus groups, archival information, and participant observations where evaluators take process notes (Patton, 1997, 2002).

Evaluation applies to work with individuals as much as work with groups, organizations, and communities. In working with a single client, it's useful to ask how he or she feels about the way we're working together, as well as the outcomes of our work. The process evaluation may be quite simple, such as writing reflections on helpful and unhelpful moments in the therapeutic relationship and sharing them with the helper.

It is best to *build an evaluation component from the outset*, even if later on you need to change it. At least you have brought to everyone's attention the need for assessing the project.

It is equally important to *build reflection into the project*. The more we learn as we go along, the greater the chances that we will catch mistakes, learn from experience, and build on successes. In our New SPEC project (designed to promote strengths, prevention, empowerment, and change in community conditions) with five community organizations, we meet as a research team twice a week for 90 minutes each time. One meeting is for administrative purposes, to make sure that we accomplish our tasks. The other is for group reflection; we share frustrations and explore alternative ways of promoting community well-being and innovative means of engaging workers and community members in the process of change. We reflect on the process of our work and give each other feedback.

Evaluation should not be relegated to the end of the change process. There is nothing more disappointing for group members or facilitators than to realize at the end that you missed the ball from the beginning, that you didn't notice some people were disengaged, that therapy wasn't working, that there wasn't ownership of the process. To prevent that, it's important to build in reflective practice: structured moments when people can express their feelings about how things are going, either in group or individual quests for change (Patterson & Welfel, 2000). This requires the creation of a truly safe space where discontent may be expressed and achievements may be celebrated. Role modeling is crucial for formative evaluations to work. The message from the facilitator of change ought to be that mistakes happen, that things can go wrong, and that it is better to express our discomfort as we feel it. A skilled facilitator balances opportunities for process reflections with concrete actions and achievements (Dimock, 1992).

Common Pitfalls   The most obvious pitfall is not to evaluate at all. Process evaluation is useful in changing course when things don't go well. A good use of the data is to inform the next phase of the project; a poor use of the information is to collect it without building into the process a feedback mechanism. Another pitfall is to create complicated evaluations that don't meet the needs of the consumers. In an ideal situation, we devise the evaluation plan with full participation of our partners. In a less than ideal situation, we create an evaluation that is not very useful or is too long. We have been guilty of imposing long evaluations on our partners. In one project, we changed the surveys after we got feedback from a community agency that the instrument was too long. We listened.

Checklist   Some questions we find useful at this stage are the following:

- Have we created a space to reflect on how we're feeling about our work together?
- What have we done to evaluate our intervention?
- Are people feeling safe enough to express disapproval?
- Am I open to challenges and criticism?
- Have we practiced how to give feedback in respectful and useful ways?

Implementer

This role calls for integrative skills. Next we try to distill some of the key features of being a competent implementer.

Role   In this capacity, we strive to integrate all the previous roles and strategies and implement the solution uniquely suited for the problem. As implementers, we match roles to situations and we follow through on the unique solution devised. We consider the factors enabling or inhibiting implementation. We anticipate and remove barriers and we strengthen enablers. We both lower resistance and increase energy for the change. Implementation is when it all comes together: when the skills are mastered, the plan is laid out, the evaluation is designed and the monitoring system is in place.

An implementer knows what strategy to use when, why, with whom, for what purpose, and for how long. She or he also knows when to change strategy. There is a measure of artistry in implementing the various roles and the best solutions. Being an implementer requires exposure to multiple situations and multiple skills. An implementer is constantly asking: Knowing what I know about the problem, the context, the players, the dynamics, the goals, and the likely solutions, what do I do now? The answer to this question is the outcome of weighing all the factors in a mental scale and choosing the best course of action under the circumstances.

There are two kinds of implementation worth differentiating. One is the immediate implementation of actions and responses taking place in a meeting. We call this *immediate implementation*. The second type, *long-term implementation*, refers to the long-range planning you do to enact major change in an organization or in a community. To achieve long-term implementation of a strategy you usually need to break it down into short-term goals and objectives. A good implementer can see small wins along the way and build on their motivating impact. As we shall see in Chapter 7, achieving short-term victories, especially when you work with organizations or communities, can be uplifting and even vital.

Ideal implementers master immediate and long-term implementation. They know how to respond to immediate situations, and they know how to plan for long-term transformation. To achieve the latter, you have to go through many small steps of immediate integration.

Strategies   Seasoned practitioners can hold in their mind several considerations at the same time. A way to approximate that level of skill is to compile a mental list of considerations affecting the process of immediate and long-term implementation. For example, a group facilitator thinks about power dynamics, keeps track of who is talking and who is not, remembers what happened the last time the group dealt with conflict, takes into account the frustrations of a minority, balances the need for process with the need for outcomes, and attends to the needs of the various stakeholders represented in the room. Taking everything into consideration, implementers ask themselves *What would be the most useful intervention at this time?* In reaching an answer, facilitators not only think about the various considerations at play, but also *weigh* their importance and *rank* them in order of priority. At any one time, there are many important dynamics and decisions to be made, but at any one time, the implementer chooses to concentrate on one or two key issues. The decision might be based on the need to satisfy a group's request for action, or for more process, or something else. These are examples of immediate implementation challenges.

The more we *practice* considering and weighing various interventions, the better we become at it. We can't implement a unique solution without paying attention to the process of doing it. A good implementer always thinks about the processes used in implementing good ideas. Good ideas without good processes die in the meeting room.

Although there is a measure of artistry in becoming an implementer, it is not a mystery. You can learn to be a good implementer. *Reflecting* on alternatives after the event can be very helpful, especially if you can do it with peers who observed you during the work. Our action research team does a lot of that in our rides back and forth to community organizations. We usually work in pairs or trios, with one of us assuming the lead role and others in supportive functions. Before and after meetings we check in with each other to learn from our mistakes and build on our successes.

Mentoring is another strategy we use to sharpen our implementation skills, especially for the type of implementation we call immediate. We usually pair an experienced facilitator with a junior one and let the latter observe. Once the junior person has gained sufficient confidence and experience, we reverse roles.

For long-term implementation, there is no substitute for study and *review of the literature* (Fixsen, Naoom, Blase, Friedman, & Wallace, 2005).

Exposure to case studies of small and large scale can help identify the challenges ahead. The types of supports needed to institutionalize an innovation are multifaceted and complex, especially in multilayered organizations.

Common Pitfalls   A common pitfall is to want to do it all prematurely. We strongly recommend that beginner consultants, therapists, and change agents work under supervision or in peer reflecting teams. This is a highly sophisticated process, for which much feedback is needed. In a sense, seasoned and green change agents alike need peer mentoring and support. We cannot emphasize enough the importance of sharing doubts, insights, fears, and achievements. To be thrown into the process without sufficient preparation can be daunting for the practitioners and not very useful for the client. As we shall see in Chapter 7, implementing an action without sufficient contemplation and preparation is a recipe for failure. As eager as we all are to do something quickly, lack of planning and preparation kill potentially good solutions. Don't run before you warm up.

Checklist   Some useful points to consider:

- Have I tried to be an inclusive host, asset seeker, good listener, and solution finder for the issue at hand?
- Have I tried to identify with my partners the most suitable solution for the long term?
- Have I made a mental list of the important considerations at play now?
- Have I considered the values, needs, and interests of all the players before making a decision or recommending action?
- Have I thought about factors enabling and inhibiting implementation of the proposed action in the short term and in the long term?

Trendsetter

The final job is making changes last. We call this role trendsetter.

Role   Perhaps the toughest part of the job is to make lasting changes, both in our personal and institutional lives. This is why we have to pay particular attention to our role as trendsetters. To achieve a change is admirable, but to make it into a new trend is even more remarkable (Mayer & Davidson, 2000; Prochaska et al., 1994). This role supports maintenance and follow-up of innovations.

Trendsetting is very challenging and very exciting. Community members like being part of something new and transformative. Motivation increases when people realize that their contributions may transcend the local level. When you think of environmental trends like recycling and composting, you can appreciate how rare they were 20 or 30 years ago, and how much more common they are today. At first, environmentalists encountered much more opposition than they face today when trying to institute earth-friendly policies and practices. The same may be said of civil rights activists, who fought an uphill battle to obtain basic human rights. Although their struggle is far from over, new trends such as affirmative action and disability rights legislation make it easier for historically marginalized groups to participate in society.

Long-term planning applies to individual, group, and community change alike. The first priority is to institutionalize the innovation at the personal and local levels. Once that has been accomplished, it's important to take the message to other communities and groups (Mayer & Davidson, 2000). An interesting example of trendsetting comes from New Zealand (Glover, Dudgeon, & Huygens, 2005). Indigenous groups, in collaboration with adult educators, strive to educate the entire population about Maori rights. Change agents have a systematic way of working with organizations so that education and affirmative actions may be institutionalized in government and private settings. It is not enough to raise the consciousness of a few people about the rights of aboriginal people: Their plan of action includes a strategy for disseminating knowledge about past wrongs and possible ways of addressing them. The essence of trendsetting is going beyond the initial goal. Remember: One swallow does not a summer make.

Strategies   It is never too early to think about setting a trend. *Early planning* for sustainability and dissemination goes a long way toward ensuring durability and impact. *Creating alliances* with like-minded groups and individuals is very useful.

Trendsetting applies not only to organizational and community efforts, but to personal changes as well. If you have ever tried to change something, you know how difficult it can be to sustain the new behavior. If you tried to stop smoking or to lose weight, you probably know that starting is not as hard as maintaining the new behavior. This is why maintenance and trendsetting are crucial (Prochaska et al., 1994). Planning for change without planning for maintenance and trendsetting is a recipe for failure. Imagine you made a decision to start exercising every other day for 30 minutes. You made a plan something like "Exercise for 30 minutes Monday, Wednesday, and Friday," but you did not plan exactly what time, what to do if somebody invites you to go out for a drink instead, or if you just have too much to study. You may have had a good beginning, but you did not have a *contingency plan or a maintenance plan*. Groups can be powerful in creating *norms of accountability*. Alcoholics Anonymous groups create pacts among their members that serve to maintain the gains newly acquired; attending the meetings and sharing the personal odyssey toward sobriety helps people with addictions to keep the risk at bay.

Setting dates for reviewing new practices, assigning roles for championing new procedures, animating processes that keep an innovation alive are all parts of follow-up. *Institutionalizing innovations* is the culmination of change.

Common Pitfalls   When starting new programs in the community, so much effort goes into project development, recruitment, and evaluation that sustainability is often not a priority. By the time funding runs out in 1, 2, or 3 years, as the case might be, there are rarely plans for the continuation of the initiative.

Rushing into action without thinking about setting a trend is a known error. This should be avoided at all costs because false starts leave strong impressions on people. People drop out prematurely. If you're on a diet and you fail to sustain gains during the first couple of weeks, you may be very disappointed and give up altogether. It is better to start gradually and to build routines rather than sprint with all your might without a plan for respite. It is important to have a plan for dealing with relapse and getting back on track.

Checklist   What can be done to make trendsetting a priority? Some questions change agents ask include:

- What have we done to make sure that the changes we plan for persist?
- How do we change the system, not just perceptions, to institutionalize innovations?
- What group norms can we establish to help members sustain new behaviors?
- How can we disseminate knowledge gained in one setting to others?
- What do we know from the literature about institutionalizing innovations?

ROWS FOR WELLNESS

Exercise 4: Putting Skills into Action

Think of yourself as a change agent. Consider what ROWS are involved in implementing the roles and strategies described in this chapter in your private life, organization, or community. You can choose to concentrate on any one of these domains of your life.

You will find in Form 4.1 the eight I VALUE IT roles under each one of the ROWS letters. Try to identify the risks, opportunities, weaknesses, and strengths involved in enacting the eight roles. Try to answer the question: What are the ROWS of implementing these values into action in (a) my life, (b) my organization, and (c) my community? After you do this, we move forward to the wellness readiness check.

The next step, as in previous chapters, is to devise a plan of action. To do that, we transfer the various items under ROWS into Form 4.2.

You can use Form 4.2 to examine how you feel about the different roles and skills required for you to become a change agent. What are your strengths? What are some opportunities for you to practice these skills? Are you better at doing than at listening? In the end, we all need these skills to become effective agents of change in our personal, organizational, and community life. You may ask your colleagues to complete the ROWS exercise and then compare notes. It may be that in your organization, most people are good at finding good solutions but nobody looks after evaluation or trendsetting. This can be a helpful diagnostic for you and for people in your family, organization, and community. Go ahead and try it.

Form 4.1   ROWS Exercise 4: Putting Skills into Action

Risks	
Inclusive host	
Visionary	
Asset seeker	
Listener and sense maker	
Unique solution finder	
Evaluator	
Implementer	
Trendsetter	
Opportunities	
Inclusive host	
Visionary	
Asset seeker	
Listener and sense maker	
Unique solution finder	
Evaluator	
Implementer	
Trendsetter	
Weaknesses	
Inclusive host	
Visionary	
Asset seeker	
Listener and sense maker	
Unique solution finder	
Evaluator	
Implementer	
Trendsetter	

(continued)

Form 4.1   (*Continued*)

Strengths
Inclusive host
Visionary
Asset seeker
Listener and sense maker
Unique solution finder
Evaluator
Implementer
Trendsetter

Form 4.2   Wellness Readiness Check 4: Putting Skills into Action

ROWS	1 I never thought about doing something about it.	2 I'm thinking about doing something about it.	3 I'm prepared to do something about it.	4 I'm doing something about it.	5 I've been doing something about it for some time.
Risks					
Inclusive host					
Visionary					
Asset seeker					
Listener and sense maker					
Unique solution finder					
Evaluator					
Implementer					
Trendsetter					
Opportunities					
Inclusive host					
Visionary					
Asset seeker					
Listener and sense maker					
Unique solution finder					
Evaluator					
Implementer					
Trendsetter					

(continued)

Form 4.2 (*Continued*)

ROWS	1 I never thought about doing something about it.	2 I'm thinking about doing something about it.	3 I'm prepared to do something about it.	4 I'm doing something about it.	5 I've been doing something about it for some time.
Weaknesses					
Inclusive host					
Visionary					
Asset seeker					
Listener and sense maker					
Unique solution finder					
Evaluator					
Implementer					
Trendsetter					
Strengths					
Inclusive host					
Visionary					
Asset seeker					
Listener and sense maker					
Unique solution finder					
Evaluator					
Implementer					
Trendsetter					

II

Personal Well-Being

Chapters 5, 6, and 7 deal with the three Ss of personal well-being: signs, sources, and strategies. Chapter 5 attends to the signs of personal well-being in the individual, in organizations, and in the community. In Chapter 6 we explore the personal, familial, organizational, and communal determinants of personal well-being and how they all interact to produce or diminish well-being. Chapter 7, in turn, looks at the promotion of personal well-being. In all three chapters we make explicit the connections among individual, organizational, and community signs, sources, and strategies for well-being.

Collectively, these chapters demonstrate that to promote personal wellness we must go beyond individual therapy and person-centered interventions. The environments where we work, live, and play exert powerful influences that must be taken into account when trying to foster individual happiness. We neglect their impact at our own peril. Unlike other approaches that concentrate on single levels of analysis, we strive to integrate multiple levels with multiple strategies. Our message for this section is that one-size-fits-all solutions are useless. They may be good for the demagogues who promote them, but they are not very good for the people who are supposed to use them. Imagine trying to cure all physical ailments with an aspirin. Simple solutions are appealing and sexy, but they don't work. If you're a professional helper, we urge you to expand your toolbox. In this section, you'll begin to collect new tools.

5

What Is It? Signs of Personal Well-Being

At the first sound of the alarm clock, 56-year-old Robert awoke from his sleep and immediately reached over to turn it off. He glanced over at Betty, relieved to see that she was sound asleep. He wouldn't want his early Saturday morning activity to rob her of an opportunity to rest for a bit longer. After all, she would soon get up herself and spend the better part of the day completing work for a course she is taking.

Robert fumbles in the dark for the clothes he laid out the night before. It is 5:00 on a Saturday morning and he is getting ready to go to his volunteer work at Habitat for Humanity. When he initially signed up 18 months ago, Robert hesitated when he found out how early he would have to get up on Saturdays. However, he decided to give it a go and never looked back. The knowledge that his work directly benefits a family in need is enough to overcome the desire for extra sleep. Besides, the good cheer and sense of camaraderie that has developed among the group of volunteers is an added bonus. After 5 hours of physical labor, Robert looks forward to a hot shower and a hearty breakfast when he returns home. By then Betty will be ready for a coffee break, and the two of them will catch up on the day's events.

Robert has a sense of contentment as he reflects on his life journey thus far. He and Betty have recently celebrated their 30th wedding anniversary, an occasion marked by a modest but joyous party organized by their middle daughter, Jennifer. Despite her busy schedule as a full-time graduate student, Jennifer took the time to carefully plan this event, enlisting the help of her older sister, Nancy, and younger brother, Mark. Of his three children, whom he dearly loves, Jennifer has been the easiest for Robert to relate to. Perhaps it is due to Jen's bubbly personality and easygoing nature. Perhaps it is because he was actively involved in her care from the very beginning. Two-year-old Nancy was particularly clingy to Betty when her baby sister arrived on the scene. By this point, Robert had gotten over his fear of newborns and prided himself on his ability to do "all but breast-feed."

At this stage, Robert enjoys a good relationship with Mark, now 19, has presented the most challenge for him. The relationship with Mark, now 19, has presented the most challenge for him. After two daughters, one characterized by quiet competence, the other by spunkiness and good cheer, Robert was ill prepared to deal with the behavioral challenges that Mark presented in his early years. Mark was stubborn and argumentative at home, and restless and at times disruptive at school. Betty was able to adapt her parenting style and managed to maintain a consistently positive relationship with him, Robert largely credits her for the eventual improvement in Mark's behavior and his willingness to take more responsibility for his actions. He is particularly grateful that Betty helped resolve the tension that at some point overshadowed the relationship between father and son. They have certainly come a long way—and they all deserve some credit. Mark has been steadily employed by a landscaping company for the past 8 months. He is considering part-time studies at a state college for the following academic year. He has recently moved to a rented apartment with a roommate, a move that has also contributed to a more positive relationship with Robert.

The improved relationship with his son is an ongoing source of fulfillment and pride for Robert. Barriers and low points notwithstanding, he feels that the family as a whole is stronger for it. It has certainly presented Robert with an opportunity to reflect on his own style and to work on some personal change. Last year he underwent intensive medical assessments following sharp chest pains and other worrisome symptoms. Although he did not have a heart attack, the tests revealed an underlying condition that required lifestyle and dietary changes. Robert initially felt helpless and deflated at the thought of having to make significant changes. He has always considered himself to be in good health and was actively involved in sports in his younger days. Although he did not exercise on a regular basis and had sported a beer belly in middle age, he had not envisioned that this would affect his health. After a few days of feeling out of sorts, Robert was mobilized into action. Being a resourceful individual by nature, he read over all of the information he was given and sat down to devise a plan. He was particularly touched by the concern that Mark showed for his health and his expressed wish that Robert would take better care of himself. Mark even suggested that the two of them join a gym together. With the help and support of his family, Robert worked on an improved diet, regular exercise regimen, and an overall reduction in stress level. He has felt a significant improvement in both physical and emotional well-being.

Robert has worked in middle management for a large firm for the past 12 years. Some recent structural changes necessitated acquisition of new skills and modification of work tasks. Unlike some of his colleagues, Robert found himself able to adapt with relative ease. Betty, who went back to nursing after many years at home, has been taking courses to upgrade her skills. She has been excited about all the new things she has been learning and encouraged Robert to view this change in a positive light. "After all," she quipped, "my going back to school and work has forced you to refine your culinary and housekeeping skills. Adjusting to changes in work should be a piece of cake in comparison."

PERSONAL WELL-BEING: AN OVERVIEW

There is nothing profound about Robert's story; similar stories with slight variations can be told about countless other individuals. In fact, chances are that you know someone like Robert. Perhaps you find parallels with your own life. The point is that personal well-being does not require exceptional wealth, talent, or fame. Although we tend to view those who possess such attributes as lucky, they are not necessarily any happier than the rest of us. There is little doubt that it is difficult to thrive when basic needs are not met. Adequate nutrition, shelter, and freedom from extreme pain and discomfort are important foundations; achieving well-being in their absence is rare. Personal well-being is compromised for those who live in abject poverty and whose lives are marked by a constant struggle to meet basic needs. Once this fundamental comfort level is achieved, objective conditions cease to be a major predictor of personal well-being in general and subjective well-being in particular (Layard, 2005; Schwarz & Strack, 1999; Seligman, 2002).

All living organisms are instinctively inclined to avoid pain and pursue comfort and pleasure. Nonetheless, a frantic pursuit of pleasure is not a formula for attaining subjective well-being. As is indicated by the term "hedonic treadmill" (Kahneman et al., 1999), one can develop an insatiable craving for pleasure and comfort that can have properties similar to an addiction: The more one has, the more one wants and the more of it that is needed to satisfy the desire. So being rich, living a luxurious life, being burden-free and able to do what we want when we want to is not necessarily a recipe for happiness and well-being. It might feel good in the short term, but its glow is likely to be short-lived, with a sour aftertaste.

Subjective well-being is about being satisfied and fulfilled with the general course of one's life. People who are high in subjective well-being tend to experience life as satisfying, enjoyable, and rewarding. They have mutually fulfilling relationships, find meaning in what they do, and feel a sense of control over many aspects of their lives. They are generally content with their life course thus far and are hopeful and optimistic about what is yet to come. They set goals, work to attain them, and mobilize their resources when they encounter obstacles along the way.

Does this mean that only superhumans can be high in subjective well-being? Let's review Robert's profile to answer this question. Although he experiences high marital satisfaction (a strong predictor) and a solid relationship with his adult children, we also learned about a history of strife in the relationship with his son, Mark. Robert was feeling anxious and despondent when he first learned about his health problems. Learning that he has a serious condition was inconsistent with his long-standing belief that he is exceptionally healthy and robust. With the support of his family, he was ultimately able to make a host of dietary and lifestyle changes that translated into improved physical and emotional well-being.

The point is that well-being is not about achieving perfection in relationships, resourcefulness, or working environments. Neither does it require being joyous and optimistic at all times and irrespective of circumstances. Although subjective well-being tends to be relatively stable across changing circumstances and environments (Diener & Lucas, 1999), there is room for personal variance. Well-being is about thriving and flourishing—rather than simply avoiding illness. "The avoidance of psychopathology, negative behavioral outcomes, or illness is no guarantee that one will also flourish and be well in multiple realms of life" (Ryff & Singer, 2003, p. 27).

Variance also exists among individual conceptions of the "good life." Some people highlight the importance of personal relationships, others place greater value on comfort and security, and yet others find that helping those in need greatly enhances their own well-being (Diener & Lucas, 1999). These variations notwithstanding, the growing body of literature in the field has provided us with invaluable information on the main factors that are associated with personal well-being. The rest of the chapter focuses on the markers and correlates of subjective well-being at the personal, organizational, and community levels. Knowing the signs of personal well-being at these three levels provides key information on how it can be enhanced.

SIGNS OF PERSONAL WELL-BEING

We explore next several indicators of personal well-being.

Optimism

I (Ora) answered the phone at the sound of the first ring: "Oh, hi, Mom. Unfortunately, I didn't win the game. I was playing this guy, rated 2300, and I was leading for most of it—but then I lost on time." It was our 18-year-old son, Matan, calling from Philadelphia with an update from the World Chess Tournament. I felt for Matan, as this was the third game in a row that he had lost in the tournament. I was about to say that it's okay—his opponent was such a strong player, after all, rated higher than Matan, whose rating is slightly over 2000. But I needn't have bothered. In typical Matan style, he went on to tell me that although "it sucks" to lose, he learned so much from these games. No, he is not sorry that he decided to enter the Open section that has all the strongest players from all over the world. This will be good preparation for future games. For the record, Matan lost the first three games of the tournament and went on to draw one game and win the next five. Despite his slow beginning, he was one of six players to tie for first place in this international chess tournament, returning home with a $750 check.

Motherly boasting aside, this exchange with Matan, which took place some 3 weeks ago, speaks volumes about optimism. Matan has been playing chess since he was 8 years old and has played in tournaments in Canada, Australia, and the United States. He loves the game, enjoys the hype of tournaments, and is always on the lookout for the next major event. Although his talent for chess undoubtedly plays a significant factor in his success, I believe his optimism enables him to continue despite an initial losing streak (Peterson & Steen, 2002).

"Optimists and pessimists differ in several ways that have a big impact on their lives. They differ in how they approach problems and challenges, and they differ in the manner—and the success—with which they cope with adversity" (Carver & Scheier, 2002, p. 231). Most important, optimists are much more likely than pessimists to be high in subjective well-being. As common wisdom has it, optimists are those who see the glass as half full, whereas their pessimistic counterparts see it as half empty. People's dispositional optimism as well as their explanatory style account for their level of optimism. Dispositional optimism has to do with one's general expectation that the future has good things in store and that positive circumstances will outnumber and overshadow negative ones. The general belief that goals will be achieved is linked to desirable outcomes in general and to effective coping skills in particular (Peterson & Chang, 2003). The tendency to expect that positive events are more likely than negative ones goes hand in hand with the belief that obstacles can be overcome and adversity can be handled successfully (Carver & Scheier, 2002).

Explanatory style is a related but separate construct that contributes to our understanding of optimism. Our explanatory style has to do with how we explain and make sense of the causes or attributions of positive and negative events in our lives (Seligman, 2002). Optimists are those who tend to explain bad events with causes that are external to themselves ("My opponent was a higher rated player" or "His lower rating doesn't really reflect his strength"). These same events are described as unstable ("I'll do better next time"), and specific ("I need to study a certain chess opening that will throw off my opponent"). Pessimists, on the other hand, will perceive negative events as internal ("I didn't play well"), stable ("I'm just not good in chess"), and universal ("I fail at most things"). On the flip side, optimists will explain good events and circumstances as internal ("I've improved so much"), stable ("I'll win more games now"), and universal ("I guess I'm pretty smart to have advanced so much"). You get the picture. As Seligman asserts, "Finding permanent and universal causes for good events along with temporary and specific causes for misfortune is the art of hope; finding permanent and universal causes for misfortune and temporary and specific causes for good events is the practice of despair" (p. 92).

Level of optimism has wide-ranging implications in varying contexts. Pessimistic students will resort to avoidance coping, whereas optimistic ones will engage in more active coping. Optimists use more problem-centered coping than pessimists, as well as a variety of emotion-focused coping techniques. When faced with difficult situations beyond their control, pessimists tend to respond with avoidance and denial, whereas optimists work to accept the reality of the situation and perceive it in the best possible light (Carver & Scheier, 2002). I'm reminded of a magazine advertisement for a cancer drug that depicts a woman in her 30s with a determined look on her face. The headline above her picture says, "I'm ready, ready to fight my cancer, ready to start chemotherapy, ready for a family vacation." This woman is an optimist.

Sense of Control and Self-Determination

> You had no say in anything . . . you didn't have a say about what you ate or when you ate it. You didn't have a say about when you got up or when you went to bed. You didn't have a say about what times you could play or have free time. Even what you were wearing . . . they were going to open the closet door and pick item a or item b . . . it was a power issue . . . they were in charge. (O. Prilleltensky, 2004, p. 125)

This powerful quote is from one of my interviews with women with disabilities. The woman I was interviewing reflected on her early years in an institution for children with disabilities. I reproduce it here because it is such a powerful description of having one's self-determination completely disregarded. You probably shuddered as you read this quote—I know I did when I heard it.

Having a sense of control over our lives is highly correlated with subjective well-being. Individuals who report that they have control over happenings in their life are much more likely to also report high levels of happiness and subjective well-being (Myers, 1993). Studies conducted in the 1960s by Martin Seligman found that dogs in experimental situations where they were unable to escape an electrical shock became passive and apathetic. Even when the experimental conditions changed and the dogs were now able to escape the shock, some of them didn't even try. These dogs had developed what Seligman called "learned helplessness." Countless studies in psychology have demonstrated the adverse effects of learned helplessness on human beings (Mikulincer, 1994).

Julian Rotter is a well-known researcher in psychology who developed the theory of locus of control. According to this theory, people have either an internal or an external locus of control. Those who have an internal locus of control believe that they have personal control over outcomes in their lives. Those with an external locus of control believe that outside forces, such as fate, God, or other people, primarily control outcomes.

Those with an external locus of control tend to feel powerless when faced with adversity because they don't feel that they have any control over the situation. They experience high levels of stress and are low in subjective well-being (Lemme, 2006).

Beyond its impact on subjective well-being, sense of control has been linked to physical health and even longevity. Researchers found that elderly people who manage to maintain control over their most valued roles live longer than those who are unable to do so (Lemme, 2006). Recall the Whitehall studies from Chapter 1: Those who experience little control over their jobs are at much greater risk for untimely death than those who experience a lot of control over their jobs.

When we say that a sense of control is important for well-being, what do we actually mean? Does it mean, for example, that loss of functional abilities due to disability or old age automatically results in low subjective well-being? Some people think so. They perceive the loss of ability to carry out all activities of daily living as synonymous with having no control over their life. People unable to attend independently to their self-care due to disability have a different explanation of control and its relation to well-being. They assert that the need for assistance in self-care, even with the most intimate tasks of daily living, does not have to result in a loss of autonomy and control (Brisenden, 1998; Morris, 1992, 1993, 1996, 2001; Shakespeare, 1996). Having a sense of control is more about the freedom to make important life decisions and have control over daily routines. It is also about the right to decide what assistance is needed, how and when it will be delivered, and by whom. Making decisions on behalf of others is what truly robs people of dignity and control over their lives (O. Prilleltensky, 2004).

Environmental Mastery and Self-Efficacy

The very little engine looked up and saw the tears in the dolls' eyes. And she thought of the good little boys and girls on the other side of the mountain who would not have any toys or good food unless she helped. Then she said, "I think I can. I think I can. I think I can." (*The Little Engine That Could*, Watty Piper, 1930, as cited in Maddux, 2002)

Albert Bandura (1977) would undoubtedly agree that the little engine had high self-efficacy. Coined by Bandura in 1977, self-efficacy is the belief we hold about our ability to complete challenging tasks. Those low in self-efficacy believe that they will be unable to meet a desired goal because they are incapable of successfully completing the tasks required for its accomplishment. Low self-efficacy "is the converse of a feeling of mastery" (Todd & Bohart, 1999, p. 342) and leads to avoidance and lack of persistence.

Both Isaac and I have worked in schools as teachers, consultants, and clinicians. We saw many children who had very low self-efficacy. They just didn't believe that they have what it takes to master academic tasks and be successful students. These students expended a lot of energy in avoiding tasks that they perceived as being too difficult for them. If they did attempt a task and were not immediately successful, they very quickly gave up. Of course, this only reinforced their beliefs that they are incapable. In a typical vicious cycle, feeling less and less capable led to lower effort and persistence. I remember one particular child who was sent for a psychoeducational evaluation. I remember writing in the report that he is motivated by the motto "Better bad than stupid." This youngster had very low academic self-efficacy and was afraid to try and fail. His acting out, I believed, was his attempt to shield himself from further feelings of failure and incompetence.

Individuals who have low self-efficacy are also prone to becoming hyper-critical self-observers. They focus all their attention on what they are doing wrong and are thereby thwarting their chances of successfully completing challenging tasks. Their ruminations and negative self-evaluations further interfere with productive behavior. They become particularly anxious when faced with obstacles, which tends to hinder cognitive processing and lower performance (Maddux, 2002; Todd & Bohart, 1999). I have seen a good number of clients in counseling whose low self-efficacy caused them much suffering and distress.

Just like the Little Engine That Could, those with high self-efficacy believe that they can be resourceful and effective when faced with complex tasks. They set high goals, expend efforts to meet their goals, and persevere when faced with challenges and obstacles (Maddux, 2002). Though they may experience frustration when faced with obstacles, they are rarely overwhelmed by them. Rather, they engage in problem solving and corrective feedback in an attempt to overcome them. When faced with challenges, those with low self-efficacy become self-diagnostic and ruminate about their inadequacies, whereas those with high self-efficacy become task-diagnostic and continue to search for solutions (Maddux, 2002). Even if they do not currently possess the skills they need to solve a problem, they entertain the possibility that these skills can be learned (Cantor & Sanderson, 1999). "Believing that you can accomplish what you want to accomplish is one of the most important ingredients—perhaps *the* most important ingredient—in the recipe for success" (Maddux, 2002, p. 277). Thus, self-efficacy is a core factor in subjective well-being.

Growth and Meaningful Pursuits

Today is Wednesday, August 3, 2005. It is early afternoon and I am sitting in my office working on this book. Isaac is in his office doing the same. The department at our university is pretty quiet these days as most students and faculty are on vacation. We have chosen to spend our summer writing and have made plans for a family vacation in the winter. I feel fulfilled and content despite the fact that I'm currently working while most others are vacationing. Writing this book on well-being is certainly contributing to my own well-being!

Most people, when asked, say that their primary goal in life is to be happy. Nonetheless, "research indicates that happiness is most often a by-product of participating in worthwhile projects and activities that do not have as their primary focus the attainment of happiness" (Emmons, 2003, p. 106). This is not to suggest that there is no need to take time for rest and relaxation, or that leisure is unnecessary. However, things that we typically associate with fun, such as a rollercoaster ride, a hot-fudge sundae, or a soothing massage, rarely have a long-lasting effect on our well-being.

Seligman (2002) makes a distinction between those kinds of *pleasures* that tend to fade rapidly once the external stimulus (hot-fudge sundae) disappears and *gratifications* that are absorbing and meaningful to us, even if they are not always fun. Examples of gratifications are pursuits that contribute to the well-being of others and those that utilize the specific strengths and gifts that we possess. The positive feelings associated with their engagement are authentic, long-lasting, and life-affirming. Robert's volunteer work in Habitat for Humanity is a gratification; the hot shower and hearty breakfast at the end of his shift is a pleasure. A good meal when hungry and a hot shower following hard physical labor are pleasurable in and of themselves. They are particularly enjoyable for Robert as they follow the gratifying activity of lending a hand to a family in need.

Robert is among the 100 million Americans who are involved in some volunteer activity (Cantor & Sanderson, 1999). A contribution to the wider society, beyond one's immediate circle of family and friends, is associated with personal well-being. Helping leads to positive feelings, and those involved in community service consistently report improved life satisfaction and well-being associated with their volunteerism (Piliavin, 2003). As economist Richard Layard (2005, p. 190) suggests, "You get more from life if you try to 'do good' than if you try to 'do well.'" Helping others provides a sense of meaning and purpose, strengthens interpersonal connections, positively impacts self-evaluation, and increases positive mood. It can also provide a temporary distraction from one's own problems (Piliavin, 2003).

Sense of purpose and contribution to the greater good can also be attained through work endeavors. Seventy-five percent of individuals assert that they would continue working even if they win the lottery and make a fortune (Myers, 1993). Some people place a high premium on the financial reward and advancement that work can provide. Others see work as a calling and are more motivated by its social usefulness (Nakamura & Csikszentmihalyi, 2003). Of course, it is not one or the other; we can appreciate the financial and professional benefits of being gainfully employed while valuing the contribution we make through our work. Furthermore, we are most likely to be satisfied in a job that provides us with an optimal measure of challenge when the job requirements and our perceived capabilities are in harmony (Nakamura & Csikszentmihalyi, 2003). Work contributes to our personal identity and provides us with opportunities for growth, self-expression, and social connection. Thus, unemployment has a corrosive impact on well-being beyond the loss of income. For those who become unemployed, the loss of work itself can be even more detrimental than the loss of income (Layard, 2005).

Spirituality and religiosity must be included in any discussion of personal well-being in general, and a sense of purpose and meaning in particular. Despite its historical neglect in psychological literature, there is mounting scientific evidence that points to the salutary effects of religion and spirituality on personal well-being. Religion and spirituality are positively correlated with longevity, physical and psychological health, and coping behavior and negatively associated with depression, risk-taking behavior, and hopelessness. Although correlation does not equal causation and the relationship between spirituality and well-being is multifaceted and complex, there is little doubt that this relationship needs to be further explored. The vast majority of Americans (95%) believe in God and consider religion an important part of their lives (86%). Thus, attending to the spiritual dimension of people's lives is an integral component of any work on well-being (Lemme, 2006; Pargament & Mahoney, 2002).

LOVE, INTIMACY, AND POSITIVE RELATIONSHIPS

"Our survival depends on the healing power of love, intimacy, and relationships. Physically. Emotionally. Spiritually. As individuals. As communities. As a culture. Perhaps even as a species" (Ornish, 1998, p. 1). Does this sound like a quote taken from last Sunday's sermon? Or perhaps from some flaky radio talk show about love and relationships? Actually, it is the opening sentence to a book by Dean Ornish, a professor of medicine at the University of California at San Francisco and director of the nonprofit Preventive Medicine Research Institute in Sausalito, California. Dr. Ornish is a renowned cardiologist whose research has demonstrated that severe coronary heart disease can begin to reverse following comprehensive changes in lifestyle. Along with advocating regular exercise and a healthy diet, Ornish highlights the healing effect of love and intimacy and the importance of positive relationships not only to emotional well-being, but to physical health and longevity.

In Chapter 1, we presented compelling evidence on the relationship between social support and survival among patients with advanced malignancies. Mere participation in a social support group accounted for a statistically significant difference in average survival rates compared to those who did not participate in supportive groups. Although a diagnosis of advanced cancer that has metastasized is associated with a shortened life span, the availability of social support appears to prolong patient survival. On a similar note, studies with heart patients in the United States and Sweden found that individuals who reported feeling loved and supported by significant others had less blockage in the arteries of their hearts than those who did not feel loved and supported. In fact, if we consider all of the causes of premature death and disease in combination, those who do not feel loved, supported, and cared for are at a 3 to 5 times higher risk of suffering premature death and disease (Ornish, 1998).

Beyond longevity and physical well-being, love, intimacy, and meaningful relationships are at the core of emotional well-being. I am part of a team that teaches a first-year course on adult development. Yesterday was the second class of the fall semester, and we had more than 100 first-year students in attendance. Using sophisticated technology that we fondly refer to as "clickers," the lead instructor posed the following question: What would make your life extraordinary? The choices were (a) being financially secure, (b) being happy, (c) loving and being loved, and (d) other. Loving and being loved won by a landslide, chosen by nearly 50% of the students. These 18-year-old incoming students have yet to learn that positive relationships are correlated with longevity or that research studies consistently point to higher levels of well-being and happiness among married people. Or, for that matter, that leading a rich and fulfilling social life was the core factor that distinguished college students who were found to be very happy from their unhappy or averagely happy peers (Seligman, 2002). Nonetheless, they intuitively understood the fundamental importance of love and social support to their personal well-being.

SIGNS OF PERSONAL WELL-BEING IN ORGANIZATIONS

In this section, we explore how the correlates of personal well-being manifest themselves in organizations such as schools and the workplace. What does self-efficacy, sense of control, and meaningful engagement feel and look like at the organizational level? If we observe children over the course of a typical day at school, what are some indications of high versus low optimism and self-efficacy? If we observe employees at an office, what signs can tell us that they're experiencing well-being?

Optimism and Self-Efficacy

A group of middle school students is busily working on a group project. Each group has been assigned a different country to research and present to the class. Today is the first of a series of group meetings where students can plan their project, assign tasks, and decide how the final product will be presented. Mallory is the first to speak up. "Okay, you guys, so according to this outline Mrs. Prasit gave us, we have to research different things about Norway." "Yeah," chimes in Robert, who is seated next to Mallory, "we need to study its geography, mode of government, economics, culture, and a bunch of other things. We'd better get going if we want to get this done and a good job—we have to present in two weeks."

If we observe this group for the next 20 minutes, we can learn a lot about its participants' levels of self-efficacy. Mallory and Robert seem to emerge as the group leaders. Mallory suggests that they begin by breaking the project into individual components: "This way it won't seem like such a huge deal." Robert notes that they should look at what resources they need to gather and who will be responsible for getting those resources. He uses the classroom computer to do an initial search while Mallory spends a few minutes in consultation with the teacher. Two other group participants seem to follow their lead: Jennifer quietly leafs through a book, while Erin asks if she should go to the library now to find more books. The four students barely take notice of Daniel, who silently plays with his pen, seemingly disconnected from his group.

Of course, Daniel's behavior might be accounted for by such transient factors as preoccupation with an argument he had with his best friend or anticipation of a game that will determine if the school basketball team, with Daniel as its captain, will progress to the finals. Nonetheless, Daniel's teacher confirms that this is typical behavior for him and that he is often passive and disengaged from academic tasks. When I worked as a school psychologist and a behavior consultant, I came across many youngsters like Daniel, youngsters who had low self-efficacy. Some were passive and quiet in class, doing their best to blend into the woodwork so that they wouldn't be called on by the teacher. Others took on the role of the class clown or engaged in various disruptive behaviors in an attempt to draw others' attention from the task—a task they felt ill equipped to complete.

Low self-efficacy is correlated with depression, anxiety, and low self-esteem, whereas high self-efficacy serves as a protective factor. In a work environment, an individual with high self-efficacy will approach a challenging task much differently from one with low self-efficacy. When faced with a difficult task, he or she will utilize problem-solving skills and mobilize a host of internal and external resources to meet the task at hand. Although some frustration and even insecurity may be temporarily experienced, these will serve as cues that a different course of action is called for.

Low self-efficacy can be misconstrued as laziness. Workers who feel ill-equipped to successfully complete assigned tasks might spend an inordinate amount of time analyzing the task and second-guessing their own performance. They will likely refrain from seeking corrective feedback from their superiors, lest their incompetence be exposed. Their ability to think clearly about the job will be overshadowed by the tendency to evaluate critically their own performance.

Sense of Control and Self-Determination

"The stress of a job does not depend on the nature of the job as much as it depends on whether workers believe that they have the ability to control the stressful aspects of the job" (Halpern, 2005, p. 406). Every spring I team-teach a first-year course on small group behavior. One of my favorite classes is a 2-hour simulation on decision making and control over one's work environment. Each lab of 12 students is randomly divided into a small group of managers, a supervisor, and a large group of workers. Students randomly pick a card that assigns them to a particular role. The managers are then taken to a separate room and given a bag of Tinker Toys. Without touching the materials, they are to come up with a detailed plan for using these resources in the construction of a tall yet steady tower, one that will be taller than the towers constructed by other groups of managers.

The managers have 5 minutes to convey their instructions to the supervisor, who constructs a diagram according to the specifications he or she is given. The supervisor utilizes this diagram in instructing the group of workers in how they are to carry out the task. The workers are to follow the instructions they are given. They are not allowed to question the design constructed by the managers or to engage in dialogue with the supervisor or with their coworkers. Their job is to follow orders and do as they are told, working under tight time constraints. At the sound of the buzzer, the workers are to step away from their respective towers, which are then measured by an external evaluator. The group that has managed to design, instruct, and construct the highest free-standing tower is declared the winner.

Although it is merely a simulation, this exercise always stirs up emotions and is a catalyst for intense discussions. Those who are assigned to be managers by the luck of the draw seem pleased that they are managers rather than workers. I've even observed one student's covert attempt to swap her worker card with an unsuspecting latecomer who drew a manager card. As the workers attempt to construct the tower, they are visibly frustrated by their inability to challenge its design, ask for further clarifications, or communicate with their fellow workers. They have very little control over their work environments, and they clearly don't like that. Given that only one group is declared the winner (and some extra quiz points are riding on the balance), subtle complaints can be heard toward managers who designed the towers, the supervisor who provided the instructions, or fellow workers who reportedly deviated from the plan. The simulation is then repeated, this time with complete freedom to collaborate on the design and construction of the tower and the ability to communicate freely ideas and strategies. The collective mood is much more positive following the second simulation.

As human beings, we strive to have control over our lives and destinies and thrive in environments where voice and choice can be exercised. In most formal organizations, such as schools and businesses, the brunt of the power is concentrated at the top of the hierarchy. "As we move down the chain of command, authority diminishes and the number of occupants at each subordinate level increases" (Forsyth, 1999, p. 132). The ubiquitous nature of hierarchies notwithstanding, organizations vary widely in the degree of power, and control, members have. A top-down management style wherein authority and obedience are emphasized will engender passivity and malcontent among the workforce. Personal well-being is clearly related to organizational well-being, the subject of Chapters 8, 9, and 10.

Challenge, Growth, and Meaning

Years ago, when I worked as a school psychologist at a child guidance clinic, the social worker and I met with a parent late one Friday afternoon. The mother in question, a sole provider for her children, had little flexibility and could meet only at the end of her working day on Friday. By the time our meeting ended and we opened the door to leave, it was well after 6:00 and completely dark outside. The principal of the school was still in the building, apparently unaware that he was not alone. We started him when we came out of the meeting room, and he seemed genuinely surprised that anyone was still in the building. Although he didn't voice this, it appeared incomprehensible to him that we chose to stay well past the end of the working day without any compensation for our overtime.

Harold (my social work colleague and good friend) and I chuckled as we left the school and headed toward our cars in the snowy evening. We even stood by our cars for a while and continued to discuss the meeting before we drove off. We had developed an exceptionally productive working relationship and felt that our collaborative efforts benefited our clients and their families. Of course, we also worked for the paycheck at the end of the month and appreciated the fact that we were off during the summer and other school breaks. Nonetheless, the satisfaction we derived from our job had more to do with the contribution we felt we were making and with the sense that we were growing personally and professionally.

Harold and I experienced *flow* on the job, a term coined and investigated by psychologist Mihaly Csikzentmihalyi. When people are completely engaged in what they are doing to the point that they are barely aware of the passage of time, they are in a state of flow. Flow can be derived from a wide range of endeavors. It is most often associated with complete absorption in a challenging and valued task that requires us to stretch ourselves yet is entirely within our ability to engage with it. The task is intrinsically rewarding, and we feel that our capacities are being fully utilized (Nakamura & Csikszentmihalyi, 2003).

Individuals who find their jobs exhilarating are those who experience flow at work. One study explored what successful professionals and business executives close to retirement identify as the most satisfying aspects of their work. The creative challenge and stimulation that their work provided coupled with the opportunities to keep learning were highlighted as the most rewarding (Goleman, 1998).

Flow is more likely to be experienced at work than in most other life arenas. Research participants outfitted with beepers were instructed to record their activities and feelings every time their beeper sounded. It was thus found that whereas people are in a state of flow less than 20% of the time during leisure activities, they are in flow about 50% of the time while at work (Goleman, 1998).

Experiencing work as personally meaningful and growth-fostering is associated with a high level of commitment to the organization. More committed workers invest more in their work. They will often put up with pressing deadlines and long hours if they perceive them as necessary for the well-being of the organization. They are more likely to take initiative, volunteer for extra tasks, and display helpful behaviors toward their coworkers. Worker satisfaction is associated with lower turnover rates, especially during times of low unemployment rates. For women in particular, satisfaction on the job is associated with a lower frequency of absenteeism (Warr, 1999).

Satisfied workers do a better job of serving customers, and productivity in general is enhanced. Productivity can be measured not only in terms of business growth. In a particular compelling study reviewed by Warr (1999), satisfaction among schoolteachers was linked to better behavior and higher academic performance among students. No fewer than 300 schools participated in the study. Just imagine the positive ripple effect on scores of students and their families. Although many factors contribute to worker satisfaction, potential for growth and meaningfulness rank high among them.

Increasingly, workers are favoring jobs that allow them to utilize valued abilities and learn new skills (Warr, 1999). For the generation of baby boomers, work was primarily seen as a vehicle for increasing purchasing power. The new generations of workers, in comparison, seem to place greater value on the fulfillment they derive from the work itself (Harter, Schmidt, & Keyes, 2003; Wrzesniewski, Rozin, & Bennett, 2003). "Surveys of recent and upcoming generations of employees clearly show a majority of employees desire greater meaning and personal development from their work and suggest many workers see their work as a calling—enjoyable, fulfilling, and socially useful" (Harter et al., 2003, p. 207).

Cooperation

A former supervisor of mine at a university counseling service liked to tell the story of a department that once existed at the university in question. The level of hostility and strife among faculty was so high that it led to the eventual demise of the department. Many people left, and those that remained isolated themselves in their offices. The department had reached a point of no return, and the only remaining option was to close it down. This story may not seem especially interesting or even worthy of mention. However, it is important to note that prior to dismantlement it was called the Department of Human Relationships. My former supervisor's tongue-in-cheek conclusion was that it closed down because its members couldn't relate.

By now, you know that decision latitude, opportunities for personal control, and lack of close supervision are associated with work satisfaction. You also understand the importance of engaging in tasks that are meaningful, absorbing, and growth-enhancing. However, these factors cannot account for the demise of the Department of Human Relationships. Academic work is anything but boring, and academics as a group have more latitude and control over their jobs than almost any other group of employees. I don't know of many other jobs that would allow me to spend the better part of the day working on my areas of interest and to decide if I'd rather do so at home or in the office.

Positive relationships, cooperation, emotional support, and a sense of belonging were the magic ingredients that were sorely lacking in the Department of Human Relationships. According to Baumeister and Leary's (1995) belonging hypothesis, we have an inborn need to form and maintain positive interpersonal relationships. Our first relational experiences are in our family of origin, but we belong to many other groups throughout the life span. Individuals strive to affiliate with others; those who are isolated experience distress (Elsdon, 2003). Cooperation is a clear sign of personal well-being in organizations, with dual benefits: The person and the organization gain by it.

SIGNS OF PERSONAL WELL-BEING IN THE COMMUNITY

If we want to live in a healthy community, we should expect to see manifestations of personal well-being in it. We should see optimism, self-efficacy, sense of control, self-determination, growth, meaning, and, of course, cooperation.

Optimism, Self-Efficacy, and Sense of Control

Just as hope and a sense of mastery are important in the workplace, so they are in the community at large. Our communities need people with high levels of optimism and self-efficacy to tackle the complicated social problems we face. As a society, we should strive to impart optimism and self-efficacy to as many of our citizens as we can. These are key ingredients of leadership and citizenship. We need change agents who believe in creating a more just and caring society. We should raise children who can master the environment and who can foster social change.

Paradoxically, though, those who have the most opportunity to exercise control over their environment may be the least interested in changing it, for they benefit from the status quo. This interesting paradox cannot be easily overcome. If privilege affords opportunities to control the environment, via education, resources, influence, and networking, and the privileged benefit from the current state of affairs, why should they use their power to change it? If the elite is invested in preserving the status quo, and the status quo is inimical to the poor and disadvantaged, it would seem that the way out is to promote a sense of control and self-efficacy in those whose well-being is tied to prospects of change.

Challenge, Meaning, and Growth

Meaningful engagement in the community is a sign of well-being as well as a marker of a healthy community. The more engaged citizens are, the higher the chances of fighting indifference and finding leaders. Both in the occupational realm (Crabtree, 2005; Krueger & Killham, 2005) and in the community sphere (Putnam, 2000), engagement benefits the agent and the setting at once. Unfortunately, there are signs of declining community involvement and social capital (Putnam, 2000), and the number of workers who report serious engagement at work is only about a quarter of the workforce (Krueger & Killham, 2005).

To halt these tendencies, we need to regain the sense of urgency in engagement and in proximal and distal caring. Proximal caring is showing compassion toward those close to us, in our family, community, or congregation, whereas distal caring is reaching out to those who are removed from us, either geographically or socially. We are not talking about miles away from us, for they often live only a few blocks away from our nice neighborhoods. Those who are removed from us are those who are socially excluded and often forgotten. To reach beyond our close circle of family, friends, and congregants is to care distally. We consider that a sign of personal well-being in the community.

Some societies excel at volunteering; others are self-absorbed. Regrettably, many of those who show the courage to devote their passion to public life are often scorned and viewed with suspicion. Ever since politics in the United States became synonymous with corruption in many people's mind, fewer and fewer people have joined public life. The downward trend in civic participation documented by Putnam (2000) in the United States only adds to the poverty of meaningful engagement in social issues.

Cooperation

Without cooperation, it's hard to imagine how any type of well-being may flourish. Cooperation is a sine qua non for personal, organizational, and certainly collective well-being. In our view, it ought to be a paradigmatic sign of personal well-being in the community. Like self-efficacy, it ought to be taught to our children and practiced by adults. No efforts should be spared to advance it. Don't expect an easy ride, though. There are no signs of decline in the litigious nature of our society.

LINKED SIGNS

Chronic high levels of stress compromise our immune system and increase the likelihood of suffering ill health. A recent study with nurses found that having latitude in making work-related decisions was an important factor in mitigating their stress. Stress among nurses was measured by the level of cortisol (the stress hormone) secreted by their endocrine glands. Cortisol levels did not vary based on objective measures of the nurses' workload. On the other hand, the degree to which they believed they could exert control over their work environment was highly correlated with their level of stress. The greatest increase in cortisol levels was found among nurses with the highest workload coupled with the least amount of control (Ganster, Fox, & Dwyer, 2001). These examples point to the interaction between environmental (workload and amount of control) and personal (belief in ability to control one's environment) factors. It is never one or the other: Personal and environmental signs of well-being are codetermined. A propitious work climate enables its workers to exercise voice and choice, which, in turn, can be used to modify the surroundings to make them more conducive to personal well-being.

ROWS FOR WELLNESS

Exercise 5: Performing Signs of Well-Being

We covered a number of signs of well-being; they ranged from self-efficacy and sense of control to love, optimism, and cooperation. What are the ROWS that enable or inhibit you from performing these signs of well-being in your personal, organizational, and community life? Review all the signs discussed in this chapter and conduct a ROWS analysis in Form 5.1. You may discover that some are easy and others are hard, that some come natural and others require more practice.

To reflect on your level of readiness for action, transfer the various ROWS to Form 5.2.

Form 5.1   ROWS Exercise 5: Performing Signs of Well-Being

Risks for Performing Signs of Well-Being	
Personal	
Organizational	
Community	
Opportunities for Performing Signs of Well-Being	
Personal	
Organizational	
Community	
Weaknesses for Performing Signs of Well-Being	
Personal	
Organizational	
Community	
Strengths for Performing Signs of Well-Being	
Personal	
Organizational	
Community	

Form 5.2   Wellness Readiness Check 5: Performing Signs of Well-Being

ROWS	1 — I never thought about doing something about it.	2 — I'm thinking about doing something about it.	3 — I'm prepared to do something about it.	4 — I'm doing something about it.	5 — I've been doing something about it for some time.
Risks					
Personal					
Organizational					
Community					
Opportunities					
Personal					
Organizational					
Community					
Weaknesses					
Personal					
Organizational					
Community					
Strengths					
Personal					
Organizational					
Community					

6

Where Does It Come From?
Sources of Personal Well-Being

In Chapter 5, our focus was on the signs of well-being: what personal well-being feels and looks like at the personal, organizational, and community level. In this chapter, our main task is to explore the core factors that account for personal well-being at these levels of analysis. Where does well-being come from? What personal, interpersonal, organizational, and community factors account for one person having a higher level of well-being than another? Understanding the sources of well-being is an important step in constructing action plans and exploring strategies for its attainment.

PERSONAL SOURCES OF WELL-BEING

There are several personal determinants of well-being. In this segment we review biopsychosocial sources of well-being.

Biological and Constitutional Factors

The most meaningful and memorable experience of my (Ora's) life surrounds the birth of our only son, Matan. It was not the birth itself that was so significant; I was mostly relieved to be no longer in pain and to know that I had a healthy baby boy. My peak experience was when I first spent time alone with my newborn baby, when he awoke for his first nightly feeding. I was so excited I could barely sleep. I knew that a nurse would bring me the baby when he woke up. Soon enough, I spotted a nurse walking briskly down the hall, a bundle in her arms. I peered at Matan's little face and into his deep brown eyes. Although less than 24 hours old and needing to be fed, he had an unmistakable expression of content and joyous wonder. It was as if he couldn't wait to meet the world and all that it had to offer. That look will remain with me for the rest of my life. It was my first glimpse of my son's spirited, spunky, and vivacious nature.

Matan, it seems, has been genetically predisposed to being happy and having high subjective well-being. He experiences a lot of pleasant affect, infrequently experiences unpleasant affect, and generally perceives his life as satisfying and rewarding. These components, according to Diener and Lucas (1999), are the mainstay of subjective well-being.

Of course, a multitude of biological, familial, social, and economic factors have contributed to Matan's development. It would be preposterous to suggest that his pleasant disposition and tendency to see the bright side of things at age 18 are solely biologically determined. Nonetheless, temperament studies of newborn infants and studies of monozygotic (identical) twins who were raised in different homes point to a strong biological basis for emotional style and subjective well-being.

Studies of newborn infants have confirmed what most parents already know: that babies are born with different temperaments. The most well-known study on childhood temperament was conducted more than 4 decades ago by Thomas and Chess (1977). Based on repeated interviews with parents of infants, Thomas and Chess concluded that there are clear individual differences among babies in level of activity, emotion, and ability to self-regulate. These differences are biologically based, although they can be modulated by the child's environment. From the first days and months of life, babies were found to differ in nine characteristics, including level of activity, adaptability, quality of mood, and intensity of reaction. These characteristics combine to form three distinct groups of infants: easy, difficult, and slow to warm up.

Many advances have been made since the early studies of Thomas and Chess (1977), and present-day researchers are cautious about making any predictions about adult personality based on early differences in temperament. Nonetheless, biologically based differences continue to be relevant to the understanding of happiness and subjective well-being. More recently, Kagan and his associates (Kagan, Snidman, & Arcus, 1992) conducted a study of inhibited and uninhibited children. They concluded that inhibited children fall into two distinct categories. The first category comprises children who become inhibited following certain experiences they have had, such as the death of a parent. Children belonging to the second category, however, have a physiology that predisposes them to adopt an avoidant style to most unfamiliar events: "These latter children differ from the former in both autonomic functioning, affect, and physical features and belong to the temperamental category we call inhibited" (p. 171). It seems, then, that babies are predisposed to experiencing differing levels of pleasant and unpleasant emotion (Diener & Lucas, 1999).

Studies of monozygotic twins who were separated at birth and raised apart provide further evidence for the biological basis of subjective well-being. Researchers have been able to track down twins who were given up for adoption and raised in different homes, at times unaware of their twin's existence. Monozygotic twins are especially interesting as they share all of their genes; genetically, they are one and the same. Even when raised in different homes, their status as a twin unbeknown to them, these twins were found to be highly similar in various measures of personality, including subjective well-being (Diener & Lucas, 1999).

Our personality, according to McCrae and Costa (1990), is based on five basic and enduring traits that combine to compose the core of our being: extraversion, neuroticism, openness to experience, agreeableness, and conscientiousness. These traits, referred to as the five-factor model of personality, are believed to be stable across time and contexts. Hence, they are enduring aspects of the self that do not readily change based on shifting circumstances (Lemme, 2006). Neuroticism and extraversion are believed to be the two factors most closely associated with subjective well-being. Neuroticism is the likelihood that a particular individual will experience negative emotions such as anxiety, guilt, and insecurity. Extraversion has to do with one's preference for relating to others. Those who are high on neuroticism tend to be anxious and depressed and have low self-esteem, whereas those high on extraversion are typically sociable, assertive, and lively (Diener & Lucas, 1999). Individuals who are high on extraversion and low on neuroticism are most likely to have high subjective well-being.

From intelligence to gregariousness to optimism, there is wide-ranging agreement among researchers that many human traits have a strong genetic component. Roughly speaking, at least 50% of the variance in our intellectual and social-emotional functioning is believed to be determined by our genes. However, that means that the other 50% of the variance is based on environmental factors. Next, we explore the role of early parenting experiences on subjective well-being, with a specific focus on the role of attachment.

Early Parenting Experiences

One-year-old David is brought into a room by his mother. The room contains a variety of age-appropriate toys designed to pique the interest of the toddler. In addition to the toys, the room also contains a stranger—someone David has never met before. With his mother in the room, David toddles over to the toys and happily explores his environment. However, his mother suddenly gets up and goes out of the room, leaving him alone with the stranger. David immediately begins to whimper, making his way toward the door. He is no longer interested in the toys. After a short while, David's mother returns. He greets her with a happy smile and outstretched arms. He is easily comforted and soon returns to exploring his environment.

The scenario is repeated with 1-year-old Sally and her mother. Sally's mother also leaves the room after a short while, leaving Sally with a stranger. Much like David, Sally fusses and whimpers at the sight of her mother leaving. She loses interest in the toys and heads for the door. Here, however, ends the similarity between the toddlers. Sally's mother returns shortly thereafter, but Sally is not comforted by her return. She continues to fuss and arches her back in protest when her mother attempts to pick her up.

After David and Sally comes Jonathan. He immediately begins to explore the room and the interesting toys contained within it. Jonathan is aware when his mother gets up to leave the room. He goes on playing, seemingly unperturbed by being left alone with a stranger. Jonathan does not respond when his mother leaves and does not acknowledge her when she returns. He appears to be completely unaffected by his mother's comings and goings.

Toddlers like David, Sally, and Jonathan participated in Mary Ainsworth's (Ainsworth, Blehar, Waters, & Wall, 1978) well-know studies on infant attachment. Ainsworth described three distinct styles of attachment. David represents the majority of infants (60%), who are securely attached. They may cry when their father leaves but are happy when he returns and are easily soothed. The solid relationship with a primary caregiver allows them to explore their world free of anxiety. Babies like Sally were labeled anxious-ambivalent by Ainsworth and are believed to comprise some 15% of infants. These babies learn early on that they cannot count on consistent care that is attuned to their needs. Their primary caregiver is at times available and at times not, and the attachment they form is mingled with anxiety and distress. Jonathan represents the third group of infants, those labeled avoidant. These babies (some 23%) have experienced rejecting and unresponsive caregiving. They have learned that they cannot trust their caregiver to attend to their needs.

Ainsworth et al. (1978) built on the work of John Bowlby (1982), who emphasized the importance of the bond between mother and child for the latter's future development. Bowlby theorized that infants are genetically programmed to elicit caring responses from their caregivers. Given the helplessness of newborn babies and their complete dependence on others, it is their ability to elicit caring responses, their cuteness, if you will, that ensures their very survival. As any parent knows, a newborn infant is a bundle of joy . . . and a bundle of needs. First-time parents are often surprised by how labor-intensive their newborn is and how every waking (and often sleeping) moment is consumed with the baby's needs. Caring for children in general, and infants in particular, requires the ability to subordinate one's needs to those of the child. Newborn infants will be soothed by anyone who attends to their physical needs, yet within the 6th month of life they begin to show a clear preference for a certain person, typically the mother or father.

When a parent is attuned to the infant's needs and is physically and emotionally available to respond with appropriate comfort and care, a secure attachment is formed between parent and child. This attachment serves as a secure base for the child to explore her environment and learn about the world around her. Bowlby and Ainsworth theorized that a secure attachment with one's primary caregiver (typically the mother) lays the foundation for healthy development throughout the life span. Based on the nature of this relationship, children develop general beliefs about their environment as safe and supportive versus hostile and alienating, and themselves as worthy or not worthy of care. This serves as an organizing framework or an internal working model that will largely determine their beliefs about self and others, the goals they will strive for, and the strategies that will be employed to attain those goals (Griffith, 2004).

Bowlby's attachment theory and Ainsworth's attachment styles have received wide-ranging attention from developmental psychologists worldwide. Some researchers, such as Hazan and Shaver (1987, 2004), reported meaningful links between early attachment styles with primary caregivers and romantic relationships in adulthood. According to their findings, individuals who are securely attached in infancy are more likely to form secure attachment later in life, whereas those whose primary attachment style was anxious-ambivalent or avoidant will tend to reenact their respective pattern.

Beyond the role of early attachment, there is little doubt that the quality of parenting affects well-being. Optimism, self-efficacy, sense of control, and self-determination are shaped and developed through environmental interactions. Parents who are responsive to a young child's attempts to affect his or her environment encourage further exploration and facilitate the development of self-efficacy and sense of agency (Maddux, 2002). Allowing children to do things for themselves even though it is far more efficient to do things for them enables them to practice important skills and perceive themselves as mastering their environment.

In one of my family visits to Israel, I was in the front seat of my brother's car while his 3-year-old son, strapped to his car seat, was having a full-blown tempter tantrum in the back. He wanted to go to the playground, and all of his father's explanations that it was too late that day and that he would get to go tomorrow were met with screams and flailing limbs. My brother parked the car by the house and went to pick up his screaming child and carry him inside. As he opened the back door, Jonathan, through his tears, gasped, "I want to go out the other door." This was a request that could be accommodated. By the time my brother went around and opened the other door, Jonathan's tantrum had subsided, and he quietly walked inside on his own, holding his father's hand. He learned that even though his wish to be taken to the playground was not met, he still had some control over how he would exit the car.

Emotional Intelligence

Let's move on now to something that happened in the back seat of my car. This was more than 13 years ago. I had two children in the back seat of my car in addition to my own 5-year-old Sara, the daughter of a good friend of mine. The youngest of the three, seated next to Sara, was my 4-year-old nephew Ben. At the time, Ben's parents were out of town and he was staying with our family. We were returning from some outing, the children were tired, and Ben became homesick for his parents. He quietly whimpered and could not be consoled. Only 3 years his senior and having just met him earlier that day, motherly Sara did all she could to comfort her new, younger friend. She sang him songs; she tried to tell him a story; she gently stroked his cheek. Nothing seemed to work. Sara had another idea. "Ben, what does your mommy do when you're upset?"

I remember how impressed I was that a child so young was capable of such insight and empathy. Not only did Sara empathize with Ben's distress and do her best to alleviate it; when all else failed, she asked him what his own mother did in such circumstances, hoping to gain knowledge that would enable her to comfort her younger friend. Now 21, Sara is a talented young woman with a strong social conscience and a passion for social activism. Among her many gifts is her caring and empathy for others, a component of emotional intelligence.

The term emotional intelligence was coined by Peter Sallovey and popularized by psychologist and journalist Daniel Goleman. Goleman's 1994 #1 best-seller, *Emotional intelligence: Why It Can Matter More Than IQ*, was followed by two other books: *Working with Emotional Intelligence* (1998) and *Primal Leadership* (2002, with Richard Boyatzis and Annie McKee). Emotional intelligence refers to "abilities such as being able to motivate oneself and persist in the face of frustrations; to control impulse and delay gratification; to regulate one's moods and keep distress from swamping the ability to think; to empathize and to hope" (Goleman, 1994, p. 34).

Goleman (1994) reminds us that for all the emphasis placed on IQ, it can predict surprisingly little in the way of happiness and general success in life. "At best, IQ contributes about 20% to the factors that determine life success, which leaves 80% to other forces" (p. 34). I think of this as I await a batch of new applications to our graduate program in counseling. As any potential graduate student knows, attaining a high GRE score is one of the key factors in gaining entry to a desired graduate program. Despite this, my colleagues and I know that whether one makes a good counselor has relatively little to do with how well one scores on a GRE. To be sure, GRE scores predict academic success relatively well, and the ability to succeed in a graduate program is a precursor to entering the profession in question. Nonetheless, emotional intelligence, described by Goleman as a meta-ability, can determine how well one can use skills and abilities, including intellectual abilities.

In their book *Primal Leadership: Realizing the Power of Emotional Intelligence*, Goleman and his colleagues (2004) describe four key dimensions of emotional intelligence: self-awareness, self-management, social awareness, and relationship management. Self-awareness, as the name implies, is about having a thorough knowledge of one's emotions, strengths, limitations, and value system. In addition to having a sound sense of their self-worth and capabilities, individuals with high self-awareness are able to read their emotions and recognize how they are impacted by those emotions. Having high self-awareness and understanding the impact of certain emotions is an important precursor to emotional self-management. Those who understand their emotions are more likely to control rather than be controlled by them. Self-management is largely about the ability to control disruptive emotions and impulses. It is a critical skill for those in positions of leadership.

Social awareness is largely about the ability to empathize with others: to take an active interest in others' concerns, understand their perspective, and sense their emotions. Finally, relationship management is the ability to cultivate and maintain a web of relationships, resolve interpersonal conflict, and work positively and collaboratively with other people. Although some people are naturally more emotionally intelligent than others are, these skills can be learned and cultivated throughout the life span.

Loving Relationships

What do you value most in your life, and what is your single greatest source of joy and satisfaction? Many individuals would rate their most intimate relationships as being of utmost importance, more so than academic achievement, work satisfaction, or financial success. "As countless novels, films, songs, plays and poems testify, our ultimate happiness and despair is founded in relationships" (Dwyer, 2000, p. 1). Having loving, supportive relationships is an important protective factor in physical as well as psychological well-being. Individuals who are married live longer and survive a host of health problems at higher rates than their single counterparts. They are also less prone to serious mental health problems such as depression and anxiety and are more likely to report that their life is satisfying and rewarding (Ornish, 1998).

The need to affiliate is a basic human need, much like the need for food and water. Young children in the presence of peers will modify their behavior to gain acceptance and avoid rejection. Freshmen in their first weeks on college campus expend a lot of time and effort forging social links. Solitary confinement is considered to be one of the harshest forms of punishment inflicted on prisoners. We are social beings from the moment of birth, and throughout our lives we affiliate with family members, friends, acquaintances, and colleagues. In fact, about two-thirds of our waking hours are spent in the presence of other people, mostly family members, friends, and coworkers. We are largely shaped by our relationships with close others. They have a powerful impact on our physical and psychological well-being, as we do on theirs (Reis & Rusbult, 2004). Not only do we live our lives in relationships with others, "when we die, the effects of our relationships survive in the lives of the living, reverberating throughout the tissue of their relationships" (Berscheid, 2004, p. 27).

Of all the various relationships we are a part of, dyadic relationships between partners have received the most attention from theorists and researchers. From types of love relationships to factors that contribute to their formation, maintenance, or demise, intimate relationships are central to happiness and well-being.

Sternberg's Triangular Theory of Love "What does it mean 'to love' someone? Does it always mean the same thing, and if not, in what ways do loves differ from each other? Why do certain loves seem to last, whereas others disappear almost as quickly as they are formed?" (Sternberg, 2004, p. 213). These are the questions that Robert Sternberg attempted to answer with his triangular theory of love.

Sternberg (2004) asserts that love is composed of three main components: intimacy, passion, and decision/commitment. Intimacy refers to feelings of bonding, closeness, and togetherness, the warmth and fuzziness of relationships. Passion has to do with drives such as the physical and sexual aspects of a relationship, and decision/commitment pertains to the short-term decision that one loves the other person and the long-term decision to remain in the relationship. The intimacy component is largely associated with feelings, the passion component is largely associated with drives, and the decision/commitment component is largely associated with cognitions. Despite this partitioning into various components, Sternberg emphasizes the importance of not losing sight of the whole, of love as a complex and dynamic experience.

Different combinations of intimacy, passion, and decision/commitment give rise to different kinds of love (Sternberg, 2004).

Nonlove represents the absence of all three components. Liking characterizes the majority of casual interactions. Liking characterizes many relationships between friends where one experiences a closeness and bonding, without feelings of passion or long-term commitment. Infatuated love is the experience of arousal in the absence of intimacy or commitment. "Love at first sight," unless complemented with intimacy and/or commitment, is typically infatuated love that is largely based on physical attraction. Empty love refers to circumstances in which couples decide to remain together, despite the absence of both passion and intimacy. Those who "stay together for the children" can be thought to exist in an empty love relationship. Romantic love is what we see in the movies, the type of love that contains both passion and intimacy but often lacks commitment. Companionate love contains intimacy and commitment but lacks passion. A stable marriage in which the partners are close and committed but no longer passionate is an example of companionate love. Passion and commitment in the absence of intimacy culminates in fatuous love. According to Sternberg (2004), this is the movie-star-style whirlwind courtship and marriage where a commitment is made based on passion without giving sufficient time for the development of intimacy. Finally, consummate love results from the combination of all three components: intimacy, passion, and a commitment to the relationship.

The components of intimacy, passion, and commitment vary along a number of dimensions and properties. In close relationships, for example, intimacy and commitment are relatively stable, whereas passion is less so and tends to come and go with less predictability. Likewise, providing we are aware of it, we can have more control over intimacy and commitment than over passion. Similarly, passion tends to be quick to rise and quick to fade; commitment gradually rises and then plateaus, but intimacy steadily grows over time. The success of relationships depends, to some extent, on our ability to attend to the various components as they change and evolve over the course of the relationship (Dwyer, 2000; Sternberg, 2004).

The Maintenance and Dissolution of Intimate Relationships   In its early years, relationship science focused primarily on the formation stage of relationships. Research studies in social psychology have advanced our understanding of why we are attracted to some people and not to others. For example, we know that we tend to be attracted to those who are in physical proximity, those who are similar to us in important attributes, and/or those who complement us in desirable ways. We also know that, as unfair as it seems, individuals who are more attractive have a definite edge in the dating and love scene.

It is only in the past 2 decades, however, that researchers began to focus their attention on factors and processes associated with the maintenance of close relationships. This trend has intensified as it became more apparent that the factors that contribute to the maintenance of relationships are quite different from those that cause us to form these relationships in the first place (Reis & Rusbult, 2004).

"Relationship maintenance—the mechanisms by which partners conserve, protect, and enhance the health of their important relationships, once those relationships have achieved some degree of closeness— is . . . essential to the longevity of a relationship" (Reis & Rusbult, 2004, p. 281). The high rates of divorce and the associated misery for individuals and families, on the one hand, and the salutary effects of loving relationships on physical and emotional well-being, on the other, heighten the need to advance our understanding of how to nurture relationships and help them to thrive.

Courtney and Michael are newlyweds in their late 20s. They met during their 1st year of college but did not start dating until the end of their junior year. Over the course of their 5-year relationship, Courtney and Michael broke up twice and got back together. They decided to marry when Michael felt compelled to move back to his hometown to join a thriving family business. What is in store for Courtney and Michael? Will their relationship blossom and thrive or deteriorate and ultimately dissolve? Will they be among the 50% of American couples whose marriage ends in divorce, or the remaining 50% who stay attached? Their relationship contains passion, intimacy, and commitment at the point of marriage; how will those evolve over the course of their married life?

According to attachment theorists, Courtney and Michael's relationship is more likely to last if it continues to meet their core needs for safety, care, and sexual gratification. Like the primary relationship with one's parents, intimate relationships are seen as providing a secure base for further growth and development (Hazan & Shaver, 2004). Courtney and Michael's primary attachment style may also play a role in the health and stability of their relationship. Individuals who formed a secure attachment with their primary caregivers are more likely to form secure attachments with their romantic partners. Having attained a secure base in infancy, these individuals are more likely to have cognitive and emotional resources that can be harnessed to regulate the quality of the relationship (Mikulincer, 2004). They are likely to perceive their partner's behavior as benevolent and more likely to seek a nonpossessive intimacy in their love relationship.

In contrast, those with an anxious-ambivalent attachment style suffer from a chronic lack of confidence in the consistent presence of their attachment figure. They are likely to expend much effort on keeping their intimate partner close by, a behavior that may be experienced as smothering and ultimately may lead to their partner's withdrawal. Finally, those with an avoidant style will tend to remain distant, avoid self-disclosure, and feel uncomfortable with a partner's attempt to attain greater intimacy (Hazan & Shaver, 2004). Notwithstanding the impact of attachment styles on adult relationships, it is important to note that one is not doomed to repeating these patterns throughout one's life. Thus, even if Michael's primary attachment style was anxious-ambivalent, this can change as he consistently experiences a loving and secure relationship with Courtney.

Self-disclosure and partner responsiveness are key components in the development of intimacy. Intimacy develops as individuals let down their guard and reveal personally meaningful information, thoughts, and feelings to their loved one. When a partner's response is typically experienced as understanding, validating, and caring, intimacy deepens and accrues over repeated interactions (Laurenceau, Barrett, & Petromonaco, 2004).

Conflict is an unavoidable component of all intimate relationships, and sources of conflict are manifold, from money, to sex, to division of labor. A lot of cross-complaining in conjunction with poor listening to the other's concern characterizes the interactions of poorly functioning couples. Whether conflicts are successfully resolved is largely contingent on the interpretations individuals make regarding their partner's annoying and irritating behaviors (Dwyer, 2000). Unhappy intimates tend to perceive their partner as the source of their marital difficulties (Fincham, 2004) and to see the undesirable behavior as characteristic of the person, long-lasting, and applying to other areas of the relationships. In contrast, the partner's desirable behaviors are perceived as circumstantial, atypical, and unlikely to generalize to other behaviors. Happy couples, on the other hand, will perceive undesirable behaviors as situational, temporary, and specific and desirable behaviors as characteristic of their partner, likely to recur, and applying to other aspects of the relationship (Bradbury & Fincham, 1990). In a similar vein, those who are satisfied with their love relationship tend to highlight and magnify their partner's virtues while minimizing and obscuring his or her faults: "Unconditional positive regard—seeing the best in partners despite their imperfections—appears to be an integral part of satisfying romantic relationships" (Murry, Holmes, & Griffin, 2004, p. 335). Thus, the kinds of attributions Courtney and Michael make about each other's behavior can serve as a barometer of their relationship satisfaction.

John Gottman (1999), a researcher and family therapist at the University of Washington in Seattle, conducts observational studies with couples who agree to spend a weekend in a university apartment, where they are videotaped, observed, and monitored for the majority of their waking hours. Within the first 5 minutes of observing a couple interact, Gottman can predict with a disturbingly high level of accuracy which couples will stay together and which are headed for divorce. Troubled relationships are marked by harsh start-ups of argument; interactions that are marked by criticism, contempt, and defensiveness; physiological reactions of fight-or-flight in times of conflict; and failed attempts to deescalate tension. In contrast, happy couples share a deep friendship and stay emotionally connected even as they deal with conflict. They know each other intimately and can easily answer questions about their partner's likes, dislikes, hopes, and dreams. They also know about important people, events, and circumstances that have shaped their partner's life and are aware of key players and events affecting their partner in the present.

Gottman (1999) claims that what makes for a happy marriage is surprisingly simple: Happy couples have a wealth of positive thoughts and feelings toward one another. This positivity and connectedness is reflected in their daily interactions and serves to protect them in times of conflict. All partners periodically experience negative thoughts and feelings about each other. In the case of happily married couples, these are overridden by the wealth of mutual affection and positivity that characterizes the relationship. Gottman equates this to the set weight theory of weight loss: "Once your marriage gets 'set' at a certain degree of positivity, it will take far more negativity to harm your relationship than if your 'set point' were lower. And if your relationship becomes overwhelmingly negative, it will be more difficult to repair it" (p. 21). Thus, Courtney and Michael are more likely to stay together if they accrue sufficient positivity in their relationship and use various "repair attempts" (p. 22) that will prevent negativity from escalating out of control.

ORGANIZATIONAL SOURCES OF PERSONAL WELL-BEING

Constitutional factors, early parenting experiences, and relationships throughout the life span influence our personal well-being. However, most people's daily lives unfold within organizational structures where they study, work, and carry out their lives. The emotional climate in these organizations and the opportunities provided for growth and engagement will affect overall levels of satisfaction and personal well-being. Furthermore, family-friendly work policies can reduce stress among working parents and result in enhanced well-being for children, parents, and the family unit as a whole.

Emotional Climate and Group Cohesion

"In human groups, cohesion is the integrity, solidarity, and sense of community of aggregated individuals" (Forsyth, 2006, p. 138). Individuals who belong to a cohesive group feel a sense of belonging and commitment to their group, enjoy spending time with other group members, and are less likely to suffer from stress related to social and interpersonal factors. They are enthusiastic about the group and its work and have positive expectations about the group's capabilities (Forsyth, 2006). Cohesive groups in the workplace create a healthier work environment where individuals can thrive.

Some years ago, I worked as a behavior consultant for a local school board. I was responsible for conducting psychoeducational assessments and providing behavioral consultation in 11 schools. I was always struck by how the emotional climate varied from one school to the next. I would look forward to spending time in some schools and dread entering others. It's not that one school largely comprised uncaring people and another had a preponderance of kind spirits. A group is more than a collection of individuals, and some groups are more cohesive and collaborative than others.

In some instances, the emotional climate was so palpable that you felt it from the moment you entered the school. People—teachers, support staff, and even students—just seemed friendlier and more welcoming in some schools. As an outside consultant who had to coordinate assessment schedules and meetings, I had to expend a lot more energy in some schools than in others. Most telling was the atmosphere in the staff room, where teachers retreat during their breaks. Given that my day involved a number of transitions between schools, I would often step into the staff room for a quick bite or a cup of coffee between meetings and assessments. Some staff rooms were characterized by little interaction. Teachers would either eat their lunch in silence while reading or grading papers, or congregate in very small groups, with little to no communication among the groups. As I became more familiar with these settings, I learned of coalitions that included some people and excluded others. Some teachers felt so excluded and alienated that they avoided the staff room altogether.

It was always a relief for me to leave such a school and head for one with a more supportive environment. A healthy school was a friendly school. People smiled more and appeared to interact with ease. They seemed to enjoy spending time with their peers, and some had developed close friendships. They would get together after school hours, and the yearly holiday party felt like a treat rather than a chore. Beyond individual friendships, there was a general sense of belonging and a commitment to group goals. Interdependence was high, and people collaborated to achieve common goals. Working teams were the rule rather than the exception, and there was a sense of pride in achieving group goals.

A supportive working environment should not be mistaken for one that experiences little or no conflict. According to the field of group dynamics, groups progress through a series of stages. The conflict stage follows the orientation stage and precedes the structure stage. These stages are usually called storming, forming, and norming, respectively. Although conflict is an unpleasant state that most individuals would rather avoid, it may actually be a required ingredient for group cohesion (Forsyth, 2006). Much like a resilient family, a psychologically healthy group is one in which disagreements can be expressed and conflict can be resolved. Only then are groups sufficiently mature to reach an optimal level of productivity. The key factor is to respond to conflict in such a manner as to keep relationships intact.

Feelings are contagious; people at work can catch feelings from one another (Goleman et al., 2002). A negative emotional climate can erode productivity in a number of ways. First of all, depressed mood interferes with memory, creativity, and complex problem solving. Furthermore, a chronically negative working environment is counterindicated with commitment to fellow workers and to the organization as a whole. Finally, a toxic environment at work often has a spillover effect into family life. Indeed, "stress hormones released during a toxic workday continue to swirl through the body many hours later" (p. 22). On the other hand, "daily occurrences that bring about joy, interest, and love (or caring) lead to a bonding of individuals to each other, their work, and their organization" (Harter et al., 2003, p. 211).

Opportunities for Growth, Engagement, and Self-Determination

If a cohesive and supportive work environment is conducive to personal well-being, so is one that provides many opportunities for growth, engagement, and self-determination. Warr (1999) has compiled a list of key features of work that are correlated with personal well-being. First on the list are opportunities for personal control, where employees have decision latitude, autonomy, and freedom of choice, coupled with the absence of close supervision. At certain times over the course of the semester, I sometimes joke about moving my bed into my office given the long hours spent there. Nonetheless, the decision to stay late is mine to make, and I have a lot of latitude over what I do and when I choose to do it.

The combination of very high demands on the job and little opportunity for control is particularly damaging to worker well-being (Warr, 1999) and, by extension, to organizational well-being. Like a tightly controlled classroom whose teacher unexpectedly leaves the room, workers who are not trusted and are micromanaged by their supervisor will lower their productivity when the supervisor is not present. Those who have other options will choose to leave the job, and those who have no choice will grow increasingly resentful and less productive. Disgruntled employees who are on the outlook for an opportunity to leave their job will often reduce their productivity as they explore other options. Most important to personal well-being, little control is associated with high levels of stress, and stressed individuals are more prone to a host of physical and psychological ailments (Halpern, 2005).

But having autonomy and self-determination is not enough. Workers also strive for environments that will enable them to utilize valued skills and abilities and provide interest, variety, and opportunities for growth and engagement. Various studies have shown that personal well-being varies as a function of changing job conditions. In one study summarized by Warr (1999), the overall job satisfaction of clerical workers significantly increased after their jobs were restructured to increase skill utilization and knowledge demands. There is an optimal level of challenge conducive to well-being. Not enough or too much challenge is associated with either boredom or high levels of stress (Warr, 1999).

"Roles influence group members' happiness and well-being in significant ways. By taking on a role in a group, individuals secure their connection to their fellow members, building the interdependence that is essential for group cohesion and productivity" (Forsyth, 2006, p. 183). Gallup (2006) polls conducted by the *Gallup Management Journal (GMJ)* categorized respondents according to their level of engagement at work. As a group, engaged workers are passionate about their work and have a strong sense of connection to the organization and to their fellow workers (27% of respondents). Nonengaged workers (59% of respondents) simply go through the motions at work with little passion for what they do. Those classified as actively disengaged (14% of respondents) act out their unhappiness by undermining the work of their coworkers.

As opposed to nonengaged and actively disengaged workers, many engaged workers reported that their interactions with their coworkers are always or mostly positive, that they are often challenged but rarely frustrated on the job, and that their supervisor mainly focuses on their strengths. Furthermore, engaged workers were much more likely to report feeling happy while on the job (86%), indicate their work is an important source of happiness for them, and report much higher levels of overall life satisfaction (Gallup, 2006).

Of course, correlation does not equal causation, and a multitude of constitutional, familial, and environmental factors likely contribute to the difference between engaged and nonengaged workers. Nevertheless, there is little doubt that a work environment that actively promotes worker engagement and in which supervisors focus on building strengths rather than accentuating faults is more likely to promote personal and organizational well-being.

The Intersection of Work and Family

The Gallup (2006) poll on worker engagement has also found that actively disengaged workers are much more likely to have a spillover of stress and unhappiness from their work life to their home life. When asked if they behaved poorly with family and friends on at least three occasions in the prior month due to work-related stress, 54% of actively disengaged workers and 31% of unengaged workers answered yes. Although this statistic provides further support for the importance of promoting cohesion and engagement in the workplace, it also speaks to the need to examine how work and family life intersect.

"Interrole conflict develops when role takers discover that the behaviors associated with one of their roles is incompatible with those associated with another one of their roles" (Forsyth, 2006, p. 184). According to the role enhancement perspective, having multiple roles, such as being both a mother and an employee, can be advantageous in that it increases potential rewards and provides multiple avenues for self-expression. Antithetical to role enhancement is the role strain perspective, whereby occupying a variety of roles can be associated with difficulty at fulfilling the demands of each role. The role context perspective views the former two as overly simplistic and emphasizes the importance of focusing not only on the number of roles an individual occupies but the nature and circumstances of these roles (Lemme, 2006).

During her term as president of the American Psychological Association in 2004, Diane Halpern formed a Presidential Task Force to review social science and research literature on the intersection of work and family and make recommendations for working families, employers, and policy makers. The task force highlighted, among other things, that the mismatch between employment norms and modern-day families is causing high levels of stress for working parents, who are often also caring for elderly or infirm family members:

Demographic data show that major changes have been occurring in the everyday lives of families over the last generation, with the majority of mothers of young children in the workforce and an increasing number of men and women assuming caregiving responsibilities for older relatives. Thus, the 2 primary identities of most adults, defined by their multiple family and work roles, need to be coordinated in ways that promote positive family outcomes, returns on investment for employers, and societal values. Despite changes in the workforce, the world of work is still largely organized for a family model that is increasingly rare—one with a stay-at-home caregiver. (Halpern, 2005, p. 397)

Halpern (2005) emphasizes that the well-being of children is not compromised by the fact that both parents work. A multitude of research on the effects of maternal employment has failed to find that working mothers produce poor outcomes for children. Poverty, on the other hand, is a detriment to children, and many families manage to avoid the negative correlates and consequences of poverty by having both parents in the workforce. Rather than the employment status of mothers, it is the lack of flexible work hours, limited opportunities for job sharing, and scarcity of high-quality affordable day care that is compromising the well-being of children and their working parents. This is particularly problematic for working poor families, who are more vulnerable than middle-income or high-wage workers. "Most low-wage earners have no health-care, paid sick leave, or other benefits, so a sick child or even a flat tire can set off a financial crisis that can take months to recover from" (p. 402). Thus, poor working parents are particularly susceptible to experiencing significant role strain and to heightened levels of stress at home and in the workplace. Furthermore, more and more middle-class parents are living precariously close to the financial edge, with little or no margin of error (Halpern, 2005). They, too, are in danger of experiencing the negative consequences of role strain and the spillover of stress from work to home and back again.

COMMUNITY SOURCES OF PERSONAL WELL-BEING

Personal and organizational sources of well-being can be enhanced or diminished by the ecological context in which they occur. Some rather powerful social forces interact with the climate in organizations and in families. Such is the power of environmental circumstances that they can undermine the positive effects of supportive climates at home and at work. Think about economic downturns in which vast sectors of the workforce feel threatened and face layoffs. It is hard to block the negative impact of such risks when we come home. As we will see in this section and throughout the entire book, social factors can create stress strong enough to undermine the foundations of resilience laid early in life through attachment and bonding. On the other hand, enabling environments and propitious social conditions can help to undo the negative sequels of a tough childhood (Ungar, 2005).

In its second edition of *The Social Determinants of Health* (Wilkinson & Marmot, 2003), the World Health Organization lists 10 sources of health and well-being:

1. The social gradient
2. Stress
3. Early life
4. Social exclusion
5. Work
6. Unemployment
7. Social support
8. Addictions
9. Food
10. Transport

This is not an exhaustive list but a very comprehensive one nonetheless. Some categories, like the first one, encompass several issues, such as poverty and lack of education. Others, like social exclusion, also entail a variety of phenomena, such as exclusion based on gender, race, or disability. We next explore briefly the influence of each determinant on personal well-being.

The Social Gradient

We already saw in Chapter 1 the effects of occupational status and associated level of control on life expectancy. As you probably remember, the lower you are on the social ladder, the higher the chances of getting sick and dying early. We return to this issue at various points in the book because it is an intricate one. We are not talking only about absolute poverty, which definitely puts you at risk for a host of physical and psychological ailments, but also about relative deprivation. That is the case when you have plenty to satisfy your physiological and security needs, but relative to other people in the community, you feel less than or inferior to them. Therefore, the social gradient, or the impact of your social status on well-being, does not operate strictly on access to resources, but also on comparative advantage.

The finding that the lower you are on the social ladder, the more likely you are to fall ill has been replicated for a host of diseases (Marmot, 2004; Wilkinson, 2005). G. Evans and Kantrowitz (2002), to name but one recent report, discussed the differential impact of environmental hazards—air pollution, water quality, hazardous waste, toxins, educational facilities, housing and work environment—on health and well-being. In their view, "It would be fair to summarize this body of work as showing that the poor and especially the nonwhite poor bear a disproportionate burden to suboptimal, unhealthy environmental conditions in the United States" (p. 323). Subramanian, Belli, and Kawachi (2002, p. 287) support these conclusions by stating that "the empirical evidence is overwhelming that poverty, measured at the level of societies as well as individuals, is causally related to poor health of societies and individuals, respectively."

Stress

To some extent we all experience tension in our life. In moderation, this is not harmful, but extended exposure to conflict and stress can create permanent physiological and psychological damage. As noted in *The Social Determinants of Health*, "If people feel tense too often or the tension goes on for too long, they become more vulnerable to a wide range of conditions including infections, diabetes, high blood pressure, heart attack, stroke, depression and aggression" (Wilkinson & Marmot, 2003, p. 13). The more anxious, insecure, and diminished we feel, the higher the likelihood of developing some of these negative responses. Climates of acceptance, tolerance, support, and inclusion mitigate the untoward effects of these noxious agents.

Stress, as Eckersley (2001, p. 54) points out, is also associated with the social gradient:

> While the stress associated with inequality can impact on health via direct adverse physiological effects, another important pathway may be through affective states or emotions. . . . Depression, hopelessness, anxiety and anger have been associated with higher risks of death and disease. . . . Conversely, happiness appears to be associated with good health. . . . All these affective states tend to show a social gradient, making them a plausible pathway.

Early Life

As noted in our discussion of attachment, the satisfaction of basic emotional and organic needs in early life is of paramount importance. The reduction of risk factors in the mother, father, and child, as well as the enhancement of protective factors must be a family and social priority. Eliminating such risk factors as smoking during pregnancy and enhancing protective factors such as caring parenting are essential sources of child well-being (Cashmore, 2001). What happens early in life can have long-lasting effects, sometimes even irreversible, as in the case of fetal alcohol syndrome (Shonkoff & Phillips, 2000). A nurturing upbringing, on the other hand, can prepare the child to cope with adverse life circumstances, such as physical illness or a learning disability. In many ways, resilience starts in the womb (Ungar, 2005).

Social Exclusion

Due to disability, race, gender, class, or immigrant status, to name but a few, thousands of people feel excluded from the mainstream of society.

Either because they cannot access buildings with their wheelchairs, or because of the glass ceiling effect that stops women from advancing in their careers, exclusion takes a toll on people. Prolonged exposure to exclusion diminishes self-worth and health (Eckersley et al., 2002; Marmot, 2004; Wilkinson, 2005).

The physical environment can also feel excluding and isolating. Deprived communities often lack transportation, services, and beauty. Physically and psychologically removed, people in these communities experience higher levels of illness, unemployment, educational failure, and crime. Several recent reviews document community barriers to well-being, including air pollution, violence, lack of access to fruits and vegetables, poorly equipped schools, and neighborhood fragmentation (G. Evans, 2003; French, Story, & Jeffery, 2001; Saelens, Sallis, & Frank, 2003).

Work

The work environment, as noted earlier, can create role strain and stress. These two phenomena are largely mediated by the level of control experienced at work. Coronary heart disease, that dreaded illness that incapacitates or kills, has a lot to do with working conditions, and especially with levels of control. As noted earlier, the Whitehall studies provide rich data to check out that hypothesis. Bosma, Peter, Siegrist, and Marmot reported in 1998 in the *American Journal of Public Health* that "low job control was strongly associated with new disease" (p. 68). They further ascertain that "the odds ratios for low job control were 2.38 and 1.56 for self-reported and externally assessed job control, respectively" (p. 68). This means that people who assessed their own level of control as low had 2.38 higher chances of coronary heart disease than those who reported high levels.

Control at work, it is important to note, is determined by a number of factors, including position, climate, seniority, age, race, and gender. Such is the prevalence of inequality at work in terms of these variables that the risk of feeling disempowered at your job is very high. Moreover, such is the number of people employed that employers must ensure that workplaces are empowering places, not just for the managers, which is usually the case, but also for the countless people who work in the front lines and assembly lines. We return to this topic in Chapters 8, 9, and 10, when we discuss the effective, reflective, and affective qualities of the workplace.

Job Security

Oh tenure, tenure, what a great thing it is. In academic circles, scholars sweat to get tenure, which is essentially the equivalent of a job for life. I (Isaac) still remember the day when I was awarded tenure at my first academic post at

Wilfrid Laurier University in Canada. The previous 4 years had been all about that: getting job security. Ever since I got tenure, I decided that we would not go to another job without it. Academics are very fortunate; a good number of them who obtain tenure do not have to worry about job security. That was a condition for moving to Australia and later to the United States. Perhaps because I grew up quite poor I value job security a great deal; but it is not just me. If you ask anybody on the street, I think most people would be willing to sacrifice a lot for this privilege. Job security alleviates financial worries and provides a meaningful identity for many, occupational stress and all. Unemployment, on the other hand, is a major source of anxiety, depression, and low self-image, not to mention economic instability and downright poverty (Frey & Stutzer, 2002; Fryer, 1998). Feyer and Broom (2001, p. 178) summarize the importance of work and job security well:

The centrality of work to health and well-being is unarguable. In industrialized societies, work consumes the greatest active time in adult life, is the most reliable source of continuous access to adequate income, and provides access to a host of key psychological dimensions such as identity, self-esteem and social networks. . . . Moreover, the absence of employment is clearly detrimental to both physical and mental health.

Social Support

As noted by Dean Ornish (1998), social support is a matter of survival. A psychological sense of community has long been identified as a source of well-being at the personal, organizational, and collective levels (Fisher, Sonn, & Bishop, 2002). Social support has been found to have direct effects on well-being and indirect effects as a buffer against stress.

As noted earlier in the book, social capital, or trusting and caring relationships in the community, is being eroded in North America and perhaps in other parts of the world contaminated by individualism (Putnam, 2000). Alienation, the antithesis of social capital, exacerbates social exclusion and conspires with it to create isolation and depression. We have lived in many cities around the world, and we can definitely feel the difference between inviting and alienating places. Inviting ones are not only friendly from a human perspective, but also from an environmental one. Shops are close together, streets are pedestrian-friendly, there is street life, and transportation is easily accessible. Interestingly, it is not only the amount of friends you have that contribute to a sense of community, but also the built environment (G. Evans, 2003; Halpern, 1995). Some places feel more isolating than others do. When you walk in downtown Nashville after 5 P.M., you walk in a desert of cement. When you walk in downtown Melbourne after 5 P.M., you walk into a party.

Addictions

Many people turn to alcohol and tobacco to numb the pain of isolation and deprivation, only to be initiated into a vicious cycle that deepens their problems. Like other social problems, this one also reflects the social gradient. Higher classes report only a fraction of the addictions that lower classes do. In Britain, for example, the most deprived experience nearly 10 times more dependence on drugs than the most affluent, and over 8 times more dependence on nicotine (Wilkinson & Marmot, 2003).

Food

While many children suffer malnutrition in sub-Saharan countries, an obesity epidemic threatens the health of millions of kids in North America. Although in the latter case there is the temptation to blame the individual for overeating and not exercising, environmental influences such as subsidies for corn (Fields, 2004), culture, prices, and community characteristics (French et al., 2001) interact with personal preferences. Lack of access to fruits and vegetables is a major source of disease and premature mortality (A. Robertson, Brunner, & Sheiham, 1999).

Transportation

Do you love your car? I (Isaac) hate it. For all my love of Melbourne, I used to commute there 1 hour to work, and for all my complaining about Nashville, I get to walk to work. We live a mere 4-minute walk to the office, and I love it. I love walking and avoiding the car. I enjoy the exercise, and it is better for the environment. However, not all neighborhoods are safe, or have sidewalks.

Mode of transportation contributes to either pollution or clean air. Access to it can decrease isolation, whereas its absence can increase it. For getting to work, to the movie theater, and to day care, transportation is essential. In a car-driven society, like most midsize cities in the United States, dependency on a vehicle interferes with job and education prospects, not to mention causing pollution generated by single-occupancy vehicles. The love affair with cars has many untoward effects, whereas a sound transportation policy can have many positive health and environmental impacts (Saelens et al., 2003; Sallins, Frank, Saelens, & Kraft, 2004).

LINKED SOURCES

The main premise of this book is that what happens in any domain of well-being—collective, organizational, or personal—affects the others. Multiple sources support this hypothesis. As noted in this chapter, economic downturns resulting in unemployment have an impact on organizational climate. When job security is threatened, tensions rise in the office, workers feel anxious, families react to the stress, and risk of disease increases. We can take any of the social determinants of health reviewed by Wilkinson and Marmot (2003) and follow their health-enhancing or -inhibiting effects. To take but one more example, neighborhoods that are high on psychological sense of community help members to feel supported, enhance coping, and breed trust among its members. Supported individuals, in turn, are more likely to have fun, share their pleasures and sorrows, and infuse their work environment with a joyous attitude. The trick is always to see the connections, for good or bad. Negative and positive chain reactions happen all the time, and if we see only isolated events, as opposed to chained events, we risk misdiagnosing the sources of problems and missing the bright lights.

ROWS FOR WELLNESS

Exercise 6: Connecting the Dots

The connections among personal, organizational, and community sources of well-being seem obvious. Yet, many people fail to make them. Due to ideology, personal experience, blinders, or lack of education, some people ascribe well-being exclusively to personal sources, leading potentially to blaming the victim, and others tend to accuse the environment for all their woes, leading potentially to lack of responsibility to do something. In either case, they are not making the connections among personal, organizational, and community sources. What are some of the ROWS preventing you or others from connecting the dots? Is it something you learned in school, church, or your family? Have you had strong experiences of discrimination that tend to overshadow other sources of well-being? Is your family so important in your life that you can hardly think of how economic policies can affect your happiness? Go ahead and write down in Form 6.1 some of the ROWS that may prevent you from seeing connections where they exist.

You can now transfer the ROWS to Form 6.2 to see what you have done, or what you can do in the future to connect the dots.

Connecting the dots is an important part of fostering well-being in your personal and professional life. Never underestimate the importance of getting the whole picture. The more you understand and act on this realization, the easier it becomes to change people's attitudes, beliefs, and behaviors, including, of course, your own.

Form 6.1   **ROWS Exercise 6: Connecting the Dots**

Risks					Opportunities				Weaknesses				Strengths			

Form 6.2   Wellness Readiness Check 6: Connecting the Dots

ROWS	1 I never thought about doing something about it.	2 I'm thinking about doing something about it.	3 I'm prepared to do something about it.	4 I'm doing something about it.	5 I've been doing something about it for some time.
Risks					
Opportunities					
Weaknesses					
Strengths					

7

How to Promote It? Strategies for Personal Well-Being

In *Who Moved My Cheese?* S. Johnson (1999) tells the story of Hem and Haw, two imaginary "littlepeople" characters who spent their lives happily running through a maze in search of cheese. One day, Hem and Haw came across a large supply of cheese in Cheese Station C. Every day they would return to Cheese Station C to nibble some cheese. They became so comfortable and complacent that they failed to pay attention to the dwindling supply of cheese. One morning they arrived at Cheese Station C only to discover that the cheese was completely gone. They were not prepared for this event, as they had not seen it coming.

Initially, Hem and Haw were stuck in cheeseless Station C due to their inability to adapt to change. They grew hungry and weak as they sat in Cheese Station C, hoping that their cheese would reappear. Haw ultimately decided not to let his fears paralyze him from acting. After days and days of remaining in his cheeseless predicament, Haw braved the unknown and ventured into the maze in search of new cheese. His friend Hem, on the other hand, could not be convinced to leave Cheese Station C. He waited, to no avail, for his cheese to return. Haw ultimately found a fresh supply of cheese and learned important lessons about adapting to change. We are not completely sure of what became of Hem.

Adapting to change is a difficult yet vital part of life. Like Hem and Haw, those who fail to notice changing conditions and circumstances are bound to find themselves in cheeseless predicaments. Some, like Haw, will ultimately pull off their blinders and prepare to do something different. Others, like Hem, will do more and more of the same, even when it is clear that it is not working for them. What enabled Haw to finally venture back out into the maze in search of new cheese? First, he had to change his outlook on the situation. Instead of constantly worrying that he would get lost and not find his way, Haw began to envision himself finding new cheese. He did not fool himself into thinking that new cheese was just around the corner. He knew that the maze would be full of obstacles, but he began to see the cheese at the end of the maze. Haw also had to change his behavior. As hungry and weak as he was, he forced himself to leave Cheese Station C and begin to jog down the maze. As his thinking and behavior changed, he began to feel differently as well. He was able to laugh at himself. He became excited about the possibility of finding new cheese. He was still hungry and weak—but he was doing something about it. Haw made cognitive, affective, and behavioral changes that ultimately enabled him to discover new cheese.

STAGES OF CHANGE

According to the stages of change theory, change unfolds over a series of stages (Prochaska & Norcross, 1998; Prochaska et al., 1994). The first stage of change is precontemplation. Individuals who are in precontemplation do not believe that they need to change anything. Some precontemplators do not think that there is a problem. Hem and Haw paid no heed as the supply of cheese dwindled before their very eyes. It's not that they didn't see the solution—they didn't even see the problem. Some people are clearly in a rut, but they are the last to recognize it. Their intimate relationships are in a terrible state, yet they do nothing about it until it's too late. We have friends who were in crisis when their relationships ended, although the writing was on the wall long before that. Other precontemplators do acknowledge their cheeseless predicament; they are miserable about the situation they are in, but they blame other people or circumstances for moving their cheese. When Hem and Haw realized that their cheese supply was gone, they thought that it was unfair and that their cheese should be returned. Hem simply wanted to get his cheese back; he was not prepared to do anything about it.

Haw ultimately moved from precontemplation to contemplation, the next stage along the continuum of change. Individuals in contemplation know that they have a problem. They begin to consider doing something about it. Contemplators are still not ready to take action—they have yet to be convinced that making a change is better than simply waiting for their cheese to be returned. Initially, Haw was very fearful about the prospect of venturing out into the maze. He almost let Hem convince him that it was too dangerous and ridden with insurmountable obstacles. Like some contemplators, Haw ran the risk of staying stuck in a perpetual state of contemplation, forever thinking about it without taking action. Those who consider taking up exercise but never make it past the stage of consideration are perpetual contemplators. They need to take some action to push themselves through to the next stage of change.

Haw finally moved from contemplation to preparation. He had had enough of sitting idle in a cheeseless station, waiting in vain for his cheese to be returned. The move from contemplation to preparation requires some behavioral change. It's not enough to simply think more about making change—some change in behavior needs to take place. Laughing at his own predicament was the first sign that Haw was transitioning from contemplation to preparation. This did not happen all at once; it followed a long period of contemplation during which he vacillated between staying and leaving. "Finally, one day Haw began laughing at himself. 'Haw, haw, look at us. We keep doing the same things over and over again and wonder why things don't get better. If this wasn't so ridiculous, it would be even funnier'" (S. Johnson, 1999, p. 43). But laughing at himself was not enough; it was followed by Haw's search for his running shoes in preparation for his run through the maze.

When we are in the process of making some change in our lives, the people we are closest to, those in our innermost circle of family and friends, can have a tremendous impact on the outcome of our change process. A long-time smoker who has thrown away his remaining cigarettes in preparation for quitting smoking will stand a much better chance of accomplishing his mission if he is surrounded by people who are supportive of his decision to quit. Unfortunately, one's decision to make a change in one's life is not always met with encouragement and support. Close others, like Hem, may even try to dissuade you if they think it will lead to undesirable consequences for themselves. Hem did not want to remain alone in Cheese Station C, and he did his best to discourage his friend from venturing out into the maze. He warned Haw of the dangers that lay ahead and suggested that he would make a fool of himself by trying and failing. When Hem realized his warnings were falling on deaf ears, he ignored his friend and did not bid him farewell.

But Haw was ready to carry out the change he had prepared for. He left Cheese Station C and started out into the maze. Haw had transitioned from preparation to action, but his process of change was far from complete. "As he started out into the maze, Haw looked back to where he had come from and felt its comfort. He could feel himself being drawn back into familiar territory—even though he hadn't found cheese here for some time" (S. Johnson, 1999, p. 47). The pull to plow forward versus the pull to stay the same is a major struggle for those who are in the action stage of change. Whether one is trying to eliminate an unhealthy behavior, such as smoking, or adopt a health-promoting behavior, such as daily exercise, staying the course can be an ongoing struggle.

Haw's journey in search of cheese was anything but smooth. On a number of occasions, he came across cheese stations that looked promising but turned out to be empty. At such times, pessimism and doubt threatened to take hold. Luckily, the few morsels of cheese he found along the way provided him with just enough nourishment to continue his journey. He even went back to Cheese Station C to share the morsels of cheese with Hem and convince him to come along. But the cheese that Haw found was of an unfamiliar variety, and Hem was still adamant about getting his old cheese back.

Haw was ultimately rewarded for his hard work when he arrived at Cheese Station N. It was stacked with cheese from top to bottom, and Haw ate to his heart's content. According to the stages of change theory, the action stage is followed by termination, when a problem behavior (smoking) has been successfully eliminated or a desirable behavior (daily exercise) has been fully incorporated into one's life. Haw journeyed though the maze despite his fears and ultimately found an abundant supply of fresh cheese.

However, making a change is still no guarantee that it will last in the long run. Old habits are difficult to break, and new behaviors are not easy to maintain. Some people quit smoking only to start again, and those who work hard to adopt health-enhancing behaviors are not always successful in maintaining them. That's why Haw decided not to become complacent again, despite the volume of new cheese he had come across. He decided to keep his running shoes close by and to monitor often the state of his newfound cheese.

THE ABCs OF CHANGE: AFFECTIVE, BEHAVIORAL, AND COGNITIVE STRATEGIES

People who have high subjective well-being experience more positive emotions than negative emotions, perceive their lives as satisfying and rewarding, and are goal-oriented and constructive in their behavior. When we strive to improve our well-being we often wish to make some change in how we think, feel, or behave. According to Aaron Beck (1976), the founder of cognitive-behavior therapy, how we feel and behave is largely determined by how we perceive and structure our experiences.

As long as Hem and Haw believed that someone had moved their cheese and that it had to be returned, they were feeling dejected and immobilized from acting. They suffered from what Beck (1976) called faulty thinking or logical errors. Hem not only believed that the cheese should be returned, he also believed that any effort on their part to search for new cheese was bound to fail.

For Haw, the change came when he managed to change his course of thinking. "Haw stuck his head out and peered anxiously into the maze. He thought about how he had gotten himself into this cheeseless situation. He had believed that there may not be any cheese in the maze, or he may not find it. Such fearful beliefs were immobilizing him and killing him" (S. Johnson, 1999, p. 47). Instead of focusing on obstacles, hardships, and images of failed attempts, Haw began to imagine himself finding and enjoying new cheese. He also used tried and true cognitive strategies such as identifying distortions in his thinking and actively challenging and disputing thoughts that were weighing him down. Perhaps Haw used Beck's (1976) strategy of looking for evidence that would support his negative belief that he would not find new cheese in the maze. Not finding any evidence that would support this negative belief may have helped him adopt a more optimistic outlook.

Challenging himself to identify and modify his maladaptive beliefs was an important first step in Haw's process of change. He began to realize that he had a choice in the matter and kept asking himself what he would do if he weren't so afraid. Nonetheless, filling his belly would take more than a changed perspective. It simply gave Haw the initial push to venture out into the maze. Haw, it seems, was psychologically sophisticated as he utilized cognitive as well as behavioral techniques to help him along the way. And he did not just keep his thoughts to himself: Whenever he came across a thought that was conducive to moving forward, he wrote it on the wall of the maze and drew a picture of cheese around it. Haw wrote a series of messages along the way, such as "What would you do if you weren't afraid"; "Movement in a new direction helps you find new cheese"; and "It is safer to search in the maze than remain in a cheeseless situation." Although he experienced his share of doubt along his journey, Haw wrote only the thoughts that would reinforce his efforts in his quest for new cheese. Of course, the few morsels of cheese he found along the way also provided important reinforcement to continue the search.

As he ran down the maze and realized that it wasn't nearly as scary as he had imagined, Haw's feelings began to change for the better.

Now he felt the cool breeze that was blowing in this part of the maze and it felt refreshing. He took in some deep breaths and felt invigorated by the movement. Once he had gotten past his fear, it turned out to be more enjoyable than he once believed it would be. Haw hadn't felt this way for a long time. He had almost forgotten how much fun it was to go for it. (S. Johnson, 1999, p. 57)

There is a reciprocal interaction among the cognitive, behavioral, and affective domains. Thinking patterns that are more constructive, along with adaptive, goal-oriented behavior, are associated with greater satisfaction and perceptions of well-being.

THE CONTEXT OF CHANGE

Family contexts can engender or block desired personal transformation. Some contexts are more enabling than others. In the 1960s and 1970s in Argentina, where Isaac grew up, the brutal regime did not like social change very much. In the Victorian era, which fueled so much of Freud's work, deviation from rigid and repressing sexual norms was sinful; in some societies, it still is today. Women in particular are subjected to oppressive customs (Nussbaum, 1999).

We can see a paradox looming large. Those who may most require opportunities for advancing their own well-being may be the least able to do so due to societal or familial restrictions. Furthermore, they may have internalized cultural prohibitions to such an extent that they may not even be aware of what they are missing. Now you ask: Who are you to tell other people they are missing something in their lives? Good point. In many cases, you are right. If there is no obvious harm caused to anyone, it may be just a matter of preferences. However, in many other cases, you are wrong. As feminist philosopher Nussbaum (1999) points out, women are subjected to practices, such as genital mutilation, which are often deleterious to their health and well-being, regardless of their level of consent. At the very least, people should be presented with options so that they can make informed decisions.

Our assumption is that well-being is best promoted in enabling environments. For environments to be enabling, they have to be subjected to influence by people whose values promote caring and compassion, self-determination, health and growth, respect for diversity, and social justice. You can see the dialectical nature of well-being. Some people have to be well enough to look after social conditions, but their own well-being and expendable energy depend on the environment to begin with. As it turns out, there is never a perfect moment to promote your own well-being while advancing others'. To some extent, this is what Reissman (1965) meant by the helper-therapy principle: Help yourself while helping others. The more love you give, the more you get.

Affective, behavioral, and cognitive strategies to engage individuals in change will be variably supported by different environments. Some people will reciprocate your affection, others won't. Some people will welcome your dieting; others will laugh at you. Some will encourage you to leave an abusive marriage; others will remind you that a woman should not leave her husband. The more aware we are of these negative influences, the more we can do to extricate ourselves from their oppressive net. We need to be mindful of the fact that affective, behavioral, and cognitive strategies do not operate in a vacuum. They are enabled or disabled by the people around us.

THE SPIRITUALITY OF CHANGE

Change is not about the mechanistic adoption of new behavior or attitudes, not in our view, anyway. Rather, it is about the meaning we ascribe to it and the purpose it serves. Each one of us has a life mission, a life path, and a life narrative. The changes we seek must connect with our webs of meaning. If they don't, if they feel foreign, they will not last. You can't just add new behaviors or perceptions the way you add another sweater on a cold winter day. There is no escaping the hard work of integrating into your webs of meaning the meaning of new customs.

Spiritual engagement, for us, involves the meaning we make out of our values, feelings, thoughts, and actions. The extent to which we can reconcile all these is a measure of our spiritual engagement. For some, it involves a higher being. For others, it involves Mother Nature. Whatever the guiding light might be, it's hard to imagine change—emotional, behavioral, cognitive—detached from it. The spiritual struggle inheres in finding out how you can live out your values without following like sheep the rest of the crowd. There is something fundamentally human about promoting well-being: the choices you can make in how to align your actions, feelings, and thoughts with your values. That, for us, is a spiritual pursuit. Changes that do not align with human values are wrongheaded at best and destructive at worst. It is entirely possible to seek new behaviors that elevate only your pursuit of power instead of your pursuit of love. That kind of change we do not endorse.

THE MORALS OF CHANGE

Fears, disappointments, rejections, mental health problems, loss, injustice—they all affect our well-being. If we are to overcome them, we must feel empowered to confront life's challenges. You may be able to engage affective, behavioral, or cognitive strategies to promote your own well-being or that of others. But what about those who seek change to promote, not their own well-being, but their own egotistical power? Moreover, what if their pursuit of power is hurting other people along the way?

Chances are, few people will seek the elevation of their own power or prestige with the explicit goal of hurting other people. It is more likely that their negative intentions will be shrouded in rationalizations, ideology, beliefs, and intellectualizations. Regardless of their explicit or implicit agenda, as helpers, friends, colleagues, and peers, we have to take a stance against the arrogation of power for unfair, unjust, and uncaring behavior. Without a set of values, that determination cannot be easily made. For what is the criterion according to which I separate legitimate from illegitimate change, if not values and ethics?

The promotion of well-being cannot proceed without a clear set of values. You may or may not agree with the set of values we presented in Chapter 3, but we don't think you can disagree with the need for *a* set of values. In *Soul Searching: Why Psychotherapy Must Promote Moral Responsibility*, Doherty (1995) articulates the dilemmas helpers encounter when their clients behave in ways that are antithetical to the well-being of their relatives or friends. Our own way of dealing with situations of this kind is to be extremely clear about our own moral stance and to assess the congruence between the type of change desired and our own values. A good match means a green light; a poor match means a yellow light; an impossible match means a red light.

So far, we have covered in this chapter a few basics: the stages, the ABCs, the context, spirituality, and morals of change. With these concepts and caveats in mind, we are now in a position to address three questions:

I VALUE IT: ONCE AGAIN

In Chapter 4, we introduced I VALUE IT roles and strategies for promoting well-being. They can be useful in addressing these three questions. To refresh your memory, the acronym stands for:

- Inclusive host
- Visionary
- Asset seeker
- Listener and sense maker
- Unique solution finder
- Evaluator
- Implementer
- Trendsetter

1. How do you engage *yourself*, affectively, behaviorally, and cognitively, in the process of promoting your own well-being?
2. How do you engage *another person*, affectively, behaviorally, and cognitively, in the process of promoting her or his well-being?
3. How do you engage *people in organizations and communities*, affectively, behaviorally, and cognitively, in the process of promoting their well-being?

In the following sections, we use I VALUE IT to engage affective, behavioral, and cognitive elements of change. Our claim is that effective and lasting change derives from combining the ABCs of change with I VALUE IT methods.

Strategies for Promoting Your Own Personal Well-Being

We start with your own well-being. After all, what you learn about promoting your own well-being can help you help others. In this section, we try to answer the following question:

How Do You Engage Yourself, Affectively, Behaviorally, and Cognitively, in the Process of Promoting Your Own Well-Being? You may already have found ways that work for you, in which case our suggestions may be superfluous. However, if you are still looking for ideas, we suggest trying to activate and synergize the affective, behavioral, and cognitive domains. Table 7.1 presents the ABC—I VALUE IT method. This approach builds on a variety of interventions: humanistic, behavioral, cognitive, existential,

Table 7.1 ABC—I VALUE IT: Strategies for Promoting Your Own Personal Well-Being

| Roles | Strategies | | |
	Affective	Behavioral	Cognitive
Inclusive host	Allow yourself to express range of emotions and be sensitive to your own feelings without repressing them.	Set aside time and space to reflect and talk with trusted people about your own issues and ways of thriving.	Start contemplating what your own needs are and how they synergize or conflict with other people's needs.
Visionary Process	Be sensitive to which processes of moving forward feel right for you.	Stick to behaviors that enable you to be active in process of change, such as talking with friends or writing a journal.	Think about strategies that keep you engaged in process of moving forward, such as sharing with others.
Outcome	Allow yourself to visualize and feel maximal well-being, without oppression or repression.	Practice behaviors that are desired and reinforce yourself.	Imagine what it would be like to achieve your affective and behavioral goals, and what meaning you would derive from reaching those goals.
Asset seeker	Celebrate what has worked well for you.	Engage in behaviors that have worked well in the past.	Search for meaning, coping, and thriving behaviors in your personal life and in your friends and relatives.
Listener and sense maker	Listen to your emotions and try to identify when you feel a certain way.	Try to make connections between behaviors you like and dislike, and antecedents and consequences.	Analyze correlation among situations, emotions, behaviors, and thoughts.
Unique solution finder	Consider various options and try to imagine what each one would feel like.	Plan and practice new behaviors and seek support from trusted people.	Take into account what would work uniquely for you and your situation and resist prefabricated solutions.
Evaluator Past efforts	Invoke feelings associated with success and failure in the past to guide your actions.	Recall what behaviors promoted feelings of well-being or lack thereof in the past.	Analyze past success and failures, and assumptions you made about them.
Present efforts	Tune in to your feelings.	Evaluate if there is any change in undesirable behaviors or increase in desirable ones.	Think about what is working well or not working well, and why, and adjust thoughts and actions accordingly.

(continued)

Table 7.1 (*Continued*)

Roles	Strategies		
	Affective	Behavioral	Cognitive
Evaluator Future efforts	Consider what could be used as an emotional indicator to tell you that you are experiencing well-being.	Predict a behavioral indicator that shows you are achieving or experiencing well-being, and build mechanisms for on going self-assessment of how you feel, without ignoring your emotions.	Ask yourself how you would know in the future if you are doing well or not.
Implementer	Reinforce yourself for integrating desired thoughts and behaviors into your life.	Have a plan for maintaining your behavior in order to prevent relapse.	Think of the help you might need to implement new positive patterns into your life.
Trendsetter	Savor helping yourself and others.	Consolidate your behavior and help others to promote their own well-being.	Monitor your gains and share your success with others to exert a positive influence.

narrative, and analytical. We acknowledge that some people relate better to insight-oriented methods than to behavioral techniques. We also recognize that some kinds of problems, such as phobias, are better handled by behavioral methods than by psychoanalytic tools. Fitting the method to the problem, the person, and the process of change requires artful calibration.

You should not be surprised to find individuals who respond better to existential meaning making than to action-oriented therapies. Humans run the gamut of preferences and variation. This is why we present a wide menu of alternatives.

By way of integrating multifaceted elements of wellness promotion, we point to the ABCs of I VALUE IT. Looking at Table 7.1 row by row, we start with being an inclusive host. Reflexively, being an inclusive host means allowing yourself the space and the time to express indignation, frustration, sadness, and loss. Getting in touch with your feelings, that worn expression, is not used in vain: It is an important step in overcoming barriers to well-being. I (Isaac) for the longest time held back tears about the loss of my parents. I don't know exactly what part of myself I was missing, but I was not whole; I was fragmented. I could not host my pain because the signals I got from the environment were repress, repress, repress. No one talked to me about my feelings, nor did anyone pick up on my enduring pain. The absence of dialogue reflected everyone's fear of talking about *it*, as if talking about *it* would make it worse. For my part, as an 8-year-old boy, I distinctly remember the proscription. Talking about it, let alone crying about it, would make my aunt sad, and surely she was sad enough already, without my adding to her burden. Why would I want to do that?

It requires an inclusive host to hold pain. You may not be able to contain your own sorrows, in which case you would do well to seek help—help from somebody who can hold you while you explore the tears you never cried.

In *Tuesdays with Morrie*, Mitch Albom (1997) describes a real-life series of encounters with his old professor, Morrie Schwartz. Morrie is dying of ALS (Lou Gehrig's Disease). Mitch and Morrie meet on Tuesdays to record Morrie's experiences as he approaches death. One of the lessons Morrie shares is the ability to hold and embrace pain as a prerequisite to moving forward:

Take any emotion—love for a woman, or grief for a loved one, or what I'm going through, fear and pain from a deadly illness. If you hold back on the emotions—if you don't allow yourself to go all the way through them—you can never get to being detached, you're too busy being afraid. You're afraid of the pain, you're afraid of the grief, you're afraid of the vulnerability that loving entails. . . . But by throwing yourself into these emotions, by allowing yourself to dive in, all the way, over your head even, you experience them fully and completely. You know what pain is. You know what love is. You know what grief is. And only then can you say, "All right. I have experienced that emotion. I recognize that emotion. Now I need to detach from that emotion for a moment." (p. 104)

Mitch recounts Morrie's despair when he could barely breathe:

These were horrifying times, he said, and his first emotions were horror, fear, anxiety. But once he recognized the feel of these emotions, their texture, their moisture, the shiver down the back, the quick flash of heat that crosses your brain—then he was able to say, Okay. This is fear. Step away from it. Step away. (Albom, 1997, pp. 104–105)

Mitch reflected on "how often this was needed in everyday life. How we feel lonely, but we don't let those tears come because we are not supposed to cry" (p. 105). How true. Social norms make it harder than it has to be to grieve, to mourn, to hold your emotions.

Containment is not necessarily an end in itself, but it is a necessary first step in moving forward. From that point, we progress to visioning. Imagining a better state of affairs is also a precondition for the pursuit of wellness. Depriving humans of such opportunity is cruel. Haw had fantasies of finding new cheese, fantasies that kept him going. Once he ventured into the maze again in search of cheese, he even enjoyed the ride. Visionaries frame not only better outcomes but also better processes. Once he became unstuck, through laughter and a healthy dose of self-deprecation, Haw begun to feel the wind at his back. The search acquired its own meaning, above and beyond the cheese. The search became an outcome. To Haw's credit, he overcame not only his own fears, but also Hem's pessimism.

The first step is the hardest to take. We can relate. So much is riding on it: risk-taking, leaving your comfort zone, abandoning defeatist but well-known narratives. Feeding yourself with stories of success is a good antidote for defeat. The role of asset seeker is meant to do just that, digging deep for little moments of victory. Big or small, chances are most of us experienced coping and thriving, however momentary and episodic. Self-efficacy depends on incremental doses of small victories. These accumulate over time and result in feelings of self-confidence, an "I can do" attitude (Bandura, 1995; Maddux, 2002).

The role of listener and sense maker is about connecting events, feelings, behaviors, and thoughts. What situations trigger what emotions? What ideas elicit what type of behaviors? This is detective work. In Prochaska's theory of change (Prochaska et al., 1994), this takes place during the contemplation and preparation stage. You're getting ready to embark on a new behavior. Once you've understood the sources of the problem, its reinforcements and patterns, you can move to the action stage.

In our framework, finding a solution that is unique to your situation supports effective action. Canned solutions can be counterproductive and go against the principle of contextualism. What works in place X for person Y may not work for person Q in place R. Therefore, action must be always customized to suit a distinctive set of circumstances.

Evaluating past, present, and future actions, as described in Table 7.1, can strengthen change efforts. It helps to monitor, often and regularly, your actions. It is part of the maintenance regimen, and it is part of fighting complacency. Regular checkups prevent descent into cheeseless situations.

Once you feel confident in the certainty of your new path, the challenge is to implement it throughout all aspects of your life—not as an add-on, but as a seamless part of your routine, your emotional makeup, your identity. This is hard to do without an intentional plan, which often requires the support of friends, relatives, and coworkers. If you just quit smoking, going to a smoky bar with your buddies after work is not a good idea. Relapse is a common occurrence, but the more you structure your environment to support the new behavior, the higher the chances of preventing it.

Trendsetting involves leadership. You may or may not feel confident enough in your convictions to spread them to other people. Alternatively, you may feel so confident that you dogmatically push your agenda indiscriminately. Give and take is necessary, and a healthy dose of emotional intelligence will help you distinguish good timing from bad timing. We have certainly witnessed scores of people sitting on the sideline, waiting for the next catastrophe to take place, at work, at school, in the community. The fear of standing out cannot be underestimated. Sticking your neck out can boomerang: You have seen what happens to other people with "good ideas."

Too much enthusiasm can turn you into a dogmatic pusher, but too little can turn you into a passive bystander. If you are a professional helper, you don't have a choice but to be part of other people's lives and to be a trendsetter, at least a trendsetter of what other people find useful in their lives.

Strategies for Personal Well-Being in Work with Individuals

From trying to improve your own well-being we move to trying to help others. The main question we seek to answer in this section is:

How Do You Engage Another Person, Affectively, Behaviorally, and Cognitively, in the Process of Promoting Her or His Well-Being? Much of what we learned in the previous section applies to the helping relationship. Your job now is to make effective use of ABC—I VALUE IT strategies to elicit wellness-enhancing responses from somebody else. The process of engagement is essential. By being an inclusive host, a listener, and a visionary, you're sending the message that it is safe here to explore anything and everything that can help. By being a unique solution finder, an integrator, and a trendsetter, you're sending the message that there is hope.

Carl Rogers (1961) did much to define the characteristics of the helping encounter. Unconditional positive regard, acceptance, empathy, and authenticity are the hallmarks of a good listener and inclusive host. Albert Ellis (1982) and Aaron Beck (1976), in turn, harnessed the power of cognitive processes in disputing faulty logic ("Everyone is talking about me"; "Whenever things go wrong, it's always my fault"). Freud (1949) was the master of insight and connections, even if he went overboard sometimes with his interpretations (a cigar sometimes is just a cigar). Existential therapists like Victor Frankl (1962), a survivor of concentration camps in the Holocaust, brought to therapeutic processes the very human quality of making choices and making meaning of whatever situation besets the human condition. Being in charge of one's destiny, perhaps like Morrie wanted to be in the face of great adversity, was Frankl's legacy. Protecting one's dignity is one of the most human features of our vulnerable existence. Being in control protects not only our health, as we saw earlier in the book, but also our dignity. This is what empowerment is all about: exercising voice and choice while maintaining our dignity and integrity.

Much of what narrative therapists do is to recover dignity lost (Waldegrave, Tamasese, Tuhaka, & Campbell, 2003). Recreating your own life narrative, while you are in charge of interpreting the events, is empowering, hopeful, and emancipatory.

The techniques presented in Table 7.2 are aids in the recovery of dignity, choice, control, and personal integrity. They are not to be used in mechanistic

Table 7.2   ABC—I VALUE IT: Strategies for Personal Well-Being in Work with Individuals

Roles	Affective	Behavioral	Cognitive
		Strategies	
Inclusive host	Make person feel safe and welcome to explore sensitive issues and ways of thriving.	Help person experiment with new modes of behavior, including asking for help or admitting insecurity.	Encourage exploration of meanings associated with issues.
Visionary Process	Ask what processes or ways of working would make person feel comfortable.	Find out what behaviors person expects from self and from you in the process.	Articulate goals and objectives for process of working together.
Outcome	Explore what feelings person would like to have or experience as result of work.	Inquire what new behaviors person would like to see in self and others.	Help visualize better state of affairs and personal role in it.
Asset seeker	Affirm person's unique feelings and abilities.	Recognize previous ways of coping and thriving that can be built on.	Identify meaning and meaning-making ways that help integrate experiences into life narrative.
Listener and sense maker	Collaborate in exploring full range of feelings.	Explore how own behavior impacts self and others, and how others' behaviors impact self.	Make connections between feelings, behaviors, thoughts, and meanings associated with them.
Unique solution finder	Overcome emotional barriers in enacting new behaviors, and reward and celebrate new behaviors.	Articulate plan of action, and break new behaviors into small chunks.	Use cognitive strategies such as reframing and challenging cognitive errors.
Evaluator Past efforts	Explore feelings associated with past efforts at change or thriving.	Evaluate past behaviors and their successes.	Examine interpretation of past efforts.
Present efforts	Explore feelings associated with current efforts.	Evaluate present behaviors and their successes.	Examine interpretation of current efforts.
Future efforts	Anticipate feelings associated with future efforts.	Identify what behaviors have to occur to explore future actions.	Plan evaluation of future actions and explore associated meanings.

Table 7.2 (*Continued*)

Roles	Strategies		
	Affective	Behavioral	Cognitive
Implementer	Explore feelings associated with making new behaviors or perceptions part of life.	Create a plan to make new behaviors or perceptions part of life and for handling barriers.	Develop cognitive strategies for making changes integral part of your life and for anticipating barriers.
Trendsetter	Explore feelings associated with taking risks and becoming a leader.	Explore steps needed to disseminate changes in other parts of your life or with significant others.	Work on self-perceptions of leadership qualities and opportunities.

fashion, without a process of owning new interpretations and new behaviors. Whatever unique solutions we devise in collaboration with our partners, they have to be fully owned (and operated) by them. Self-determination, collaboration, and democratic participation, respect for diversity, caring and compassion and social justice must guide our actions. Techniques without values are dangerous things.

To implement these values and techniques, great listening skills are required. Ivey and Ivey (2003) have developed very well-refined ways of training in listening skills. We recommend their work and their approach, as they provide the foundation for enacting the right method (cognitive, humanistic, existential, behavioral, narrative, solution-focused, or psychoanalytic) at the right time.

Strategies for Personal Well-Being in Working with Groups

From your personal work, to working with others, to working with organizations and communities, we keep expanding the circle of influence. In this section, we address the following question.

How Do You Engage People in Organizations and Communities—Affectively, Behaviorally, and Cognitively—In the Process of Promoting Their Well-Being? Although Prochaska's (Prochaska et al., 1994) stages of change are applicable for work in organizations, they have to be expanded to account for the fact that organizational and community change involve many actors. In *The Heart of Change*, Kotter and Cohen (2002; see also D. Cohen, 2005) describe eight necessary stages to bring organizational and community change to fruition. Our assumption is that to improve worker well-being or citizen well-being, the organization and the community have to engage in comprehensive change. Consistent with our view that sustainable change cannot be mounted by lone rangers, they highlight the role of the change team. Like us, they emphasize the need for clarity and dissemination of the vision, and they claim that buy-in of the message is a key strategy for change. These are their eight steps for making changes in organizations or communities stick:

1. *First step: Increase urgency.* Not much will change if people think the status quo is acceptable. The starting point must be the need for change. Rallying support for the need and urgency of change will help you build momentum. Reducing fear of failure enables people to unfreeze. If you want to change something about your life, but you feel no urgency to do so, you won't go very far.

2. *Second step: Build the guiding team.* Pick well and nurture you team. Cohesion and solidarity among the team will create an atmosphere of support that will be very much needed during turbulent times. As Margaret Mead pointed out, "Never doubt that a small group of thoughtful, committed citizens can change the world. Indeed, it is the only thing that ever has." Your team will become your agents of change. If you want to change something in your own life, gather around you supporters who will cheer you up when you succeed and pick you up when you fall.

3. *Third step: Get the vision right.* A clear vision must convey clearly and concisely the essence of the purpose. Sufficient time should be allocated to getting it right, and getting it to reflect the views of most people in the organization or community. This is a step that many managers have no patience for, as it seems to waste time, but the better the vision, the better the process of change. Fuzziness around the vision translates into fuzziness around practices. Know where you're going before you go there. You can get nowhere fast.

4. *Fourth step: Communicate for buy-in.* Spreading and sharing the new philosophy is a sine qua non for sustainable change. The vision must not be the sole province of the elite, but of the entire organization or community. Multiple media and multiple opportunities must be used to communicate the message. Forums, workshops, retreats, and professional development days must be devoted to digesting, absorbing, and questioning the vision.

5. *Fifth step: Empower action.* By removing barriers and creating an atmosphere of risk taking, action is enabled and reinforced. Fail often to succeed sooner. Reward preliminary efforts at change in line with the vision. This is what Haw did in his pursuit of cheese. He took some steps, failed, and started again.

6. *Sixth step: Create short-term wins.* Nothing speaks louder than success. Identify winnable challenges that can be told and retold. Be strategic in achieving small wins and build momentum. Make sure people are reinforced by tangible accomplishments along the way. Break the big change

into small chunks. Reward yourself for small wins. Haw found little pieces of cheese along the way, and most important, he felt invigorated by doing something, as opposed to waiting for somebody to return his cheese.

7. *Seventh step: Don't let up.* The temptation to give up when you're in the middle of a storm is strong indeed. Normalizing the neutral zone, where the old is gone but the new is yet to come, can prove useful in calming anxieties. Ask others to help you, to make you accountable.

8. *Eighth step: Make changes stick.* Institutionalizing the changes into the life of the organization or the community, through induction, policies, bylaws, training, mentoring, and promotion, can go a long way toward sustainability. We call this trendsetting.

The work of Kotter and Cohen (2002) is very compatible with our ABC—I VALUE IT framework. In Table 7.3 we outline our own version of working with groups in either organizations or communities. Although the target audience is somewhat different in communities and organizations, the work usually happens in groups. Hence, we chose to combine these two entities under the heading of working with groups.

The main strategies will look familiar to you by now, although there are some key differences in the work with groups, most notably the creation of a safe space for large numbers of people and the formulation of a vision that requires consensus of many players and teams.

In working with large groups, there is always the risk of losing people along the way. It is much easier to blend into the woodwork when there are so many people around. The key to prevent this problem is to create small communities of practice of about eight people. In such teams, people get to problem-solve, formulate local visions, learn from each other, support each other, and evaluate together. It is far easier to create an inclusive environment with 8 people than with 50. Remember that a key principle is to engage people in meaningful work or activities that speak to them. You cannot do that when you're trying to please 20 or 40 people at a time. A lecture is not a very engaging way of promoting transformational change, nor is a memo or a video.

In the Better Beginnings Better Futures (BBBF) prevention program in Ontario, Canada, community involvement in small teams proved essential for citizen participation. From the planning to the demonstration to the sustainability phase, citizen engagement was vital. For community change to survive past the initial stages of planning for change, ownership and communication for buy-in must be emphasized. In large part, it was resident participation that accounted for the many positive child, family, and community outcomes achieved in BBBF, including better mental health and educational attainment for the children and higher levels of parental and teacher satisfaction. By carefully nurturing relationships and partnerships with residents, schools, and local agents of change, the BBBF team

Table 7.3 ABC—I VALUE IT: Strategies for Personal Well-Being in Work with Groups

Roles	Strategies		
	Affective	Behavioral	Cognitive
Inclusive host	Create safe environment for people to express views and emotions.	Structure time and space where safe and fun dialogue can occur.	Promote sharing of personal narratives and interpretations of events and beliefs.
Visionary Process	Foster feelings of affiliation and solidarity in group work.	Engage people in activities to devise a vision for working together.	Address basic assumptions about working in groups.
Outcome	Make the vision alive and foster ownership of it throughout the organization or community.	Involve people in the development of a vision for team, unit, organization, or community.	Analyze gap between actual and desire state of affairs.
Asset seeker	Make sure you recognize and affirm people's strengths.	Help people develop inventories of own strengths.	Reframe life experiences and ways of coping as strengths.
Listener and sense maker	Establish processes for people to feel heard and valued.	Structure opportunities for people to speak, learn, and problem solve together.	Learn how to listen to each other and problem solve in teams.
Unique solution finder	Small wins keep people engaged and energized.	Assign specific actions in line with goals and objectives.	Identify which values, beliefs, and assumptions either promote or inhibit new actions.
Evaluator Past efforts	Make it safe to explore past failures and successes.	Get people involved in evaluation criteria that is meaningful to them.	Analyze links between sites, signs, sources, and strategies of well-being.
Present efforts	Reward people for sharing sources of stress.	Use empowerment-based evaluation and appreciative inquiry to evaluate efforts.	If change is needed, create cognitive dissonance between aspirations and actual actions.
Future efforts	Build trust by showing your own personal commitment to act.	Institutionalize mechanisms to monitor well-being of staff and community members.	Create narrative of ongoing growth and development.

Table 7.3 (*Continued*)

| Roles | Strategies | | |
	Affective	Behavioral	Cognitive
Implementer	Celebrate attempts to implement new behaviors and attitudes into life of organization or community.	Build structures that support new behaviors and attitudes and foster sustainability.	Tell stories of success and how they have helped other people improve well-being.
Trendsetter	Generate enthusiasm among peers about being leaders in a field.	Have a participatory plan for disseminating lessons learned.	Spread the message across organizations and communities in compelling ways.

secured ownership and sustainability of a model project (Nelson, Pancer, Hayward, & Peters, 2005).

ROWS FOR WELLNESS

Exercise 7: ABC Self-Assessment

Affective, behavioral, and cognitive strategies—some of us are stronger in some of these domains than in others. When Isaac did this exercise in class with his students, several of them discovered they were better at "brainy" things (cognitive strategies) than at "feeling" things (affective strategies). Others realized that they had little patience for listening when the person who was being listened to contradicted himself. By asking yourself what are your ROWS with respect to ABC strategies, you may discover your own strengths and weaknesses, as well as opportunities and risks for practicing these skills.

Think about these three sets of strategies and ask yourself what are your strengths and weaknesses and what risks and opportunities are present in the environment that may either help you to improve your profile or impede your own growth. For example, in an organizational culture of "fix it" and "fix it fast," there may not be adequate time for proper listening; it's all about action. Thus, the environment works against our best practices. Complete Form 7.1 thinking about your ROWS vis-à-vis the ABCs.

In transferring your ROWS to Form 7.2, you create a profile of your own readiness to do something about what you just found. Now that we covered in this chapter the stages of change theory, we hope that you can appreciate fully the importance of the readiness check.

Form 7.1   ROWS Exercise 7: ABC Self-Assessment

Risks for using ABC				
Opportunities for using ABC				
Weaknesses for using ABC				
Strengths for using ABC				

Form 7.2   Wellness Readiness Check 7: ABC Self-Assessment

ROWS	1 I never thought about doing something about it.	2 I'm thinking about doing something about it.	3 I'm prepared to do something about it.	4 I'm doing something about it.	5 I've been doing something about it for some time.
Risks					
Opportunities					
Weaknesses					
Strengths					

III

Organizational Well-Being

Organizational well-being may be defined by the presence of effective, reflective, and affective environments, ERA environments in short. We make the point that for organizations to thrive, these three conditions must obtain. Otherwise, a key component of organizational well-being is missing. We present a three-dimensional framework consisting of ERA continua. Settings that are high in all three can expect productive and supportive learning environments where workers are not afraid to take risks and innovate. Safety is a precondition for reflection, and reflection is a precondition for growth. That is the subject matter of Chapter 8.

In Chapter 9, we discuss the interplay of values, interests, and power (VIP) and their influence on the effective, reflective, and affective qualities of the workplace. We discuss conflicts that emerge within people and among groups who differ on their VIPs. We use the example of the city of Alborg in Denmark, where various constituencies clashed around the use of city space. It is obvious from the case study that VIPs matter.

In Chapter 10 we apply I VALUE IT strategies to advance organizational well-being. Using examples from a variety of sources, we show how this set of strategies can be applied in a variety of settings.

In each of the chapters we demonstrate the connections among personal, organizational, and community dynamics and how they affect organizational health and wellness. Organizations are mediating structures that can either enhance or diminish well-being for the population at large. Whether we are workers or recipients of services, organizational structures affect our lives in multiple ways. This part of the book calls attention to organizational dynamics and potential ways to make organizations more humane and efficacious at the same time.

8

What Is It? Signs of Organizational Well-Being

It's hard to get it right. Some workplaces are very friendly but not very effective. Others are friendly and effective, but not very stimulating. Yet others are stimulating and perhaps even reflective, but nobody talks to anybody. Universities can be like that: very stimulating work, deeply reflective, but each professor is a virtuoso soloist, or so he or she thinks. We're happy to report that our department at Vanderbilt is not like that; in fact, it's pretty close to being really good on all accounts: affective, reflective, and effective.

Early on in my career I (Isaac) had a job at a very friendly place. People talked to each other, shared family stories, and asked each other about their weekends, but the place wasn't very productive. I didn't feel very stimulated or particularly supported there. In contrast, I had another job where people were supportive, committed, accountable, and pretty effective, but not necessarily reflective about what it was all about. That was the Child Guidance Clinic of Winnipeg, a place for which I have very fond memories. I worked there for 6 years, soon after my arrival in Canada. There was devotion to the well-being of children and families, and the 220 or so clinicians were a most committed bunch. Both Ora and I, who were psychologists working in the schools, felt supported, appreciated, and respected. The place was high on friendliness and effectiveness, but there was no time to reflect deeply on the services we were delivering. There was an incredible pressure to see one more child, to do one more psych assessment, to do one more home visit, to do one more consultation. But when I put forth the proposition that perhaps all this diagnostic and therapeutic work was off the mark and that we should do more prevention, my coconspirators and I couldn't get time to explore new avenues of serving children and youth. The pressure to do more, instead of doing it differently, was overwhelming and eventually frustrating. I still maintain contact with the people there, and I know how hard it is to become more reflective about the overall mission of the place. More of the same is not necessarily the way to go.

How is your workplace? How high is it on friendliness? What about task completion? Does it promote learning about what you're doing? In most cases, you can get two out of the three options, although more and more organizations are beginning to realize that to keep talent, and to serve the community best, they have to excel in the three domains. They have to be affective, effective, and reflective (Senge, Scharmer, Jaworski, & Flowers, 2004).

In this chapter, we examine the signs of organizational well-being. For us, organizational well-being consists of effective, reflective, and affective environments (ERA, in short). We will examine the personal, organizational, and community signs of such environments.

ENVIRONMENTAL CHARACTERISTICS OF ORGANIZATIONAL WELL-BEING

Evidence shows that healthy organizations, those that attract and maintain good workers, perform their duties well, and serve the community, create three kinds of positive environments: effective, reflective, and affective. Therefore, we can say that organizational well-being consists of highly effective, reflective, and affective environments where workers, managers, and the community served by the organization have their needs met in ways that are congruent with the values of self-determination, freedom, personal growth, health, caring, and compassion; accountability, transparency, and responsiveness to the common good; collaboration, democratic participation, respect for human diversity, support for community structures, and social justice. What a mouthful! We know. But we didn't want to neglect any of the values that sustain personal, relational, and collective well-being. We reviewed in Chapter 3 the reasons behind all these values, but we haven't yet explored the ERA dimensions of organizational well-being.

Effective Environments

Organizations exist to perform a job, to meet some needs, and to serve their workers, clients, and the community at large. Justifiably, they can be evaluated on the degree to which they do all of these things well. To achieve their goals, they have to be efficient, well organized, task-oriented, accountable, and responsible, and they have to believe in their ability to do so. This is the organizational analogue of self-efficacy (Bolman & Deal, 2003; Chowdhury, 2003).

Workers have to feel, as individuals and as a collective, a sense of efficacy and mastery. Effectiveness, then, is both a means to an end and an end in itself. It is a means to an end in the sense that it enables a smooth operation for the achievement of a mission, and it is an end in itself in that it is intrinsically rewarding for workers to see that they can achieve goals.

People in effective environments communicate well, set realistic goals, assign jobs based on expertise and interests, respect time lines, deliver products or services as promised, problem-solve, anticipate challenges, and learn from experience. Effective environments create structures of accountability, review, and monitoring. No organization is perfect, and there is always room for improvement, but you can tell which organizations come close to the effective end of the continuum and which don't.

It takes a pretty wounded or disengaged worker not to care about inefficiency, and it takes a pretty dysfunctional and unreflective organization not to worry about goal achievement. Sad as it may sound, both exist in large quantities (Bolman & Deal, 2003; Doyle, 2003; Hager, 2001; Maslow, 1965). And both point to the interdependence of effectiveness with affectivity and reflexivity. The existence of an effective environment depends, to a large extent, on the presence of affective and reflective qualities. Figure 8.1 shows the interdependence of the three kinds of environments. We aspire to reach the top, back, righthand corner of the cube, as the arrow indicates. That is the best spot to be, but there are forces keeping organizations

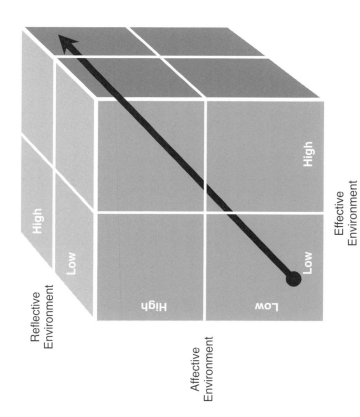

Figure 8.1   Environmental Characteristics of Organizational Well-Being.

from reaching that stage. Lack of reflection and disengagement are two of those forces.

Reflective Environments

It is possible to be efficient without being reflective. You may be very good at reaching the wrong goals. If you haven't taken the time to ask what this is all about, or to think about the big picture once in a while, it is possible that you are not in tune with the times. You may be out of sync. This happens to a lot of organizations that continue to provide therapeutic services but never ask if prevention might not be more efficient or humane, or if participatory approaches may not be more empowering than expert-driven methods (Hall, Juhila, Parton, & Poso, 2003; Ife, 2001; Mullaly, 2002; I. Prilleltensky & Nelson, 2002).

Reflective organizations ask big questions, such as What is the mission of the enterprise? They think outside the box. They create structures for questioning, and they respect dissent. In fact, some of them encourage dissent as a way of being creative. In the literature, these are called learning organizations precisely because they are constantly evaluating what they are doing and how they are doing it (Senge et al., 2004).

In the field of human services, the incredible pressure to provide psychosocial emergencies has kept counselors, social workers, psychologists, and others from asking the big questions, such as how to prevent the crises in the first place or how to work in natural settings instead of professional buildings. Even agencies that are created with the explicit purpose of doing prevention often revert to counseling mode due to the endless barrage of "urgent cases" (Nelson & Prilleltensky, 2005).

This was exactly what happened to a brand-new operation in Australia where I (Isaac) did some work. A colleague and I were asked to consult with a new organization designed to prevent behavioral and emotional problems in children and youth. This was in a picturesque little town northeast of Melbourne. The 2-hour drive from Melbourne was beautiful and provided my colleague, students, and I an opportunity to reflect on what was going on. We used to drive twice a month to help the organization with consultation and program evaluation. It turns out that as soon as they set up shop in the center of the town, families started asking for help with counseling. The workers, who had a big heart and wanted to be responsive to the community, began to deliver reactive instead of proactive services, which was the whole point of the operation. As external consultants, we worked together with them to concentrate on the main mission, which was prevention.

The Child Guidance Clinic of Winnipeg, Canada, experienced a similar, if somewhat more acute problem. Emergencies were plenty: suicidal youth, bullying at school, child abuse, school dropout, alcoholic parents, and educational failure. No shortage of crises. There was an urgent need to do something about the mental health of children, youth, and their families. But the pressure was so intense that there was rarely an opportunity to consider whether our approach, which was basically "diagnose and treat," was the most efficient one. There were many opportunities to do prevention, to promote strengths, to empower children and youth, and to improve the conditions for families. But instead, we did a lot of deficit-oriented assessments, crisis intervention, and expert-driven consultation, and didn't do much to change the conditions in schools. It is a struggle that the clinic faces still today.

How to become a reflective organization amid emergencies? It's a difficult challenge, and one that requires leadership. If we're going around in circles, somebody better call it for what it is. But this requires a safe environment and a little time. Few people will take risks in unsafe environments. Leaders have a role to play in nurturing spaces for free dialogue (Senge et al., 2004).

Affective Environments

Despite rhetoric of lofty missions and professional development, people become attached to organizations primarily through human bonds. Affective bonds go a long way to secure employee satisfaction and efficiency. Feeling accepted, appreciated, valued, and honored are strong predictors of worker well-being, as are flexibility, decision-making power, and social support (Marmot, 2004; Warr, 1999).

An affective climate of acceptance, appreciation, and affirmation not only promotes mental health, but it also enables examination of basic premises. Feeling safe is a prerequisite for questioning the status quo. When there is animosity and insecurity, it is much harder to voice disapproval or question sacred cows than when there is mutual respect (Perkins et al., in press).

An affirming psychological atmosphere can breed empowerment, but it can also foster complacency. Friendliness can work both ways: It can create a safe space for dialogue and elucidation of the mission, but it can also relax expectations. This is why an affective environment must be complemented by an efficient and reflective climate. Something or somebody must call attention to the latter two.

Linked Environments

Just as there cannot be personal wellness in the absence of relational, organizational, or collective well-being, there cannot be organizational well-being in the absence of any one of the ERA environments. Too much affection without reflection can lead to complacency, whereas too much efficiency without reflection can lead to dogmatism. Too little affection without reflection can lead to alienation and neglect of values, whereas too little efficiency without reflection breeds dysfunction.

The reflective piece serves as a conscience for the other two, and the affective state operates according to Maslow's (1965) basic needs. Without safety, it is hard to take risks and stretch yourself. The drive for efficiency, in turn, keeps in balance accountability and stewardship.

Organizational well-being flourishes at the intersection of highly affective, effective, and reflective environments, as the arrow in Figure 8.1 points out. If this is the definition of organizational well-being, how can we tell when we've got it? What are the personal, organizational, and community signs?

SIGNS OF ORGANIZATIONAL WELL-BEING IN INDIVIDUALS

If I look at an employee, leader, or client of an organization, how can I tell that the organization is working well? One way is to look for signs of ERA environments in their thinking, feelings, and behavior. Thus, I can look for signs of effectiveness by asking employees about role clarity and task accomplishment. If they tell me their roles are clear and that they have resources to achieve expected tasks, I get a sense that this is an effective environment. If I want to know about the affective domain, I can ask employees about support and acceptance. If they tell me that they feel supported and welcomed in the workplace, I have some confidence that there is a friendly climate. Finally, if leaders of an organization welcome constructive criticism and workers feel free to give it, we get a sense that this is a reflective place.

Work environments can be infective, both in the positive and negative sense of the word. Workplaces that are low on ERA qualities are negatively infective. Low commitment, enthusiasm, productivity, growth, and support infect the settings with negative vibes. In contrast, institutions high on ERA are infectiously energetic and engaging. We want highly effective, reflective, and affective environments that turn into positively infective organizations. When that is achieved, we end up with *engaged* workers who are passionate about what they do. We want behavioral, emotional, and cognitive engagement (Harter et al., 2003).

Personal Signs of an Effective Environment

If we were interviewing or observing workers in organizations, what would we see and what would they tell us? What signs of an effective environment might we see? They would probably tell us that their *roles are clear* and that they *understand their managers' expectations* of them. Role ambiguity and confusing guidelines diminish productivity and demoralize the workforce (Harter et al., 2003; Warr, 1999).

We would also see people *communicating effectively* (Hayes, 2002); exchanges among workers and between workers and clients are easy to follow. To make sure tasks are accomplished, we would see people *taking minutes at meetings, having agendas, assigning responsibility* for various jobs, and *summarizing the next steps. Follow-through* on decisions are monitored and reported to the group.

We would see that workers have the *resources* they need to perform their duties. They have access to materials, equipment, literature, and information to do their jobs well. Workers would likely tell us that their skills are valued and put to good use. In other words, there would be a *good match between skills and tasks.* Our imaginary interviewee would also tell us that her peers are *committed* to doing high-quality work; it is a team effort.

We would also see attention being paid to *physical conditions.* Workers are not exposed to dangerous materials, and every effort is made to prevent injuries, physical or emotional. We would see workers well trained in health and safety procedures.

When doing solitary work, we would see them engaged in their jobs, problem solving, creating, writing, thinking, and otherwise being *productive.* If we tracked attendance, we would likely see *low absenteeism.* If we asked our interviewee about *overall satisfaction,* she'd probably tell us that she feels quite happy with the place (Bolman & Deal, 2003; Doyle, 2003; Harter et al., 2003; Warr, 1999).

Now, for all we know, these descriptions can apply to a hospital, a family service, or a bomb-making facility. The Nazis were very effective at what they did: supremely so. Which begs the question: Effective for what? To entertain, let alone answer that question, we need a reflective environment.

Personal Signs of a Reflective Environment

Reflective environments serve two primary goals. One is to provide *cognitive stimulation, variety, learning, and intellectual growth in workers.* These are all basic human needs worthy of serious consideration (Harter et al., 2003; Maslow, 1965). Hence, we want to see signs of learning, debating, integrating, and synthesizing in workers. We want to see employees taking courses, upgrading their skills, and making use of professional development opportunities.

The second function of reflective environments is to *ponder the vision, mission, and values of the organization.* Therefore, we want employees, managers, and leaders to engage in reflective processes about the why, what, and how of the organization; herein lies the answer to the question Effective for what: effective to make bombs, to perpetuate the status quo, or to bring about radical change in the way we serve people and promote social justice? Workers with a vocation for helping don't want to just put on Band-Aids; they want to transform the conditions that lead to suffering in the first place. To avoid a mere perpetuation of the status quo, we have to see workers *engaged in debate about the sources of suffering, the role of injustice, power differentials, and conflicting interests* (Perkins et al., in press; Senge et al., 2004). Some argue that to do so is to pollute professional discourse with politics (Wright & Cummins, 2005); we argue that not to do so is to be ignorant of the workings of politics (Flyvbjerg, 1998, 2001; Fox & Prilleltensky, 1997; I. Prilleltensky & Nelson, 2002). We avoid politics and ignorance at our own peril.

Two kinds of reflection about the vision, mission, and values can take place: first- and second-order reflection (Perkins et al., in press). First-order reflection does not question the structure of the organization, or its very mission, but rather seeks to improve functioning and to bring the operations more in line with the vision and mission. *Workers engaged in first-order reflection are a sign of a reflective environment.* Though useful and important, this type of reflection doesn't go far enough. Second-order reflection refers to a questioning of the values at play in the organization, to the alignment of values with mission and vision, and to the role of power and interests in the whole enterprise. Parallel to thinking about first- and second-order change (Watzlawick, Weakland, & Fisch, 1974), first-order reflections do not challenge the system within which questions take place, whereas second-order reflections do question the system, its very premises, and its values. *Workers engaged in second-order reflection are a sign of a deep reflective environment.* Simply put, we can have shallow or deep reflective environments. In our view, the deeper the reflections, the healthier the organization can become (Perkins et al., in press; Senge et al., 2004).

But, you say, how can you tell when a reflection is deep or superficial? Good question. In our view, questions about practices and policies that don't alter or question the mission, vision, or values of the organization tend to remain at a superficial level. On the other hand, questions that involve those aspects, in addition to issues of power, conflict, and interests, delve more deeply into fundamental organizational dynamics. When we see workers asking *whose interests are being promoted in the organization, whose power* is being exercised, and *what values* should guide the mission, we can be pretty confident that this is a reflective environment. A mnemonic for this seemingly complicated issue is VIP: values, interests, and power (I. Prilleltensky, 2000): What values, whose interests, and what power dynamics are at play? In the next chapters, we explore the tension among these three forces in more detail. For now, suffice it to say that a *questioning attitude* and a healthy dose of *skepticism* are good tonics against dogmatism.

Personal Signs of an Affective Environment

Dignity matters, a lot actually. It is at the heart of *empowerment.* A feeling of dignity is built on recognition, caring, affirmation, support, voice, and choice. Lack of dignity breeds despondence, ill health, and disengagement (Marmot, 2004).

Dignity is reflected in the little things and in the big things. Being treated with respect, being recognized, and being seen build dignity. Daily interactions contain the ingredients of dignity in the little things. Workers who feel valued and supported miss fewer days of work, are more productive and engaged, and experience better mental health than those who feel alienated (Harter et al., 2003; Layard, 2005; Warr, 1999).

But dignity is also related to the big things, such as organizational justice and fairness in pay. Workers who *experience the workplace as just and fair* are also more productive and healthier than those who report recurring instances of injustice. When workers perceive *concordance between effort and reward*, their feelings of fairness increase and their overall work satisfaction goes up (Conlon, Meyer, & Nowakowski, 2005).

The little and big things that constitute dignity have a lot to do with a sense of acknowledgment and control. *Feeling acknowledged and valued by others* creates the ground for creativity, enjoyment, and the lowering of defenses, which is so valuable in innovation (Hornstein, 2003; Menzies Lyth, 1988, 1989). A sense of control, in turn, grows out of latitude and decision-making power. When workers experience low demands and high levels of control, their health improves. On the contrary, when they encounter high demands and low decision-making power, their health status deteriorates (Marmot, 2004).

Employees experience multiple anxieties at work, especially workers dealing with human beings. Suicide attempts, child abuse reports, domestic violence—these are all draining. Low levels of support and few opportunities to share doubts and dilemmas can lead to burnout and disaffection. A supportive environment is reflected in *workers who stick with it despite the challenges*. Another sign is the *ability to express concerns and doubts without fear* of reprisals. Feeling threatened, which is rampant in some organizations, leads to distancing. Feeling put down, which is also not uncommon, leads to sabotage and lack of caring (Conlon et al., 2005; Doyle, 2003).

While positive emotions lead to higher work and personal well-being, having a voice leads to engagement. Workers whose work is recognized and whose efforts are praised report more loyalty and commitment than those whose contributions go unnoticed (Harter et al., 2003).

In sum, a positive affective environment is reflected in employees who report *control, support, recognition, and friendliness, and who demonstrate caring* through little and big actions such as asking how others are doing and working together to make the place more just, fair, and equitable (Conlon et al., 2005; Harter et al., 2003; Marmot, 2004; Warr, 1999).

A brief visit to Chapter 3 reveals that effective environments meet basic needs through the enactment of value-based policies and practices. Most signs of personal well-being reflect one or more of the core values presented in Chapter 3. Self-determination and freedom are reflected in signs of control, autonomy, and decision-making power. Personal growth is closely tied to a reflective environment; in the absence of stimulation, personal and professional development stalls. Health, caring and compassion, collaboration, and democratic participation are values embedded in the signs of participation, workplace empowerment, and social support. The more control, the more vitality in the organization. Transparency and responsiveness to the common good, as well as respect for diversity and promotion of social justice, are brought to life in reflective environments. Without a reflective climate, these values are sacrificed. They are often the first casualties of "effectiveness." No time to philosophize, says the time-pressured manager. No time to forget our values, say we.

SIGNS OF ORGANIZATIONAL WELL-BEING

What signs can tell us that the organization is either well, on the path to wellness, or in trouble? We can look for the vital signs of health and for signs that not all is well. We look at vital signs in ERA domains.

Signs of an Effective Environment

Effective organizations do not rely on luck or spates of motivation, but create *enabling structures* for the work to be done. To avoid erratic performance, organizations build *mechanisms and monitoring systems*, such as meetings, reports, reviews, and planning sessions to make sure the operation runs smoothly. These enabling structures serve as decision-making bodies and as follow-up vehicles (Shafritz, Ott, & Jand, 2005).

Organizations that function well establish *communication channels* that *disseminate essential information*. Documents and processes that *clarify roles and expectations* are a sign of health. Organizations that function well have *participatory structures* to make decisions. In a human service we consulted with, several formats were used to elicit employee participation. We created councils and task forces that mixed people from various branches. They all made pretty consequential decisions. The time and space allowed by management to do this ensured a great deal of buy-in.

Participatory structures do not replace the need for *effective leadership* (Goleman et al., 2002). Optimal division of labor and integration of efforts are visible in healthy organizations. *People's skills are matched to jobs*. Healthy organizations have a *time perspective* on the services and products they deliver. They keep up with the times and have ways of adapting to the circumstances (Doyle, 2003; Shafritz et al., 2005).

Availability of resources to perform the job is a sine qua non. In many environments today, you couldn't function without a computer, proper software, proper training, books, or, of course, proper space. Working as itinerant clinicians in schools, the two of us experienced lack of space in a big way. We all had stories about working in the proverbial closet—that was all the school could provide for us. Office space, working space, meeting space, lunch space, coffee space—we have all been in discussions where those coveted resources were vied for.

Optimal use of time is a key constituent of effective organizations. In how many meetings have you felt that the goal could have been accomplished in a quarter of the time? And in how many meetings have you felt that decisions were rushed? Neither extreme is good. Healthy organizations demand from people just about the right amount of their time.

Many of these qualities are learned via trial and error. How much time is sufficient to accomplish a task, or how many times do you need to see a client before you get a feel for his or her issues? These are lessons you learn over time, provided you function in a reflective environment.

Signs of a Reflective Environment

We see three kinds of reflections as signs of organizational well-being. The first pertains to *personnel development*. A reflective environment is one where employees are given constructive feedback in formal and informal ways. Through peer support, mentoring, or supervision, workers are given an opportunity to think about their work, to share sensitive issues, and to get useful feedback. Professional development opportunities are pertinent and frequent (Bolman & Deal, 2003; Friedman, 2001).

The second kind of reflection refers to *organizational improvement* through ongoing program evaluation efforts and strategic planning. These are structured opportunities for the entire organization to pause and ask whether the actions are matching the vision and the philosophy. Formative and summative evaluations notify workers and management of areas of strength and weaknesses. Planning sessions build on evaluations and formulate strategies for fine-tuning, sharpening, or replacing practices, programs, and policies (Argyris, 1993; Chowdhury, 2003; Schein, 1992).

The third type of reflection pertains to *organizational learning* (Watkins & Marsick, 1993). These are efforts to engage the entire workforce in deep reflections about mission, vision, and growth. Unlike the second kind of reflection, this mode of learning goes beyond fine-tuning and probes the enactment of values, the role of interests, and the exercise of power—the same VIP issues (values, interest, and power) we discussed earlier. Why is this kind of exploration a sign of organizational well-being? Socrates said that the unexamined life is not worth living. We say that the unexamined organization is a risky venture. Time and again, we have seen corporations collapse, plans disintegrate, or agencies evaporate simply by doing the same old thing in highly unexamined ways (J. Bakan, 2004; Flyvbjerg, 1998; Hager, 2001). The risks of the unexamined organization range from the evil to the banal, from Enron deceiving millions of share-holders and wiping out their life savings to mere inefficiency and benign neglect of the client and the mission.

It's hard, if not impossible, to become a reflective organization without structures that institutionalize this in the culture. We have all been to work-shops where some new fad or some new guru is presented as the quickest fix to the latest organizational woes. This does not a reflective environment make. Ideas have to be digested, debated, and disseminated throughout the organization in engaging and meaningful ways. Frontal lectures and moti-vational videos are not the way to promote a reflective culture. The chal-lenge is to find ways to make personal development, team improvement, and institutional learning an integral part of organizations (Addleson, 2000; De Vita & Fleming, 2001). We explore this further in the next two chapters.

Signs of an Affective Environment

The look in people's faces can say a lot about organizational climate. Gloomy faces tell you this is not a fun place to be. *Laughter and convivial-ity,* on the other hand, signal "I want to be here," or at the very least, "I don't mind being here" (Kets de Vries & Florent-Treacy, 2003).

Interactions also say a lot about the environment. Do workers chat often? Do they come close when they speak to each other? Do they come in contact often, or do they avoid each other? Looks and patterns of interac-tion are useful indicators of emotional climate (Goleman, 1998).

An affective environment is manifested in *acceptance and in excitement* (Maslow, 1965). The former makes you feel that you can be yourself, and the latter makes you feel alive. How can you tell if there is acceptance and excitement? If there is acceptance, there is little tension and there are few defenses when people communicate; if there is excitement, you can see ac-tion around the place. These feelings are created and maintained by *norms of conviviality.* Rituals and celebrations make such norms. Taking time be-fore meetings to check in with people, sharing a sense of excitement and en-thusiasm about people's accomplishments, praising colleagues for a job well done, and developing camaraderie are signs of an affective environment. These practices develop over time and require sustenance. The best part of laughter and positive emotions is that they are contagious. The more people who exhibit these signs, the more they become part of the culture.

The ease of flow in meetings, the sounds of laughter, the look of smiles, and the relaxed attitude of workers point to an upbeat place. But when things don't go well, workers stick with each other and don't blame each other. *Support* in difficult times is as important as fun in enjoyable times. In moments of grief, affective places rally behind their people. Colleagues show caring and compassion; words of encouragements are softly spoken. It's not a blaming place, but an affirming one.

For an outsider, cultural norms are not so easy to discern, but for an insider, a few days suffice to read the cues. Each of us has an emotional barometer. The level of affirmation and elation generated by a workplace can be gauged in our emotional barometer. We need to pay attention to it.

SIGNS OF ORGANIZATIONAL WELL-BEING IN THE COMMUNITY

Public organizations in general, but especially health, human, and community services, exist to promote the common good. If they are doing a good job, we can justifiably expect community improvement. Over the long run, if schools are providing high-quality education, we can predict an enlightened citizenry. If health care is affordable and accessible and health education is effective, we should see less disease. These are reasonable expectations, provided government and nongovernment organizations work in unison and not at cross-purposes (Gore, 1993). Often we see one branch of government investing in early education while another is dropping people off the medical care system. Well-being is a holistic concept that requires holistic approaches. We have to watch for signs of organizational and interorganizational coordination. If individually and collectively, public agencies are responsive to the community, we should see some vital signs of health and well-being. This is the focus of this section: Looking at communities, how can we tell if organizations are being effective, reflective, and affective?

Community Signs of an Effective Organizational Environment

I (Isaac) have not been blessed with tolerance for inefficiency. In fact, I often think that my mental health is directly related to the mood of public servants. Upon arrival in Nashville, Tennessee, in 2003, we tried, in vain, on numerous occasions, to obtain a driver's license. We visited various offices of the Division of Motor Vehicles (DMV) several times, only to find a new obstacle every time. The waiting lines, which circled each office like a serpent, were interminable, as was my exasperation. We wasted several days trying to get our driver's license. Each time there would be a new hurdle to overcome—all irrational, as far as I was concerned. The most ludicrous one was the "severe weather" clause. Ora and I had driven in Canada for 15 years under conditions of snowstorms and black ice. Each of us had had a license for over 20 years when we came to Nashville. In one of our recurrent pilgrimages to the DMV, carrying multiple photocopies of untold documents, we finally made it! They called our number: Hallelujah! When we reached the counter, the uniformed lady told us that they couldn't do any more driving tests today due to "severe weather conditions." Looking outside for signs of severity, we could barely see a drop. It was turning slightly cloudy, and the officials resolved to invoke the severe weather clause. Ora pleaded with the officers, explained to them that she had over 2 decades of driving experience, that this was the nth time we had come to the DMV, and that we couldn't take any more time off work. Nothing worked.

Eventually, after countless and fruitless trips to the DMV, Ora and I got our licenses. Each of us had a test that lasted 2 minutes. We were asked to drive out of the parking lot, turn into the parking lot of an industrial site a hundred yards to the left, and come back.

A couple of years later I was retraumatized when I took Matan, our son, for his driving test. On this occasion, Matan's school attendance certificate didn't have the proper signature. I begged the officer to let me go get the signature and come back to see him without waiting hours in line again. In an uncharacteristic gesture of DMV compassion, he let me submit the document without waiting. Eventually Matan got his learner's permit. When it was time to do his driving test we came to the office at 6 A.M., 2 and a half hours before they opened the door. We were second in line! By the time they opened the door the serpent had circled the building several times.

My traumatic experiences at the Nashville DMV epitomize, for me, the peak of inefficiency. Day in and day out thousands of citizens waste hours of productive work in lines. I had been spoiled: In Canada, civil servants are efficient, courteous, educated, and respectful. This was my experience over a period of 15 years in two provinces. I had come to expect this service everywhere. Was I ever wrong!

Indignity adds insult to injury in the public service. Being professional immigrants, we had to negotiate with more immigration and customs officers than we care to remember. More than once, we were subjected to indignities and treated like children by officers who abused their power. And we're pretty educated people with big mouths. Imagine those who cross borders with refugee status and no language.

Community satisfaction with public services is a sign of organizational efficiency (I was never given a customer satisfaction survey at DMV). From transportation to taxation, from education to human services, the public is the subject of organizational efficiency (Gore, 1993). The signs are all over the place: Do schools produce high-quality education? Does local government provide sufficient affordable housing? Is health care affordable and accessible to all citizens? Do child and family services prevent child abuse? These questions pertain to *program evaluations* of public services. Do they do what they are supposed to do? Do they do it well?

Community signs of government and organizational efficiency can be measured in *public health indices* such as prevalence of infant mortality, literacy, teenage pregnancy, and addictions. Each public organization has a different focus. But whatever the focus is, they are supposed to be *accountable to the public.*

But there are limits to efficiency. An organization, such as the Child Guidance Clinic where we worked, can be very efficient but still be unable to stem the tide of new cases. This is because the demand always exceeds the supply for services. No matter how effective child and family services personnel are, if community conditions do not improve, demand will continue to grow, exponentially, which is currently the case in many communities. There is no question that public services can be made more efficient, but it is all too easy to blame an agency for social problems that originate outside the organization.

Efficiency can be a double-edged sword. The community is well justified in expecting prompt and high-quality services from government and not-for-profit organizations. But this expectation carries certain risks. Professionals in these agencies, and especially their managers, are pressured to do more with less. As a result, there is less time to reflect on what are the sources of community problems. Instead of working with communities to get to the root causes of problems, we economize by seeing clients less in time and less often.

A community sign of an effective organization is an effort to create *partnerships* across sectors and awareness of the social causes of problems. In the long term, consortia of services, private institutions, and governments will have to deal with economic disadvantage, educational failure, and norms of violence. Bringing together partners that share responsibility for the public good is a reflection of organizational strategic planning (De Vita & Fleming, 2001). It is totally unfair to put the burden of fixing society on social workers and health professionals alone.

Community Signs of a Reflective Organizational Environment

How do communities learn? Think about it: It is not a question we often ask. We ask how children learn, how professionals get their skills, but we rarely ponder how communities as a whole learn. How do communities reflect on their achievements and their failures? I can think of no public forum where such deliberations take place regularly. When community members come together to debate a school proposition or a bylaw, it is usually not a learning experience but a confrontational one: residents who oppose the halfway house and those who support it; parents who want more special education services and school officials who have to cut them. Before elections, it is all about your candidate beating the other; it is rarely about dialogue or learning.

A community sign of a reflective organization would be *forums that engage citizens in learning and planning.* The Plan of Nashville (PoN), headed by the Civic Design Center, was such a project (www.civicdesigncenter.org). Extensive community consultation took place over 2 and a half years to produce a comprehensive plan for the future of the city of Nashville. The Civic Design Center sought input from many communities and devised participatory strategies to gain meaningful involvement from neighbors across the city. Between 2002 and 2004, citizens met with experts to dialogue about the strengths and weaknesses of various designs. The PoN afforded a learning opportunity to understand the interface between the built environment and urban life.

Projects such as the PoN help the community see the connections between different parts of well-being. In the PoN, the impact of public transportation on the environment could be discerned, as well as the effects of safety on quality of life. A reflective community is one that sees connections among different spheres of wellness. To the extent that organizations help achieve these goals, they are making an important contribution to the promotion of well-being.

Community Signs of an Affective Organizational Environment

Clients of any kind of service can readily tell you if they were treated with *respect, dignity, and compassion*. The affiliation of workers within the organization has to radiate outward, toward those they serve. *Affirmation* has to come for workers and clients alike.

Earlier in the book, we proposed SPEC principles (strengths, prevention, empowerment, and changing conditions) for the promotion of community well-being. Among other ways, strengths and empowerment are promoted via affective means. We want *community members to feel valued and appreciated for their strengths*. We want them to build on their coping skills and their resilience. But for them to take these steps, they have to trust workers, and they have feel accepted for who they are, regardless of their life situation. It is only when community members feel unconditionally accepted that they can begin to build on strengths. Feeling judged by service providers only reinforces their life experiences of marginalization (Hall et al., 2003).

Likewise, community members must be *empowered to exercise voice and choice*. Empowered community members are a sign that the organization lives up to SPEC principles. Whatever the problem community members experience, empowerment is not an adjunct to problem solving, but an intrinsic part of the solution.

Strengths and empowerment generate *engagement in the community*. If we are looking for community signs of an affective organization, we have to look at the type of relationships clients develop with service providers. Do they want to come back? Do they feel blamed? Are they getting the support they need? These are important symbols of affectivity.

LINKED SIGNS

The emotional and productive state of workers depends not only on internal drives and motivators, but also on the cultural norms of the environment.

Organizational practices, in turn, depend on the actions of individual employees and workers. It is they who create and reproduce, or kill, effective, reflective, and affective organizations. When the ERA qualities of workplaces are low, the place becomes negatively infective; when the ERA standards are high, the setting is positively infective, generating energy and engagement for workers and clients in the community (Harter et al., 2003).

The organization as a whole, through its structures, procedures, regularities, and habits, can foster ERA climates. Workers need to be rewarded for supporting enabling structures, and structures have to be user-friendly and participatory. When the place is internally together, signs of organizational well-being start to be reflected in the community. ERA qualities are intrinsically beneficial for workers and the community at large.

Without personal contributions, the organization doesn't function, and without enabling structures there is nothing to support and institutionalize good intentions. Ultimately, the merits of ERA in individuals and agencies have to translate into signs of community well-being, which is the whole point.

SIGNS OF TROUBLE

Not so fast, though! They sure sound nice, but all these signs of organizational well-being are very hard to achieve. Often, the norm is inefficiency, recalcitrant habits, and disaffection instead of efficiency, reflection, and affection. The cube presented in Figure 8.1 introduces three continua along ERA dimensions. Organizations can be in the low, middle, or high range of the continuum. Those closer to the low end had better think about moving up the ladder. Why they are stuck and how to get moving is the focus of the next two chapters.

ROWS FOR WELLNESS

Exercise 8: Vital Signs and Signs of Trouble

By now, you're familiar with ROWS. Looking at an organization where you work or volunteer or where you study, can you think of ROWS in terms of its effective, reflective, and affective environments? Is it possible that your organization does well in terms of efficiency, but it's still learning how to be reflective? Using Form 8.1, try to identify ROWS for the ERA environments discussed in the chapter. This exercise can be a diagnostic tool for you and your coworkers. Once you all do it, you can summarize the results and present it at a meeting for discussion. It can be used as part of a strategic plan or simply as part of a staff meeting.

Now you need to transfer the ROWS mentioned in Form 8.1 to Form 8.2 and come up with some actions. If you place the ROWS mostly under columns 1, 2, or 3, you need to plan some actions. If you have some ROWS already under numbers 4 or 5, you are already doing something. Keep it up.

Form 8.1   ROWS Exercise 8: Vital Signs and Signs of Trouble

Risks that can make the organization less	
Effective	
Reflective	
Affective	
Opportunities that can make the organization more	
Effective	
Reflective	
Affective	
Weaknesses that make the organization less	
Effective	
Reflective	
Affective	
Strengths that make the organization	
Effective	
Reflective	
Affective	

Form 8.2   Wellness Readiness Check 8: Vital Signs and Signs of Trouble

ROWS	1 I never thought about doing something about it.	2 I'm thinking about doing something about it.	3 I'm prepared to do something about it.	4 I'm doing something about it.	5 I've been doing something about it for some time.
Risks					
Opportunities					
Weaknesses					
Strengths					

9

Where Does It Come From? Sources of Organizational Well-Being

W hat are the sources of effective, reflective, and affective organizations? In short, what are the sources of organizational well-being? There are obviously many answers to that question, but we choose to concentrate on three key factors that are often acknowledged, but whose interactions are seldom understood: values, interests, and power (I. Prilleltensky, 2000). There are superficial and subterranean meanings to these three words. The superficial meanings are all too well-known. They are part and parcel of our vocabulary: values adorn mission statements, interests are reflected in WIIFM (What's in it for me?), and power is ascribed to commanding leaders and CEOs. But deeper meanings require elaboration, for contradictions among values, interests, and power abound.

Management books sometimes portray the values and interests of managers and employees as equivalent, which is misleading (e.g., Senge, Ross, Smith, Roberts, & Kleiner, 1994). Social justice, a value that is often invoked by social services, is in contradiction with the philosophy of individualism—the lift-yourself-up-by-your-bootstraps mentality—which also pervades human services (Mullaly, 2002; Wineman, 1984). Much talk about democracy in the workplace doesn't diminish the power of executive directors to undermine employee decision making.

How do values, interests, and power interact to promote or inhibit organizational well-being? What special combo will render a value-based culture? Such is the subject of this chapter.

VALUES, INTERESTS, AND POWER

It is true that VIPs (very important persons) influence organizational well-being, but in this chapter, we want to talk about a different kind of VIPs—

values, interests, and power. Here we use the VIP acronym to refer to the latter, less well-known version. Values, interests, and power are key sources of organizational well-being. These VIPs determine the effective, reflective, and affective climate of your workplace, your school, your hospital, your sports club. Their reconciliation, or lack thereof, impacts organizational culture in a big way.

It's not hard to imagine that VIP machinations would shape organizational culture, but it's quite difficult to decipher how they do that. Consider that each worker, manager, employer, and community member has a different set of VIPs, and that for an organization to function properly, a good deal of alignment is warranted. That makes for a complicated picture.

Our point is that VIPs can influence organizations in positive or negative ways. It is entirely possible for private interests to undermine a reflective culture; in a reflective space, one's hunger for power may be exposed. Similarly, it is probable that misunderstood values, like autonomy, would undercut client well-being, another fundamental value. When autonomy is made synonymous with self-sufficiency, and self-sufficiency is made equivalent to not depending on external help, we forget that true autonomy comes with supports. Values exist in a web. Autonomy is dependent on social supports, a fair distribution of resources, and self-efficacy (Loewy, 1993). If we push onto clients the idea that it is always "within their power" to solve their problems, and we neglect the surrounding conditions, we can set them up for failure.

But VIPs can be a source of organizational health as well, especially if we can foster congruence among various constituencies. When the meaning and interdependence of social justice, self-determination, respect for diversity, and caring and compassion are shared among staff, managers, and communities, we foster value-based practice.

But before we get ahead of ourselves, let's define VIPs. *Values* refer to morally desirable outcomes and processes that people pursue and enact in their actions and in their thoughts. The dual objective of desirable outcomes and processes is meant to promote personal and collective well-being at the same time. To quote Kekes (1993, p. 44), values are "humanly caused benefits that human beings provide to others." As an example, he claims that "love and justice are moral goods" (p. 44). In contrast, *interests* refer to the narrow pursuit of personal benefit in disregard of consequences for the collective (Flyvbjerg, 1998, 2001).

Power, in turn, is a combination of the capacity and opportunity to promote values and/or interests (I. Prilleltensky, in press). Capacity and opportunity derive from a number of factors, including the availability of resources (e.g., money, education, status, information, privilege) and skills (e.g., eloquence, leadership, training). A culture that promotes organizational well-being is one that uses power to advance values in recognition—as opposed to denial—of personal interests. Organizations ignore personal interests at their own peril. The way organizations resolve the tension between what's good for me and what's good for the collective shapes organizational culture.

There is no point denying that people have diverse and conflicting interests; the best we can hope for is that most people will be able to control their predilections and so minimize harm. The more we can get people to satisfy their own needs along with other people's needs, the easier it will be to manage personal interests (Maslow, 1965).

The VIP model is predicated on the fact that the three features are always present. Their interactions determine to a large extent organizational culture. If we want to change the organizational culture, and thus its well-being, we have to pay attention to their dynamic interplay.

If we did not have values to protect communities and individuals, harm would readily increase. If we did not have regulations against intoxicated driving, more innocent people would be killed; if we did not have norms against smoking in public spaces, more children would be sick. We need these norms to protect citizens against abuses of power and excesses of individual rights.

In some cases, personal and collective values come into conflict. Smokers demand the right to engage in the habit, but public health officials uphold the public good; teenagers want to have babies, but social workers try to prevent them (Loewy, 1993).

Whereas values promote the welfare of others in society, interests represent an investment in our own well-being. Workers, leaders, and community members have their own economic, social, and psychological interests to protect. For as long as personal interests are not threatened, and vision and values are clear, individuals are likely to engage in value-based actions. But once their interests are at risk, their commitment to the collective diminishes (Brumback, 1991).

Instead of hoping that colleagues, workers, and clients will pursue values just because they have been clearly articulated, leaders should learn how interests interfere with value-based practice. It's not realistic to expect human beings to suppress their subjectivity in the name of altruism, nor is it reasonable to expect leaders to ignore their own biases (DiTomaso & Hooijberg, 1996).

Power can be defined as the ability and possibility to influence the course of events in one's own and others' lives. The ability to promote personal well-being depends on economic, social, and psychological power. If a person commands sufficient power to fulfill and protect her personal interests, chances are that she might pursue value-based actions. But if she lacks basic resources, her inclination will be toward survival rather than altruism (Kanungo & Mendonca, 1996). Power may be a necessary, but is not a sufficient, condition for the promotion of value-based culture; some people use power to arrogate more power to themselves, instead of sharing it with

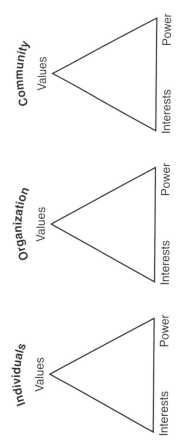

Figure 9.1   Values, Interests, and Power Affecting Organizational Well-Being.

others (DiTomaso & Hooijberg, 1996). Whether you give it or keep it, power remains a mediating force between interests and values.

In organizations, power suffuses every aspect of the enterprise. Power can be exercised through overt or covert means. Some democratic gestures may be explicit, but powerful dynamics of system maintenance go on at deeper levels (Bradshaw, 1998).

How can we visualize the complex interactions among VIPs? Figure 9.1 shows three separate triangles. Each triangle represents the VIPs of various groups with a stake in the organization. For simplicity's sake, the figure shows only three groups: individuals, organization, and community. But we could further break down individuals into staff, managers, volunteers, and board members, and organizations into teams, branches, and the like. Communities can also be separated into clients, external partners, and funding bodies.

In this figure, the triangles do not intersect. That means that the three groups share none of the VIPs. Their level of congruence is zero. Usually, though, there is some congruence among the values of workers, managers, and the communities they serve, as shown in Figures 9.2 and 9.3.

ZONES OF CONGRUENCE

Overlap among triangles represents congruence among the VIP of players in the organizational drama. Figure 9.2, for instance, shows a very small zone of congruence among three groups: staff, managers, and clients. The figure also shows a small zone of congruence between managers and staff but a fairly large one between clients and managers. The larger the zone of congruence is, the smaller the likelihood of conflict, and vice versa.

Figure 9.3 depicts the zone of congruence among three staff members. In this case, there is a fair amount of overlap among their VIPs; they share many common values, interests, and degrees of power within the organization.

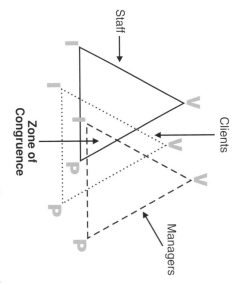

Figure 9.2 Zones of Congruence among Staff, Managers, and Clients.

Now it is your turn to experiment. On a piece of paper, draw triangles for all the relevant stakeholders of your organization. Then write on the vertices their respective VIPs. For example, on the V end of a triangle, write the values of a particular group or individual; then repeat for I and P. Do the same thing for a second and third group, until you have a good picture of all the players in the organization.

Based on the similarity of VIPs, draw a second picture showing their overlap, if any. Do you see any differences in their VIPs? What about congruence? Are some groups more congruent than others? How about the board of directors? This can be a diagnostic tool for understanding synergy and friction in your organization.

To detect the origins of organizational well-being we have to be very good detectives indeed. It is not enough to ask people what their values and

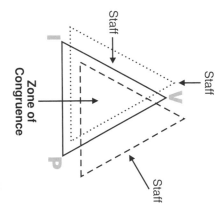

Figure 9.3 Zone of Congruence among Three Staff Members.

their interests are. Instead of just listening to what they have to say, we have to observe what they do. If leaders claim to be collaborative, do they mean it in practice, or do they only proclaim it? If workers commit to empower clients, do they really share power in sessions? How congruent are their actions with their statements? If the first zone of congruence was between players and groups, the second zone of congruence is concordance among words and deeds. Words are important, but deeds are essential. The gap between them is what we call hypocrisy. The overlap between them is what we call integrity. Let's have a look at a case.

Kerri Kershaw (2005) set out to explore conflicts among the values, interests, and power of prison guards and therapists in the State of Victoria, Australia. After working in prisons for many years, she doubted there was much concordance between the two groups. Although staff in prisons ostensibly abided by the principles of rehabilitation and mutual respect, some guards displayed utter contempt toward prisoners and therapists alike. And although custodial staff and psychologists shared the principle of rehabilitation, the former practiced it in very punitive ways that seemed incongruent with a therapeutic philosophy. Guards were secretly jealous of the time therapists spent with prisoners. Guards saw themselves as doing the dirty work of discipline, and they perceived the therapists as doing the cushy job of talking. Moreover, guards suspected therapists' work of empowerment as undermining their own work of controlling. Inmates, the guards thought, needed less and not more control. Such was the resentment that guards felt toward therapists that they played tricks on them, such as "forgetting" them in locked rooms with dangerous prisoners. Kershaw's analysis won her a much-deserved PhD and delivered a set of recommendations for bringing interdisciplinary teams closer together.

You may be tempted to dismiss this example as too dramatic or uncharacteristic of social services. But it exists in different degrees in most teams. In some welfare services, workers' wages are barely above the poverty line, and they have a lot to be angry about. They work with hard populations, they don't make enough money, and they have to learn byzantine rules of eligibility. No wonder many of them leave soon after they finish their training. Do their frustrations justify doing a poor job? We don't think so. Should we pay more attention to their private interests and lack of power? We do think so.

If we just go by mission statements, we should think everyone is an angel, but in actual fact, people don't behave like the words on the wall. If we want them to enact the organizational vision, we have to pay attention not only to values, but also to interests and power and how they interact with the words on the wall.

Organizations that strive for congruence among VIPs and among diverse groups have a higher chance of creating effective, reflective, and affective environments than those that ignore conflict. The way to congruence, as we shall see in the next chapter, is not to make people ashamed that they have personal interests, but to provide a safe space to explore their frustrations. That's not the whole path toward value-based practice, but it sure is a good beginning.

PERSONAL VIPs

What are your VIPs? How do they influence the organizational environment? Let's go in order of appearance. Values, as we said, are principles that guide behavior toward moral outcomes and ethical processes. This sounds too abstract, though. What does it mean to hold the value of self-determination or social justice? It means that I should do whatever I can, within my reach, to promote the autonomy of people who are currently deprived of opportunities to exercise control over their lives. This can be children, youth, the elderly, or the poor. Self-determination manifests itself in actions to promote the empowerment of those whose life circumstances deprived them of voice and choice.

What about social justice? In practice, this value means that I interpret the conditions of the people I work with in light of equality and fairness in the community. It also means resisting the temptation to blame them, or their parents, for their woes. It is all too easy to assign culpability and responsibility to a single person and exculpate the people and the structures that created disadvantage in the first place. Social justice means addressing the origins of inequality and supporting policies that distribute resources equitably. It means fighting for universal health care, for high-quality public education, and for affordable housing (Ife, 2001; Loewy, 1993).

But self-determination and social justice have to be practiced within your own organization as well, not just with clients or communities. In your own workplace, self-determination means trying to give your peers and subordinates room to maneuver. It means giving them the opportunity to learn, to exercise control over their jobs, and to be accountable for their actions. Literally, in every interaction with your coworkers, you have the opportunity to increase or decrease their self-determination. Every interaction is an opportunity to provide confidence, respect, and empowerment or their opposite: put-downs and sarcastic comments.

Justice at work means sharing the load equitably and preventing burnout in your colleagues and employees. It means recognizing and praising work well done and making accountable those who don't carry their weight. If justice is about the fair distribution of resources and obligations, you have to ask yourself what role you can play in making it happen. Self-determination and social justice, as two of many possible values, contribute to organizational well-being. They make the workplace more effective, reflective, and affective.

After you articulate your own set of values, ask yourself what gets in the way of enacting them. Is it your personal interests? Is it your lack of power in the organization? Or is that you have too much power and have a hard time sharing it?

A good way to understand personal interests is to ask the WIIFM question: What's in it for me? What do I get out of my job? Money, relationships, prestige, benefits? It's okay to have these wishes and resources. The problem starts when these wishes get in the way of enacting values such as social justice or self-determination or caring and compassion. In the case of Kershaw's (2005) prison guards, some of them felt that their own sense of fairness was violated by what they considered the preferential treatment accorded to inmates and the benign neglect they experienced from management. Unconsciously or otherwise, some of the guards sabotaged therapy by restricting access to inmates. Guards' interests interfered with the values of caring, compassion, health, and rehabilitation.

When we feel undermined, unheard, or unappreciated, sabotaging or neglectful behavior is not uncommon. It takes an astute manager or an observant colleague to recognize this in others. But it takes courageous and self-reflective workers to recognize this in themselves. Everyone agrees that it's okay to ask the WIIFM question, but few ask how that attitude undermines organizational and collective values. For as long as interests and power in the VIP triangle are neglected, it will be very hard to reconcile private motives with collective wellness. The solution to this tension is not to suppress it. On the contrary, the more people are aware of their conscious and unconscious desires, the more they can deal with them in a constructive way (Maslow, 1965).

But for people to subject their inner conflicts to public scrutiny, several conditions must obtain. First, this must be a safe place where sharing is appreciated and not used as a weapon to get back at people. Second, for a safe place to evolve there must be trust and mutual respect. Third, the creation of such space must be sanctioned and fully supported by leaders. Fourth, people have to be trained in how to talk and, more important, how to listen. Fifth, this cannot be a one-time event but a permanent feature of the organizational culture. In conditions of that nature, people's lives become whole through the integration of their working and personal selves (Senge et al., 2004). By developing a climate where sharing is permitted and honored, collective support and ingenuity will help workers confront their struggles. But let's be clear: None of this can happen if people abuse their power.

An abuse of power can kill the most constructive and creative ways of dealing with tension. As soon as people feel exposed, their system reverts to automatic shutdown. It's a flight response. Sharing takes so much effort and courage, and so little to destroy it. Anyone can weigh in with their power in these situations. You can defend your peer's right to share without being judged, or you can make a sarcastic comment. But as with sharing, you have to feel safe to use your power. And this sense of safety has to be nurtured by the leadership and supported by the organizational culture.

We've come, then, to a major realization: Your VIPs may be very personal, but they are not independent. The organizational climate and the community context play a vital role in the construction and perpetuation of your VIPs. A climate of safety and support will enable you to be honest with yourself and explore the sources of inner struggles. That climate, in turn, will be determined partly by leaders and partly by your peers. Together, you all knit the safety net (I. Prilleltensky, Walsh-Bowers, & Rossiter, 1999).

The community context plays no less of a role. If you work for an agency that is not valued by the public, where the salaries are poor and the status is low, your personal interests will decidedly suffer. When you compare yourself to your neighbors, who are making more money and enjoying better benefits and higher respect, you will feel devalued. That feeling affects not only your self-esteem but also your health (Marmot, 2004). The way organizational and community VIPs promote or inhibit effective, reflective, and affective environments is the subject of the next two sections.

ORGANIZATIONAL VIPs

Organizations are made of people, but not only of people. Human beings develop traditions that outlive the individuals who created them. Embedded in these traditions are values and ways of dealing with power and personal interests. Rituals, ceremonies, myths, stories, habits, meetings, newsletters, and parties are all part of the organizational culture. The way issues are resolved is transmitted from old-timers to neophytes in water cooler conversations and over a beer (Tushman & O'Reilly, 2002).

Organizations have formal and informal structures to deal with VIPs and socialize newcomers. The former approach consists of mission statements invoking lofty values, personnel reviews to plan goals and objectives for the coming year, and codes of conduct to curtail abuses of power. However, the strength of these mechanisms often pales in comparison to informal networks, the grapevine, and conversations behind closed doors. The latter is a more powerful way to get the lay of the land than rules and regulations. You get to know an organization by spending time in meetings and shadowing people, as opposed to reading rule books.

How does your organization deal with VIPs? If you are a manager, what do you do to enable productive conversations about the potential conflicts within VIPs and between stakeholders? The answer to these questions reveals much about the sources of organizational well-being. Think about the ERA features of organizational well-being: effective, reflective, and affective environments. Being effective requires loyalty to organizational values of customer satisfaction, and being reflective requires consideration of how private interests might interfere with collective values; being affective, in turn, calls for the enactment of values such as caring, compassion, support, and growth. The achievement of ERA qualities results in meaningful engagement of workers in the life of the organization (Senge et al., 2004).

However, it's hard to achieve ERA status without achieving VIP conscience. Sustainable organizations attend to the tensions, create structures to deal with them, and empower workers to find unique solutions to their particular dilemmas. Top-down strategies alienate workers and create an imbalance between their values and their interests.

You're probably thinking of what you can do to foster a reflective culture, one that doesn't shy away from conflict, ambiguity, and uncertainty. It takes time to nurture a climate of exploration and reflection (Bridges, 2003, 2004). You can start small, with a few peers, sharing your own dilemmas around VIPs. Gradually expand it to involve more people, and use the I VALUE IT strategies described in Chapter 4 (more on this in Chapter 10).

With the advent of welfare reform in the 1990s in the United States, many social services had to change organizational goals, structures, and mission. They had to retool their workforce and get into the business of community development, instead of the traditional eligibility assessment. Some of these organizations had to reconsider their perceptions and expectations of clients and workers alike (Austin, 2004). Resistance to the changes derived in part from workers who developed an identity that had to be altered. In place of being the experts, they were now required to share power with clients. Successful adaptation required responsiveness to the VIP struggle of workers. Under the new philosophy, the value of empowerment seemed to undermine staff authority and affect their self-perception. From being experts, they had to morph into collaborators (Austin, 2004). Although most agreed with the new philosophy, few were untouched by the seeming reduction in status.

Ed embodied such a dilemma for us. He was a social worker at a community organization. He was not in welfare administration but in community outreach. Our project was about implementing a strength-based and empowering approach. Upon discussion of these principles, Ed proceeded to tell us that the organization had already been doing this for a long time, and that he had been personally involved in such efforts for over a decade. With time, we had occasion to see Ed in action. His demeanor was reflective of neither strengths nor empowerment; on the contrary, his approach emphasized deficits and gave clients no chance to express their views. He did all the talking; clients did all the listening. In his eyes, he was doing empowerment at all. In our eyes, he wasn't doing empowerment at all.

In another instance, the organization planned to conduct a drug prevention project with youth. Affirmation of SPEC (strengths, prevention, empowerment, and changing conditions) principles notwithstanding, the program reflected none of these tenets. Instead, it evolved into scare tactics and frontal lectures about the ills of addictions—more tough love.

Ed could not be easily challenged. He practiced tough love with his peers as well. He had leadership qualities and was an influential figure. But some of his private interests and beliefs were incongruent with the values of the project. His stature was threatened by the presence of external consultants (us), and his beliefs in tough love were undermined by the discourse of empowerment. He meant well, no doubt about it. But we disagreed profusely, and we couldn't talk about it because the culture of the place was one of silent discontent. There was plenty of VIP tension in his attitudes and within the team. We tried slowly and gradually to establish sufficient trust to address the contradictions. We were only moderately successful. Had the value of conflict resolution been held in high regard, we might have made progress faster. Had there been a tradition of sharing concerns, we might have averted passive resistance.

Our experience is not unique, however. When private interests are threatened, even mildly, organizational effectiveness declines, essentially due to preoccupation with face-saving. Instead of enacting collective values of community wellness, people enact barriers of self-protection. When dialogue is not the norm, reflectivity and affectivity suffer. Norms matter. Organizational practices that encourage value clarification, interest exploration, and power examination generate effective, reflective, and affective environments. As Lao Tzu said in about 600 B.C. "kindness in words create confidence, kindness in thinking creates profoundness, and kindness in giving creates love" (Elsdon, 2003).

COMMUNITY VIPs

People don't operate in a vacuum, nor do organizations. Community VIPs, in the traditional meaning of very important persons and in our meaning of values, interests, and power, exert considerable influence on organizations and the people influenced by them.

By way of illustration, consider a true case from the city of Ålborg, Denmark, as told by Bent Flyvbjerg (1998) in a fascinating tale of values, interests, and power. Over 2 decades ago, the city's planning department embarked on an ambitious project to reduce traffic accidents in the downtown area, to increase public transportation, and to reduce pollution. These were some of the values of the city planners and their political masters. Another key value was public input into the planning process itself. Such was the effort invested in public participation that the city won a prize for its innovative and inclusive approach. The planners' efforts, however, would soon encounter resistance from a titanic opponent, the 500-year-old Chamber of Commerce. The Chamber disliked the idea of preventing motorists from entering the business district. Leaders of the Chamber worried that this would diminish sales from wealthy Ålborgians. As a result, they mounted stiff opposition to the entire plan. They spared no effort in blocking the city's aspirations. In the end, only a portion of the city's plans were implemented.

The planning office had embraced collective values such as sustainability, health, clean environments, and public transportation. The Chamber, on the other hand, had promoted its own interests in selling high-priced goods to rich residents, in large disregard for those who used public transport. The values of the city collided with the interests of the Chamber. To resolve this conflict, both sides used their power and political muscle. The local newspaper sided heavily with the Chamber of Commerce because it owned an expensive piece of real estate downtown and didn't want prices to go down due to restricted vehicular access. The cyclists' association, on the other hand, supported the city, but its voice didn't carry much weight.

Figure 9.4 shows the zones of congruence, or lack thereof, among five players in the Ålborg saga. The local newspaper and the Chamber of Commerce share economic interests, as shown on the righthand side of the picture. On the lefthand side, we see considerable congruence among the planning department, elected officials, and the cyclists' association. Although elected officials supported their own staff for the most part, they didn't want to be seen as ignoring the opposition lest the newspaper and the Chamber interfered with their political futures. On the surface, at least, politicians attended to their concerns. By looking at the zones of congruence, you can understand what kind of coalitions were going on and who had to stretch the most to appear reasonable to all sides.

If we take the planning department as our focal organization, and the cyclists' association, the local paper, and the Chamber of Commerce as community voices, we can see that their influence is remarkable. Politicians, who mediated between community groups and the planning department, were also the subject of much pressure from these groups.

What's the lesson from Ålborg? A local organization, especially one concerned with the public good, is subject to multiple VIPs from external sources. Planners in Ålborg faced considerable pressure from politicians,

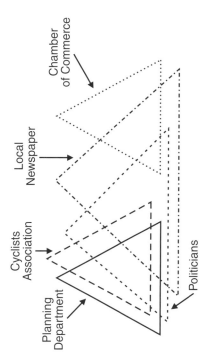

Figure 9.4   Zones of Congruence among Five Groups in the City of Ålborg's Urban Development Project.

Note: As in previous figures, the top of each triangle represents values, the lower left-hand corner represents interests, and the right side represents interests.

lobbyists, and the press. The well-being of their department was heavily taxed. They paid a price for standing up for what they thought was right.

If you are an executive director, you can think back to instances when the board of directors pressured you to move in directions you didn't think healthy for the organization. If you are a development officer, you can relate to instances when funding bodies wanted you to engage in activities that were not in line with your mission. The ways you resolve VIP conflicts have an impact on organizational well-being. If you cave in to pressures and acquiesce to unreasonable requests, you are not protecting the mission. On the other hand, if you totally ignore others' suggestions, you risk crucial support. Ultimately, your ability to negotiate community and organizational VIPs is essential for the well-being of the organization.

LINKED VIPs

Planners in the city of Ålborg were a cohesive bunch: They shared values, they were able to keep their private interests in check, and they all had a limited amount of power to see the project through to completion. They were highly invested in the well-being of their department and in its mission of public service. Nevertheless, their influence, which derived essentially from scientific and professional argumentation, was barely protected by their political masters and severely undermined by external forces. The team of planners, however, did not take conflict lightly. They devised strategies to make their point and to keep the project alive. They believed in their mission and spent many hours countering bogus claims with detailed evidence. From Flyvbjerg's (1998) accounts, we can tell that the planning department was effective, reflective, and affective. We can also surmise that there was a fair amount of VIP congruence within the team. Had the department been weak, it's quite likely that the assaults they endured would have destroyed, if not its stamina, at least its morale. That did not seem to be the case.

VIP LEADERSHIP

Leadership is not everything, as many contend, but it's a big part of organizational well-being. Leadership is a major source of organizational wellness or illness. Note that we talk about leadership and not singular leaders. Although each organization has a formal leader, there are many active informal leaders, and many more latent ones. You may not be your organization's formal leader, but you can play an informal leadership role. The more people who assume responsibility for the fate of the organization, the higher the chances that collective values will come to fruition.

You may not think of yourself as a potential leader, but if we reframe leadership in terms of active engagement, as opposed to just formal authority, you may begin to see yourself as a latent leader. It is true that there are many organizational barriers to inclusion and worker empowerment, but it is also true that there is a fair amount of surplus powerlessness (Lerner, 1991), that is, a self-prescribed diminution of power, above and beyond what actual circumstances might predict.

So, whether you are a formal or informal, actual or potential leader, there are some things you can do to promote VIP congruence within your organization. Based on previous work (I. Prilleltensky, 2000), we describe next four central tasks, along with their respective challenges and opportunities:

1. *First task: Clarify the position of the organization with respect to values for personal, organizational, and collective well-being.* A key role for leaders is to help the organization clarify its vision and values. Once that is achieved, they have to worry about maintaining equilibrium among personal, organizational, and collective well-being. Value clarification requires the engagement of relevant stakeholders. Participatory visioning encourages collective ownership (Maton & Salem, 1995; Racino, 1991; Senge, 1990). In such a process, we need balance between the principles arising from the group and the principles arising from moral reasoning. After all, it is possible for a group to primarily choose values for personal wellness and neglect the collective sphere. The group might, unwittingly perhaps, foster individualism instead of collectivism; given the prevalence of individualism in our culture, it wouldn't be surprising. If that were the case, it is up to the leader to suggest a more balanced approach.

Although leaders may be sincere in their desire to formulate a cogent set of values, their good intentions may be threatened by a number of risks. The first risk is to remain at a level of abstraction that makes for an internally coherent set of values but for a useless practical guide. Values have to be articulated in such a way that they can be translated into concrete policies. Table 9.1 provides some concrete suggestions.

Another risk is confusing personal preferences with morally legitimate principles (Becker, 1998). What workers and managers prefer is important, but it's not necessarily right. Values derive their legitimacy from grounded input, but also from moral philosophy. Unless they are morally defensible, statements of values amount to no more than preferences (Becker, 1998). Citizens are known to have wished on others reprehensible things, such as sterilization in the name of racial purity and segregation in the name of racial superiority. Collective opinion does not equate with moral practice.

2. *Second task: Promote a state of affairs in which personal power and self-interests do not undermine the wellness or interests of others.* This role entails, first of all, the development of leaders' awareness of how personal power and vested interests suffuse all aspects of their work (Boonstra & Bennebroek Gravenhorst, 1998). This awareness should spread throughout the organization. Workers and leaders should reflect on how their biases influence what they value for the organization, for themselves, and for the public at

Table 9.1 Guidelines for Promoting a Value-Based Organizational Culture

Values For	Guidelines
Personal Well-Being	
Self-determination	Promote the ability of workers and community members to pursue their chosen goals in life *in consideration* of other people's needs.
Health	Promote the physical and emotional well-being of workers and community members through acquisition of skills and behavioral change *in consideration* of structural and economic factors impinging on the health of the population at large.
Personal growth	Promote the personal growth of workers and community members *in consideration* of vital community structures needed to advance individual health and self-actualization.
Organizational Well-Being	
Accountability	Promote responsiveness to the community *in consideration* of the workload of your employees and their own needs.
Respect for diversity	Promote respect and appreciation for diverse social identities *in consideration* of the need for solidarity and the risk of social fragmentation.
Collaboration and democratic participation	Promote peaceful, respectful, and equitable processes of dialogue whereby citizens have meaningful input into decisions affecting their lives, *in consideration* of the need to act and not just avoid conflicts.
Community Well-Being	
Social justice	Promote fair allocation of bargaining powers, resources, and obligations in community and organization *in consideration* of people's differential power, needs and abilities.
Support for community	Promote vital structures that meet the needs of workers and communities in consideration of the risks of curtailing individual freedoms and fostering conformity and uniformity.

Adapted from "Value-Based Leadership in Organizations," by I. Prilleltensky, 2000, *Ethics and Behavior, 10*(2), pp. 139–158. Used with permission.

large. Awareness, however, is only a first step; the satisfaction of personal needs is also an important requisite. Workers are more likely to abide by collective values and norms when they feel looked after by the organization.

Research consistently points to the need for a safe space where workers and leaders can express their doubts without feeling judged (Goleman, 1998; I. Prilleltensky et al., 1999; Rossiter, Prilleltensky, & Walsh-Bowers, 2000; Weisinger, 1998). Professionals yearn for a space where they can dialogue with peers about their internal and interpersonal conflicts. An organizational climate of acceptance can foster such a dialogue.

Nevertheless, the process of balancing interests with values can be subverted in multiple ways. One way is developing a discourse that legitimizes self-interests: I deserve what I have because I'm smarter; I don't have to share power because other people don't know how to handle difficult situations; I can't really empower people who don't know how to help themselves; and so on.

Another potential subversion is the creation of spaces that don't challenge participants to change, but rather appease their guilty conscience. A safe space for sharing dilemmas can easily turn into a confessional; people are absolved of personal responsibility, and nothing changes.

It is not easy to temper personal power or vested interests. Serving others is an admirable goal, but it is forever plagued by personal interests. To enhance leaders' accountability, their efforts should be transparent. Nevertheless, leaders can use covert strategies to maintain unfair policies. There are many ways to support the status quo; ironically, sharing power is one of them. When power on minor issues is shared, the demand for power on major issues often diminishes (Bradshaw, 1998).

3. *Third task: Enhance the zone of congruence among communities, workers, and leaders.* The VIP model of leadership is based on expanding zones of congruence. First, leaders try to establish concordance among their own personal values, interests, and power. Second, they spread this process throughout the organization: They ask workers to do the same thing they did. Third, they try to enhance the zone of congruence among citizens, workers, and leaders. Unfortunately, this process can be easily subverted.

When consumers sense that their voice is minimally heard but maximally exploited for public relations, a great deal of damage is sure to follow. Adulterated consultations inflict deep wounds. These take months, if not years, to heal. But partnerships can also falter because of lack of skills, not only on the part of leaders, but also on the part of community members. Meaningful participation in advisory committees is not easy to achieve. Many community members lack the skills or confidence to make their views known.

4. *Fourth task: Confront people and groups subverting values, abusing power, or allowing self-interests to undermine the well-being of others in the organization or in the community.* Efforts to promote value-based practice notwithstanding, chances are that some people will behave in ways that undermine the vision and values of the organization. This is when leaders need to step in. In a climate of respectful debate, opposing parties can negotiate an agreement. But a healthy atmosphere cannot always avert disagreements.

Confrontation may be used for the good of the organization or for the good of the public, but it may also be used to suppress legitimate discontent. Leaders can use their power to silence opposition; yet, they can also refrain from necessary conflict. In an effort to avoid it, some leaders sweep under the carpet unacceptable behavior. Leaders, beware of hyper- or hypoconfrontational styles. Whereas the former may be a manifestation of anger, the latter may be an expression of fear. Better find a middle ground between these two extremes.

Table 9.2 summarizes the various roles, tasks, facilitating factors, potential subversions, and measures of accountability we just reviewed. Together,

Table 9.2   The Role of the Leader in Promoting a Value-Based Organizational Culture

Role of Leader	Tasks	Facilitating Factors	Potential Subversions	Measures of Accountability
1. Clarify position of organization with respect to values for personal, organizational, and community well-being.	Engage stakeholders in dialogue about ways to balance personal, organizational, and collective well-being.	Knowledge with respect to need for balance among values and with respect to process of consultation.	Confuse personal preferences with values and remain at level of abstraction without translating values into action.	Consult with others about limitations and contradictions in values selected.
2. Promote state of affairs in which personal power and self-interests do not undermine well-being or interest of others.	Develop critical self-awareness of how personal interests and social power suffuse leadership and may undermine collective wellness.	Creation of safe space for dialogue about value and ethical dilemmas.	Replace need for personal change with self-acceptance and/or distort values to coincide with narrow personal interests.	Subject personal and organizational process of consciousness-raising to scrutiny by other stakeholders.
3. Enhance zone of congruence among citizens, workers, and leaders.	Create partnerships among public, leaders, and workers.	Prolonged engagement in the organization and community and establishment of mutual trust.	Engage in token consultative processes that do not afford public meaningful input.	Create leadership structures with meaningful input and representation from various stakeholder groups.
4. Confront people and groups subverting values, abusing power, or allowing self-interests to undermine the well-being of others in the organization or in the community.	Engage in constructive conflict resolution with individuals or groups undermining vision and values.	Clear procedures for conflict resolution, and a culture of openness and critique.	Use power and legitimacy to confront people in order to suppress opposing views, or use conflict resolution to avoid excluding people from organization.	Subject to scrutiny of partners the efforts by leader to confront people and groups subverting vision and values.

Adapted from "Value-Based Leadership in Organizations," by I. Prilleltensky, 2000, *Ethics and Behavior, 10*(2), pp. 139–158. Used with permission.

these leadership functions nurture the type of value-based culture that is needed for organizational well-being.

ROWS FOR WELLNESS

Exercise 9: The VIPs of a Value-Based Culture

A value-based culture attends to values, obviously, but also to interests and power. In your view, how do VIPs influence the value-based culture of your organization? What are the risks, opportunities, weaknesses, and strengths of your organization when it comes to promoting a value-based culture? Think about VIPs under each of the ROWS and diagnose the forces inhibiting and enabling the emergence of a value-based culture. A risk may be that people talk a lot about values but neglect to consider power issues. An opportunity might be peer supervision where contradictions can be raised. A weakness might be a tradition of silencing discontent; an organizational strength might be the level of trust among your peers. Think also about the tensions among VIPs and the conflicts among different players in the agency. Then write them down in Form 9.1.

Each of the statements you made in Form 9.1 can be turned into an action. In Form 9.2, insert in the wellness readiness check below the ROWS statements and put a checkmark under the appropriate column. The profile will serve as a guide for planning and action.

Form 9.1   ROWS Exercise 9: The VIPs of a Value-Based Culture

Risks

Example: People in my organization don't talk about power issues because they are afraid of repercussions.

Opportunities

Example: We can use the next strategic planning session to discuss conflicts among VIPs within the organization.

Weaknesses

Example: My organization does not have clear values.

Strengths

Example: My team is very cohesive and I feel like I can talk about conflicts between my values and my personal interests.

Form 9.2   Wellness Readiness Check 9: The VIPs of a
Value-Based Culture

ROWS	1 I never thought about doing something about it.	2 I'm thinking about doing something about it.	3 I'm prepared to do something about it.	4 I'm doing something about it.	5 I've been doing something about it for some time.
Risks					
Opportunities					
Weaknesses					
Strengths					

10

How to Promote It? Strategies for Organizational Well-Being

In case of an emergency, you should put on your oxygen mask first and only then assist other passengers." You've heard that before, haven't you? This is what flight attendants tell you every time you fly. You can see the logic: It's hard to help other people when you're not breathing, isn't it? When you're bleeding, there is little energy left to aid others. Similarly, it's hard for organizations to achieve their external mission or goals when they are not doing well internally. You can't really provide excellent service when you're hurting, can you?

The way we see it, organizational well-being is a precondition for the promotion of community well-being. It doesn't mean you have to wait for years until your own house is completely in order. But at the very least, you should begin cleaning up your own mess as soon as possible. We've consulted with workplaces where workers felt so disempowered, alienated, deceived, or just plain discounted that it was hard for them to even concentrate on the external mission.

This chapter is about maximizing organizational well-being for the benefit of the people who work in organizations and for those who receive their services or products. Time and again, we encounter conflicts of interests and power differentials undermining the proclaimed organizational values. If you stop and think about the various agendas at play in your workplace, you will soon discover that power and interests obstruct the fulfillment of values. Which begs the question: What's the point of having values if power and interests are forever undermining them? The answer is that without values at all we have no compass. And without a compass it's a free-for-all. We are neither angels nor egoists all the time; most of us fall somewhere between. The surrounding conditions influence our behavior a great deal. If we can foster ecological alignment among values, interests, and power, as described in the previous chapter, we stand a good chance of working for the commonwealth as opposed to sabotaging or ignoring it. To approximate alignment, where the values and interests of workers, managers, employers, and clients alike are fairly congruent, we need specific strategies. We invoke in this chapter I VALUE IT strategies described first in Chapter 4. We apply them to identify the sources of organizational well-being, and to promote it as well. In our own language, we use I VALUE IT strategies to identify VIP (values, interests, and power) sources of organizational well-being and to foster ERA (effective, reflective, and affective) climates.

Figure 10.1 offers a bit of a road map to organizational well-being. We use I VALUE IT strategies to identify VIP sources of organizational well-being. Based on our VIP analysis, we choose the best strategies to create synergy among changes at the personal, organizational, and community levels. After all, organizational well-being depends on individual behaviors, structural changes within institutions, and community attitudes and support for the enterprise. New behaviors of workers and managers have to be reinforced by organizational policies and structures, just as much as innovative practices have to enjoy public support. When the three levels of change (personal, organizational, and community) work in unison, we have a good chance of effecting lasting improvements. When they don't, it's an uphill battle. The more synergy we achieve across levels, the better off we are.

Compare public support for government Medicare in Canada and Tennessee. In Canada a few years ago, the government was struggling with increased health care costs, as most nations around the world do. A series of hearings took place to study public attitude and sustainability. The Commission on the Future of Health Care in Canada (Romanow, 2002) made multiple recommendations, including support for health care providers and

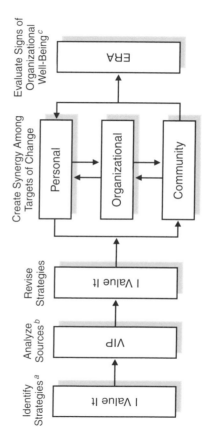

Figure 10.1 Steps in Promoting Organizational Well-Being.

[a]Strategies: Inclusive host, visionary, asset seeker, listener and sense maker, unique solution finder, evaluator, implementer, trendsetter.
[b]Sources: Values, interests, power.
[c]Signs: Effective, reflective, and affective environments.

their respective institutions. Fast-forward to Tennessee, where in 2005 a financial crisis precipitated the near collapse of the system and the elimination of any support for 323,000 people. Medical benefits were severely reduced for another 500,000 citizens. The public in Tennessee, which is tax averse, was fairly apathetic, and TennCare languished.

The level of community support makes a big difference for the quality of services and for the resources channeled to them (Hahn, 1994; Wineman, 1984). In Canada, health care providers benefited from the Commission's report and from public hearings. In Tennessee, with the exception of some activists, the community at large remained apathetic to the future of public health insurance. As a result, the funding for health care facilities diminished drastically. Community involvement makes a big difference in attitudes and support toward health and human services.

Or take the example of for-profit organizations in the late 1990s and the beginning of the century. For a while, communities allowed corporations to operate without much scrutiny or government regulation. When the Enron, Tyco, and WorldCom corporate scandals broke out, public sentiment changed and more regulations were put in place to avert similar crises (J. Bakan, 2004).

In the welfare system, reforms introduced by President Clinton in the 1990s transformed its philosophy, services, and ways of doing business (Austin, 2004). Staff in human services had to undergo training and learn a new way of serving the poor. They were expected to change roles, from eligibility assessors to career counselors, and in some cases to community developers. In short, what happens in the outside affects the inside.

Careful consultants and agents of change foster and monitor development at the personal, organizational, and community levels. The aim is to construct effective, reflective, and affective environments where organizational well-being can thrive.

Figure 10.1 summarizes the steps we describe in this chapter to promote organizational well-being. We start with strategies. We use selected letters, or roles, to analyze the dynamic interplay among values, interests, and power within the organization. Based on that diagnostic examination, reflected in the second column from the left, we revise our strategies (Tushman & O'Reilly, 2002). From the menu of options, we decide to do more listening, or more searching for assets. If all is well, we make sure we create trends to sustain organizational well-being. The context will determine the combination of strategies to use. Once we settle on the strategies, we try to influence individuals, organizational structures, programs and policies, and community attitudes and support at the same time. By having a multipronged approach, we increase the chances of making lasting changes. During and following the intervention, we want to see if signs of organizational well-being improve. The vital signs include effective, reflective, and affective practices. If we were successful, we would have enhanced organizational well-being, which, as defined in Chapter 8, consists of highly effective, reflective, and affective environments where workers, managers, and the community served by the organization have their needs met in ways that are congruent with the values of self-determination, personal growth, health, caring, and compassion; accountability, transparency, and responsiveness to the common good; democratic participation, respect for human diversity, support for community structures, and social justice.

I VALUE IT STRATEGIES

The first step in promoting organizational well-being is to have a strategy. As introduced in Chapter 4, we have a menu of complementary and sequential strategies. Captured in the acronym I VALUE IT, the strategies embody different roles for the agent of change:

- Inclusive host
- Visionary
- Asset seeker
- Listener and sense maker
- Unique solution finder
- Evaluator
- Implementer
- Trendsetter

Review Chapter 4 if you need a refresher on the specifics of I VALUE IT. Their merit will become apparent as we discern sources of well-being and devise interventions. To use our strategies, you can be an internal or an external agent of change—they work the same. Similarly, they can be used by frontline staff or managers. Remember our discussion on formal and informal leaders in Chapter 9? You don't have to be a formal leader to initiate change. Anyone can act as an inclusive host to invite input into organizational matters. Equally, anyone can be a visionary, asset seeker, or any of the roles embodied in I VALUE IT. At some point, if you are not a formal leader within the organization, you will need endorsement from upper management. But that's not necessary to start the process.

We can think of really only one prerequisite for using the strategies: believing you can make a difference. No small thing when you think about how much we have been conditioned to defer to leaders. But unless you try to make a difference, however small, you won't have an opportunity to see what you are really capable of. The only way to enhance self-efficacy is to try things out. Of course, support from others helps, but somebody has to get the ball rolling. If it's not you, nobody else might—a sure way to preserve the status quo.

STRATEGIES TO IDENTIFY VIP SOURCES

No amount of gadgetry will make your organization effective or reflective if you don't address tensions, especially tensions among values, interests, and power. Workshops, training, readings, software, and other resources are secondary to creating an environment in which people want to learn and where it's safe to express your view.

To get to the bottom of VIP dynamics, we need to start from the beginning: with the "I" for *inclusive host*. An inclusive host, you or somebody else, needs to use an existing space, or create a new one, where workers can express their values, interests, and power, probably in that order.

Let's start with values. Value clarifications are usually part of visioning exercises or strategic planning processes. If your organization is not clear about its values, that's the best place to start. What do people believe in? What are the preferred outcomes for the population they serve? As you'll remember from Chapter 3:

Values guide the process of working toward a desired state of affairs. These are precepts that inform our personal, professional, and political behavior. But values are not only beneficial because they guide behavior toward a future outcome, for they also have intrinsic merit. We espouse values such as self-determination and caring, not just because they lead toward a good or better society, but also because they have merit on their own accord.

Your organization may espouse the values of empowerment and compassion or social justice. Whatever they are, the very process of creating them builds ownership and meaning in the workforce. This is an exercise in big picture thinking. If properly done, and if properly followed up, value clarification can be your foundation for organizational well-being. On the other hand, if poorly done, and without follow up, it will foster cynicism in an often skeptical workforce (Senge et al., 2004).

You start the process as an inclusive host, but pretty quickly you need to enact other roles: *visionary* and *asset seeker*. Values are about a better future and a better present. As a visionary, you want to stimulate dreaming and hoping. What is the future we want to create? What role models can we use? Have others done this before? A visionary presents options of a better state of affairs but also encourages people to devise their own futures. The same applies to processes of collaboration. You can share knowledge from other workplaces where decisions are made more democratically or where workers feel more empowered, but ultimately, people have to own their process, and they have to decide what works for them (Maton & Salem, 1995).

To make those decisions, you invoke their existing skills. As an asset seeker, it's your job to recognize talent and build on existing resources.

Once you identify resourceful people or useful practices, you enlist them to your cause. Building on existing skills is a way of honoring what people already know and do well. It's a matter of respect. As a change agent, you need to make sure you capitalize on that.

The organization may very well have a coherent set of values and a cogent mission, in which case, you may want to explore whether it's been implemented effectively. If that is in fact the case, you act as *listener and evaluator*. You can help the process by reflecting on what values are being implemented and how. Remember, it's possible to have skewed values: those that privilege personal self-determination but neglect relational or collective well-being. Or the opposite: those that put so much emphasis on the collective that choice and personal control are sacrificed (Loewy, 1993). As an evaluator, listener, and *implementer*, it's your job to be attentive to the balance among the different values.

From values, let's move to interests. Talking about the former is safer than discussing the latter; our culture encourages the expression of values, but not of private interests. Although the entire capitalist system is built on the pursuit of personal interests (remember WIIFM?), it's deemed unrefined to talk about them openly. How often have you been to a meeting where the agenda was to talk about your personal interests?

We neglect private interests at our own peril. If we ignore them, they will come back to haunt us. It is simply unrealistic to expect workers to quash their personal interests for the good of the collective. A modicum of altruism is possible, desirable, and often present, but usually not enough to eliminate selfish pursuits. The way to deal with selfishness and egoism is not to wish them away, but to confront them and allow people an opportunity to express them without shame. The process of balancing private interests with collective values is always a negotiation. It is always liberating to say "I need this or that from this organization" or "My passion is this or that, and I need help" (Maslow, 1965). Against a background of repressive organizational decorum, it takes guts to open a dialogue about "what I want out of this." You shouldn't have to be heroic or foolish to suggest such a conversation. How can you get it started?

From the menu of strategies, a few come to mind. First, you literally have to *host* such a conversation, among trusted peers initially, and later on with a wider circle. You can also *envision* a state of affairs where values and interests are as congruent as possible. But if you *listened and evaluated* the situation, and it turns out that vast disagreement exists, within people and among teams, you will need to work on a *unique solution and implement it*. By definition, unique solutions defy prescriptions; they have to emerge from the process. You can certainly have input, but you'll need help from others. The constellation of factors enabling or inhibiting the expression of interests is usually complicated, and beyond what any one person can see.

The task of identifying conflict between values and interests is most delicate. People can be justifiably reluctant to talk about it with peers or superiors. In such a case, the role of inclusive host may be better served by an external consultant. Via interviews, focus groups, or anonymous surveys online, an external consultant can elicit information that internal agents of change usually can't; there is too much at stake sometimes. This is what we found out when we consulted with a number of organizations on a process of renewal. When staff had an opportunity to speak freely, they usually did so. When managers were present, self-censoring took place in a big way. The incongruence between appearance and reality is often striking. On the surface, many organizations look calm and serene, but underneath there are rivers of discontent flowing like rapids. A trusted external consultant can help in diagnosing the tension between values and interests and the discrepancy between appearance and reality. If you happen to be the external consultant, you would start the process as an inclusive host and move up the ladder of strategies as appropriate, until you get to work on *unique* solutions, *implement* them within the life of the organization, and establish a positive *trend*.

If talking about interests is uncouth, talking about power is a complete taboo, especially in autocratic cultures where you're not supposed to challenge leadership. The reasons for this silencing are complex. Fear of reprisal is an obvious one, but other explanations exist. Like the word *politics*, the terms *interests* and *power* are filled with negative connotations: dirty, corrupt, beneath me. No wonder people refrain from talking about them. I can be tainted by association if I get involved in politics or power issues (Bradshaw, 1998; Kershaw, 2005).

At the interpersonal level, many people just don't know how to confront those in power, or how to assert themselves. And many people in power just don't know how to take feedback. When you think about what's involved in naming power issues, who needs it? You might get reprimanded and accused of "seeing" things, or buying into the negative culture of politics. However, unless you talk about it or, at the very least, understand the power dynamics operating in your system, it will be hard to make progress toward VIP reconciliation.

One way or another, either as an internal or an external consultant, in open forums or anonymous surveys, it's vital to get a reading on how people feel about power issues in the organization. Are they resentful of upper management? Are they resentful of peers? Is there favoritism in the culture? Who is in and who is out in major decisions? Not long ago we discovered in an agency we consult with that organizational learning was going on in most teams, except the one with the least amount of power and the hardest jobs. We needed to democratize learning. As an external consultant, I (Isaac) could name the issue: the marginalization of an entire team. I had sufficient credibility with management and *wasn't* afraid to call it what it was: exclusion and elitism. It was the well-educated groups—the elite—who were benefiting from organizational renewal. The proletariat within the agency remained excluded.

As a *unique solution finder*, you won't be able to predetermine the course of action. Yet, once you identify dilemmas associated with power differentials, conflicts of interests, and discrepant values, you will be able to host conversations to normalize the situation and search for assets. It is possible to build on good, or at least civil relationships between management and workers. In fact, we would say that 90% of the solution lies in hosting a good process. Under propitious conditions, strengths are recognized, people are listened to, unique solutions emerge, and new trends are established. The hosting can take place in existing or new structures, such as staff meetings, confidential focus groups, peer supervision, retreats, or strategic planning sessions. Part of the solution is, in fact, finding the time and space to search for one. If you can get one concession from management, get them to free people to participate in this process.

By using I VALUE IT strategies, you can set a process in motion, nurture it, listen to all sides, create unique solutions, integrate them into the life of the organization, and start positive trends. Together, these strategies promise to open up previously illicit issues, liberate people from internally and externally imposed censorship, and enhance honest communication. Once you understand VIP dynamics, you can move on to influence individuals, organizational structures, and community forces to enhance organizational well-being.

This is what James Freedman did when he was appointed president of Dartmouth College in New Hampshire in 1987 (Gardner, 2004). The school was in dire need of improving its academic reputation. Freedman was the board of trustee's choice for the job. But everyone knew there would be opposition to his appointment, especially from the *Dartmouth Review*, the student publication and a bastion of conservatism financed largely by the Olin Foundation. Freedman was brought in to infuse intellectual vitality; the *Review* was more concerned with the football team and campus life. Freedman was the first Jewish president since the college's inception in 1822. Such was the opposition from the *Review* that vitriolic commentaries on his leadership were often published. Supported by the conservative *National Review*, students engaged in vicious attacks, including rumors that he and his wife had moved from the presidential mansion because it was not good enough for them. The student publication also attacked African American professors and compared Freedman to Hitler. With support from alumni, the *Review* engaged in constant provocation.

Freedman was advised to ignore the juvenile and offensive publication. This went on for months, until Freedman had had enough. He devised his own unique intervention: He decided to criticize the student publication at a faculty meeting. And to make sure everyone knew where he stood, he sent copies of his speech to national media. The *New York Times* and the *Wall Street Journal* picked up the story, as did CBS's television program *60 Minutes*. Freedman won support from several quarters, and the anti-Semitic and racist overtures of the *Review* subsided. Freedman had won on several fronts: The school's rank went up, the intellectual atmosphere improved, and entrance scores were much higher than before. To make sure he won faculty support, he created presidential scholar awards for academic excellence.

Dartmouth's case illustrates VIP conflicts on several fronts. Freedman's values of intellectual excellence were not shared by the student publication, which was more into the football team and the party scene. Not only were his professional and academic values assaulted by the narrow interests of the *Dartmouth Review*, but his personal dignity was as well. Various players threw their weight around: The board of trustees and the faculty were behind the president, whereas alumni, the Olin Foundation, and the *National Review* were behind the student newspaper.

Freedman used his power to reward faculty and students who embodied his values. Prizes and fellowships were used to recognize passion for intellectual pursuits. He used the resources at his disposal to undermine the influence of the *Dartmouth Review*, including access to national media. The organizational well-being of the college could not have been improved without close attention to VIP dynamics. Internal and external allies rallied on behalf of both sides, and something had to be done to temper the negative influence of the *Review* on the student body. Freedman went beyond damage control: He revamped an institution with some recalcitrant players whose values and interests he did not share.

The president devised his *unique solution*—denounce the publication in the national media—and instituted a new *trend*: academic rigor and intellectual vitality. He *listened* to all parties, *implemented* a strategy, and managed to turn the situation around. External indicators, such as national rankings and entrance scores, showed that his actions benefited the institution.

STRATEGIES TO CREATE ERA ENVIRONMENTS

To recap from Chapter 9, ERA stands for effective, reflective, and affective environments. It would be easy to prescribe recipes for making teams more effective—automation, accountability, and the like—but unless workers feel the changes are in line with their values and interests, the chances of success are small. Staff members need to be consulted; otherwise, resistance will surely take hold. Only a few days ago we heard from a group of employees that a restructuring imposed by management to make the operation more efficient resulted in high turnover and resentment. What seemed very rational to management looked very capricious to workers.

This is to say that technical solutions must be preceded by human solutions. VIP alignment deals with the human and psychological roots of organizational well-being. Imagine a tree: Its branches and fruit are only as strong as its roots. VIP alignment solidifies roots on which to build ERA environments. We maximize innovations when the workforce is not distracted by either discrepant values or interpersonal resentment. The best return on investment can be gotten when human potential is liberated from restraining forces such as abuse of power. The relationship of VIPs to ERA environments is analogous to that of the unconscious to the conscious: VIP dynamics, like the untamed unconscious, bubble up to the surface in uncontrolled bursts; unfinished business in the unconscious perturbs the quiet of the conscious. If conscious efforts to be efficient, amicable, and reflective are to endure at the surface, we have to domesticate the forces below the surface (Bion, 1961; Menzies Lyth, 1988, 1989).

Life is dynamic, however, and we never quite achieve organizational nirvana. In other words, the process of discovering the unconscious is a perpetual one. And it requires collaboration from multiple parties and entities. To achieve high levels of productivity, reflexivity, and affectivity, we need to work with individuals, structures, and bodies external to the operation.

Personal Change Leading to Organizational Well-Being

To achieve any sort of organizational development, you need to engage the leadership and the workforce. Bottom-up and top-down strategies are complementary, not mutually exclusive. If the organization is not living up to its values, you need to infuse some changes. Some of the changes you need to make are in people's minds. No small job, to be sure. Managers may ascribe to theory X, according to which workers are lazy and need tight control and supervision (McGregor, 1960). Workers, in turn, may blame clients for their problems. Hidden assumptions are deeply entrenched in people's minds. Changing their minds is part and parcel of improving organizational well-being, but how to do it?

Few people have studied this question more in depth than Howard Gardner. In *Changing Minds: The Art and Science of Changing Our Own and Other People's Minds* (Gardner, 2004), the Harvard professor delineates seven factors conducive to mind changing:

1. Reason
2. Research
3. Resonance

4. Re-descriptions
5. Resources and rewards
6. Real-world events
7. Resistances

Most of these are self-explanatory, but some require elaboration. Reason has to do with the use of logic and rational thinking in making an argument: You make your case by showing causality or the correlations among phenomena. Research complements reason: You find empirical evidence that supports your well-reasoned points. Resonance means that your point makes intuitive sense with the audience; they can relate to it because you have made it tangible and palpable for them. Re-description means the ability to express the same idea in different formats for different audiences; for example, you might use stories with one group and graphs with another, or you might combine several media to make your point more compelling. Resources and rewards are used to make a positive reinforcement. Re-sources and rewards are used to make a positive reinforcement. James Freedman, the president of Dartmouth College, used his resources to reward academic excellence. Real-world events are just that: daily occurrences that you can use to your advantage. When the *Dartmouth Review* compared Freedman to Hitler, it gave the president the excuse he needed to denounce the student newspaper in public. Finally, resistance is the force inhibiting the power of the foregoing factors. Through an examination of expert mind changers, from Gandhi to Clinton, Gardner (2004) demonstrates the powerful effect of combining these strategies.

To make sure we understand Gardner's (2004) theory, and know how to apply it, let's illustrate it with an example close to home. For most of my professional career, I (Isaac) have been trying to persuade professional helpers on the merits of a SPEC approach. As explained in Chapter 2, SPEC stands for strengths, prevention, empowerment, and changing conditions. My point is that focusing on strengths is better than focusing on deficits; that prevention is more efficient and humane than crisis management; that giving people voice and choice is more dignified than telling them what to do; and that changing conditions is often more effective than changing people one at a time. The rationale for this approach is described in detail in Chapter 2. As a frontline child psychologist for several years, I discovered firsthand the limitations of what might be called the DRAG approach: deficit-oriented, reactive, alienating, and guilt tripping (of parents and teachers especially).

I don't consider myself an expert at mind changing, not at all, but in retrospect, a lot of what I've been doing reflects Gardner's (2004) seven Rs. Over the years, I've been trying to perfect my case for SPEC, so that whenever I have an opportunity to talk about it I can maximize the effect. One such event took place soon after my arrival in Nashville. Scot Evans, my former doctoral student and now research partner, asked me to come to Oasis Youth Center and talk about my philosophy of mental health. Scot, who was a counselor at Oasis for many years, introduced me to the agency and its wonderful people. On February 25, 2003, Scot and I made our way from the Peabody Campus of Vanderbilt University to Oasis on 16th Avenue South. I had heard much about the agency and was looking forward to meeting its people.

I gave a powerpoint presentation that dealt, essentially, with SPEC. I showed graphs, I used empirical data, I told stories, used personal examples, and showed photos of myself standing next to the Broad Street pump we told you about in Chapter 2. I showed a picture of Venice and told them that individual efforts of residents would never stop their houses from sinking; the solution had to be a collective one. My talk was apparently quite effective in stimulating discussion. So much so that the agency wanted me to come back and begin a conversation about changing the way the Center did its business. At the time—I hadn't come up yet with the name SPEC—we called the new paradigm Webs of Wellness. Not only did I come back to talk to them, but I was introduced to the United Way of Metropolitan Nashville, where I proceeded to give a similar spiel. The United Way was quite taken with this approach, and they, in turn, took me to several agencies, where I repeated my dog and pony show about prevention, empowerment, and all the rest. Each agency, in turn, asked me for a repeat performance in front of their boards and funding agencies. And on and on it went. It got to the point where I could have done this speech in my sleep.

One interesting development was noteworthy, though. People in human services in Nashville started talking about the famous water pump. *Removing the handle* became a popular metaphor. The metaphor entered the local jargon and became part of human service lingo for prevention and changing community conditions. In due course, this series of speeches turned into a 3-year project to help health and human services move from ameliorative to transformative paradigms, from DRAG to SPEC.

Apparently, I had convinced some people and changed some minds about the merits of SPEC. Looking back, I realize that I had used all of Gardner's (2004) Rs:

- *Reason*: I made a logical case that no mass disorder afflicting human kind has ever been eliminated or brought under control by treating the affected individual. You don't eliminate child abuse, poverty, or HIV/AIDS by treating the victims; all that does, at best, is alleviate their suffering. You don't eliminate the problem in society by treating the people already affected by the problem because you're not getting to the root cause of the problem. If you follow this logic, you realize the limitations of counseling and therapy and begin thinking about prevention instead.
- *Research*: I made a second point based on empirical research. Even if therapists were successful 100% of the time with people afflicted by a certain psychological problem, there would never be enough therapists to look

after sick people. The demand for professionals would always exceed the supply. I also used research to show that well-designed and implemented prevention programs can successfully prevent child abuse, school problems, delinquency, welfare dependency, and other negative outcomes.

• *Resonance:* This one was not hard. People in health and human services know all too well the revolving-door syndrome and the long waiting lists. People are rarely "cured," and there are always more people waiting to be seen. My call for prevention resonated very well with workers. The Broad Street pump story also resonated intuitively with my audience. Instead of rescuing children and youth one at a time, it would be much more effective to get to the root cause of the problem.

• *Re-description:* I used multiple means to tell my story. I told stories from different parts of the world to make the point that you don't have to be rich to do prevention. I used international examples, graphic representations, inspirational stories, rhetoric, and pictures to advance my argument. When the United Way asked me to present my approach to their community investment board, I was trying to come up with a name that would resonate with them and fit the occasion. Their main task was to decide how to invest United Way funds in the community. Examining my own approach, I decided that "investing to SPEC" would fit the occasion indeed. After all, if you are going to invest, you want to do it intelligently and according to the best standards in the industry. That was the connotation I was trying to attach to SPEC. The name caught on, and it has since become shorthand for our approach to health and human services. The power of a name is quite remarkable. SPEC is now a symbol.

• *Resources and rewards:* I had no rewards to give my audience, but I did have resources, primarily in the form of bright doctoral students willing to invest in SPEC, so to speak. I also had knowledge of the research literature and was available for consultation and collaboration. We had only recently arrived in Nashville, and this looked like a great project.

• *Real-world events:* Tennessee does not do well by its children; every human service leader and professional knows this only too well. The grim reality of child abuse, homelessness, unemployment, teenage pregnancy, and depression hit home. Tennessee usually ranks among the lowest seven states in the country in its child well-being record (Kids Count, 2005). There was no question that time was of the essence, and something had to be done.

• *Resistance:* Lots of those, for sure. Even though many people showed initial enthusiasm for our ideas, some of them declined to participate, and some others found it difficult to implement the SPEC philosophy.

If you are charged with changing people's behaviors, attitudes, cognitions, and feelings about work, changing their minds is a good place to start (Burke, 2002). Gardner's (2004) strategies complement I VALUE IT roles very well. You can use them in combination. The seven Rs are well suited to help you become a visionary. Without a vision, it's hard to move people. But without organizational changes, individual transformations do not last.

Organizational Change Leading to Organizational Well-Being

Assume you've convinced a few key people that organizational change is needed. You've managed to enlist their support; they agree with your philosophy, and want to see it implemented. This is in fact what happened with several of our partners in the SPEC project.

The hard part is to transform organizational structures that can support the new approach. Unless the new paradigm is converted into new practices, its value is marginal at best. Put simply, organizational change entails the transformation of practices and policies for the operation to be in line with new priorities. Whatever the new philosophy happens to be, you want to make sure that it is implemented in an effective, reflective, and affective way. In other words, it has to improve productivity in the long run, involve an evaluative component, and engage people. Put simply, innovations must pass the ERA test: effective, reflective, affective.

Take the case of SPEC. We wanted our partner organizations to become more effective, to learn from the process, to be inclusive, and, of course, to be aligned with the SPEC philosophy. We knew we couldn't do it all at once, so we divided the project into four phases. Most project development theories use a variant of what we call CIID (Burke, 2002). It's a useful acronym to remember four typical phases:

1. Conception
2. Inception
3. Implementation
4. Dissemination

The CIID metaphor (pronounced *seed*) connotes progression from germination to fruition. Conception entails the thinking phase, wherein people contemplate an innovation. Inception is the beginning phase, when possibilities are explored and alternatives considered. Implementation is when we actually launch innovations, and dissemination is when we try out our lessons in new lands.

Figure 10.2 illustrates a plan for organizational change based on the four phases. Within the phases you can see four sets of players: two groups of promoters on the top part of the graph and two groups of beneficiaries at the bottom. The innermost section represents the key factors associated with change.

The inner line connecting the circles represents the relationships among the four groups of players. The words "sustain and evaluate" pertain to the

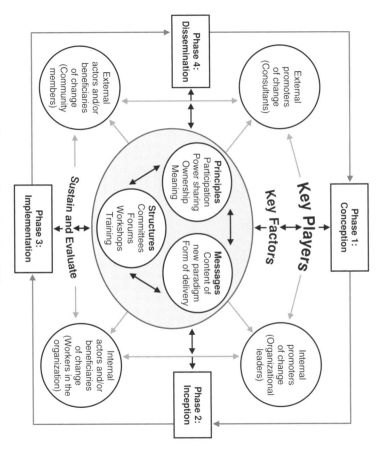

Figure 10.2 CIID Phases in Organizational Change.

entire diagram. The organizational intervention model includes several basic assumptions:

• The progression from one phase to the next is not entirely linear. Sometimes we need to go back and do more planning, even if we're already in the implementation phase. For each phase of the intervention to succeed (four phases in outer line), we need to pay attention to the contents of each circle in the figure and to the relationships among them (Burke, 2002). For example, we need to ask ourselves how well we're conveying the need for, and the contents of, a new paradigm in human services. We also need to consider to what extent we're being participatory, promoting ownership and meaning during the process, and also how involved the external actors are in each phase. Each element within the key factors circle can be translated into a question that can guide the intervention.

• The key factors influence and are influenced by the key players and the relationships among them. This is illustrated by double-headed arrows going from key factors to the relationships among key players.

• The roles of key players change during different phases. During the first phase, external promoters of change play a large role and external actors or beneficiaries a relatively small one. This can be illustrated graphically by enlarging or reducing the size of the circles of the various players.

• Each circle within the diagram is worthy of a diagram on its own. Within key factors, under principles, we need to understand how power sharing or lack thereof can affect participation and ownership of the process. Within the messages circle, we need to understand how the contents of the new, transformative paradigm we're trying to promote are communicated. We need to know how the form of the delivery interacts with assimilation of the content. Within the structures circle, we need to pay attention to the optimal structures that maximize participation without losing efficacy and accountability.

• The circles are interdependent. Each one satisfies a necessary but insufficient condition for the success of the intervention. A good and clear message about the new paradigm is wasted if there are no stable structures to sustain it. Stable structures, in turn, cannot foster ownership among workers unless they are participatory.

For an evaluator, there are several implications stemming from this plan:

• Each circle and the relationships among circles can be subjected to process and outcome evaluations. Remember that process evaluations deal with how we're doing our work, and outcome evaluations with the results of our work.

• Similarly, each phase needs to be subjected to process evaluations. We produce and deliver a summative evaluation at the end of the project; process evaluations need to take place along the way.

• To proceed with the process evaluation, we can take each circle within this overview map of the project and assess how well its factors are contributing to the intervention. For example, we can assess how participatory each phase of the process has been. Similarly, we can evaluate how well the different structures are working. If we have task forces within each organization, we can periodically ask participants for their view of the committee's effectiveness, processes, and the like.

Now that we're in a position to unfold a change process, we need a theory to make sure that our intended outcomes can be delivered by the action. We call this a *logic model*. Basically, we need to make sure that there is congruence among inputs, activities, outputs, outcomes, and impact, as demonstrated in Figure 10.3. Inputs are the resources going into a process of change. Activities are the actual innovations we undertake. Outputs are the observable changes deriving from the activities, and outcomes are the eventual results. The difference between outcomes and impacts are that the former are fairly specific and the latter quite general. The first two columns represent our planned work, and the last three denote our intended results.

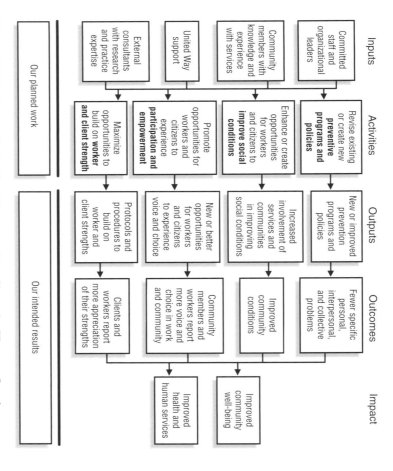

Figure 10.3 is an illustration from our SPEC project. It is highly advisable to spend time doing this kind of exercise before launching any kind of innovation (Tushman & O'Reilly, 2002). A disconnect between intentions and resources can be as fatal as incongruence between activities and outcomes. Bottom line: Take time to plan.

During any phase of the CIID cycle, and in any part of the logic model, you can, and probably should, use I VALUE IT strategies. The multiple interactions with partners require a lot of inclusive hosting, asset searching, and listening. The logic model requires visioning and evaluating as well as implementing. The whole process calls for unique solutions, and the dissemination phase is all about trendsetting.

Whereas the conflicts among values, interests, and power highlighted the political aspects of change processes, and the environmental qualities of organizations its desired outcomes, this section emphasized the technical aspects of change. The previous section focused on mind changing, this one on institution changing. Attention to the rational elements of change complements inquiry into its unconscious currents. To get a more complete picture of organizational well-being, we also need to understand the social context.

Figure 10.3 Logic Model for Changing Paradigms in Human Services.

Community Change Leading to Organizational Well-Being

Health and human services can be only as good as the support they get from the public. And the support they get from the public is only as good as the dominant ideology. Day in and day out our local newspaper, the *Tennessean*, is replete with calls to reduce taxes, eliminate taxes, reduce services, eliminate services. Just last week there was a campaign by the local Republican Party to commit politicians to a pledge not to raise taxes after the upcoming state election. This week we read some confessions about how people feel about the poor who are going to be cut from the state Medicare program, TennCare. A candid woman, Bev Chandler, shares her opinion with a reporter. In her view, many of the TennCare enrollees "are people who have fallen ill because of poor lifestyles choices such as smoking cigarettes, drinking too much alcohol or overeating." She goes on to say that "it's probably not a nice thing to say, but it's true" (Wissner, 2005, p. 2A). Like her, dozens of others flood the newspaper with accusations that the poor are to be blamed for their misfortune. In Tennessee at least, this is a prevalent discourse. It permeates politics, economics, and social issues. With such a predominant mentality, public officials struggle to get sufficient funding for state agencies. Many of them are under siege, surrounded by pundits and mavericks intent on eliminating public support for the needy. This local example is reproduced across the United States and across the world hundreds of times every day. What the community thinks matters, for better or for worse.

To get communities to support communal endeavors, such as health and human services, we need to radically oppose the radical individualist agenda that would dismantle any kind of public assistance to disadvantaged groups. Chapter 3, on values, already deconstructed these and other myths. Suffice it to say here that it's challenging, to say the least, to embark on efforts to enhance the common good when the popular sentiment is all for more money in your pocket and fewer services. Chandler thinks that she "should not be required to continue to subsidize the medical care of people who have not taken their own health seriously" (Wissner, 2005, p. 2A). In a sweeping generalization, she goes on to condemn a vast number of people who, for different reasons she does not know about, require TennCare. But she is certain that she should not subsidize others. Welcome to Tennessee.

With meager resources, there is only so much local authorities can do to promote health and prevent disease. Yes, systems can always be made more efficient, but there is a ceiling effect. Unless you collect more taxes (in Tennessee there is no state tax, only a sales tax that requires the poor to pay as much as the rich for every purchase), there won't be a possibility to invest in health infrastructure and support. And if you don't invest, you don't collect.

Ms. Chandler epitomizes for us the voice of the community. Multiply her voice by several thousands, and you get great animosity for any kind of shared ownership of collective health and well-being. To obtain the resources you need to run health and human services properly, you have to bolster public support for it. Coalitions, political campaigns, needs assessments, and public outcry are all valid and legitimate ways to build support for institutions entrusted with the common good. Professionals in these sectors have a responsibility to look beyond the provision of direct services, for if they neglect the big picture, pretty soon they won't have a job to help others, or help themselves either. We explore in the next section of the book the intricate task of community change writ large.

Linked Changes for Organizational Well-Being

This chapter called attention to the interactions among personal, organizational, and community change. To change public opinion to enhance funding for human services, you need to change minds. To change minds, you need a communication strategy (Bales & Gilliam, 2004). A strategy can use I VALUE IT tactics and the various techniques encapsulated in Gardner's (2004) seven Rs: reason, research, resonance, re-description, rewards and resources, real-world events, and resistance. These tools can be used to effect change at the personal, organizational, and collective levels. These dimensions are so interdependent that unless we tackle all of them in concert, we risk failure. You can slice processes of change in thirds: individual, organizational, and collective. The more you give to each of them, the higher the chances of creating lasting and meaningful changes. This is how synergy works (Capra, 1996, 2003).

ROWS FOR WELLNESS

Exercise 10: Multilevel Change

Think of a change you want to introduce in your workplace, school, or voluntary association. Think of the various ROWS involved at the personal, organizational, and community levels. Based on the strategies, techniques, and steps reviewed in this chapter, consider how people, organizational structures, and community opinion may react to your change. Outline in Form 10.1 ROWS for each one of these levels. Later on, you will transfer them to the Wellness Readiness Check.

To create a plan of action, transfer the various ROWS to Form 10.2. You may surprise yourself and realize you're already doing several things to make your desired change happen. Or you may realize that you need more help. If most of your items are under column 1, you should consider getting together with a trusted colleague or friend and start devising a strategy.

Form 10.1   ROWS Exercise 10: Multilevel Change

Risks for the change I want to introduce
Personal level
Organizational level
Community level
Opportunities for the change I want to introduce
Personal level
Organizational level
Community level
Weaknesses at various levels for the change I want to introduce
Personal level
Organizational level
Community level
Strengths at various levels for the change I want to introduce
Personal level
Organizational level
Community level

Form 10.2 Wellness Readiness Check 10: Multilevel Change

ROWS	1 I never thought about doing something about it.	2 I'm thinking about doing something about it.	3 I'm prepared to do something about it.	4 I'm doing something about it.	5 I've been doing something about it for some time.
Risks					
Personal					
Organizational					
Community					
Opportunities					
Personal					
Organizational					
Community					
Weaknesses					
Community					
Organizational					
Personal					
Strengths					
Community					
Organizational					
Personal					
Community					

IV

Community Well-Being

Different countries have different strengths. We open Chapter 11 with a comparative analysis of well-being across countries. The entire chapter deals with signs of community well-being, so it is appropriate to discuss what other countries have to offer by way of social policies, child abuse legislation, family support, and a host of practices that enhance community well-being. What we find is that equality figures pretty high as a correlate of well-being. The more egalitarian a country is, the better its health.

We explore next in Chapter 12 three key determinants of communal well-being: poverty, power, and participation. These three Ps are pretty powerful sources of health and well-being at a large scale.

In Chapter 13 we draw a distinction between ameliorative and transformative interventions in the community. We compare and contrast the civil rights movements with local community efforts to alleviate suffering.

Throughout the chapters we discuss the importance of developing critical consciousness, critical experiences, and critical action to overcome oppression and exploitation. We claim that critical consciousness about power, poverty, and participation is a necessary but insufficient condition to bring about transformative action; critical experiences are also required. In the absence of critical experiences that move you, upset you, and motivate you, it's hard to convert the fruits of critical consciousness into critical actions.

11

What Is It? Signs of Community Well-Being

Assume you had to choose between living in a country that was very rich but that had a fair amount of inequality, and a country that was not as rich but had a fair amount of equality. In the former country, you don't pay a lot of taxes; in the latter you do. Both are developed countries, both belong to the Organization for Economic Cooperation and Development (OECD), and both are technologically advanced. Two questions for you: Where would you choose to live? Where do you think you might be better off?

Not so fast, you say. Being the rational person that you are, you want more information before you make a decision. To begin with, you want to know where you belong in the social ladder. If you are rich, you may choose to live in the richer society, so you don't have to pay a lot of taxes and you can enjoy your riches to the fullest. But if you happen to be poor, the picture might change. You may want to live in the more egalitarian society so you don't feel the blows of inequality so much.

Alternatively, you may choose to live in the more egalitarian society, even if you knew that you could be richer in the richer country, and even if you knew that you would be paying more taxes. You are an egalitarian type, you are willing to give up some of your own wealth in the form of taxes, and you like the possibility of contributing to the well-being of others in the community.

To break the suspense, let us tell you that on average, developed countries that are more egalitarian produce longer lives and better health outcomes for the population on a number of indicators (Marmot, 2004; Wilkinson, 2005). If you had a choice, you could move to a place where the quality of life is higher than where you live now. But unfortunately, for many people there is no choice.

Moving among countries is not an easy proposition. Immigration laws being what they are, moving to the most desired countries is not that simple, especially if you happen to be poor or uneducated. For a great many people, this is a moot point. But there is a point to this exercise, and it is this: We need to think about what kinds of social arrangements are more beneficial to well-being and what type of societies are healthy and friendly. What can we learn from other societies?

The July 26, 2005, international edition of *Newsweek* magazine had an article entitled "The Best Countries in the World." In it, Jeffrey Sachs, director of Columbia University's Earth Institute, claims:

While big countries like the United States like to tout their achievements, it is the smaller nations of northern Europe that can boast the greatest success in solving the problems of balancing competition and cooperation, capitalism and social security. Consider just about any social indicator—income per capita, health, democracy, economic competitiveness, environmental consciousness, honesty—and the Nordic world of Iceland, Norway, Denmark, Sweden, and Finland is sure to shine. These are small countries with homogeneous populations. Their incredible successes are sometimes easily put aside as "special cases." Yet they have much to tell bigger nations about paths to the good life.

Being the skeptic that you are, however, you ask: How does Sachs know that these are the best countries in the world?

For years the U.N. Development Program has measured human progress by including measures of literacy and life expectancy alongside per capita income. On the combined Human Development Index, Norway and Sweden ranked first and second in 2004 out of 175 countries, with the United States coming in eighth, and the larger countries of continental Europe ranked in the teens. Nordic health and wealth build on high-quality governance. These are also the countries where corruption finds zero tolerance. The global-corruption watchdog Transparency International ranks Finland, Iceland, and Denmark right at the top of the list of the world's "cleanest" governments. France and Spain are tied for 23rd. (Sachs, 2005)

Now the obvious question: How did they do that?

Broadly speaking, the Nordic region took three basic decisions. First, it prioritized education—study and science. Second, it decided that it would leave no countryman behind. Social insurance—pensions, public health care, public education—became a basic shared commitment in each of these countries. And third, the region built a vigorous private sector. Ericsson and Nokia are not government creations. Outsiders predicted that the Nordics' high tax rates would stifle their private sectors, but the region has an enviable record not just of innovation but of wringing profits out of high-tech breakthroughs. And while these countries benefit from natural resources—fish, oil and gas, timber, iron ore—they do not rely on these resources for their long-term economic future. Iceland does not merely sell fish to the world. It sells know-how about sustainable fisheries management. The beauty of globalization is that every corner of the world can learn from the others. A little less ideology, and a little more openness to the ideas adopted by the Nordic states, would do us all a world of good. (Sachs, 2005)

Before you experience an upsurge of nationalism and begin to recite the well-worn arguments that they are exceptional cases, we ask you to keep an open mind. Stick with it a little longer. In this chapter, you will see not only the benefits of egalitarian societies, but also the benefits of social cohesion in different parts of the United States, so that if you are ever presented with a choice, you could make an educated decision about where to move. In general, this chapter is about what is a healthy community, and how you would know it if you ever saw one. To start, let's offer a working definition of community well-being.

Community well-being consists of physical, geographic, cultural, economic, political, and psychosocial environments where community members have their needs met. Healthy communities meet the needs of their constituents in ways that are congruent with certain values: self-determination, freedom, personal growth, health, caring, and compassion; accountability, transparency, and responsiveness to the common good; collaboration, democratic participation, respect for human diversity, support for community structures, and social justice. Another mouthful! Sorry.

The immediate implication of this definition is that we have to foster certain kinds of environments for people to have their needs met and for them to thrive. This definition enables us to make comparisons across communities, regions, and countries. Take, for instance, the economic environment. Some countries are richer than others; others are poorer but more egalitarian. Which model is the best? What's the best option: to be rich or to be egalitarian? Is there a third option? Can you be both egalitarian and rich? This is pretty much the case with Nordic countries, as Sachs (2005) argues. They are fairly wealthy, but egalitarian at the same time. Sweden, for instance, one of the most egalitarian countries on earth, boasts also one of the best life expectancy records. But if you happen to live in Norway or Sweden, your taxes are likely to be double what you pay in the United States. Yes, you'd pay lots of taxes, but you'd also get free university education and free health care for all, not to mention extended paid maternity or paternity leave and very reasonable unemployment insurance. As you can see, there are many facets to community well-being, including some trade-offs as well. Let's unpack a little of the benefits and disadvantages of different social configurations.

Following the moral philosopher John Stuart Mill (2001), we're interested in the greatest good for the greatest number of people. And, also like Mill, we assume that each person counts for one and not more than one, meaning that everyone in society deserves the same treatment and opportunities. Feudal notions that peasants should sacrifice to honor the king and the queen bestow more dignity on royalty than on the rest of us and are fundamentally immoral. If we all count the same, and if we seek to maximize well-being for the largest possible number of people, we are bound to reject some social orders, such as feudal ones, and we are bound to prefer some others. To determine which environments are preferable, we need to understand a little better what they do to people. In this chapter, and the next, we discuss the signs of community well-being at the personal, organizational, and collective levels, as well as their respective sources. But before we delve into the personal, organizational, and communal signs, we need to attend to two major reflectors of community well-being that influence all the rest: inequality and privilege.

SIGNS OF INEQUALITY, SIGNS OF PRIVILEGE

It won't surprise you to hear that poor people usually live shorter lives than rich people. It also won't surprise you that poor people are usually more vulnerable to a whole host of risk factors than are wealthy people (Hofrichter, 2003). What may surprise you is that the difference in levels of well-being and quality of life continues even within the upper echelons. The difference in life expectancy, for instance, is not merely between rich and poor, but also between rich and richer. The higher in education, income, and social status you are, the better off you'll fare in terms of health and well-being. This is rather unexpected. You would predict that people with nice houses, good income, and higher education would be just as healthy as their neighbors who have slightly higher job status and a higher graduate degree. After all, what difference does it make for health if you live in a three- or four-bedroom house, or if you have a PhD? As long as families are well housed and adequately clothed, why should a PhD matter? As it turns out, social status matters—a lot actually. Apparently we compare ourselves to our neighbors constantly, and the more they get, the lesser we feel, and the lesser we feel, the worse our health becomes. Conclusion: It is not only material wealth that matters for well-being, but psychological perceptions of inequality as well. Michael Marmot (2004), whom we met in Chapter 1, calls this condition the *status syndrome*.

Why, asks Marmot (2004, p. 3), "should educated people with good stable jobs have a higher risk of dropping dead than people with a bit more education or slightly higher job status?" He goes on to ask why "living in a four-bedroom house [should] be better for your health than living in a clean, dry, warm, three-bedroom apartment? Why should someone with a master's degree have a longer life expectancy than someone with a bachelor's?" These questions open Marmot's fascinating odyssey into social inequality in his book *The Status Syndrome: How Social Standing Affects Our Health and Longevity*. After 25 years of research, Marmot was able to answer these questions. "For people above a threshold of material well-being," he claims, "another kind of well-being is central. Autonomy—how much control you have over your life—and the opportunity you have for full social engagement and participation are crucial for health, well-being, and longevity" (p. 2).

If you imagined a continuum of social status, going from very low to very high, you'd discover that for people above the material threshold Marmot (2004) talks about, differences continue to exist all the way to the very end of the spectrum. Those below you are expected to suffer more ill health than you, and those above you are expected to do better. Marmot calls this phenomenon *the social gradient.*

To illustrate how social hierarchy impacts life expectancy, Marmot (2004) invites us to take a short subway ride from the southeast of Washington, DC, to Montgomery County, Maryland. "For each mile traveled, life expectancy rises about a year and a half. There is a 20-year gap between poor blacks at one end of the journey and rich whites at the other" (p. 2). The social gradient demonstrates not only the difference between people at opposite ends of the ride, but also the difference between each subway stop. In other words, the status syndrome is about degrees of difference. Although the widest gap in life expectancy is between the first and the last station, life gets longer with each stop. It is not just a difference between first and last, but also between those who live close to each other. This is why it's called a gradient. Marmot explored this phenomenon within and across countries. Wherever he looked, he found it.

In wealthy countries, psychiatric conditions, diabetes, chronic respiratory disease, violence, and accidents "all follow a social gradient—the lower the ranking in society, the higher the risk" (Marmot, 2004, p. 6). That means that you and I are affected by it. It is not a phenomenon that happens in remote countries; it happens right here in North America and in other industrialized countries. It happens pretty much wherever there is inequality.

To a large degree, these negative results occur because people compare themselves to others, and relatively speaking, they feel diminished by the wealth and success of others. You may be tempted to conclude that negative outcomes beset only those people who are silly enough to compare themselves to their wealthier neighbors, but the truth is that it happens to most people. When Marmot (2004) compared the health and longevity of thousands of people, including the population of entire states and countries, he confirmed the status syndrome, which may lead you to the conclusion that we are all silly people because we worry about how green our lawn is and because we care about such things as control and participation in social life. Be that as it may, there is something very real here worth paying attention to.

The status syndrome isn't something that happens only to control freaks or to people obsessed with social status. If it happens to entire populations, as it does, there is something going on in the very environments where people live. Indeed, according to Marmot (2004, p. 6):

The causes of the social gradient in health are to be found in the circumstances in which we live and work; in other words, in our set of social arrangements.

That is important. It is not the calamities that most determine well-being, but the way we go about our daily lives, in offices, banks, factories, houses, and neighborhoods. It is about the fact that control over life circumstances and full social engagement and participation in what society has to offer are distributed unequally, and as a result health is distributed unequally. . . . The psychological experience of inequality has profound effects on body systems.

In a double punch that is hard to match, Richard Wilkinson (2005), Marmot's collaborator, marshals overwhelming evidence on the negative repercussions of hierarchies in his new book *The Impact of Inequality: How to Make Sick Societies Healthier*. Both books by Wilkinson and Marmot make the point that inequality has both material and psychological consequences, and that social standing affects not only the poor, but all of us. As Wilkinson put it, "Although each person has his or her unique psychology, we are all affected by circumstances, by common patterns of meaning in our society, and by impact of social structures on our emotional and psychological life" (p. 60).

The social gradient affects the psychology of individuals, the culture of organizations, and the norms and policies that communities and governments put in place. Indeed, many of the signs at the personal, organizational, and community levels that we shall explore here are related to signs of inequality and privilege.

PERSONAL SIGNS OF COMMUNITY WELL-BEING

The well-being of a community is reflected in personal and family life. There are definite markers of social well-being in the way we conduct our lives, how we treat our children, and where we look for growth opportunities. A very objective indicator of community health is how long people live in different countries and in various neighborhoods within regions. These markers fall into four categories of personal signs: early life development, life span development opportunities, lifestyle, and life expectancy.

Early Life Development

Some neighborhoods across the United States have much higher levels of infant mortality than others do. In the city of Milwaukee, for instance, infant mortality rate (IMR) for African American children in 2003 was 15.9 per 1,000. Compared to the national average of 6.9 or the local rate of 5.8 for Whites, African American babies are dying more than twice and close to three times as often. In Nashville, our situation for African American babies is even worse. The discrepancy in IMR for African American and White babies was approximately 3.7 in the year 2000 in the Music City. Only San Diego had a worse discrepancy rate, at 4.5 times more African

American infants in a survey of big U.S. cities (City of Milwaukee Health Department, 2005).

Premature death is only the most dramatic instantiation of poor community well-being in the life of an infant. Another physical manifestation is birth weight. Low birth weight has been associated with myriad problems later in life, including cognitive, emotional, and physical complications. The risk of diabetes increases dramatically with lower birth weight. Compared to those who had a birth weight of 4.3 kg or higher, men age 64 whose birth weight was 2.5 kg or lower had a sevenfold increase in risk of diabetes (Barker, 1998).

In addition to these physical manifestations of health early in life, there are a series of influential psychological signs of health and well-being. Pre- and postnatal levels of parental stress, as well as bonding, attachment, and cognitive stimulation during early life, are crucial for development in infancy. Children whose parents are more relaxed and spend time bonding with them and nurturing a secure attachment develop much better than those whose parents lived in stress and were too worried about money, debts, or addictions (Barker, 1998; Shonkoff & Phillips, 2000).

At this point, you might think that these are not signs of community well-being, but rather of personal or family well-being. But, as Wilkinson (2005, p. 100) notes, "Individual characteristics are rarely, if ever, the explanation of why one society has 2% unemployment and another 20%, or why one society has less than two homicides per hundred thousand population while others have ten times that rate."

It is true that many of these negative signs are more highly concentrated in certain families, but these families, in turn, are more concentrated in certain communities. The fact that certain cities attend better to their disadvantaged communities and attain higher levels of well-being and lower levels of death and disease says something about the community as a whole. "If we want to understand why a larger or smaller proportion of the vulnerable run into difficulties, we must understand how the wider economy and social structure damage more people in one society than another" (Wilkinson, 2005, p. 100).

As a society, we should strive to minimize child abuse and child poverty, and we should aim to maximize bonding, early stimulation, and secure attachments. These are positive signs of early life development that last a lifetime.

Life Span Development Opportunities

Another sign of community well-being is the opportunities people have to continue their journey of lifelong learning, spiritual development, and meaningful engagement. Opportunities are not distributed equally among the population. Those with adequate preparation go on to college or land jobs with prospects of advancement and stimulation. Those without preparation or resources cannot afford the luxury of higher education.

Meaningful engagement in arts, sports, spirituality, work, volunteer positions, or recreation enhances one's sense of control, civic participation, and overall satisfaction (Marmot, 2004; Putnam, 2000). The more opportunities for meaningful participation a community affords, the better off its people will be. Commitment to a cause and passion for a pursuit are both intrinsic and extrinsic goods. They are innately rewarding at the same time that they advance an external goal. Granted, not all collective pursuits are for the common good, as in participation in the Ku Klux Klan, but this is not a reason for avoiding participation in communal affairs. Rather, it is a cause for engaging in causes and pursuits that promote justice and equality. As Putnam has amply demonstrated, participation in civic pursuits has declined dramatically in the United States in the past 3 decades. People are participating less in the common good and more in solitary activities like shopping.

With declining civic duties and ever ascending consumerism, people spend more time in front of the tube and browsing in shopping malls. The negative impact of consumerism on personal development cannot be underestimated. As B. Schwartz (2004) has persuasively argued in *The Paradox of Choice: Why More Is Less*, more and more people spend more and more time shopping and comparing themselves to their neighbors in an endless treadmill of consumption that robs people of satisfaction and opportunities to engage in meaningful pursuits. Under the guise of exercising your own choice, people expend inordinate effort finding the right clothes, cars, life insurance, health insurance, and even vacation packages that suit them.

In some tribal communities, people worried about food and survival. In some instances, there were very few choices in life: hunt and eat or starve. Anthropologist Robert Edgerton (1992) documents the immediate concern with survival of remote tribes in Africa and South America. Personal development could not enter the realm of possibility for some of these hunters. The incredible irony is that we now live in an era of plenty where instead of being consumed by scarcity we are consumed by goods. Life was supposed to get easier and simpler with technology and the availability of food, clothing, and shelter, but in a paradoxical twist of fate, we have become slaves to abundance. "In the past few decades," B. Schwartz (2004, p. 23) argues, "that long process of simplifying and bundling economic offerings has been reversed. Increasingly, the trend moves back toward time-consuming foraging behavior, as each of us is forced to sift through more and more options in almost every aspect of life." As a result, there is less and less time to dedicate to spiritual pursuits and personal development that matter.

But wait a minute, you say. Who are you, or who is Schwartz, for that matter, to determine that shopping and consumerism is not a viable method of personal development? Judging by the numbers, it seems to be an appealing pastime. Some have even called it a national sport. You have the right to question our judgment, and of course Schwartz's, but you're not going very far with the argument that because many people do it, it must be good. Quantity does not replace quality. The question to ask is not how many people do it, but what it does to those who engage in it. Let's explore this a bit further.

Lifestyle

Contrary to popular opinion, more choice is not always better. "Having too many choices produces psychological distress, especially when combined with regret, concern about status, adaptation, social comparison, and perhaps most important, the desire to have the best of everything—to maximize" (B. Schwartz, 2004, p. 221). You might say that these ills affect only a few people who don't know how to enjoy the benefits of choice—too bad for them. Well, Schwartz documents that this is not just a fringe group obsessed with perfection. Rather, it is a cultural phenomenon penetrating every corner of society and every soul. It is the norm and not the exception. Like it or not, we are social and gullible animals who pay attention to commercials and fashion. We compare ourselves to the Joneses, and we never cease to want what others have. When we discover that our choices have not made us lastingly happy, we blame ourselves for making the wrong choice, and back we are in the saddle, galloping toward better choices—only to find out that it is an endless treadmill of choice. Choice is no longer serving us; we are serving it.

B. Schwartz (2004) makes the compelling point that an overload of choice contributes to dissatisfaction, primarily through comparisons we make. We compare experiences against three main criteria:

1. What we hoped it would be like
2. Other experiences we had in the recent past
3. Experiences others have had

The constant comparisons in which we are engaged, fostered largely by commercialism, suck us dry. We are never quite satisfied because there is always something new to be tested, or because the Joneses have tried something exotic we ought to taste. One way or another, people in rich countries have developed a consumerist lifestyle that depletes instead of enriches our lives. As material prosperity has more than doubled in the past 30 years, the proportion of people reporting happiness and satisfaction with their lives has been steadily declining (B. Schwartz, 2004). If happiness is a measure of well-being, or at least a very good proxy for it, we have to consider what consumerism and choice are doing to it. Schwartz recommends moderation and temperance, not choice, as indicators of a sane lifestyle.

Besides shopping, there are other markers of well-being. The amount of stress is also a telling sign. Although manifested in high blood pressure and immune system deficiencies, stress originates in social and psychological circumstances. Often, stress derives from not having sufficient control over these very social and psychological events. Persistent stress can result in vulnerability to infections, diabetes, heart attack, stroke, aggression, depression, and high blood pressure. By implication, we want to see people who are relaxed, who know how to balance work and leisure, and who exert control over their life circumstances (Wilkinson & Marmot, 2003). The more societies foster that lifestyle, the better off we all are. Unfortunately, workplaces are imposing longer hours on employees. In some places, people boast of working 60 or 70 hours per week. It has become a badge of honor to be a workaholic.

A side effect of stress is addictions. Smoking, alcohol consumption, and drug use derive from social conditions and worsen health inequalities at the same time. Addictions of various kinds are closely associated with indicators of economic and social marginalization. Scholars claim that causality is likely to run both ways: The socially excluded turn to alcohol and drugs to escape the pain of exclusion, and drug dependence contributes to downward mobility. Temporary escape aside, drug abuse exacerbates both the pain and the exclusion.

The social gradient is very much present in addictive behaviors. When you compare five social groups, from most affluent to most deprived, there is a gradual decrease from fifth to first in dependence on alcohol, nicotine, and drugs. In comparison to the most affluent group, the most deprived consume nearly 10 times as much drugs, over 8 times as much nicotine, and nearly 3 times as much alcohol. When it comes to drug dependence, the data presented by Wilkinson and Marmot (2003) show that the fourth group uses drugs nearly 5 times as much as the first, the third group 3 times as much, and the second group twice as much. Similar declines are observed for nicotine and alcohol. In a healthy community, we hope to see very few addictions, both in rich and poor neighborhoods. At present, it's very clear that the heaviest burden of substance dependence takes place among the most deprived.

Two other personal signs of community well-being have to do with basic functions: eating and moving. What people put in their mouths is not only a reflection of personal taste, but also of accessibility and availability. "Access to good, affordable food makes more difference to what people eat than health education" (Wilkinson & Marmot, 2003, p. 26). Affordability and proximity to fresh fruits and vegetables make a huge difference to people we work with in poor communities in Nashville. Tennessee ranks seventh among states with obese and overweight adults, at 61.9%. In one of the neighborhoods where we work, there is no nearby supermarket or fresh fruit market. People don't have cars, and it's very hard for them to afford taxis to take them shopping. As a result, they end up buying canned goods that only contribute to a host of related diseases. The social gradient we observed in addictions is also present in obesity (Bruner, Juneja, & Marmot, 1998).

Related to obesity are walking and exercising, two vital functions for health. The more we rely on cars as part of our lifestyle, the more we pollute the environment and the more we deprive ourselves of opportunities to walk and cycle. It's hardly fair to blame people for using their cars when public transportation systems leave much to be desired and when the streets are unsafe for walking. Although personal choices can be improved to help the environment and the individual, the infrastructure plays a big role in the choices people make. The more convenient public transport is, the more use it gets (Saelens et al., 2003; Sallins et al., 2004). In addition to public transport, safety is a factor in walking and cycling. Residents of a neighborhood in east Nashville told us in no uncertain terms that they're afraid to walk the streets. They would like to, but they're just afraid.

Life Expectancy

We started this section with early life development and we conclude, at the other end of life, with mortality. There is no stronger physical sign of well-being than being alive. As noted earlier, life expectancy follows a social gradient. What is interesting to note here is that even in fairly egalitarian societies, such as Sweden, there is still a noticeable gradient in mortality. As reported by Marmot (2004), research conducted in the Nordic country shows that, compared to those holding doctorate degrees, men with only compulsory education had a threefold increase in mortality rate. Mortality rate increases steadily along the following continuum of education: doctorate, higher tertiary, lower tertiary, secondary, vocational, and compulsory. Education matters not only for income and status, but apparently also for longevity.

Together, early life development, life span opportunities, lifestyle, and life expectancy show something about the communities where we live and work and play. It is clear from the research that a heavier burden of illness, mortality, addictions, and psychological problems fall on those with the least resources. Saner societies would be reflected in lower rates of infant mortality, child abuse, obesity, and premature mortality, not only among the poor but among all.

ORGANIZATIONAL SIGNS OF COMMUNITY WELL-BEING

We can think of two kinds of organizational signs of community well-being. In the first instance, we can regard the very existence of some organizations as a reflection of well-being. In Sweden, for instance, they have a government office designed to protect and promote the rights of the child:

the Children's Ombudsman. The presence of such an organization may be regarded as a sign of concern for the rights and well-being of children. This is a necessary but not a sufficient sign of community well-being, for we need to explore what the office does, and whether it does it well. This is the second level of signs: the quality of organizational work.

Let's start with the type of organizations that are present in a society. In general terms, we can divide the organizational world into for-profit and not-for-profit. Not-for-profit organizations can be privately or publicly run. Many private charities and nongovernment organizations seek to promote the common good. Government organizations, in turn, are public institutions entrusted with the promotion of collective well-being through education, health, housing, and transportation. We start exploring what type of not-for-profit organizations, private and governmental, exist and what is it that they do.

Governments have more resources than any one charity or social service. This is a good enough reason to start with Big Brother. What type of governmental organizations may be regarded as signs of community well-being? Governments that value education, health, welfare, housing, and the environment would invest in departments that foster these domains of well-being. We might say that a country with a ministry or department specially designated to promote the rights of the child is better than one that doesn't have such an entity. But it is entirely possible to have great-sounding government departments that do nothing or do a very poor job, existing only in skeletal form. So, we have to explore not only their names but also, and especially, the quality of their operations.

The same applies to nongovernmental organizations. All over the world, there are millions of not-for-profit organizations dedicated to improve well-being from cradle to grave and everything in between. A key question is whether they are adequately funded to do their job. And if they are, are they making a difference? We explore these two issues next.

Organizational Infrastructure in Rich Countries

Countries and communities differ in how they allocate resources for communities through public organizations. The SPEC (strengths, prevention, empowerment, and changing conditions) lenses can help us assess what is a good investment in organizational infrastructure. Those that promote SPEC, in its entirety or in portions, have a better chance of enhancing collective well-being than those focused on deficits, crises, alienation, and one-person-at-a-time rescue operations. We consider various examples from different countries in the North and in the South.

We start with Sweden. Over the past 4 decades, there has been a growing understanding that government needs to intervene to prevent physical maltreatment of children. As a society, Sweden decided that physical discipline is unacceptable. As a result, it created government and nongovernment organizations to make sure that legislation protecting children was enacted and respected. The cultural rejection of child abuse culminated in legislation in 1979 banning corporal punishment and in the appointment of a Children's Ombudsman in 1993. This government office, along with two nongovernmental organizations, the Swedish Save the Children Federation (Rädda Barnen) and the Swedish Children's Rights in Society (Barnens Rätt i Samhället), promote children's well-being through legislation, public education, parenting courses, and overall advocacy (Durrant & Olsen, 1997). The outcomes are very encouraging. A recent article by Durrant and Jansen (in press) reports that "acts of violence against children have declined dramatically in Sweden over recent decades; corporal punishment is infrequent, serious assaults are uncommon, and child abuse fatalities are extremely rare."

Compared to Sweden, in Canada, where there is no legislation banning the use of force against children, mothers favor and engage more frequently in physical punishment (Durrant, Rose-Krasnor, & Broberg, 2003). Sweden invested in infrastructure that promoted children's strengths, prevented child abuse, empowered children, and changed cultural conditions. Through legislation, advocacy, and education, Sweden considerably reduced cases of child abuse.

From Sweden and Canada we move south to the United States. Only days ago, this country suffered its worst natural disaster in history. Hurricane Katrina destroyed the city of New Orleans, much of the Louisiana coast, and parts of Mississippi. Ten days after the hurricane, the country still doesn't know how many people perished, although the toll is estimated in the thousands. On September 2, 2005, the *Washington Post* reported that "in recent years, Bush repeatedly sought to slice the Army Corps of Engineers' funding requests to improve the levees holding back Lake Pontchartrain, which Katrina smashed through, flooding New Orleans" (VandeHei & Baker, 2005, p. A16). The article goes on:

Local and federal officials have long warned that funding shortages in the New Orleans area would have consequences. They sounded the alarm as recently as last summer when they complained that federal budget cuts had stopped major work on New Orleans east bank hurricane levees for the first time in 37 years. Al Naomi, the senior project manager for the Army Corps of Engineers, reported at the time that he was getting only half as much money as he needed and that much of the funding was being used to pay contractors for past work. "When levees are below grade, as ours are in many spots right now, they're more vulnerable to waves pouring over them and degrading them," Naomi told the Times-Picayune of New Orleans. (p. A16)

Infrastructure to prevent floods is absolutely vital. It is day 10 after the flood and the cost so far is around the $60 billion mark. The financial cost of reinforcing the levees would have paled in comparison, not to mention the lives that might have been saved. But prevention was neglected not only in averting the floods that ensued, but also in the evacuation plans. Poor families, most of them African Americans, had no transportation or money to get out of the city. The government urged people to leave but did not provide the means to do so. Katrina was not the first hurricane to visit the Gulf Coast or New Orleans. There were several missed opportunities here to do prevention. Without infrastructure, private citizens are left to fend for themselves. This was a catastrophe waiting to happen. As commentator Michael Parenti (2005) put it: "The catastrophic flooding of New Orleans had been foreseen by storm experts, engineers, Louisiana journalists and state officials, and even some federal agencies. All sorts of people had been predicting disaster for years, pointing to the danger of rising water levels and the need to strengthen the levees and pumps, and fortify the entire coastland." Similarly, David Brooks (2005) of the *New York Times* claimed that "Katrina was the most anticipated natural disaster in American history, and still government managed to fail at every level."

Two organizations that might have reflected concern for community well-being failed miserably during Katrina. The Army Corps of Engineers and FEMA, the Federal Emergency Management Agency, did not do their job. The Army Corps of Engineers cannot be blamed for having its budget cut by the Bush administration. This is not a poor reflection of the workers on the ground, but rather of the political masters who chose to eviscerate FEMA and cut funding to prevent flooding. From its glossy annual reports and high-tech web site, you would think that FEMA stands for the highest standards of public safety, but when you dig a little deeper, you realize that the agency was populated with presidential cronies who had zero experience in handling disasters. As the *Washington Post* reported on September 9, 2005:

Five of eight top Federal Emergency Management Agency officials came to their posts with virtually no experience in handling disasters and now lead an agency whose ranks of seasoned crisis managers have thinned dramatically since the Sept. 11, 2001, attacks. FEMA's top three leaders—Director Michael D. Brown, Chief of Staff Patrick J. Rhode, and Deputy Chief of Staff Brooks D. Altshuler—arrived with ties to President Bush's 2000 campaign or to the White House advance operation, according to the agency. Two other senior operational jobs are filled by a former Republican lieutenant governor of Nebraska and a U.S. Chamber of Commerce official who was once a political operative. (Hsu, 2005, p. O1)

FEMA is a perfect example of a missed opportunity. Here you have an organization that can potentially save lives, but due to incompetence and political manipulations failed miserably. As Hsu (2005, p. O1) reports in the *Washington Post*:

Experts inside and out of government said a "brain drain" of experienced disaster hands throughout the agency, hastened in part by the appointment of leaders without backgrounds in emergency management, has weakened the agency's ability to respond to natural disasters. Some security experts and congressional critics say the exodus was fueled by a bureaucratic reshuffling in Washington in 2003, when FEMA was stripped of its independent Cabinet-level status and folded into the Department of Homeland Security. Emergency preparedness has atrophied as a result, some analysts said, extending from Washington to localities.

FEMA "has gone downhill within the department, drained of resources and leadership," said I. M. "Mac" Destler, a professor at the University of Maryland School of Public Policy. "The crippling of FEMA was one important reason why it failed."

Katrina's repercussions are perhaps symptomatic of the decimation of the public sector in this country. Human services are expected to do more with less, while the number of desperate people grows exponentially with the ever-expanding gap between rich and poor. The health and human services sector in this country faces an unprecedented retrenchment occasioned by unprecedented tax cuts for the upper echelons (Feikema, 2005). There is no doubt that without a strong safety net, properly financed and adequately maintained, human services will continue to be so stretched that there will never be time or resources to build people's strengths, to engage in prevention, to empower citizens, or to promote social change. Instead, they will continue to patch people up and send them back to the same gruesome conditions they came from (Hahn, 1994; Wineman, 1984). The level and type of infrastructure that a government puts in place surely reflects its investment in collective well-being.

What happens in the United States is not an anomaly. Rather, it is part of the global neoliberal agenda that forces governments to shrink. This unpleasant phenomenon is most vividly experienced by poor countries indebted to the International Monetary Fund. The depletion of the public sector in developing nations, as we shall see, has devastating effects.

Organizational Infrastructure in Poor Countries

Governments create international institutions that serve primarily nations and corporations in the North. As poor countries depend—often because of histories of colonization—on foreign loans, lending institutions like the International Monetary Fund dictate terms and conditions that wipe out social services, health care, and public education. Economic growth and efficiency, touted as the only way to prosperity, require the privatization of public utilities and services, resulting in massive unemployment of public sector workers and in restricted access to health, education, and sometimes even water (Korten, 1995). The case of rice producers in Haiti illustrates the international dynamics quite well. Governments are forced to open markets and lift restrictions on imports, and local producers have to compete with cheaper foreign products that are either subsidized or produced with equipment that is more efficient. Once the local competition is eliminated, prices go up and fewer and fewer people have access to them (Aristide, 2000; Korten, 1995; Weisbrot, 1999).

At the national level, poor countries indebted to the International Monetary Fund and to the World Bank spend considerable amounts of money servicing their debts. In the case of Mozambique, the country spends 25% of its income from exports on debt payments. This prevents the country from investing in its own population. If only half of the debt service payments were spent on health care, the lives of 115,000 children and of 6,000 mothers who die in childbirth would be saved (Weisbrot, 1999).

The dominant doctrine that economic growth inflicts short-term pain for long-term gain in poor countries is challenged by economics Nobel Prize winner Amartya Sen (1999a, 1999b, 2001). Sen claims that investments in education, health, and social services in fact contribute to economic strength. He challenges the received wisdom that "human development is a kind of luxury that a country can afford only when it grows rich" (1999a, p. 10). With evidence from East Asia, including Japan, Sen demonstrates that policies in favor of comprehensive human development do not retard but rather enhance economic prosperity:

These economies went comparatively early for massive expansion of education, and other ways of broadening the entitlements that allow the bulk of the people to participate in economic transactions and social change. This happened well before breaking the restraints of general poverty; indeed, that broad approach greatly contributed to breaking the restraints of poverty. (pp. 10–11)

Investments in education, health, and social facilities enabled East Asian economies to work on economic deprivation quite successfully. Their major shortcoming, however, was not to plan for the possibility of sudden destitution that comes with economic cycles and recessions. As a result, during the 1997 economic crisis, millions of working people became suddenly poor or even destitute in countries like Indonesia, Thailand, and South Korea. "Even though a fall of 5 to 10% of total national income (or of GNP) is comparatively moderate, it can decimate lives and create misery for millions" (Sen, 1999a, p. 40). According to Sen, protective security is as important as economic progress. Many of the Tiger economies of Asia neglected to install safety nets that would catch the victims of economic downturns. This is when the lack of democracy can be most severely felt, for recessions hit most harshly the poor, who, without unions or protective institutions, fall rapidly into destitution. "The victims in Indonesia may not have taken very great interest in democracy when things went up and up. But when things came tumbling down for some parts of the populations, the lack of democratic institutions kept their voices muffled and ineffective" (p. 40).

In Latin America, economic crises have had the similar effect of increasing poverty and exacerbating inequality. Based on data from 48 growth and recession periods for 12 Latin American countries, Janvry and Sadoulet (2001) argue that recessions are systematically devastating for the poor. They also note that the gains lost during recessions are not recovered in future spells of growth:

A 1% decline in GDPpc in a recession episode eliminates the gains in urban poverty reduction achieved by 3.7% growth in GDPpc under early growth, the gains in rural poverty reduction achieved by 2% growth under early growth, and the gains in inequality reduction achieved by 9% growth under late growth. Recession has a particularly strong ratchet effect on inequality since subsequent growth is unable to compensate for the higher level of inequality achieved. (p. 37)

The pressure on poor countries to open their markets, combined with repressive policies of authoritarian regimes, conspire to widen the gap between rich and poor. Globalization works for powerful corporations while authoritarian regimes work for the corrupt elites that pillage the nation and its resources. As Sen (1999a, 1999b) has eloquently argued, democracy at the *national* level is a prerequisite for the prevention of destitution. As Aristide (2000) and Korten (1995) have persuasively shown, without *international* justice, the downward spiral for the majority of poor countries cannot be averted.

The power dynamics operating at the international scene and in developing countries bear a resemblance to what happens in developed countries. The same corporations that put pressure on international bodies to open new markets put pressure on domestic governments to reduce public services and cut taxes (Dobbin, 1998). The growing inequality in developed countries is unprecedented. In industrialized countries, economic growth without redistributive policies widens the gap between rich and poor, with adverse health and social effects for the large middle class that is experiencing declining standards of living (Allahar & Cote, 1998; Wilkinson, 1996, 2005).

SIGNS OF COMMUNITY WELL-BEING

How can we tell, by looking at a community, that it is doing well? A simple way to answer this question is by looking at what type of resources, material and psychological signs, are present in the community. That's a start, but that's not good enough, for it is entirely possible that most resources will go to a small segment of the population, as is often the case, leaving the poor with few resources to thrive. Therefore, we have to ask a second question: How well is society doing by those with few resources? In the following two sections, we answer both questions.

Material Signs

Green spaces, strong levees to resist floods, technologically advanced hospitals, well-equipped schools, bike-friendly roads, public transportation systems, money, recreation clubs, clean air—these are material and objective resources for quality of life. These are things that exist out there to serve the community. We distinguish them from psychological resources such as social support or feelings of inclusion, which are also very important and are related to material resources, but of a different quality. Let's explore first what type of objective resources would lead us to designate a community as healthy.

In *Visions of Development*, author David Alexander (2002) confronted the question of what constitutes human development and well-being. In a comprehensive review of conceptions of well-being, Alexander identifies four sets of capabilities:

1. Physical capabilities
2. Mental well-being and intellectual development
3. Relating and interacting
4. Personal autonomy and freedom

These capabilities, which complement the personal signs of community well-being, are supported by material conditions. Alexander offers a very thorough list of conditions supporting well-being. *Physical capabilities* such as health and a long life are supported by access to:

- Basic necessities such as nutritional food, clean water, clothing, sanitation, and fuel for cooking
- Adequate housing
- Medical and health care
- Appropriate means of transportation

Mental well-being and intellectual development, including the ability to read and be creative, is essentially supported by access to:

- Education
- Information
- Growth opportunities

Relating and interacting, in turn, are predicated on access to:

- Care and support of family and friends
- Meaningful civic and social activities
- Employment opportunities

Last, *personal autonomy and freedom* are built on access to:

- Economic resources, including income from jobs and wealth
- Goods and services
- Safe environments

These signs of community well-being are corroborated by vast empirical research. An impressive study of indicators of community well-being was conducted by the World Bank. The Poverty Group of the World Bank wanted to know what would constitute, in poor people's eyes, adequate material resources. By asking poor people themselves, the Group hoped to discover the essential ingredients of a good community. With this goal in mind, the Group conducted interviews with more than 60,000 people in more than 47 countries. The team provided a reliable account of the conditions that poor people need to live with dignity (Narayan, Chambers, Shah, & Petesch, 2000; Narayan, Patel, Schafft, Rademacher, & Koch-Schulte, 2000).

Poor people seek (a) to experience *social justice, security, and peace*; (b) to benefit from *material well-being and assets*; and (c) to live in places with accessible and responsive *community services and organizations*. In the South in particular, poor people talked at length about the wish to have reliable government agencies. They want to have a police force that will protect them, health professionals that will treat them with respect, and safety nets that will support them in times of crises. Almost uniformly, they wish an education for their children. Among others, these results were independently confirmed by Alexander (2002), who conducted similar studies in South African villages.

People in the South suffer from two sets of devastating experiences: (1) insecurity, chaos, and violence, and (2) economic exploitation. Narayan and colleagues (Narayan, Chambers, Shah, & Petesch, 1999; Narayan, Chambers, et al., 2000; Narayan, Patel, et al., 2000), who interviewed thousands of people in the World Bank study, heard frequently about the fear of living with uncertainty and lack of protection. Lack of order and lawlessness exacerbates the plight of the poor and adds a dimension of terror to the material deprivation. A poor woman in Brazil pointed out that "there is no control over anything, at any hour a gun could go off, especially at night" (Narayan et al., 1999, p. 7). Chaotic environments in politically unstable regimes are fertile grounds for crime and violence. The poor are the most vulnerable of all as they are often homeless and exposed to random acts of violence. Many observed that the police can be quite brutal and heartless in their dealings with the poor. Many participants complained about the lack of institutional protection afforded by the state (Narayan, Chambers, et al., 2000).

Economic exploitation is felt as a trap without escape. Children and adults working at slavery or near slavery levels have no choice but to relinquish their freedom and abide by rules of despotic employers:

> Officially, slavery no longer exists in Haiti. But through the lives of children in Haiti who live as *restavèks* we see the remnants of slavery. *Restavèks* are children, usually girls, sometimes as young as 3 and 4 years old, who live in the majority of Haitian families as unpaid domestic workers. They are the first to get up in the morning and the last to go to bed at night. They carry water, clean house, do errands and receive no salary. . . . They eat what is left when the others are finished, and they are extremely vulnerable to verbal, physical and sexual abuse. (Aristide, 2000, p. 27)

Economic policies that result in poverty and unemployment affect people in the South and in the North. Based on research in developed countries, Fryer (1998, p. 78) asserts that "unemployment is centrally involved in the social causation of mental health problems." Furthermore, he claims that unemployment is psychologically debilitating because it "disempowers by impoverishing, restricting, baffling and undermining the agency of the unemployed person. . . . Unemployment generally results in psychologically corrosive experienced relative poverty" (p. 83). The impact of recessions can be felt in unemployment and in many other levels as well. Wages go down, health and working conditions deteriorate, and minorities are more visibly excluded from the job market (Fryer, 1998). There is no question that the poor carry the heaviest burden of social decay. "Poor people report living with increased crime, corruption, violence, and insecurity amidst declining social cohesion" (Narayan, Patel, et al., 2000, p. 222).

A woman's lifetime chance of dying in pregnancy or delivery in the least developed countries is 1 in 16. In industrialized countries, the chances are 1 in 4,085 (UNICEF, 2001). Although most poor mothers living in industrialized countries receive much better prenatal care than their counterparts in developing nations, they nevertheless face higher risks than mothers in higher socioeconomic groups. Poor mothers in developed countries have a greater incidence of premature and low birth weight babies. In general, lower socioeconomic groups have greater health risks associated with poor diet, hypertension, physical inactivity, smoking, and lack of breast-feeding (A. Robertson et al., 1999).

Life span and the global burden of disease also demonstrate the health effects of poverty. In some regions of Africa, life expectancy for women is 35.4 years, whereas in parts of the Western Pacific region it is 80.8. Southeast Asia has about 13 times more communicable diseases, poor maternal and perinatal conditions, and nutritional deficiencies than Europe. The ratio between Europe and Africa is about 1:19 (MacFarlane, Racelis, & Muli-Musiime, 2000).

When probability of death between ages 15 and 60 is compared between richer and poorer countries, the former have outcomes that are about 3 times better than the latter. Reasons for death include infections; poor perinatal, nutritional, and maternal care; cardiovascular and respiratory disease; cancer; and other external causes (see Marmot, 1999). Lack of shelter and sanitation are major causes of killing diseases around the world. Feuerstein (1997) reports that in 34 of the 47 least developed countries, only 46% of the population has access to safe water.

Within countries, the poor, the unemployed, refugees, single parents, ethnic minorities, and the homeless have poorer indices of health than more advantaged groups. This applies not only to poor countries, but to rich countries as well. Homeless people in Western countries, for example, are 34 times more likely to kill themselves than the general population, 150 times more likely to be fatally assaulted, and 25 times more likely to die in any period of time than the people who ignore them on the streets (Shaw, Dorling, & Smith, 1999).

Inevitably, economic recessions and material deprivation lead to poor outcomes for communities and individuals alike. Mental health deteriorates markedly, and symptoms of depression and helplessness ensue (Fryer, 1998). Affected individuals feel disempowered and diminish their contribution to society at large. The data presented so far overwhelmingly suggest that inequality exists, in rich and poor countries, and that the poor suffer most of the untoward consequences.

Social and Psychological Signs

Objective and material conditions matter, but so do social and psychological factors. Overall quality of life depends greatly on the availability of social support, inclusion, and participation in civic life.

According to the World Bank study, psychological signs of community well-being include (a) *respect and tolerance for diversity*, (b) *democratic participation*, (c) *sense of community and solidarity*, (d) *social support*, (e) *freedom of choice and action*, and (f) *capacity for action*. In spite of great adversity, many poor people not only wish for but enact many of these qualities, primarily those related to solidarity and support. "Maintaining social traditions, hospitality, reciprocity, rituals, and festivals are central to poor people's defining themselves as humans, despite dehumanizing economic and environmental realities" (Narayan, Patel, et al., 2000, p. 217). A poor woman in Ukraine noted that "without these simple humane signs of solidarity, our lives would be unbearable" (p. 217).

In the struggle for survival, social relations suffer. Social suffering is marked by (a) *heightened fragmentation and exclusion* and by (b) *fractions social relations*. An Ecuadorian participant in the World Bank study put it succinctly: "What is mine is mine, and what is yours is yours, in this community people are very stingy" (Narayan, Patel, et al., 2000, p. 222). In addition, poor communities are often characterized by (c) *powerlessness*, (d) *limitations and restricted opportunities in life*, (e) *physical weakness*, (f) *shame and feelings of inferiority*, and (g) *gender and age discrimination*. Impotence in light of ominous societal forces like crime and economic displacement fuels the sense of powerlessness.

People feel they have dreams for their children that will never be fulfilled. Illness and disability were frequently mentioned, not only because of the physical pain endured by malnutrition and harsh labor, but also because a physical disability means inability to work. With their bodies as their main working tool, a physical impairment translates into hunger. The body has to endure the lack of shelter, food, water, and clothing. Illnesses and injuries are frequently experienced but infrequently treated. "If you don't have money today, your disease will take you to your grave" (an old man in Ghana, quoted in Narayan, Patel, et al., 2000, p. 218).

Shame was a strong feeling expressed by poor people in the South and in the North. It can be captured by the following quotes from Canadian children:

> Poverty is . . . pretending that you forgot your lunch, being teased for the way you are dressed, feeling ashamed when my dad can't get a job, not getting a hot dog on hot dog day, being afraid to tell your mom that you need gym shoes, not getting to go to birthday parties, not buying books at the book fair. (Grade 4 and 5 children, North Bay, Ontario, Canada, quoted in Interfaith Social Assistance Reform Coalition, 1998)

Discrimination based on gender and age was a prominent issue in most accounts of poverty. Gender discrimination is strongly felt in the north and northwest of India and in some parts of East Asia. Studies demonstrate that in these regions there is excess female infant and child mortality. There is also evidence that with the advent of amniocentesis, there is selective abortion of female fetuses. In parts of sub-Saharan Africa, women have heavier workloads than men and have very little say in decision making (Razavi, 1999).

Reports indicate that poor women are also very often the subject of domestic violence. In 1996 Health Canada produced a report called *Breaking the Links between Poverty and Violence against Women*. The authors noted that "many thousands of Canadian women experience poverty and violence every day . . . for many women, poverty adds another dimension to the pain and suffering they experience as a result of violence" (Gurr, Mailloux, Kinnon, & Doerge, 1996, p. 1).

Children and the elderly are also discriminated against. "During 2003, an estimated 2.9 million referrals, including 5.5 million children, were made to CPS [child protective services] agencies. The national rate was 39.1 referrals per 1,000 children for 2003 compared to 35.9 referrals per 1,000 children for 2002" (U.S. Department of Health and Human Services, 2003). Studies show that a preponderance of child abuse cases take place, in fact, in poor families (I. Prilleltensky, Nelson, et al., 2001). Discrimination against the young and the old happens not only in family quarters, but also at the state level. The majority of old people in developing countries are uninsured by any type of social security plan. In sub-Saharan Africa, less than 10% of the old population is covered. In East Asia less than 30% of old people have any pension or social security. Only the very wealthy can age securely in these countries. In contrast, in most OECD countries, between 90% and 100% of old people are covered (E. James, 2001).

The lived experience of poverty, at all levels of analysis, is characterized by powerlessness. "Poverty is like living in jail, living under bondage, waiting to be free" (a young woman in Jamaica, quoted in Narayan et al., 1999, p. 8). When rice farmers in Haiti work as hard as they can, abide by all the rules, and still cannot compete with American producers, there is a profound sense of powerlessness and lack of control. When little *restavek* girls work day and night and sustain multiple forms of abuse, hopelessness ensues. When poor women are subjected to humiliation, exclusion, and violence, powerlessness is the most common outcome. Power differentials sit at the core of suffering for poor people of all ages.

The power inequality expressed by poor people is not exclusively psychological or political, but always both. Material and economic power are intertwined with feelings of shame and inferiority. In light of so much adversity, it is against the odds that poor people still engage in acts of meaning, solidarity, and wellness.

LINKED SIGNS

Although feelings of happiness and well-being are important, they cannot be treated in isolation from the cultural, political, and economic signs of well-being. They are all connected (Eckersley, 2000). We require "well-enough" social and political conditions, free of economic exploitation and human rights abuses, to experience quality of life. Eckersley has shown that subjective experiences of well-being are heavily dictated by cultural trends such as individualism and consumerism, whereas Narayan and colleagues (Narayan, Chambers, et al., 2000; Narayan, Patel, et al., 2000) have claimed that the psychological experience of poverty is directly related to political structures of corruption and oppression.

Sen (1999b) frames poverty in terms of both capabilities and entitlements. Without the latter, the former cannot thrive. Capacities and resources are at once intrinsically meritorious and extrinsically beneficial. This means that a sense of mastery and control is both an end in itself and a means of achieving wellness or reducing poverty. Access to preventive health care is not only a means to human development but also an end in its own right. Wellness at the collective level is not measured only by the health and educational outcomes of a group of individuals, but also by the presence of enabling institutions and societal infrastructures.

Sen (1999a, 1999b) articulates the complementary nature of diverse social structures in fostering community well-being. He invokes the interaction of five types of freedoms in the pursuit of human development:

1. Political freedoms
2. Economic facilities
3. Social opportunities
4. Transparency guarantee
5. Protective security

Each of these distinct types of rights and opportunities helps to advance the general capability of a person. They may also serve to complement each other. . . . Freedoms are not only the primary ends of development, they are also among its principal means. In addition to acknowledging, foundationally, the evaluative importance of freedom, we also have to understand the remarkable empirical connection that links freedoms of different kinds with one another. Political freedoms (in the form of free speeches and elections) help to promote economic security. Social opportunities (in the form of education and health facilities) facilitate economic participation. Economic facilities (in the form of opportunities for participation in trade and production) can help to generate personal abundance as well as public resources for social facilities. Freedoms of different kinds can strengthen one another. (Sen, 1999b, pp. 10–11)

ROWS FOR WELLNESS

Exercise 11: Assessing Your Community

Think of the community where you live. It can be as small as your neighborhood, or as big as your city or your country. How are the ROWS affecting the well-being of your chosen community? Think of all the personal, organizational, and community signs we reviewed in this chapter and apply them to your community. What you see may surprise you.

To get you thinking about changes in your community, transfer the ROWS from Form 11.1 to Form 1.2, the planning tool. If you belong to a community association or to a political action group, you may want to do this with your peers. You may start something big.

Form 11.1   ROWS Exercise 11:   Assessing Your Community

Risks for my community's well-being

Opportunities for my community's well-being

Weaknesses that diminish my community's well-being

Strengths that enhance my community's well-being

Form 11.2   Wellness Readiness Check 11: Assessing Your Community

ROWS	1 I never thought about doing something about it.	2 I'm thinking about doing something about it.	3 I'm prepared to do something about it	4 I'm doing something about it.	5 I've been doing something about it for some time.
Risks					
Opportunities					
Weaknesses					
Strengths					

12

Where Does It Come From? Sources of Community Well-Being

Poverty, power, and participation are three very important Ps when it comes to sources of community well-being. What individuals, organizations, and countries do about these three Ps is very consequential. The repercussions of power, poverty, and participation can be felt in rich and poor countries alike, as well as in rich and poor neighborhoods. Before we explore the personal, organizational, and community sources of community well-being, we need to understand some things about the three Ps.

POVERTY

First, let's examine the scope of the problem. In the time that it takes you to read this page, approximately 60 children under 5 will die. Every hour, about 1,140 young children die, most of them from malnutrition and preventable diseases. Annually, it is about 10 million lives. In sub-Saharan Africa, the rate of under-5 mortality is 172 per 1,000 live births. In industrialized countries, the rate is 6 per 1,000. While many in the West worry about obesity in children, 149 million children in developing countries experience malnourishment. Some people drink bottled water, others drink only filtered water; 1.1 billion people around the globe have no access to safe water at all (UNICEF, 2001).

But poverty is not something that happens only in remote places to different people. It happens in industrialized countries as well. One in every six children in the OECD nations lives in poverty. "Despite a doubling and redoubling of national income in most [OECD] nations, a significant percentage of their children are still living in families so materially poor that normal health and growth are at risk" (UNICEF Innocenti Research Centre, 2000, p. 5). "Relative" poverty is a common definition used in industrialized countries. It refers to families with income below 50% of the national median. According to that formula, child poverty in OECD countries ranges from 2.8% of all children in Sweden, to 7.9% in France, 12.6% in Australia, 15.5% in Canada, and 22.4% in the United States (UNICEF Innocenti Research Centre, 2000).

Another way to appreciate the toll of poverty is in life expectancy. In 1986, life expectancy for males in Russia at age 15 was 52 years. In 1994, after the collapse of the economy, males at age 15 could be expected to live only to age 45 (Marmot, 1999). For males, probability of death between ages 15 and 60 in the year 2020 is 32% for former socialist economies of Europe and sub-Saharan countries, 18% for Latin America, and 12% for most OECD countries (Marmot, 1999).

In Britain, life expectancy at age 15 varies considerably among social classes. Data for the period 1987 to 1991 show that women in the bottom two social classes are expected to live 3.4 years less (to age 62.4 years) than those in the top two classes (to age 65.8). For men, the disparity is greater: Those in the lower classes will live 4.7 years less (to age 55.8) than those in the upper classes (to age 60.5 years; Shaw et al., 1999).

In a recent report of the United Nations Development Program, May (2001, p. 25) summarizes the main definitions of poverty. According to the minimal acceptable standard, poverty refers to the "failure of individuals, households or entire communities to command sufficient resources to satisfy their basic needs. . . . The inability to attain minimal standards of consumption to meet basic physiological criteria is often termed absolute poverty or deprivation." Lack of power to benefit from vital entitlements is at the core of this definition (Sen, 1999b).

The Human Poverty Index is another common measure of poverty. It uses basic dimensions of deprivation to assess poverty: lack of access to public and private resources, a short life, and lack of basic education (May, 2001). Although many people in developed countries have access to basic resources such as food and shelter, their life is marred by exclusion and ill health (Shaw et al., 1999). To be sure, inequality of resources exists in the North and in the South, in rich countries and in developing ones.

On a global scale, absolute poverty is concentrated in the South—but relative poverty and real deprivation also exist in the North. In the United Kingdom, over a quarter of people live in low income households, with worse health, lower life-expectancy, lower levels of social participation, and worse life chances than those above the poverty line. Children are disproportionately disadvantaged. (Maxwell & Kenway, 2000, p. 1)

There is no question that the economic and political environment influences health in potent ways (Bruton, 2001). Consider the following examples provided by Wilkinson (1996). Perhaps contrary to expectations, a child born and raised in Harlem has less chance of living to age 65 than a baby born in Bangladesh. Also in the United States, life expectancy is 7 years longer for Whites (76 years) than for African Americans (69 years). In lower social classes, infant mortality in Sweden (500 per 100,000) is less than half the rate in England (1,250 per 100,000).

The data compiled by Marmot and Wilkinson (1999) clearly indicate that, in addition to economic prosperity, equality and social cohesion are also powerful determinants of health.

In the developed world, it is not the richest countries which have the best health, but the most egalitarian. . . . Looking at a number of different examples of healthy egalitarian societies, an important characteristic they all seem to share is their social cohesion. . . . The epidemiological evidence which most clearly suggests the health benefits of social cohesion comes from studies of the beneficial effects of social networks on health. (Wilkinson, 1996, pp. 3–5)

The negative outcomes of poverty and inequality worsen in times of economic crises or environmental disasters such as earthquakes, floods, and landslides. Lustig (2001) reviews the health and educational effects of recent economic crises in Argentina, Mexico, and Indonesia. In Argentina, per capita GDP fell 4.1% and per capita private consumption fell 5.6% in 1995. That same year, per capita daily protein intake fell 3.8%. Growth in primary school enrollment declined from 2.2% in 1993 to 0.8% in 1996.

In 1995, Mexico experienced a serious economic crisis. Per capita GDP fell 7.8% and private consumption fell 11.1%. The health repercussions were severe. Among children under age 1, mortality from anemia increased from 6.3 deaths per 100,000 live births in 1993 to 7.9 in 1995. The rate for children age 1 to 4 rose from 1.7 to 2.2.

Indonesia had a severe economic crisis in 1998. Per capita GDP fell 14.6%. School dropout rates for children age 7 to 12 in the poorest quartile rose from 1.3% in 1997 to 7.5% in 1998. For children age 13 to 19, the rate rose from 14.2% to 25.5%. The share of children age 7 to 12 in the poorest quartile not enrolled in school rose from 4.9% in 1997 to 10.7% in 1998. In the 13 to 19 age group, the rate rose from 42.5 to 58.4%.

However you define it, poverty matters, no question about it. The poor are often marginalized and deprived of opportunities to participate meaningfully in societal structures such as schooling and the workforce. They are often secluded in ghettos, politically disenfranchised, and economically unable to participate in cultural life; they are powerless in the face of ominous barriers to inclusion, which is precisely the second determinant of community well-being: the power to make a difference (Smith, 2005).

POWER

The power to make a difference is vital for personal and communal well-being. There is physical and psychological power, there is the power of the individual and the power of the corporation, the power of the citizen and the power of the state, the power of the employer and the power of the employee, power to define poverty and power to reject definitions.

We can't understand community well-being unless we understand power. Let's start with a definition: Power refers to the capacity and opportunity to fulfill or obstruct personal, relational, or collective needs (I. Prilleltensky, in press; I. Prilleltensky & Nelson, 2002). Not all power is good or bad. There is power to promote well-being, power to deprive people of basic needs, and power to fight for one's rights. Power can be exercised by individuals, groups, communities, institutions, countries, and the courts, to name only a few of its multiple agents.

As power is an amalgam of capacity and opportunity, poor people may experience the former without the latter, in which case the desire to work is insufficient to overcome poverty. Without opportunities for employment or without efficient safety nets, no amount of good can undo the severe effects of structural poverty (Lustig, 2001; Sen, 1999a, 1999b). It is true that some personal characteristics—such as Schizophrenia, which in some cases affects ability to work—lead to downward mobility. But for the vast majority of the population it is not personal habits or traits that lead to poverty or ill health. Rather, it is the other way around: Poverty and inimical environmental conditions lead to ill health (Marmot, 2004).

It is often argued that people have the power to change bad habits such as smoking. Proponents of this theory claim that everyone has the capacity to change and improve. To some extent this is true, but only to some extent, for the power to make a difference is conditioned by the availability of opportunities. As just defined, power consists of capacity and opportunity. The former without the latter cannot do much. To fulfill potential we require favorable conditions. The force of circumstances can lead to positive or negative outcomes. It can bring to fruition innate potential, such as art classes for the talented, but it can also decimate the vulnerable (Marmot, 2004). As amply demonstrated by Hurricane Katrina, the circumstances of poverty prevented many residents of New Orleans from evacuating the city. Many of the poor in the city understood the need to evacuate but lacked the resources to do it. The microcosm of Katrina reflects the struggle of many poor people. They all understand that certain things need to be done to improve the lot of their families, such as sending their kids to good schools, but they lack the resources.

Just as talent that is not nurtured is wasted, environmental assaults that are not averted are catastrophic. Without proper schooling there is only so much that a brilliant poor kid can achieve, and without adequate protection against environmental risk factors there is only so much that the vulnerable can do to resist devastation. Capacity without opportunity is only a promissory note; overbearing negative circumstances are a certain ticket to marginality. Yes, there are heroes and inspiring stories of resilience, but they are a very small minority (Ungar, 2005). The fact that some kids overcome adversity is a testament to their exceptionality, a very poor foundation for formulating social policy. Most of us are average, just plain average. Most kids exposed to chronic adversity do not overcome it. Rather, they succumb to it. It is not a matter of beating the odds, but of changing the odds (Pittman, 1995).

Many hold steadfastly to the ideology that if you want to overcome the odds bad enough you can do it. But this ideology is not based on empirical evidence. Rather, it is based on a set of beliefs that have not been proven empirically. When you compare individuals from the same social group you can find some who are more industrious than others and you can explain the difference on the basis of genes and education. But when you compare entire groups, you realize that the impact of genetics is much smaller than the impact of environments (Marmot, 2004). The data on Argentina, Mexico, and Indonesia discussed earlier clearly demonstrate that school attendance and levels of health, among other things, are greatly determined by changing circumstances and not by changes in the gene pool. The gene pool of an entire country or social class does not change in a couple of years.

Compelling evidence regarding the influence of environments derives from studies of height and intelligence. In the middle of the nineteenth century, adult men in the United States were almost 7 cm taller than Germans. The former were on average 174.1 cm, and the latter were 167.3 cm. Over time, and with improved nutrition, toward the end of the twentieth century the average German grew taller (180 cm) than the average North American (178 cm). Similarly, over time, levels of intelligence have gone up in every one of 20 countries studied. In some instances, such as in the Netherlands, the IQ of the entire population went up 20 points from 1952 to 1982. Better education, better nutrition, and healthier and richer environments account for these changes. It is true that within populations, certain people fare better than others, but as an entire population, the changes are attributable to environmental improvements and not to personal will (Marmot, 2004).

These sources support the assertion that the power to make a difference is conditioned by environmental circumstances. This is not to deny that a small percentage of the population gets poorer due to disability or gets richer due to diligence, but this is true for only a small percentage. For the vast majority, it is not disability that gets them down or diligence that gets them up, but the nature of the favorable or unfavorable circumstances in which they grow up (Frey & Stutzer, 2002). As Marmot (2004, p. 55), who reviewed these studies, concludes, "Individual differences appear to have a big genetic component, but group differences, in particular improvements over time, are surely the result of environmental changes."

Power plays a crucial role in experiencing, inflicting, and repulsing poverty. Power's effects can be discerned when we examine the various facets of poverty. Entire communities and entire countries experience economic exploitation. Poor communities working for starvation wages in fields feel trapped (Feuerstein, 1997). Poor countries feel equally trapped by international lending institutions that force governments to drop social services and lift tariffs on imports in the name of efficiency and economic growth. Korten (1995) reviews the cases of Costa Rica and Brazil. In both instances, structural adjustment programs imposed by the International Monetary Fund and the World Bank displaced millions of agricultural workers. Furthermore, many countries have "become dependent on imports to meet basic food requirements" (p. 49). Aristide (2000), in turn, reviews the case of rice production in Haiti. In a matter of 10 years, from 1986 to 1996, Haiti increased its import of rice from 7,000 to 196,000 tons per year. During that period Haiti

> complied with lending agencies and lifted tariffs on rice imports. Cheaper rice immediately flooded in from the United States where the rice industry is subsidized. . . . Haiti's peasant farmers could not possibly compete. . . . Haitian rice production became negligible. Once the dependence on foreign rice was complete, import prices began to rise, leaving Haiti's population, particularly the urban poor, completely at the whim of rising world grain prices. (pp. 11–12)

These stories repeat themselves throughout the South (Korten, 1995). The price of structural adjustment policies in countries like Haiti, Brazil, and Costa Rica is unemployment and displacement for millions. Measures imposed at the collective level are felt very much at the personal level as well. These countries have great capacity for production and progress, but they lack opportunities. External debt and competition with products from highly mechanized and subsidized countries diminishes their power to make a difference. Once again, capacity without opportunity renders more powerlessness than power.

PARTICIPATION

Negative effects of poverty and lack of power notwithstanding, participation in civic affairs and political life can mitigate risk factors and build social capital. Social capital, in the form of connections of trust and participation in public affairs, enhances community capacity to create structures of cohesion and support. These structures of participation lead to positive health, welfare, educational, and social outcomes. Research indicates that cohesive communities and civic participation in public affairs enhance the well-being of the population. Communities with higher participation in volunteer organizations, political parties, and local and professional associations do much better in terms of health, education, crime, and well-being than communities with low rates of participation. This finding has been replicated at different times across various states, provinces, and countries (Putnam, 2000).

Putnam (2001, p. 48) created a measure of social capital based on the degree to which a given state is either high or low in the number of meetings citizens go to, the level of social trust its citizens have, the degree to which they spend time visiting one another at home, the frequency with which they vote, the frequency with which they do volunteering, and so on.

He then compared how states with different levels of participation and social capital perform on a number of indicators. Putnam ranked states on measures of educational performance, child welfare, TV watching, violent crime, health, tax evasion, tolerance for equality, civic equality, and economic equality. The results: States with high levels of social capital and social cohesion enjoy better rates of health, safety, welfare, education, and tolerance.

Of particular interest to us is whether social capital and social cohesion can increase health and wellness. There is evidence to support this claim. In a survey of 167,259 people in 39 states, Kawachi and Kennedy (1999) lend strong support to Putnam's (2001) claim that social capital reinforces the health of the population. Whereas earlier studies investigated the effects of social support on individuals, researchers like Putnam, Kawachi, and Wilkinson assessed the effect of social cohesion on entire populations, proving that participation in social affairs and a sense of community can lead to population health and wellness.

In our view, social capital refers to collective resources consisting of civic participation, networks, norms of reciprocity, organizations that foster trust among citizens, and actions to improve the common good. Social capital entails networks of trust and reciprocity that lead to positive outcomes for psychological, family, community, and social well-being.

We should note, though, that communities may define themselves in exclusive terms reminiscent of apartheid or in inclusive terms reminiscent of solidarity. Communities that define themselves in exclusive terms are closed to others. They tend to have a negative effect on the whole community because they develop exclusionary policies that discriminate against the "other."

Indeed, social capital may be used to increase bonding or bridging. The former refers to exclusive ties within a group; the latter refers to connections across groups. Country clubs, ethnic associations, farmers' associations, and men's groups increase bonding. Coalitions, interfaith organizations, and service groups enhance bridging. There is a risk of bonding overshadowing the need for bridging. If every group in society were interested only in what was good for its own members, there would be little or no cooperation across groups. Bridging is a necessity of every society. It is a basic requirement of a respectful and inclusive society. However, there are examples of groups investing in bonding to prevent bridging. Classic examples include the Ku Klux Klan and movements that support ethnic cleansing.

"Networks and the associated norms of reciprocity are generally good for those inside the network, but the external effects of social capital are by no means always positive" (Putnam, 2000, p. 21). Positions such as NIMBY (not in my backyard) and coalitions of elite businesses exploit their power and connections to achieve goals that are inimical to social justice.

Social capital, in short, can be directed toward malevolent, antisocial purposes, just like any other form of capital. . . . Therefore, it is important to ask how the positive consequences of social capital—mutual support, cooperation, trust, institutional effectiveness—can be maximized and the negative manifestations—sectarianism, ethnocentrism, corruption—minimized. (p. 22)

Just as power can be used for good or ill, so can participation. History is replete with examples of participating in the wrong cause, such as Nazism, fascism, Stalinism, and other forms of ethnic cleansing. But history is equally full of examples of inspiring participation, such as liberation movements in India and civil rights movements in the United States.

In the next three sections, we apply the poverty, power, and participation trilogy to understand how individuals, organizations, and communities can make use of the three Ps for community well-being. In all instances, we see critical consciousness, critical experiences, and critical actions related to poverty, power, and participation. Gandhi and Dr. Martin Luther King embraced poverty, power, and participation to further their causes, as did organizations promoting Maori rights in New Zealand/Aotearoa and groups of women in Kerala, India.

PERSONAL SOURCES OF COMMUNITY WELL-BEING

Mahatma Gandhi and Dr. Martin Luther King shared similar experiences, values, and, to some extent, fate. Both of them faced discrimination, knew poverty and injustice, and created social movements through nonviolent participation. Both of them were also killed for their convictions. On January 20, 1948, Gandhi was assassinated during prayer. Twenty years later, on the evening of April 4, 1968, Dr. King was shot on the balcony of his motel in Memphis, where he was to lead a protest in support of striking garbage workers.

Both leaders knew poverty, power, and participation up close. They knew the suffering of the Indian and African American people; they knew the power oppressing them and the power to change that situation through massive participation in nonviolent actions. They had a critical consciousness of how oppressive power and poverty can be overcome through people power and participation. They understood that poverty and discrimination were rooted in injustice and that social change cannot happen without massive support for their causes.

But they had not only critical consciousness. Critical experiences of personal discrimination and collective injustice were also influential. Experiences complement intellectual knowledge. Both factors, critical consciousness and critical experiences, inform critical action.

We ascribe the word "critical" three separate but related meanings. In critical consciousness, we imply criticism of social conditions leading to poverty and injustice, and awareness of our ability to change the situation. Critical consciousness is the realization that injustice is not predetermined or natural but socially created and, therefore, socially modifiable.

In critical experiences, we imply phenomena that leave a strong impression, as in critical incidents or critical moments in history. These are situations that can change the course of one's life. Gandhi and King had a series of critical experiences that solidified their resolve: Gandhi when he experienced discrimination in South Africa and King during the Alabama bus boycott.

Critical action evolves from the previous two descriptions. It is action against social injustice, and it is action capable of shaping the course of community. Actions that prevent suffering and promote well-being are critical actions.

Critical Consciousness

In *Critical Consciousness: A Study of Morality in Global, Historical Context*, Mustakova-Possardt (2003) differentiates between expediency motivation and moral motivation. In the former, self-interest dominates over moral concerns; in the latter, moral concerns rule over self-interests. In some exceptional cases, such as Gandhi and King, there is a unity of self and morality—the highest stage of moral development. Mustakova-Possardt describes in detail Gandhi's evolution from mere moral interest to the highest level of morality: critical consciousness.

Although not everyone is Gandhi or King, we are all moral agents and we are all capable of contributing to the common good. The question is how to move people from expediency to moral motivation, a question that has concerned moral philosophers for centuries. In *Utilitarianism*, originally published in 1861, John Stuart Mill (2001, p. 17) claims:

The happiness which forms the utilitarian standard of what is right in conduct is not the agent's own happiness but that of all concerned. As between his own happiness and that of others, utilitarianism requires him to be as strictly impartial as a disinterested and benevolent spectator. In the golden rule of

Jesus of Nazareth, we read the complete spirit of the ethics of utility. "To do as you would be done by," and "to love your neighbor as yourself," constitute the ideal perfection of utilitarian morality.

Mill concerned himself not only with the definition of a moral act, but also with ways to promote moral behavior. In his view, society and education play a crucial role:

Laws and social arrangements should place the happiness or . . . the interest of every individual as nearly as possible in harmony with the interest of the whole; and . . . education and opinion, which have so vast a power over human character, should so use that power as to establish in the mind of every individual an indissoluble association between his own happiness and the good of the whole. (p. 17)

Mill was right. Psychology has proven that socialization and education contribute to the development of the moral mind (Batson, Ahmad, Lishner, & Tsang, 2002; Schulman, 2002). Over the past 40 years, psychological research has taught us a great deal about these sources of moral behavior. In essence, there are three pathways:

1. Fostering empathy
2. Identifying with moral figures
3. Instilling values and principles

Schulman (2002) makes the point that some people can behave morally based on their empathic responses to others, whereas other people do the right thing based on either identification with moral leaders or a strong sense of values. In other words, there is more than one motivation for contributing to the common good, and there is no one way to get there. Batson (Batson et al., 2002) and Schulman (2002) describe the connections among empathy, principles, and altruism. But altruism is not tantamount to critical consciousness, for the former may amount to charity, whereas the latter seeks social transformation. As Mustakova-Possardt (2003) points out, more than charity is required for the promotion of critical consciousness and community well-being. Altruism may be a necessary but is not a sufficient condition for the social good. If it ends up in charity, and if it does not challenge injustice, altruism is not good enough.

For altruism to become critical consciousness, it has to entertain the roles of power, poverty, and participation. These were pivotal for Gandhi and King. Neither believed that charity was the highest manifestation of moral behavior. Critical consciousness came to them not from charity, but from an understanding that power can create and perpetuate poverty and that participation can overcome both illicit power and unacceptable poverty. Participation in the marketplace, in education, in community, and in social movements can indeed make a difference (Della Porta & Diani, 1999; Tarrow, 1998).

Critical Experiences

Gandhi and King suffered colonization, exclusion, discrimination, verbal abuse, and detentions. Despite their devotion to nonviolence, both were assaulted and taunted. In both men's lives, we find critical experiences that enhanced their capacity for empathy, their identification with moral figures, and their commitment to values. In fact, Gandhi was one such figure for King; the African American leader derived much inspiration from him. King identified with the principles of nonviolence and promoted them in the face of great adversity and at great personal risk.

Like Schulman and Batson, we believe that empathic training, a value-based education, and affiliation with ethical leaders contribute to moral behavior. But that is insufficient. Coming close to the experiences of the poor can change your life. But again, that is not enough to achieve critical consciousness. You have to connect your compassion to injustice. You have to see how the suffering of the poor and the oppressed is not natural but is the result of inequality and abuse of power. You don't have to live these inimical circumstances to believe they exist, but you have to feel their repercussions, either directly or vicariously, to engage in action.

Critical Action

M. Pancer and colleagues (M. Pancer, Pratt, Hunsberger, & Alisat, in press) studied the determinants of volunteerism in young people. They wanted to know what factors are associated with involvement in community and political action. To do that, they divided youth into four groups according to their level of participation. In descending order of involvement in the community, the four groups were activists, helpers, responders, and uninvolved.

A number of factors distinguished among these groups. Most findings reveal a clear distinction between the top three and the uninvolved segment. The latter cluster reported the lowest scores on self-esteem, social responsibility, optimism, social support, and identity development. It is very telling that this group also perceived their parents as lacking in warmth and strictness, the hallmarks of negligent or rejecting parenting styles. In contrast, the more engaged groups reported much higher levels of self-esteem, social support, and optimism; similarly, they displayed a stronger sense of identity. The activists and helpers, the more active bunch, experienced more interactions with peers and parents. M. Pancer and colleagues (in press) summarize the differences among the four clusters as follows:

The Activists were involved in a wide range of activities. They were well-adjusted, had well-developed identities, a sense of social responsibility, and engaged with their parents across a variety of issues. The Helpers, as their label implies, were active in helping others, but eschewed political action and formal community organizational work. They also were well-adjusted, had well-developed personalities and a sense of social responsibility, but were less engaged with their parents than were the Activists. The Responders were active only when those activities were initiated by others. They were relatively well-adjusted, but had lower levels of social support, and a less developed sense of identity. They interacted less with parents and peers. Finally, the Uninvolved showed a substantially lower level of involvement in all activities than did youth in the other clusters. They were more poorly adjusted, showed the least identity development, came from poorer-functioning families and interacted less with both parents and friends.

The authors are careful to point out that the correlation among involvement and other variables such as interaction with parents and friends does not imply causation. That is to say, the research did not prove that better family relationships led to greater community participation. An experimental design would have been required for that. However, the finding that activist youth come from families of activists is suggestive of parental influence and socialization.

When we integrate findings from Mustakova-Possardt (2003), M. Pancer et al. (in press), Batson et al. (2002), and Schulman (2002), we can confidently say that instilling values in young children, sensitizing them to the plight of others, exposing them to positive moral figures, treating them kindly, and talking with them about social issues is indeed a good recipe for moral action. But whether moral action turns out to be critical action depends, in our view, on connecting moral proclivities with an understanding of how power, poverty, and participation interact. This is the main lesson we derive from Brazilian educator Paulo Freire (1972, 1973), who worked with the poor to illuminate the relationships among power, poverty, and participation. When the peasants realized, through participatory and experiential learning, that oppressive power kept them excluded and poor, they began to develop critical consciousness, which, based on critical experiences, led to meaningful critical actions.

ORGANIZATIONAL SOURCES OF COMMUNITY WELL-BEING

In 1840, the British Crown signed the Treaty of Waitangi with the Maori people of New Zealand/Aotearoa. The treaty established a framework for the relationships between the colonial power and the local indigenous population. It allowed the formation of a settler government while guaranteeing the sovereignty of tribes over property and cultural rights. The agreement promised that Maori would enjoy citizenship equal to that of New Zealanders of European descent. Over the years, however, the treaty has been all but neglected, depriving Maori people of rightful participation in society and access to resources. The treaty has become the subject of legal contestation, as Maori people claim that the autonomy and sovereignty assured to them in the treaty have been violated.

Since the 1970s there have been many efforts by Maori and Pakeha (residents of European descent) to recognize the entitlements of Maori inscribed in the treaty. Although the original wording of the document is debated due to bilingual versions in English and Maori, vast sectors of the population, and not just Maori, recognize that a great injustice has been perpetrated in the way colonial settlers marginalized the original settlers of the land (Glover et al., 2005; N. Robertson & Masters-Awatere, in press).

Contemporary attempts to revive the Treaty of Waitangi offer a microcosm of what it takes for organizations to contribute to community well-being. Here we have a marginalized population, experiencing a great degree of poverty, deprived of participation, and subject to colonial powers, trying to claim its rights and improve its communal well-being. It is obvious that without the cooperation of Pakeha organizations not much progress can be made—they control most of the social, political, and economic resources—which is why a group of treaty educators has been working with Pakeha institutions on promoting Maori well-being (Huygens, 2004; Huygens & Humphries, 2004).

For Pakeha organizations, private and public, to promote Maori well-being, they have to confront their own power and privilege and their own participation in the poverty and oppression of a minority group. Not an easy task, to say the least. This is what treaty educators are up against: nothing less than a century and a half of status quo. Their work, currently being studied by Ingrid Huygens (2004), demonstrates the confluence of critical consciousness, critical experiences, and critical actions when organizations strive to promote or restore communal well-being.

Critical Consciousness

Organizations can diminish or promote communal well-being. In most cases, they do both. In some cases, as Joel Bakan (2004) extensively documents in *The Corporation: The Pathological Pursuit of Profit and Power*, they mostly undermine community well-being—ecological, social, economic, political—for the exclusive maximization of profit for stakeholders. In other cases, they try to improve public health, mental health, social capital, economic equality, or inclusion, as many health and human service organizations do.

Although some try very hard to enhance community well-being, we should not confuse intentions with consequences. This is where critical consciousness comes in. To what degree are organizations aware that their actions might end up hurting more than helping? A seemingly caring attitude toward Maori people might belie more paternalism than concern for their autonomy. Creating more soup kitchens can feed a few more hundred people but does nothing to eliminate the source of hunger. Organizations have a hard time looking at themselves critically; some don't even want to. But even those that are genuinely interested in examining their practices have a hard time discerning positive and negative outcomes. To some extent, this is a question of levels. What seems beneficial at the personal level—feeding a hungry child—may be detrimental at the community level: tolerating hunger.

Treaty workers in New Zealand/Aotearoa encounter multiple organizational responses to their consciousness-raising efforts. These range from resistance to enthusiasm, from "Maori expect too much" to "Maori deserve so much more." In our work with health and human services, we have found that critical consciousness is a sine qua non for change. Unless organizations explore their treatment of poverty, power, and participation, in their internal dynamics and in their community work, their role in community well-being will continue to be hazy at best (S. Evans et al., in press).

Internally, organizations distribute power and participation, usually in hierarchical fashion. There may not be economic poverty in the workforce, yet there is often poverty of participation, leading to feelings of exclusion and marginality. It has been argued that without internal critical consciousness there cannot be a full embrace of external critical consciousness (S. Evans et al., in press). That is, without experiencing equality, justice, and participation in the workplace, it is hard, if not impossible, to propagate them in the community.

Critical Experiences

Critical consciousness may derive from either positive or negative critical experiences in organizations. Some of these experiences reside within the organization, whereas others take place in the community but are brought to organizational consciousness by their workers.

Of all places, one might not expect oppression and discrimination within social movements that promote justice and equality. But this is precisely what Linda Stout (1996), a community activist, experienced in peace and justice movements. The very oppression her organization was fighting out there in the world was being reproduced right at home, within the organization, among peers.

Linda Stout (1996) is a community organizer and social activist. She founded the Piedmont Peace Project in North Carolina and worked on many political campaigns, including voter registration, literacy projects, nuclear disarmament, workers' rights, and welfare issues. Linda grew up poor and could not get the education she always wanted. Among activists, she was different. She didn't speak like them and she didn't have the middle-class manners other activists had. She was a lesbian in a mostly straight culture. Linda did excellent organizing work and always believed in fighting for the poor and the oppressed. She knew that fighting oppression would not be easy. She encountered opposition from local government, police, and angry citizens who didn't agree with her views. What she didn't expect, however, was the discrimination that she would face from progressive social movements. This is what Linda had to say about her plight:

Because we are all products of the world we live in, it is understandable that oppression is also a problem within progressive movements. Most people involved in progressive organizations see themselves as fighting oppression that is "outside," in the larger society. We all agree that our goal is to end oppression in the world. However, what we have found is that very often it is oppression on the inside that keeps us from achieving our goals. Progressive people from the oppressor group carry into their organizations all the things they've been taught about the group they serve and oppressive ways of behaving toward the "other." Usually without intending it or seeing it, middle-class progressive people behave in ways that disempower low-income and working-class folks; whites do the same to people of color, men to women, and heterosexuals to gay, lesbian and bisexual folks. (p. 89)

Linda's experiences are very telling because they demonstrate that there can be gaps in critical consciousness. Her peers in the organization were probably able to analyze the sources of oppression out there in the world, but were not able to see how they were treating their own peers. These gaps have to be named and discussed within organizations. Critical experiences have to be felt, not only by the Lindas of the world, but also by the people perpetrating the injustice within organizations. Treaty workers like Ingrid Huygens (2004) speak of disempowering the powerful and not only empowering the disempowered. Critical experiences within organizations can be catalysts for productive conversations. The more contradictions we can point to within organizations, the more we enhance the opportunities for having critical experiences.

In Linda's case, she felt a poverty of voice, participation, and power. Her critical experiences were negative. There are other cases, however, in which hitherto marginalized staff or community members develop voice and choice within organizations. Nelson and colleagues (Nelson, Lord, et al., 2001) documented such process in the case of organizations serving people with severe mental health problems. Being heard, acknowledged, and consulted are positive critical experiences indeed.

Critical Action

Actions that promote social justice and shape community for the better are hard to come by. Yet when they do happen, they are powerful. Organizations struggle to find a balance between softening the effects of injustice and eradicating injustice in the first place. It is hard to find time to get to the root causes of the long waiting lists. Yet, there is no alternative but to find time.

How to do both? How to feed a hungry child and fight hunger at the same time? Doing the former without the latter reinforces the status quo; that much is clear. What is not clear is how to restructure work to attend to the wounds and their sources concurrently. Many agencies try to find *the* book with the *answer* to these questions. The truth is, there is no such book. Each institution has to write its own book on critical actions. Through participation of the workforce, power equalization, and attention to poverty of voice and resources, it is possible to write a new book on how your organization can attend to multiple levels at the same time.

Several mental health organizations in Canada, Australia, and New Zealand/Aotearoa have partnered with their clients to promote advocacy and participation of service recipients in treatment plans and in the very management of the organization (Community Mental Health Project, 1998; Nelson, Lord, et al., 2001; Waldegrave et al., 2003). Although these organizations cannot easily reverse the economic poverty of their clients, they can do much to reduce their poverty of participation. As we know, poverty comes from lack of dollars but also from lack of meaningful engagement. These are not interchangeable. Overcoming both types of poverty is important and necessary for well-being.

Some organizations in Ontario, Canada, have gone as far as creating employment opportunities for their members with mental health problems, thus addressing both kinds of poverties: lack of resources and lack of participation (Nelson et al., in press; Ochocka, Nelson, Janzen, & Trainor, in press). These organizations, called consumer survivor initiatives (CSIs), are led and controlled entirely by former psychiatric patients. These are mutual help organizations based on critical consciousness, critical experiences, and critical action. All participants have a critical understanding of the role of stigmatization and exclusion in their disability, they have all suffered critical experiences through their interactions with the psychiatric system, and they have taken action to overcome barriers to community integration. Activities undertaken by CSIs include peer support, self-help, and development of economic opportunities. Guided by values of empowerment, social justice, participation, and community building, these settings show positive effects for the quality of life of their participants, as well as reduced visits to psychiatric services. After a 3-year follow-up, compared to a control group, active participants in CSIs scored significantly higher on measures of community integration, employment and education, and quality of life (Nelson et al., in press; Ochocka et al., in press).

Nelson's findings support previous research demonstrating that CSIs reduce hospitalization and contact with psychiatric services and save millions of dollars to the health care system. Prior to participation in CSIs, members had an average of 48.36 hospital inpatient days; this number dropped to 4.29 after joining a CSI. The estimated savings for the CSIs in Ontario are approximately $12 million. People who were connected to CSI peer mentors were discharged from hospital 116 days earlier than those who did not have a CSI peer mentor (Canadian Mental Health Association, Centre for Addiction and Mental Health, Ontario Federation of Community Mental Health and Addiction Programs, & Ontario Peer Development Initiative, 2005).

Through participation and empowerment, citizens with psychiatric disabilities are able to overcome, at least in part, their social poverty and decision-making poverty. By managing their own affairs, they recover much of the dignity lost in the process of being stigmatized by institutions and are able to establish bonds of support. Though modestly, CSIs also address economic poverty by creating alternative businesses. Finally, through their advocacy efforts CSIs continue the struggle to defend the rights of people with severe mental health problems (Janzen, Nelson, Trainor, & Ochocka, in press). It is important to note that professional associations such as the Canadian Mental Health Association and the Ontario Federation of Community Mental Health and Addiction Programs provide assistance to these initiatives but do not run them. It is a role that embodies advocacy on behalf of a marginalized population without taking over the process. There are many lessons for health and human services from the CSIs, not the least of which is that traditional helping bodies can play advocacy roles in the empowerment of people who are often participation- and power-poor.

COMMUNITY SOURCES OF COMMUNITY WELL-BEING

Economists and community developers debate the merit of rapid economic growth as a means of overcoming poverty (Bruton, 2001). Amartya Sen, 1998 Nobel Laureate in economics, makes the point that the impact of economic growth depends a great deal on how the *fruits* of economic growth are put to use. He further observes that the positive connection between life expectancy and growth of GNP per head works primarily through investments in health care and poverty removal. In other words, growth per se does not necessarily translate into human development, unless it is properly invested in health, education, social security, social services, and employment programs. Indeed, during the economic crisis of 1997 the failure of some Asian countries to invest the gains of growth in human development resulted in devastation for millions of people. However, there is another route to community wellness and poverty alleviation that is not linked to rapid or elevated economic growth. Sen (1999b, p. 46) claims that "in contrast with the growth-mediated mechanism, the support-led process does not operate through fast economic growth, but works through a program of skilful social support of health care, education, and other relevant social arrangements." The success of this approach is evidenced in countries such as Costa Rica and Sri Lanka and in the State of Kerala in India. These places achieved rapid reductions in mortality rates and marked improvement in living conditions without much economic growth.

In the State of Kerala, human development indicators rise despite poor economic growth. This case demonstrates that distribution of resources, and not necessarily economic growth, can contribute to wellness. In Kerala, the population has very high rates of participation in community development, leading not only to social progress but also to personal and collective wellness. The case of Kerala illustrates how fraternal values of social cohesion and democratic participation, along with collective values of justice and equality, contribute to improvements in community wellness. Positive actions at the collective level bring about desirable outcomes at the personal level, not the least of which is a sense of empowerment and control.

With a GNP per capita of less than $700 per year in 1994, Kerala and Sri Lanka had life expectancy at birth of 73 years. In contrast, with a GNP per capita of $4,000, Gabon had a life expectancy of only 54 years. Brazil, with a GNP of nearly $3,000, had a life expectancy of 63 years in 1994. Sen (1999b) concludes from these figures that it is not only growth that will bring prosperity but a wise distribution of available resources across the entire population.

The celebrated case of Kerala deserves attention because it reflects trends vastly different from the rest of India. Kerala achieved human development rates that are comparable to developed nations. As a percentage of total adult population, Kerala has a literacy rate of 94%, compared to 65% in the rest of India and 96% in the United States. Life expectancy for females is 72 in Kerala and 80 in the United States. This is very interesting in light of the fact that Kerala's GNP per capita is $324 and the United States' is $28,740. Infant mortality per 1,000 in Kerala is 13, compared to 65 in low-income countries and 65 in the rest of India.

Critical Consciousness

Kerala's story has a few implications for critical consciousness in poor and rich countries alike. The lesson for poor communities is that investment in education, health, and human rights can generate wonderful benefits for public health, even if the investments are small. Remember that Kerala is not any richer than most other states in India, yet it achieves much better quality of life through policy reforms. In most cases, economic poverty is exacerbated by participation poverty. Not in Kerala, however, where women's movements since the beginning of the past century made the connections between social and economic poverty and endeavored to gain political power to improve the well-being of children and families. As Sen observed, it is not only how large the pie is, but how you divide it.

The lesson for richer countries is that popular participation through critical consciousness can make a difference. If it works in countries with few resources, there is a good chance that it can work in communities with access to the Internet, advanced communication systems, and political networks. The problem in rich countries like the United States is that critical consciousness, at a massive scale, is close to nil. Even people who are horribly affected by racism and poverty often espouse the American dream proposition that if you work hard enough you can overcome any obstacles.

Critical consciousness depends on the degree of openness of the population, which, in turn, depends on the degree of ethnocentrism in the nation. The United States is highly averse to learning from other places. Although a little bit of reverse colonization would do this country some good, it remains fiercely insular and afraid of foreign influences, not only from exotic places like Kerala, but also from European counterparts.

The fear of strangers and strange ideas combined with the fervent belief in the American dream conspire against critical consciousness: Our system is the best, and if you don't succeed in it, it's your fault. Don't blame the system, blame yourself. So deeply does that dictum penetrate the national psyche that, paradoxically, it is freely reinforced by those who suffer from it most.

Critical Experiences

The women in Kerala endured discrimination and poverty. They suffered with their children and experienced firsthand the toll of second-class citizenship. A daily dosage of indignity fueled their rightful indignation toward a caste system that condemned them to lives of despair. But despair they did not. On the contrary, their pain solidified their resolve to do something about it. The result was not hopelessness but resistance, resilience, and revolt. Organize they did, launching a century-long campaign to improve child and family health and well-being.

The critical experiences of Kerala's women were not confined to poverty; participation and political power also shaped their destiny. Their engagement in a human rights struggle empowered them and reinforced them to continue to fight for their children. Participation in civic and political institutions was both intrinsically and instrumentally beneficial. They helped themselves while helping others—the famous helper therapy principle (Reissman, 1965).

Critical Action

How did Kerala achieve these positive indices of human development? Through a series of land reform and redistribution of resources, as well as highly participatory social programs, Kerala managed to invest in social programs dedicated to economic equality and to improvement in health and education. In the village of Nadur, for instance, the abolition of rice land tenancy contributed dramatically to reductions in inequality. Improvements in tenant protection had equally positive effects. School and nursery lunches throughout the state improved caloric intake of children in the poorest households by 5%. Provisions made available through ration shops also decreased hunger. Agricultural labor pension helped a great percentage of the population. The ration shop, school lunches, and agricultural labor pensions benefited the female-supported households more than male-supported households. They thus contributed to reductions in one aspect of gender inequality. Franke and Chasin (2000, p. 24) conclude that "Kerala's quality-of-life achievements result from redistribution. But why has redistribution occurred in Kerala?" According to the authors, the answer lies in the century-long history of popular movements in the state. "These movements have gone through many stages, from caste improvement associations to trade unions and peasant associations to . . . the Kerala People's Science Movement" (p. 24). These social movements have forced the government to listen to the concerns of the poor and have lobbied successfully for the introduction of poverty-alleviation measures. Narayan, Chambers, and colleagues (2000, p. 265) claim that "coalitions representing poor people's organizations are needed to ensure that the voices of the poor are heard and reflected in decision making at the local, national and global levels."

LINKED SOURCES

Poverty, participation, and power are closely related sources of community well-being. Money matters for well-being, no question about it, but especially for the poor. As Frey and Stutzer (2002, p. 90) indicate, "Higher income clearly raises happiness in developing countries, while the effect is only small, if it exists at all, in rich countries." More than money is needed to achieve well-being. Once you have it, your attention turns to other nonmaterial goods, such as participation and control over your life. There is a bit of a ceiling effect for people who already have enough money to cover basic needs. Evidence suggests that income above $10,000 adds very little to happiness (Frey & Stutzer, 2002). You can put more money into your pocket, but if you don't have a sense of control and meaningful participation in life your gains in happiness will not be substantial.

So far, we talked about making money. Now think about the relationship between losing money and well-being. Extensive research documented by Frey and Stutzer (2002) unequivocally states that unemployment greatly diminishes life satisfaction. The lack of meaningful participation and the costs to one's identity take a toll on well-being. But in addition to income and unemployment, there is a third economic indicator worthy of mention: inflation. "Inflation has a marked effect on people's happiness. . . . Studies suggest that inflation harms people" (p. 115).

All in all, these three economic variables have repercussions on people's well-being, but their effects can be attenuated by other psychosocial variables. For example, people who are unemployed don't feel as bad when many of their acquaintances are also unemployed. And, as we saw earlier, beyond a certain threshold, money doesn't add too much to happiness; meaningful relationships and sense of control are required to elevate quality of life (Eckersley, 2005).

Strong demonstrations of the effects of power and participation derive from comparisons among Swiss cantons conducted by political economists Frey and Stutzer (2002). Their studies showed that cantons with higher levels of political participation via referenda experience higher levels of well-being than cantons with fewer opportunities to influence political decisions. Given that Switzerland's 26 cantons exhibit great variability with respect to possibilities for direct participation in the political process, the investigators had a wonderful opportunity to correlate political participation with measures of well-being. What they found was that "more extensive political participation rights, as well as more autonomous communes, increase people's subjective well-being" (p. 150).

Their groundbreaking research made two more important points. They were able to show, "for the first time, that good political institutions do indeed raise happiness" (Frey & Stutzer, 2002, p. 150) and that people value direct participation not only for the outcomes they obtain, but also for the mere act of participating in decisions affecting their lives. The point is that citizens value open and participatory decision-making processes above and beyond the specific outcome of the decision. Following the values introduced in Chapter 3, we can clearly state that self-determination is enhanced in democratic models that favor direct participation in communal affairs.

The implication for happiness, then, is as follows: In poor countries, money matters more than in rich countries, but in all countries, regardless of economic resources, democratic participation is crucial to achieve higher levels of satisfaction (Bruton, 2001). And let's not forget that in rich countries there are many poor communities for whom economic well-being is a chimera. In their case, the power to make an economic difference through participation in the political process is vital.

ROWS FOR WELLNESS

Exercise 12: The Three Ps of Community Well-Being

Community well-being depends on power, poverty, and participation. In this exercise, we ask you to identify a community of interest to you and assess the ROWS of the community in terms of the three Ps. With respect to power, consider to what extent people in the community feel in control of their lives; regarding poverty, examine the level of economic well-being of its members; and with respect to participation, explore how people get involved in social and political affairs. Together, these three factors are powerful predictors of community well-being. After you complete the ROWS exercise (Form 12.1), go on to the Wellness Readiness Check.

By now, you are familiar with the wellness readiness exercise. Insert in Form 12.2 the ROWS statements and put a checkmark under the appropriate column. The profile can help you conceptualize an intervention in your community of interest.

Form 12.1   ROWS Exercise 12:   The Three Ps of Community Well-Being

Risks	
Power	
Poverty	
Participation	
Opportunities	
Power	
Poverty	
Participation	
Weaknesses	
Power	
Poverty	
Participation	
Strengths	
Power	
Poverty	
Participation	

Form 12.2   Wellness Readiness Check 12: The Three Ps of Community Well-Being

ROWS	1 I never thought about doing something about it.	2 I'm thinking about doing something about it.	3 I'm prepared to do something about it.	4 I'm doing something about it.	5 I've been doing something about it for some time.
Risks					
Power					
Poverty					
Participation					
Opportunities					
Power					
Poverty					
Participation					
Weaknesses					
Power					
Poverty					
Participation					
Strengths					
Power					
Poverty					
Participation					

13

How to Promote It? Strategies for Community Well-Being

December 1, 1955. An African American woman boards a bus in Montgomery, Alabama. She sits in the fifth row with three other African Americans. This is the first row African Americans could occupy; the first four rows are reserved for Whites. When the driver sees a White passenger standing, he orders the African American passengers in the fifth row to vacate it, as people from the two races were not supposed to sit together, and the White passenger took precedence. Three African Americans stood up. One person refused to vacate her seat. She was Rosa Parks. Rosa Parks stayed seated, not just for herself, but for many of her people who for far too long had to cede their seats. Rosa Parks ignited the famous Montgomery bus boycott that would become a milestone in the struggle for civil rights in the United States. She went to prison for her defiance and became a symbol of freedom for her oppressed sisters and brothers (Loeb, 1999). She passed away on October 24 of 2005. In the wake of her death, many commentators appropriately praised her heroism and defiance toward a racist system of segregation.

Her bravery notwithstanding, Rosa Parks did not do this by herself. Neither her her refusal to give up her seat nor the boycott that came afterward were cases of singular leadership. On the contrary, a whole movement stood behind her when she refused to cede her place on the bus, and a whole movement supported her efforts to make sure her courageous act was not in vain. The movement that ended segregation in this country was truly *transformational*.

About 30 years prior to the Montgomery boycott in Alabama, Chicago was struggling with another all-too-common social ill: delinquency. In the 1920s, Clifford Shaw and Henry McKay studied the distribution of crime in the city, discovering that delinquency was higher in areas exhibiting the most "social disorganization," which consisted of high rates of mobility and poverty (Greenwood, 2006). Based on their study, a group of community-based organizations created the Chicago Area Project (CAP). In his thorough study on the prevention of delinquency, Peter Greenwood (2006) describes in *Changing Lives* how the Russell Square neighborhood in the south part of the city became the focus of the project. Closely attached to St. Michael's Church, the project trained community volunteers in mentoring youth at risk and provided afterschool and recreation programs. In addition, local leaders advocated on behalf of troubled youth with the courts, schools, and police. CAP assisted youth on parole and mobilized local residents to give youth a chance to rehabilitate. Through community organizing and networking, CAP "was undeniably a success in building an indigenous structure, fostering local leadership, eliciting widespread community support, and altering the way in which youth-serving agencies dealt with the neighborhood" (pp. 22–23). Although outcome research could not ascertain causation, there was a decline of two-thirds in delinquency rates in the areas targeted by CAP. Chicago Area Project is an example of *amelioration* of a serious social problem.

When you compare the civil rights movement with CAP it becomes obvious that the former is more transformational than the latter. Though useful and terrifically important, CAP did not transform society the way the civil rights movement did. Ameliorative projects usually do not get to the root causes of problems. Instead, they mostly deal with the symptoms of social ills, such as delinquency, teen pregnancy, child abuse, and domestic violence. Victims of these circumstances require immediate help, no question about it, but it's important to distinguish between treating symptoms and getting to the bottom of things.

George Albee (1998, p. 373), one of the most ardent proponents of social transformation in psychology and the helping professions, illustrates the distinction between amelioration and transformation by contrasting the contributions to humanity of some prominent figures:

> Most people, if asked to rank in order of importance Albert Schweitzer, Mother Theresa, John Snow, and Ignatz Semmelweiss, would put the first two names at the top and confess ignorance about the latter two. Yet, in terms of contributions to humankind, like the number of lives saved throughout the world, Snow and Semmelweiss tower over the other two. It may seem subversive or mean-spirited to fail to praise Schweitzer and Theresa as recent-day saints, but I greatly prefer the canonization of Snow and Semmelweiss.

Albee makes the point that Schweitzer and Mother Theresa, the former with his hospital in Africa and the latter with the poor in India, were trying to save humanity one person at a time. Snow, whom we encountered earlier in the book, discovered that cholera was a water-borne disease. Semmelweiss, in turn, realized that physicians in Budapest were carrying poison and disease from one section of the hospital to another. Unbeknown to them, doctors and trainees delivering babies were causing child-bed fever and maternal death. Semmelweiss ordered all physicians to wash their hands for 10 minutes before delivering babies. All of a sudden, child-bed fever and maternal deaths stopped almost completely. Snow and Semmelweiss saved thousands of lives by going to the root cause. They realized that health cannot be improved one person at a time. They both discovered ways to prevent problems in the first place.

The same situation applies to social and psychological problems. While some devoted counselors and social workers treat people one at a time in ameliorative fashion, like the volunteers in CAP did, other people like Rosa Parks and Dr. Martin Luther King try to change the root causes of segregation and oppression in the first place. The trick is how to do both, and how to build on our ameliorative efforts to move us toward transformation. It is not one or the other, as the prevalent mentality dictates. Counselors, parole officers, and food bank workers—they all come into contact with poverty and suffering and they all know a great deal about the root causes of the problems their clients face.

A major limitation in embracing both amelioration and transformation has been a rigid definition of our roles as helping professionals. Somehow, we've indoctrinated millions of professionals into thinking that they have to do one or another: You either put on psychological Band Aids or you become a revolutionary and try to change the world. Our job in this chapter is to explore how to bridge the all-necessary ameliorative work of tending to the wounded with the all-necessary transformative work of social change. One of the most frequent questions audiences pose to us is how to bridge the ameliorative-transformative divide. We hope to show in this chapter that, with a little imagination and commitment, everyone can do both. To help us figure out how to blend the two, we present in Table 13.1 key parameters of both paradigms that Geoff Nelson and Isaac (Nelson & Prilleltensky, 2005) developed for their book on community psychology.

BRIDGING AMELIORATION AND TRANSFORMATION

Whereas ameliorative work soothes wounds, as in the efforts of Mother Theresa and Albert Schweitzer, transformative work alters the social conditions that lead to suffering and ill health, as in the efforts of Rosa Parks, Dr. Martin Luther King, and Gandhi. There is no question that social services need to help the homeless when they are cold and hungry, but there is also no question that homelessness needs to be eradicated. Whereas the former has traditionally been the province of social workers, the latter has been the province of politicians and policy makers. This dichotomy has resulted in the muting of very important voices. Social workers and street workers know a lot about homelessness, but their rescue job has not offered them a meaningful opportunity to play a role in the eradication of the problem.

Table 13.1 Distinguishing Characteristics of Ameliorative versus Transformative Interventions

Characteristics	Interventions	
	Ameliorative	Transformative
Framing of issues and problems	Issues and problems are framed as technical matters that can be resolved through rational-empirical problem-solving; power dynamics are ignored. Scientific problem-solving is in the foreground; power is in the background.	Issues and problems are framed in terms of oppression and inequities in power that require emancipatory solutions, as well as research and problem-solving. Power, oppression, and liberation share the foreground with scientific problem-solving.
Values	Since issues and problems are framed in technical terms, the value emphasis of the intervention is often ignored. However, the values of health, caring, and compassion are implicitly given the most emphasis. Values are in the background.	Values play a central role in the conceptualization of the intervention. While the values of health, caring, and compassion may be present, greater emphasis is placed on the values of self-determination, participation, social justice, respect for diversity, and accountability to oppressed groups. Values are in the foreground.
Levels of analysis	Issues and problems are examined in terms of an ecological perspective that is attuned to multiple levels of analysis. However, interventions are often targeted at improving personal and organizational well-being. Intervention at the personal and organizational levels is in the foreground.	Issues and problems are examined in terms of power dynamics that are conceptualized as occurring at multiple levels of analysis. Intervention occurs at all levels of analysis, but there is concerted effort to improve collective well-being. The collective level of analysis is in the foreground, even for interventions at the personal and organizational levels.
Prevention focus	Prevention is aimed primarily at the enhancement of protective factors, including skills, self-esteem, and support systems.	Prevention is aimed primarily at the reduction of systemic risk factors, including racism, sexism, and poverty.
Desired outcomes	The primary desired outcome is enhanced well-being, which is conceptualized apolitically and narrowly at the individual level of analysis. Specific outcomes include the promotion of individual well-being, which	The primary desired outcome is enhanced well-being, which is conceptualized in terms of power at multiple levels of analysis. Specific outcomes include increased control, choice, self-esteem,

Table 13.1 (*Continued*)

Characteristics	Interventions	
	Ameliorative	Transformative
	includes self-esteem, independence, competence, the prevention of psychosocial problems in living, and the enhancement of social support. Outcomes at the individual level of analysis are in the foreground.	competence, independence, political awareness, political rights and a positive identity; enhanced socially supportive relationships and participation in social, community, and political life; the acquisition of valued resources, such as employment, income, education, and housing, and freedom from abuse, violence, and exploitation. Outcomes at multiple levels of analysis that emphasize power-sharing and equity are in the foreground.
Intervention process	The intervention process may be "expert-driven," but usually involves collaboration with multiple stakeholders from the community.	The intervention process involves a partnership in which professionals work in solidarity with oppressed groups and possibly other stakeholders from the community. Conscientization power-sharing, mutual learning, resistance, participation, supportive and egalitarian relationships, and resource mobilization are in the foreground of the intervention process.
Roles for helping professionals	Since issues and problems are framed as technical matters that can be resolved through rational-empirical problem-solving, the role of professional helpers is to lend their professional expertise to the community to solve problems. Program development and evaluation are emphasized. The professional expertise is in the foreground, while the political role of the helping professional is in the background.	Since issues and problems are framed in terms of oppression and inequities in power that require resistance and empowering solutions, the role of professionals is to work in solidarity with oppressed groups to challenge the status quo and create social change. Social and political action is emphasized, along with program development and evaluation. The political role of the helping professional shares the foreground with the professional role.

Adapted from *Community Psychology: In Pursuit of Liberation and Well-Being*, by G. Nelson and I. Prilleltensky (Eds.), 2005, London: Palgrave Macmillan.

We often hear the argument that it is for experts in social policy to eradicate homelessness, or that it is up to medical experts to eradicate HIV/AIDS. The truth is that so far, social policy makers and health scientists have not eradicated the major social and health problems of the day. This is not because they lack the proper expertise, but because these are not only technical but also social problems. Many social issues, such as the lack of universal health care in the United States, remain intractable because the public has not become sufficiently enraged by the gross injustices that are perpetrated in the name of the capitalist system. Helping professionals have an essential role to play in explaining to the public the connections between private interests of the medical profession and insurance companies and the lack of universal health care. The same can be said of the private interests of pharmaceutical companies and the astronomical prices of medications. The closer a professional is to suffering, the more it behooves him or her to speak up against injustice.

How can we make sure that the invaluable information that social workers have does not get lost? How can we make sure that the voices of counselors and nurses are heard? How can we create a seamless opportunity for helping professionals to do amelioration and transformation at the same time? The answers lie in developing critical consciousness, critical experiences, and critical action. As illustrated in the previous chapter, these are vital components of community well-being. But to develop each one of these three critical faculties, we need to invoke another strategy introduced earlier in the book: I VALUE IT. Hence, this chapter advocates bridging amelioration and transformation through critical consciousness, critical experiences, and critical action by the use of strategies contained in the I VALUE IT model. Whereas before we concentrated on the roles contained in the model, here we develop a series of strategies concordant with each letter of the system. Table 13.2 describes the roles and strategies derived from each of the letters.

Our task now is to implement these strategies to promote personal, organizational, and community practices that blend amelioration with transformation.

PERSONAL CHANGE LEADING TO COMMUNITY WELL-BEING

To refresh your memory from the previous chapter: Critical consciousness consists of a reflective attitude toward social and political structures that questions their legitimacy, explores interests at play, and analyzes who wins and who loses from structures of inequality. Furthermore, critical consciousness scrutinizes the ideology that supports systems of unfairness. In other words, critical consciousness does not take for granted that the current state of affairs is the only possible one. On the contrary, critical con-

Table 13.2   Roles and Strategies Derived from the I VALUE IT Model for the Promotion of Critical Consciousness, Critical Experiences, and Critical Action

Roles	Strategies
Inclusive host	Develop inclusive environments for the development of CC, CE, and CA
Visionary	Promote visions of community well-being through CC, CE, and CA
Asset seeker	Search for assets in partners that can foster CC, CE, and CA
Listener and sense maker	Listen carefully to experiences of peers, clients and marginalized populations and frame them in terms of CC
Unique solution finder	Work with partners to find the most contextually sound CA
Evaluator	Establish culture of reflection to evaluate CC, CE, and CA
Implementer	Make CC, CE, and CA part of the everyday activities of your organization, movement, community, public and private life
Trendsetter	Once you have established practices for CC, CE, and CA within your own organization, community, and life, try to set a trend for others to follow

Note: CA = Critical action; CC = Critical consciousness; CE = Critical experiences.

sciousness discloses the many contradictions inherent in our social system. As Diemer and colleagues (Diemer, Kauffman, Koening, Trahan, & Hsieh, in press, p. 4) put it, "In essence, critical consciousness represents the capacity to critically reflect and act upon one's sociopolitical environment."

Critical consciousness can be nurtured by watching documentaries, reading critical essays, joining book clubs, or simply attending to alternative media such as *Z* magazine (zmag.org), TomPaine.com, democracynow.org, commondreams.org, TheNation.com, and *The New Internationalist* (newint.org). On a daily basis, people are fed very uncritical renditions of the news that never challenges the status quo. Although they create the illusion of democratic debate in programs such as *Crossfire* and *Meet the Press*, the discussions never challenge the prevailing state of affairs but only tinker with policies that support the status quo.

Some people may have a knee-jerk reaction to this list of media. Some of you may be thinking that these are all radical media that are totally out of the mainstream. To that we say: Try it. It is very common for the dominant media to propagate knee-jerk defensive reactions to all matters nonconventional.

How can you, as a citizen, create an inclusive environment for you and others to contemplate alternative renditions of how the world goes round, of what makes society tick? Paulo Freire (1972, 1973), the great Brazilian educator, used to start by asking people to reflect on their lives: Is there something they find oppressing in their families, in their workplaces, in society at large? It all starts with a certain degree of introspection, with checking your own emotions and reactions to perceived oppression. In a climate of safety and acceptance, people feel secure to explore their own critical experiences. Some people repress memories of oppression, but most can elicit from their repertoire of experiences instances when they might have felt diminished, put down, dismissed, or ignored. Once the presence of oppression is recognized in a personal life, the jump to the political is not huge. But critical consciousness and critical experiences do not readily translate into critical action.

In *Soul of a Citizen: Living with Conviction in a Cynical Time*, Loeb (1999) argues that people shy away from social action because they feel unprepared or inadequate. He talks about the perfect standard, according to which no action can be taken until you know all there is to know about a subject and until you feel completely ready. Truth is, you will never know all there is to know about an issue, and there will never be a perfect time. Children, work, family, travel, and the like will always be there. Moreover, nobody knows all there is to know about a subject. The best we can do is to be as informed as we can be and enact our values in pursuing justice. We reviewed at length in Chapter 3 the values we support. Of course, you don't have to agree with our principles, but you surely have your own, which should guide you toward action.

The perfection standard is a strategy designed to silence people and to defer to experts. So far, the experts have not come up with great remedies for child abuse, homelessness, domestic violence, corporate welfare, crime, teen pregnancy, war, white-collar crime, or tax evasion. It is a downward spiral: You don't believe you know enough, and therefore you don't become involved. Because you'll never know enough to be an expert, and only experts can speak, you'll never speak. Because you'll never speak, you'll never discover your own voice and you'll never be able to influence social affairs. In the end, you lose and society loses. Loeb (1999) does a magnificent job of documenting the prevailing myths that operate against social action.

The pernicious effects of the perfection standard operate in health and human services. Although professionals in these fields know a lot about their clients' plight, they keep deferring to authorities for major policy making, thereby muting themselves. But not always; thankfully, some people are vocal and do not shy away. The Just Therapy team in New Zealand (Waldegrave et al., 2003), for instance, addresses issues of poverty, exclusion, and gender discrimination in therapy sessions and in the community, just as the Dulwich Centre does in Adelaide in South Australia. In our own work with local human services, we have seen professionals discover their social action voice and become involved in local politics, bridging amelioration with transformation through advocacy and community organizing.

If you want to promote critical consciousness, you can think of critical experiences that you and your colleagues can undertake to educate yourselves. In our graduate program in community research and action, we instituted a field school in Latin America. Students have gone to Ecuador and are going next to Argentina to experience firsthand the negative consequences of the economic policies of the International Monetary Fund. Nothing like being there to understand what policies can do to people.

The opportunities for critical experiences are literally endless. You can watch movies together, invite members of the community to share with you some of their struggles; you can travel to developing countries, or you can just have a conversation with your colleagues about society and some of its conformist and constraining norms. What's important is that in each of these opportunities you try to be an inclusive host, you try to listen respectfully, and you try to come up with an action plan that creates small wins for you and your partners in social change. It can be as small as attending a demonstration together, or as big as adopting a cause, such as gentrification or the environment, and having action plans that can be pursued as a collective.

It is important to always ask the question, How can we build from our ameliorative practice toward transformative action? No need to change the world overnight; one step at a time will suffice. No need to do it all by yourself, either. You could never sustain yourself without support, nor would you go very far. These are little antidotes against the hero complex.

When Rosa Parks died in 2005, very few commentators noted the many frustrations she experienced in the civil rights movements, the vast movement of supporters and the many hours of training she underwent to become an agent of social change. She was portrayed as a hero who made it all happen by herself. In fact, Rosa Parks had received training in community organizing in Highlander in Monteagle, Tennessee, and had participated in many organizing sessions with peers in the civil rights movement (Loeb, 1999). For every famous Rosa Parks, there are many unsung heroes who do great work behind the scenes. This teaches us a few things. First, you don't need to be famous to work for social change. Second, for every famous actor there are lots of foot soldiers doing incredibly important work behind the scenes. Third, nobody can mount a social movement overnight. Fourth, you have to be ready for occasional defeat, and you have to celebrate little accomplishments whenever you have them. Fifth, you have to know how to work with colleagues and how to harness critical consciousness and critical experiences for critical action.

As noted in earlier chapters, in recent years researchers have come to realize the influence of emotional intelligence in dealing with groups and organizations. Daniel Goleman and colleagues (Goleman, 1998; Goleman et al., 2002) have emphasized the role of personal and social competences in leading teams. Goleman concentrated primarily on organizational change, but his lessons about emotional competencies can be applied all the same for the promotion of community well-being through critical consciousness, critical experiences, and critical action. Table 13.3 summarizes the key emotional competencies required for dealing successfully with people, including yourself, and their transformational potential for critical consciousness, critical experiences, and critical action. Table 13.3 speaks to the emotional competencies required for advancing each. The more you can develop in yourself and others these capacities, the more successful you'll be in promoting with others community well-being.

ORGANIZATIONAL CHANGE LEADING TO COMMUNITY WELL-BEING

The story of the United Way of Metropolitan Nashville illustrates how I VALUE IT can help in developing critical consciousness, critical experiences, and critical action. Concerned with its impact in the community, this well-recognized foundation engaged in a process of self-reflection. My students and I (Isaac) created a team to evaluate the foundation's policies and practices. We created an inclusive environment, we listened attentively, we built on their assets, and we evaluated systematically their funding to health and human services. We're now in the process of finding unique solutions to their challenges, integrating our SPEC model into their operations, and setting a trend. Of all the I VALUE IT strategies, we've used especially I, V, A, L, and E. The E for evaluating policies and practices was invaluable in promoting critical consciousness and critical experiences. We assessed to what extent the organization was funding projects based on the SPEC model presented earlier in the book. In other words, we wanted to see whether their funding was supporting strength-based, preventive, empowering, and community-change efforts.

The United Way's new vision was to build on community strengths, to do more prevention, to empower communities, and to change communities. After we conducted a systematic analysis of their funding of community projects, we realized that their funding was out of sync with their vision. Out of 166 projects funded, 112 emphasized individual strengths, and only 5 built on community strengths. Of the remaining 49 projects, 48 were not strength-based at all. As can be seen in Figure 13.1, this was a big realization. They immediately learned that funding priorities needed to change to build more on community strengths. A similar graph was found for dollar allocations. Most of the money went to individual-based programs.

A similar incongruence between vision and funding allocation was found with respect to prevention. The United Way wanted to move toward universal and primary prevention projects addressing entire communities, yet the findings revealed that most of the funding, and most of the projects they supported, were reactive and treatment-oriented as opposed to proactive.

Table 13.3   Emotional Competencies and Potential for Promoting Critical Consciousness, Critical Experiences, and Critical Action Interventions

Competence				
Personal			**Social**	
Self-Awareness	**Self-Regulation**	**Motivation**	**Empathy**	**Social Skills**
Emotional competencies				
Emotional awareness	Self-control	Achievement drive	Understanding others	Influence
Accurate self-assessment	Trustworthiness	Commitment	Developing others	Communication
Self-confidence	Conscientiousness	Initiative	Service orientation	Conflict management
	Adaptability	Optimism	Leveraging diversity	Leadership
	Innovation		Political awareness	Change catalyst
				Building bonds
				Collaboration and cooperation
				Team capabilities
Potential for promoting CC, CE, and CA				
Self-awareness	Monitoring effects of oppression on behavior	Pursuit of liberation and well-being	Appreciating others' experiences of oppression	Persuasive in promoting need for justice
Recognizing personal experiences of oppression	Ethical behavior in all domains of life	Commitment to change, well-being	Promoting others' sense of agency	Active listening and use of plain messages
Understanding impact of oppression on self	Accountability for actions	Ability to mobilize self and others	Transformational orientation	Fair resolution of differences
Sense of agency	Appreciation of impact of change on self	Work with others to maintain hope	Respecting and valuing minorities' experiences	Inspiring self and others to do their best
	Willingness to be challenged		Perceiving effects of power dynamics in group	Promotion of change for liberation and well-being
				Solidarity with people who are marginalized
				Value-based partnerships
				Fostering synergy, fun, and satisfaction in group

Note: CA = Critical action; CC = Critical consciousness; CE = Critical experiences. Adapted from *Community Psychology: In Pursuit of Liberation and Well-Being*, by G. Nelson and I. Prilleltensky (Eds.), 2005, London: Palgrave Macmillan. Used with permission of Palgrave Macmillan.

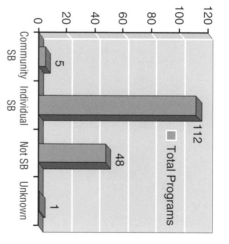

Figure 13.1   Number of Community or Individual Strength-Based (SB) Programs (Out of 166) Funded by the United Way of Metropolitan Nashville.

This finding is graphically depicted in Figure 13.2. When the amount of dollars allocated to prevention versus treatment was plotted, a similar graph was found. In other words, most of the programs funded and most of the money allocated were for treatment as opposed to prevention, and most of the prevention efforts were for people already at risk or showing signs of problems. Most of the problems dealt with by these programs reflect the kind of ameliorative work Mother Theresa and Albert Schweitzer were doing. According to our findings, very little effort was devoted to the legacy of John Snow and Ignatz Semmelweiss.

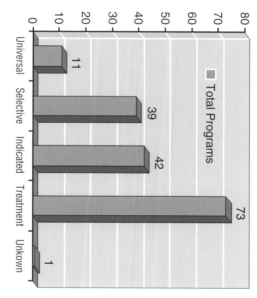

Figure 13.2   Number of Programs funded by the United Way of Metropolitan Nashville (Out of 166) Devoted to Universal, Selective, Indicated Prevention or Treatment.

As noted, the foundation was interested in empowering communities, not only individuals. Figure 13.3 shows once again that most of the programs were aiming to empower individuals as opposed to communities. When the dollar amount was considered, a similar result was found.

The final component of SPEC is community change. The foundation was interested in promoting changes at the community level, thereby addressing some of the root causes of physical, psychological, and family suffering. As with the previous letters of SPEC, the findings showed that most of the programs and most of the money went to change individuals as opposed to communities. Figure 13.4 shows the dollars allocated to changing community conditions as opposed to individuals.

These findings contain important lessons for organizational change for community well-being. First, by evaluating what the organization was funding systematically, the collective consciousness of the agency was raised about its priorities. Second, it provided an avenue for change: They could concentrate on funding more preventive and community-based efforts. Third, it gave them a baseline from which to assess progress. This exercise in evaluating their own efforts added to the strategies of being inclusive hosts, good listeners, and asset seekers as an important component. With these data, they are about to set a new trend of emphasizing community-based and preventive action. Their decision will have ripple effects throughout many health and human services, locally and perhaps even nationally.

This case shows that there are many potential points of entry into an organizational change process. In this case, the research turned out to be a key piece in creating some critical consciousness. This organization is not

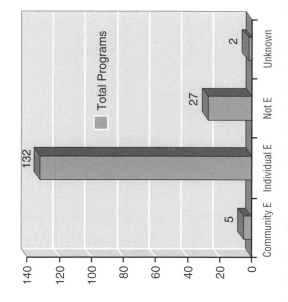

Figure 13.3   Number of Programs fuded by the United Way of Metropolitan Nashville (Out of 166) with Community or Individual Empowerment Focus.

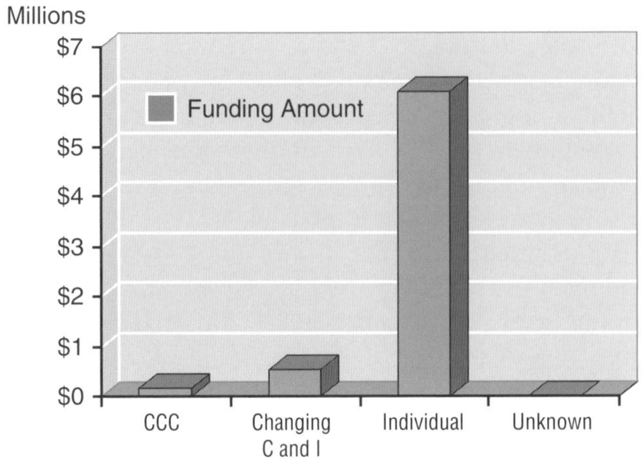

Figure 13.4   Amount Allocated to Changing Community Conditions (CCC), Changing Both at the Same Time (C and I), and Changing Individuals in Programs Funded by the United Way of Metropolitan Nashville.

yet at the stage of generating massive critical experiences or critical action, but it is a start.

In contrast to this organization, which is in the beginning stages of critical consciousness, critical experiences, and critical action, the Grameen Bank in Bangladesh is a leader in these capacities for community well-being. It all started when Muhammad Yunus, a Bangladeshi, came to our school, Vanderbilt University, to study economics in the 1960s. Upon completion of his studies at Vanderbilt, he returned to Bangladesh to discover that the type of economics he had studied at Vanderbilt were not very helpful to his country or his people. As head of the Rural Economics Program at the University of Chittagong, he started a program to provide credit to poor men and women without collateral. With his own money, he started an enterprise called microcredit, whereby the poor are given small loans to start their own businesses. His small pilot projects grew into the Grameen Bank (Grameen means "rural" or "village" in the Bangla language), which now serves 5 million people and is 90% owned by the rural poor it serves. The project has lifted millions of people out of poverty.

When Muhammad Yunus returned to Vanderbilt to give a talk about his experiences with the Grameen Bank, I (Isaac) immediately realized that the Grameen Bank embodied the best qualities of SPEC. He built on the strengths of the rural poor; they were hard-working and enterprising people. The bank helped prevent poverty and a host of associated maladies. In addition, the bank empowered poor people to help themselves. Yunus shared with us how he went from village to village convincing people that they could lift themselves out of poverty with a little help. He convinced people that they were worthy of credit and that they could make a living without being totally indebted to the loan sharks who used to exploit them. He believed that the poorest of the poor could help themselves if they were given a decent chance. For him, the chance was in microcredit. Finally, he created an institution that was truly transformative. He changed community conditions for millions of poor people.

Yunus is an exemplar of I VALUE IT. He created a space for poor people's voices to be heard; he was a visionary who created a model institution that rigorously evaluated its steps and that expanded and created a new trend in Bangladesh and throughout the world. He went against received wisdom in giving people loans without collateral, and he fought a system of injustice that exploited the poor with exorbitant interest rates. He promoted critical consciousness among the poor, who had their fair share of critical experiences. He brought it all together in creative critical actions. The actions of the Grameen Bank challenged conventional precepts about who can get loans and who can run a bank. The bank is now involved in diversified investments in the telecommunications and health care industry and continues to thrive (see www.grameen-info.org, www.grameen.org). When Yunus came to Vanderbilt he made the point that if the poorest of the poor could work when given an opportunity, other people could, too. His work is most transformative. He tackled not people's laziness, as many who blame the poor for their misfortune are quick to do, but conditions of injustice and exploitation. Once the conditions were favorable, the poor embraced the opportunity to work without being indebted for life to unscrupulous lenders.

Different points of departures and different contexts distinguish the story of the Grameen Bank and of our local United Way. Whereas the former operated in a very poor rural context, the latter did most of its business in an urban Western setting. Their differences called for unique strategies, but both cases used aspects of the I VALUE IT strategies to foster critical consciousness, critical experiences, and critical action. What our local partner could learn from the Grameen Bank is that even highly institutionalized and regulated bodies such as banks can engage in transformative work.

Two other business ventures show how organizations can promote community well-being. One story is from my native Argentina and the other from Spain. When I returned to Argentina in 2004 after an absence of nearly 30 years, I went to visit a print shop in Chilavert, Buenos Aires. There I met Cándido. He told me an inspiring story. When many businesses in Argentina were declaring bankruptcy at the beginning of the century, a workers' movement emerged. Factory and service workers throughout the country organized to keep businesses afloat. In many cases, owners had all but abandoned the factories without paying overdue wages or honoring their creditors. In the case of Chilavert, workers in the print shop decided to take over the business. At first, they encountered legal problems, as the owner intended to sell the machinery and close the shop. Later they were challenged by the police, who threatened to arrest all the workers when they refused to vacate the premises. Upon hearing of the police threat, the entire neighborhood mobilized to protect the workers; they literally circled the shop and prevented the police from coming in. When the workers were prevented from distributing their merchandise, a next-door neighbor offered to be their distributor. As the shop was under police surveillance, the workers used an air conditioning vent to pass their products to the neighbor. The neighbor left in the middle of the night to distribute the merchandise on behalf of the workers. Today, Chilavert continues to operate in a cooperative fashion (Magnani, 2003; there are many stories that can be read on the Internet about Chilavert and other worker-run businesses; see, e.g., http://www.newint .org/issue368/pollen.htm).

The worker-run "recovered" businesses, as they are called, is a movement that spread throughout Argentina. Most workers report higher wages, more life satisfaction, more solidarity, and improved output. The film *The Take* by Avi Lewis and Naomi Klein, distributed by the National Film Board of Canada, depicts this new social movement. Workers in these recovered businesses had plenty of critical experiences. They used their experiences to foster critical consciousness and critical action. They transformed business organizations that were hitherto run in very hierarchical and exploitive fashion into cooperatives that enhanced the well-being of workers, their families, and their communities.

The cooperative movement, though not very popular or well-known by mainstream measures, is a viable alternative to business as usual. Mondragon, in the Basque region of Spain, is an industrial conglomerate with 5 decades of experience running a very successful cooperative. Based on principles of cooperation, social responsibility, participation, and innovation, this organization has provided jobs for thousands of people and is the seventh largest corporation in Spain and the first in its region (www.mondragon.mcc.es). Altogether, the four examples provided here demonstrate that alternatives to the status quo are possible, in business, in the service sector, and in the caring professions. From the Just Therapy Centre in New Zealand, to our local United Way Foundation, to Bangladesh, Spain, and Argentina, more humane, preventive, and just ways of coexisting and helping are viable. These organizations are in different stages of blending ameliorative with transformative paradigms. What they have in common is a desire to unite the two modalities: to provide jobs today but to create a more just society for tomorrow; to help abused women today but to eradicate domestic violence for tomorrow.

COMMUNITY CHANGE LEADING
TO COMMUNITY WELL-BEING

In the early 1990s I was very taken by the research on self-help and social support. I wanted to promote their beneficial effects in a community of refugees. While living in Ontario, I contacted a group of Latin American refugees. These were families that had escaped the political turmoil of countries like El Salvador and Colombia. As an immigrant myself, I was very aware of the challenges involved in moving to a new country with a new language and completely different customs. I had lived in two other countries before and had had to learn two new languages (since then, I've moved to Australia and to the United States). I knew that refugees would struggle with language, employment, cold weather, and a new educational system for their kids.

Some had only recently arrived; others had been in Canada for a couple of years. In all cases, parents complained about the way schools treated their children. In some cases, children were misdiagnosed as having intellectual disabilities; in others teachers didn't want to worry the parents and didn't report learning problems to them at all. What to do?

We convened a meeting of concerned parents and discussed various options. In the end, we trained parents in interviewing techniques and asked them to interview other parents and children about their immigration experience. We called it a needs and resources assessment. When the findings were in, we realized that challenges were widespread and that not much help was available. That needs and resources assessment started a 6-year project that involved the creation of the Latin American Educational Group. Together with residents of the Sand Hills community of Kitchener, Ontario, we started parenting groups, a volunteer-run Spanish school, ESL classes, a job search club, computer training, summer camps, a smoking prevention program for children and youth, and various community activities. One of our first jobs was to advocate on behalf of the children in the various schools. Most schools were very responsive, and they promptly improved communication with the families.

Throughout the 6 years that I was involved with the project, we put into practice the principles of social capital and self-help. As a community psychologist, I helped with the evaluation of various programs. The positive results that we found invigorated the community and persuaded government funding bodies that our efforts were worthwhile.

Not only had we created a sense of community, but we made a bit of an impact as well. As part of the smoking prevention project, we engaged families in social action. Families prepared posters and demonstrated in shopping malls against the ill effects of smoking. I loved in particular the presentation the children made at City Hall; they had collected petitions to ban smoking from public spaces and presented them to city council. It was a very empowering occasion for the kids, most of whom were still in primary school.

Our modest experience connected amelioration with transformation, albeit in a small way. Our smoking prevention plan raised awareness of commercial interests causing harm to kids and engaged families in social action (1. Prilleltensky, Martell, Valenzuela, & Hernandez, 2001; I. Prilleltensky, Nelson, & Sanchez, 2000). It was a small step, but it illustrates how helping professionals can expand their circle of influence from the individual to the collective and from the psychological to the political. In our project, we made a concerted effort to promote critical consciousness, critical experiences, and critical action. We used the various techniques inherent in I VALUE IT with a measure of success.

Building on our experience, one of my students in Australia, Julie Morsillo, worked with youth in Melbourne on several social action projects. The project, appropriately called SAY (Social Action with Youth), made explicit the links between the marginalization of some youth, such as gays and lesbians, and their political and ideological bases (Morsillo & Prilleltensky, in press). Julie was a master at I VALUE IT. She perfected the art of creating inclusive spaces, engaging the young people, and listening carefully to their wishes. She helped them craft projects uniquely tailored to their interests, and she worked with them to evaluate the adventure.

The more explicit the connections between personal and family woes and community injustice, the more empowering the interventions are going to be. For one, they remove from people who are usually oppressed the enormous burden of self-deprecation. Once they realize that the source is not their own inability, but imposed structural barriers, as Yunus amply demonstrated, they leap at the opportunity to make a difference in their communities. This is what Stephen Smith (2005) discovered in his global journey to fight poverty. In *Ending Global Poverty: A Guide to What Works*, the George Washington University professor documents at length external poverty traps. Among others, he includes these:

- Family and child labor traps
- Illiteracy traps
- Working capital traps
- Debt bondage traps
- Information traps
- Undernutrition and illness traps
- Low skill traps
- High fertility traps
- Subsistence traps
- Farm erosion traps
- Powerlessness traps
- Mental health traps

Smith concludes that "from the study of poverty traps we get confirmation that not only is poverty not the fault of the poor, neither are the things usually blamed on the poor, such as high fertility, the underlying cause of poverty—they are a result of poverty" (p. 17). Learning about these traps is a first step in critical consciousness. Coming into close contact with poverty is a powerful critical experience: Witnessing firsthand what poverty does can be transforming. In my own experience, living in Argentina in the 1960s and 1970s provided ample witness opportunities. In my case, it was not only poverty I got to see up close, but also injustice, repression, and brutality. These critical experiences left an indelible mark.

I don't believe you can jump from critical consciousness to critical action without going through critical experiences. Multiple modalities can induce critical experiences; witnessing is only one of them. Whichever avenue you choose to experience personally and deeply what it's like to be poor or marginalized, it has to be more than intellectual discourse. It has to touch you and leave you feeling confused, angry, and resentful. If it doesn't, I'd venture to say it wasn't powerful enough and another dosage may be needed. I'm not advocating for masochism—far from it. Certain realizations cannot be intellectualized but must be perceived in your soul. I think that many efforts at community change fail because people obviate the all-important critical experience step and jump from critical consciousness to critical action. It's like jumping from visioning to solutions without listening.

Smith (2005) provides a series of keys for connecting the personal to the political in overcoming poverty. We can think of them as keys for critical action:

- Health and nutrition for adults to work and children to grow to their potential
- Basic education to build the foundations for self-reliance
- Credit and basic insurance for working capital and defense against risk
- Access to functioning markets for income and opportunities to acquire assets
- Access to the benefits of technologies for higher productivity
- A nondegraded and stable environment to ensure sustainable development
- Personal empowerment to gain freedom from exploitation and torment
- Community empowerment to ensure effective participation in the wider world

All these are critical actions for helping poor communities. You can think of similar critical actions to address other issues affecting your community, such as pollution, commercialization, Wal-Martization of business, corporate corruption, government violence, cuts to essential services, lack of universal health insurance, corporate welfare, violence, teen pregnancy, and union busting.

In a comprehensive review, the authors of the Community Tool Box (2006), a great web tool for community development, identified the following key steps in promoting community health and well-being:

- Analyzing information about the problem or goals
- Establishing a vision and mission
- Defining organizational structures and operating mechanisms
- Developing a framework or model of change
- Developing and using action plans
- Arranging for community mobilizers
- Developing leadership
- Implementing effective interventions
- Assuring technical assistance
- Documenting progress and using feedback
- Making outcomes matter
- Sustaining the work

This list covers some general change principles as well as some specific ones to communitywide change, such as engaging community mobilizers. Several I VALUE IT strategies are noted along the way: establishing a mission and vision (visionary), analyzing information about the problem (listener and sense maker), implementing effective interventions (unique solution finder and implementer), making outcomes matter and documenting the work (evaluator, implementer, trendsetter), and documenting progress and using feedback (evaluator). Although not explicitly mentioned in this list, we highly recommend not skipping the inclusive host aspect of change, mentioned in other parts of the Tool Box, especially under the rubric of participation.

As with processes of personal or organizational change, the steps are never linear but spiral. Some steps overlap and some steps you have to revisit, but in general, it's useful to have guideposts such as the ones in the Community Tool Box. We recommend always keeping in mind the various stages of personal and organizational change in working with communities and the stages of community and organizational change in working with individuals. I VALUE IT is our shorthand for remembering key dimensions of personal, organizational, and community change.

Using I VALUE IT, you can help your community link the personal to the political, the ameliorative with the transformative, and critical consciousness with critical experiences and critical action. And remember: You don't have to do it all by yourself. For every Rosa Parks and every Martin Luther King there are thousands working to make a difference, one step at a time.

LINKED STRATEGIES FOR COMMUNITY WELL-BEING

In *Better Together: Restoring the American Community*, Putnam and Feldstein (2003) survey the United States for projects that promote social capital, from libraries in Chicago to the Dudley Street neighborhood in Boston, to Portland, Oregon, to Saddleback Church in Lake Forest, California, and back to Boston, where they studied Harvard's Union of Clerical Workers. In total, they studied 12 initiatives throughout the country where social capital has served to improve literacy, build cohesion, advance businesses, bridge across ethnic groups, and otherwise foster community well-being. The projects ranged from the ameliorative to the more transformative and political, but they all had something in common. They all used networking, small groups, and face-to-face meetings to create bonding within homogeneous groups and bridging among diverse groups. All the projects involved a measure of personal, organizational, and community change. What they learned was that linking these three domains is fundamental. They also learned that for meaningful dialogue—about critical consciousness or critical experiences—to take place, groups should not exceed 10 people. In fact, small is good. When you are part of a small group, you cannot fade into the background and let others do the work, nor can you be easily ignored.

Some groups studied by Putnam and Feldstein (2003), such as the Harvard Union of Clerical Workers, were highly political in their aspiration. Others were more interested in the arts. But they all engaged people in ways that affected their core identity. In all cases, members of these little cells were touched by a vision and a mission. The power of solidarity and teamwork is what links personal, organizational, and community change. It is the relational aspect of community well-being that binds and sustains people in a just cause. As noted earlier in this book, teaming up for a good cause is not only good for the community, but it's also very good for those who join the team. It is the stories people tell each other and the narratives they create in concert and when their voices are heard, new possibilities emerge. As Smith (2005, p. 43) observed:

Well-being is fundamentally individual, but is also social. Direct participation in one's immediate community, and indirect participation in the larger society, can affect well-being. At the basic village, neighbourhood, or township level, to escape from poverty you must have a voice within your community that is taken seriously when you have a legitimate concern. Your community, or communities, however humble, must be informed, empowered to stand up for their interests, and able to defend their rights.

Putnam and Feldstein (2003, p. 282) claim that "organizing is about transforming private aches and pains into a shared vision of collective action." This is precisely the way to move from amelioration to transformation and from critical reflection to critical action.

ROWS FOR WELLNESS

Exercise 13: Critical Consciousness, Critical Experiences, and Critical Action

In this and the previous chapter, we focused on the notions of critical consciousness, critical experiences, and critical action. In our view, these are vital—not to say critical—components of moving from amelioration to transformation and from individual to collective actions. ROWS can either inhibit or facilitate critical consciousness, critical experiences, and critical action. When you think about a community of interest to you, what are the ROWS for these three critical components? List them in Form 13.1. The exercise might help you identify gaps and avenues for moving a community project forward.

If you're interested in the three critical domains of community well-being, transfer the various ROWS onto Form 13.2. Use this exercise with peers with whom you share a passion for a community issue.

Form 13.1   ROWS Exercise 13:   Critical Consciousness, Critical
Experiences, and Critical Action

Risks that get in the way of	
CC	
CE	
CA	
Opportunities that can promote	
CC	
CE	
CA	
Weaknesses in fostering	
CC	
CE	
CA	
Strengths in fostering	
CC	
CE	
CA	

Form 13.2   Wellness Readiness Check 13: Critical Consciousness, Critical Experiences, and Critical Action

ROWS	1 I never thought about doing something about it.	2 I'm thinking about doing something about it.	3 I'm prepared to do something about it.	4 I'm doing something about it.	5 I've been doing something about it for some time.
Risks					
CC					
CE					
CA					
Opportunities					
CC					
CE					
CA					
Weaknesses					
CC					
CE					
CA					
Strengths					
CC					
CE					
CA					

V

Challenges and Conclusions

The next three chapters deal with challenges to well-being. In Chapter 14, Ora discusses at length the connection between disability and well-being. She contrasts the social model with the medical model of disability and recounts the history of the disability rights movement and the many gains made by its supporters. The chapter brings together many of the concepts discussed earlier in the book and shows their application to the lives of people with disabilities. Ora asserts that many of the challenges experienced by people with disabilities are not inherent in the disability itself, but rather in the way society deals with them.

Chapter 15 tackles the issue of injustice. A detailed analysis of cultural practices demonstrates a mismatch between criteria used to distribute goods and resources and the social context. Although the context dictates distribution of resources based on needs, the dominant ideology dogmatically insists on distributing them according to effort and merit. We discuss in depth the incongruence between the regnant social conditions of the poor and the blind adherence to rigid criteria for distributing gains and pains.

Chapter 16 deals with the many blinders that hinder social progress. The barriers range from the psychological to the educational to the historical. Private interests, socialization, and anxieties get in the way of enacting value-based practices for social justice and well-being. If we are serious about embracing an agenda of justice and well-being, we need to get acquainted with the forces of opposition. Good intentions notwithstanding, the status quo is powerful and habituation is fierce.

To wrap up, Chapter 17 presents 10 conclusions that integrate some of the main lessons of the book. We end by reminding the reader that change for its own sake is more of the same. There is plenty of change going on. The point is to infuse change with values and evidence for well-being.

14

Disability

"BUT I DIDN'T HELP YOU UP, MOM"

It was a bitterly cold winter morning in Winnipeg, the sort of morning when you want to stay in a nice cozy bed. Of all days, Isaac had an early morning meeting at work and could not take 3½-year-old Matan to preschool. I would have to take him on my way to work. There was only one child to be dropped off and the preschool was immediately next to our home. However, this seemingly simple task was not easy for me as a mother with a mobility impairment. There was no parking right next to the building, so I decided to walk Matan to preschool and then come back for my car.

Matan was somewhat fussy that morning; young children have a special talent for taking their time when they sense parental pressure to hurry. We left later than we should have, I walked faster than I should have, and I promptly found myself on the cold, snow-covered ground. For a moment, I felt a mixture of irritation and concern. I was irritated with Isaac, who had to leave early, and with my young son, who took his time. Befittingly, my knee-jerk reaction was: "We should have left earlier." However, Matan's question, "Is it my fault, Mom?" quickly dissipated my irritation. I assured him that he was in no way responsible and that we would find a solution. I was still on the ground, however, unable to get up unassisted. Concern took over. It was –25 Celsius (–13 Fahrenheit) and there was no one in sight. Several cars passed by; however, I doubted that they could see us behind the colossal snow banks that separated the sidewalk from the road. Matan extended his little arm: "I'll help you get up, Mom." I explained as best I could under the circumstances that he was not strong enough to lift me up; only an adult could do that. I felt the chilling wind and noticed that Matan's face was getting red from the cold. Doing my best to stay calm, I told him to walk to the building and ask someone to come and help me. He took several steps forward and then backtracked. "But the door is too heavy for me, I won't be able to get it open." He was on the verge of tears; I did my best to reassure him as I considered my next step.

Another few cars passed by and the two of us waved at them frantically. I breathed a big sigh of relief when I saw a woman getting out; I always feel more comfortable getting this type of assistance from women. I still remember the petite and cheerful teacher who lifted me to my feet. I was impressed that a woman so small could be so strong. We thanked her and, ever so carefully, walked to the preschool. We went in and got Matan out of his boots and snowsuit and into the class. His teacher was very sympathetic and helped me comfort my clearly distressed child.

Along with my concern for Matan, I started to think about the meeting at work that I would undoubtedly be late for. I was a clinician in the school system, and on that morning, I had arranged to meet with a parent and with the school. It was a young single mother who was highly reluctant to come to the school. It took some convincing on my part to get her to agree to the meeting. I had assured her that I would be there. I phoned the school to inform them that I would be late and slowly, carefully walked to my car. Luckily, I had an extra set of car keys in my wallet, as my key holder was buried somewhere under a pile of snow. When I arrived at work, I was relieved to hear that the mother called to say that she would be late. After phoning the preschool to hear how Matan was doing, I sat down in the staff room for a cup of coffee. Finally, I had a few moments to think about myself and about the impact that this experience had on me. I could not deny that it left me shaken.

Safely at home at the end of the day, Matan and I told his dad what had happened. The distress no longer there, Matan was nonetheless bothered by the incident. "But I didn't help you up," he kept repeating. I sat him on my lap and explained that he did the best he could. Following my instructions as well as he did was the best help he could have provided. A little later, Matan came up to me with some of his little toy cars. He wanted to play what had happened. "One car goes by and doesn't stop. Another car goes by and doesn't stop. Another car goes by and stops." He demonstrated with his cars as he spoke. Going along with his game, I said, "This must be the nice lady who came to help us." Matan raised his head from his cars and looked at me with his big brown eyes. "No, Mom, this is me when I am big. I get out of the car and help you up."

This is a cherished story in our family, one that continues to move us despite the 15 years since the incident took place. I share it with you because I think it speaks volumes about the topic of this chapter: wellness in disability and ill health. Much has happened in our lives since that cold winter day 15 years ago. Matan is now almost 19 years old and taller than both his parents, there have been changes in jobs and schools, and our family has moved from Canada to Australia to the United States. In addition to typical transitions that families go through, we are also responding to the progressive nature of my disability and to the need to modify certain tasks and routines. Life isn't always easy, and some days the disability is more of an issue for me than other days. Notwithstanding the challenges, I continuously strive for meaning, fulfillment, and a sense of well-being. For the most part, I am successful. I see these as attainable rather than as lofty goals even in the context of chronic illness and disability.

Disability: Separating Myths from Realities

- People with disabilities suffer from poor health.   True/False
- The most distressing thing about having a disability is having to live with physical limitations.   True/False
- Having a disability is a tragedy that causes considerable suffering.   True/False
- People with severe disabilities are not sexual beings.   True/False

Do you think that all or any of the above statements are true? If your answer is yes, I'm afraid that you are misinformed. Myths about the experience of disability are very common. For example, many people with disabilities enjoy very good physical health. Although some disabilities are associated with chronic illnesses, others are not. Irrespective of that difference, people with disabilities as a group are frequently perceived as medically fragile. For example, some are denied job opportunities due to unfounded concerns that they will take frequent sick days.

Expressions of anger are frequently understood as emanating from frustrations about the impairment. Psychological counseling may be automatically assumed to be a necessity. Being in an intimate relationship and having children may be regarded as unattainable.

In the not so distant past, physical impairment was regarded as a personal tragedy that clouds all other components of personal identity. People with disabilities were perceived as unfortunate beings requiring our sympathy and care. Parents were encouraged to place disabled children in institutions rather than raise them at home. The children attended special schools where little emphasis was placed on their scholastic progress; after all, they weren't expected to grow up and become productive members of society. People with disabilities were usually placed away from the pubic eye, to be displayed only for fund-raising purposes. On such occasions, they would be portrayed as unfortunate individuals who must endure great suffering due to their afflictions. Such images would typically appeal to people's sympathies and would result in donations to various organizations.

To this day, many charity drives depict the lives of people with disabilities as incompatible with fulfillment and well-being. The predominant message in the yearly muscular dystrophy drive is that nothing short of a cure will do. Although the individuals depicted throughout the drive are often referred to as "heroes" and "remarkable people," the focus is still on a diminished quality of life.

It's not that individuals with muscular dystrophy are not interested in a cure, or that those with spinal cord injuries see research as irrelevant. Rather, it is the depiction of people with disabilities as hapless beings, unavoidably devastated by their impairment, that is oppressive and harmful. The past few decades have seen people with disabilities around the world protest their portrayal as passive victims. Individually and collectively, they have resisted the "disability as tragedy" model that they regard as at the core of their plight. Rather than accept their diminished status as emanating from the impairment itself, they have focused on their oppression by the nondisabled majority.

RECOGNIZING, NAMING, AND RESISTING OPPRESSION

In fact, people with disabilities have long claimed that disability is not a personal tragedy that requires medical solutions. They have decried the medical model of disability that regarded the problem as residing solely within the disabled individual. The focus on bodily abnormality meant that medically driven solutions were called for. Treatment was designed, implemented, and evaluated by a host of professionals, with the disabled individual having little input regarding the process. What could not be cured had to be rehabilitated, and what could not be rehabilitated had to be accepted. Psychological theories focused on the need to adjust to one's misfortune and make the best out of a tragic and limited life. Those who did not despair despite their disability were often perceived as being in a state of denial.

People with disabilities have argued that it is society, rather than the impairment itself, that is the source of their disablement:

In our view, it is society which disables physically impaired people. Disability is something which is imposed on top of our impairments by the way we are unnecessarily isolated and excluded from full participation in society. Disabled people are therefore an oppressed group in society.

Thus declared the Union of the Physically Impaired Against Segregation in 1976 (quoted in Barnes, Mercer, & Shakespeare, 1999).

Proponents of this alternative social model of disability have demonstrated the multiple ways in which people with disabilities are socially and economically disadvantaged. Being historically excluded from mainstream schooling, many did not attain the skills necessary to further their education and make them competitive in the job market. Some encounter discriminatory attitudes and a lack of willingness to make simple accommodations in the workplace.

Those who require assistive devices and/or attendant care often encounter paternalistic policies designed to retain professional control over resources. Physical barriers have also been a source of exclusion, as public spaces were historically designed with able-bodied people in mind. A shortage of affordable accessible housing and inaccessible public transportation further marginalize people with disabilities.

Michael Oliver (1996), a disabled academic in the United Kingdom, was one of the first people to talk about the social versus the individual model of disability. Along with other disability activists, he argued that the very term "disability" is about exclusion and disadvantage. For example, Oliver suggested an alternative format to a disability survey conducted by the Office of Population Census and Surveys (OPCS) in the United Kingdom. Whereas the standard version focuses on the impairment as the source of limitation, Oliver's version shifts the focus to disabling barriers and attitudes. Compare the following examples:

OPCS: Can you tell me what is wrong with you?
Oliver: Can you tell me what is wrong with society?
OPCS: Do you have a scar, blemish, or deformity that limits your daily activities?
Oliver: Do other people's reactions to any scar, blemish, or deformity you may have limit your daily activities?
OPCS: Does your health problem/disability make it difficult for you to travel by bus?
Oliver: Are there any transport or financial problems that prevent you from going out as often or as far as you would like?

So what, you may be asking, does all this have to do with well-being? For one thing, the political action and struggle of disabled people around the world has resulted in significant progress. No longer willing to put up with inadequate resources and professional control, people with disabilities have collectively fought for economic, legislative, and social gains. In the United States, the formation of the "independent living movements" in the 1960s and 1970s has been associated with greater individual autonomy as well as more political and economic freedom.

Passage of the Americans with Disabilities Act in 1990 has ensured that many of the aforementioned gains are not contingent on people's goodwill, but are enforceable by law. For example, it is illegal to discriminate against a worker based on disability status, to hold a civic gathering at an inaccessible venue, or to fail to accommodate the needs of a disabled patient at a health clinic.

Although there is still a long way to go, there is little doubt that these practical gains in legislation, economic resources, and social participation do a long way toward the enhancement of well-being. Furthermore, the new focus on disabling societal barriers and systematic powerlessness has done much to improve the self-esteem and well-being of people with disabilities. Consider the following quote from a disabled activist in the United Kingdom who describes the impact that the social model has had on her life:

> My life has two phases: before the social model of disability, and after it. Discovering this way of thinking about my experiences was the proverbial raft in stormy seas. . . . For years now this social model has enabled me to confront, survive, and even surmount countless situations of exclusion and discrimination. . . . It has played a central role in promoting disabled people's individual self-worth, collective identity, and political organization. I don't think it is an exaggeration to say that the social model has saved lives. (Crow, 1996, pp. 206–207)

Say no more.

THE PERSONAL EXPERIENCE OF DISABILITY, IMPAIRMENT, AND ILLNESS

We all stood around and watched her.

She was sitting on a mat on the floor, clad in shorts and an undershirt, struggling to put a top on. Time and time again, she attempted, unsuccessfully, to pull the top over her head. In the fourth or fifth trial, she finally succeeded. Her treating therapist provided warm words of praise, and we all smiled. We were a group of first-year counseling students who were on a field visit to a school for children with cerebral palsy. She was a 7- or 8-year-old girl in the midst of an occupational therapy session. We were many, she was one; we were standing, she was sitting on the floor; we were professionally dressed, she was in an undershirt. She had a disability. We did not.

This scenario took place some 25 years ago, when I was a young counseling student, barely aware that I had a condition that would one day impair my own mobility. Nonetheless, I remember the distinct discomfort I felt at the moment. No one asked this little girl if she was okay with some 20 young students walking in on a dressing session. I've thought about her many times since, as my own disability awareness has developed. The following quote is from research I conducted in the late 1990s on the lived experiences of women with physical disabilities:

> There would be no privacy screens or anything. . . . They'd have us literally running around in our underwear . . . at ages 9, 10, 11, 12, you know, when you become painfully aware of your body and you're becoming aware of the opposite sex as well. . . . They weren't sensitive at all to how it would make you feel and how it would impact on you later on. . . . I really see this as a sort of systemic abuse. (O. Prilleltensky, 2004, p. 115)

The interviewee, in her late 30s at the time, was reflecting on her physiotherapy sessions at a school for children with disabilities in Canada in the late 1960s. It is almost identical to the former scenario that took place in Israel some 10 years earlier.

In recent decades, personal narratives by women and men with disabilities have given voice to their lived experience. Often, such narratives include testimonies of oppressive experiences and threats to self-determination. These oppressive stories are balanced with personal experiences of triumph, support, and resistance. Far from wanting to sensationalize images of oppression, I believe that both ends of the spectrum can teach us a lot about enabling or hindering wellness.

Personal accounts of living with a disability give voice to the pain associated with exclusion and marginalization. Women have been particularly vocal in this arena, arguing that their stories are another indication that the personal is indeed political. In other words, personal stories, pain and all, tell us much about the impact of oppressive practices and attitudes.

In my own research on women with disabilities and motherhood, some participants came across discouraging messages about their sexuality and reproductive options. Ultimately, some decided to become mothers, others did not. Without exception, all discussed the importance of choice and self-determination and the hindering effect of restrictive messages. In the voice of one participant:

I think that every individual, whether you're disabled or not, has the basic human right to make that choice. And nobody should tell you that because you have a disability, whether it be developmental, or physical, or whatever it may be, that you cannot become a mother or be a parent. . . . Society or anyone else should not make that decision for you. . . . The choice should be clearly our own. (O. Prilleltensky, 2004, p. 148)

This is an example of how the expression of oppressive attitudes has fueled resistance and mobilized self-determination. In addition to describing the effects of discriminatory attitudes on their lives, some disabled women and men reflect on the impact of the impairment itself. Some have argued that, its benefits notwithstanding, the social model of disability tends to silence the impairment experience.

If we focus only on the impact of oppressive attitudes and practices, we invalidate some people's struggles with their body. Liz Crow, who credited the social model with saving lives, also argues for the importance of acknowledging impairment-related distress. Jenny Morris is another disabled feminist who argues for the inclusion of personal experience; this is what she wrote in 1991:

There is a tendency within the social model of disability to deny the experience of our own bodies, insisting that our physical differences and restrictions are entirely socially created. While environmental barriers and social attitudes are a crucial part of our experience of disability—and do indeed disable us—to suggest that this is all there is to it is to deny the personal experience of physical or intellectual restrictions, of illness, of fear of dying. (p. 10)

The dilemma for Morris is that being vocal about impairment-related distress may bring back skeletons of the "disability as tragedy" model.

So where does this leave those of us who want it all? For my own sense of well-being, I'd like to feel free to explore and sometimes share different aspects of my disability experience. Sometimes, it is more about exclusion and attitudinal barriers than bodily struggles. For example, when we lived in Melbourne, the local Muscular Dystrophy Association held an information day about research and management issues. Although it was held in one of the hospitals in an accessible room, there was no parking anywhere near the venue. As someone who drives easily but walks with great difficulty, I had a problem. Isaac was out of town, so I was stuck. Unable to walk for more than a few steps, I wanted to take my scooter in the van. I attempted to make prior arrangements with the conference organizers to assist me with my scooter. No, apologized the nondisabled coordinator of client services; no one could meet me at the hospital parking lot. Could I possibly take the train? Was I sure that it was really important for me to attend?

Come I did, after a good friend agreed to park his car at my house at 7:00 A.M., drive my van and help me with my scooter, and then pick me up at the end of his working day. He didn't hesitate for a minute when I asked for help. Thank goodness for good friends. Although I certainly registered my protest at the conference, both orally and in writing, I didn't show the full extent of my wrath at the injustice. It was clear to me from a previous encounter that this coordinator didn't quite know how to handle me as a disabled assertive woman. I am sure I was labeled "a difficult woman."

There. I feel vindicated, having put this incident in writing. I hope that you, the reader, whether disabled or not, are sharing in my outrage at this experience of exclusion. Having shared this story with you, I also want to state that these types of experiences are the exception rather than the rule in my life. I have a loving and supportive partner and a delightful 18-year-old son. When Matan was a middle school student, he was not always thrilled to have me around his friends; however, he was equally self-conscious about his very fit and able-bodied father. A teenager should be allowed to be a teenager; he doesn't have to be a saint because he has a mother with a disability.

My professional life is dedicated to writing, teaching, and training master's level counseling students—all of which I enjoy. I have caring friends and feel appreciated by students and clients. In Melbourne, I worked in a rehabilitation hospital with patients who had illness-related or accident-related impairments. They taught me much about resilience in the face of adversity. Helping them respond to some of the hurdles and challenges in their lives also served as a reminder that we still have a long way to go before oppressive factors are completely eradicated.

Somehow, sharing the productive, fulfilling aspects of my life seems to make it safer for me to discuss bodily struggles and the associated frustrations and distress. My disability has progressed markedly in recent years, making mobility increasingly more difficult. At times, I feel like my trunk and all four limbs are encumbered with weights. I fall down frequently, and while I rarely really hurt myself, I have to be lifted back to a standing position. This is not a problem at home—Isaac and Matan pick me up in a split second—but it is a problem for me out of the house. I don't like getting this type of assistance from other people. Even with my knowledge of disability discourse, I am not immune from having issues regarding dependence and independence. I also experience periods of fatigue and am at times frustrated with how effortful everything is for me. As I look ahead, I know that I will require a greater level of physical assistance in various domains. That is not easy for me.

The challenge for me, and I suspect for some other people with a disabling chronic illness, is to be able to explore and share disability-related as well as impairment-related distress. It is a challenge because in doing so, one risks being pitied, felt sorry for, and seen as helpless and needy. In other words, one risks being "othered." It is ironic that although I write these words with publication and public exposure in mind, I very rarely share these dilemmas with nondisabled friends and colleagues.

At home, with my partner, I feel totally safe to explore different dimensions of the disability experience. He is equally as indignant about disability insensitivity and exclusion and is supportive in a very affirming way. I would never think of him as feeling sorry for me. Pity is not something that I, or any other disabled person I know, need.

A few years ago, we visited some friends in their summer home and took along my manual wheelchair. Their 10-year-old son enjoyed wheeling himself around when it was not in use. At some point, his psychologist father said, "Get up dear, or people will feel sorry for you." I chose to spare everyone the discomfort that would have resulted had I asked him to explain further. Sometimes, it's simply not worth the effort.

SELF-DETERMINATION, SOCIAL SUPPORT, AND OTHER RAMPS TO WELLNESS

Earlier I noted some of the positive movement that has taken place in the past 3 decades in the field of disability. Legislative changes have resulted in fewer discriminatory practices in workplaces and in greater physical access to public spaces. People with disabilities are becoming more visible, not only in the public sphere but also in the media and in advertising. I am reminded of a Royal Bank commercial in which the client is a working mother who is utilizing the services of the bank. Only toward the end of the commercial do we learn that she is also a blind woman who reads her bank statements in Braille. It would be naive to refer to this as social transformation, yet more ads of this type can contribute to a healthier, more realistic portrayal of people with disabilities.

Of course, access to funded assistance for parents with disabilities would make such images more feasible and familiar; cosmetic changes in media images are not enough. However, more allocation of resources toward that end requires further transformation in our thinking about disability. People with disabilities have fought hard for their right to self-determination and control over their lives. They have argued that determining one's course in life is not to be equated with the ability to function independently. In other words, even severely disabled people who require assistance with the most intimate tasks of daily living can maintain control over their lives.

Self-determination is inherent in wellness. Physical independence is not. Yet, my own work in rehabilitation settings has exemplified the degree of importance that is often accorded to physical independence. Much of the work carried out by occupational and physical therapists is focused on patients' ability to carry out independently activities of daily living.

Whereas most people would prefer to be as independent as they can in self-care, it is critical that this is not regarded as necessary for autonomous adult functioning. If a person does not find meaning in preparing breakfast for herself, a task that may take her 45 minutes and drain her of energy that may already be in short supply, perhaps another person could do it for her in 5 minutes.

I am reminded of a patient I worked with who had to negotiate with one of his treating therapists that it is pointless for him to attend a breakfast group. A stroke had left this man with significant physical impairments, although his cognitive functioning remained largely unaffected. It was very clear to him that he would not be attending to his own breakfast at home given the time and energy that this required of him. Given the emphasis placed on physical rehabilitation, convincing his therapist of this was no easy task. Making such decisions on behalf of others is what truly robs people of dignity and control over their lives.

Along with maintaining control over their own lives, people with disabilities wish to contribute to the lives and well-being of others. In 1991, the American Psychological Association granted a prestigious award to Emory Cowen for his work on the promotion of wellness. In his acceptance speech, Cowen (1991, p. 405) defined wellness as "having a sense of control over one's fate, a feeling of purpose and belonging, and a basic satisfaction with oneself and one's existence." To have a feeling of purpose and belonging, we need to be able to share our lives with others, be supported by those we care about, and contribute to their lives. Having a disability, however severe, does not mean that one is always on the receiving end of care and support. A few years ago, when Matan was 15, I wrote the following about my life as a mother with a disability:

If you see me walking with my son, you will notice that my left arm, crossed with his right one, is not merely a display of affection. He is clearly helping me walk. You might even come to the erroneous conclusion that he carries out many care-giving tasks for me. You only have to come to our house as I prepare his lunch in the mornings, drive him to one of his activities or discuss curfews, to realize that I am clearly a parent in charge. He has never had any doubts about the caring role I play in his life, even though I was not able to lift him after the first few months of his life. A caring role is much more than caring functions.

Feeling satisfied with oneself and one's existence is the third component of Cowen's (1991) definition of wellness. This is often associated with the ability to form and maintain friendships and intimate relationships. For many years, people with disabilities have had to fight the stereotypical myth that they are asexual beings. Being excluded from sexual expression and perceived as unsuitable sexual partners has been associated with poor self-esteem and a lower level of life satisfaction overall. However, there is some positive movement on that front as well. More information is available on sexuality and disability; adults with disabilities are asserting their rights to intimacy and sexual expression; parents are becoming more aware of the importance of promoting a healthy psychosexual identity for their children with disabilities.

Public perceptions also need to be targeted for change. Media images of people with disabilities as working, studying, parenting, and doing other ordinary things need to counterbalance the gloomy images perpetuated by charity drives. Likewise, sexuality and its expression need to be portrayed as the domain of everyone, not only those who are young, physically fit, and conventionally attractive.

Disability and wellness are not a contradiction in terms, just as health and youth are not a guarantee for happiness and fulfillment. Given the rising rate of illness and disability as we advance in age, chances are that we will all be affected one way or the other by a limitation, either directly or indirectly. Enhancing the well-being of people with disabilities is ultimately everyone's business. Let's see now how Fran confronts myths and realities in her pursuit of wellness.

FRAN'S STORY

"Hey, Fran, you look like you're in another dimension. Come on, it's coffee time." Fran looked up and saw Cathy's friendly smile. She remembered about Cathy's date last night and knew that her friend was eager to talk about it. She grabbed her crutches and the two slowly headed toward the staff room.

Fran is a 26-year-old systems analyst at a large accounting firm. She has been recently promoted and is now supervising five junior colleagues. Fran was born with cerebral palsy. She walks with crutches, and her speech, though comprehensible, is somewhat affected.

Fran lives in a one-bedroom flat in the city, a 15-minute drive from her work. She comes across as a bright, assertive young woman who is well liked and respected by those who know her. In fact, some of Fran's colleagues regard her with wonder. Somehow, this bright, articulate, and attractive woman does not fit their perception of a person with a disability. Just the other day Fran completed a project that she had been working on for several weeks. When she delivered it to Dave, one of her team members, he told her that she was absolutely amazing—that he doesn't know how she can do it.

After the interaction with Dave, Fran felt moody and deflated. She likes Dave and enjoys working with him. However, this "you're amazing" business is something that she's heard before, and it doesn't make her feel good. Fran knows that Dave wouldn't tell Cathy she is amazing just because she handed in a good piece of work. Rather than seeing her as just Fran, a talented systems analyst, he sees her as a person with a disability who has "made it."

Confronting Dave with this wouldn't be easy, though, as he merely gave her a compliment! Somehow, it is much simpler to deal with behavior that is clearly ignorant or disablist. Like the woman she saw at the parking lot on her way to the building. Seeing Fran walking with her briefcase and crutches, the woman hurried over and grabbed Fran's briefcase from her, nearly knocking her off her feet. Fran politely yet assertively told her that she was fine, thank you, and that it is better to ask if help is needed.

Fran is well versed in this. She was brought up to believe in herself, her abilities, and her right to be an assertive and autonomous person. From a young age, she learned to articulate what she needs and refuse help that is not wanted. She is grateful for her parents' supportive yet demanding parenting style that contributed so much to her positive sense of self—if only they didn't ignore the sexual part of her identity. This was one area that had been carefully avoided at home.

Although it was never stated, Fran had always assumed that her parents had no expectations that she would be in an intimate relationship. Recently, Fran shared some of these frustrations with her brother Timothy. She told him about some of her past relationships that he was unaware of. She also told him about Jason.

Fran met Jason through her volunteer work at the Independent Living Center. They were both serving on the same committee. Jason is a 30-year-old attorney who sustained a spinal cord injury as a young boy. He is a paraplegic and uses a wheelchair to get around. Jason's interest in Fran was apparent from the moment they met. He made attempts to engage her in conversation, frequently glanced in her direction, and was the first to volunteer his help on a project she was overseeing. Initially, Fran didn't even consider the possibility of a relationship with Jason. However, she found herself looking forward to their weekly committee meetings and took extra care with her appearance on those days. She was nonetheless confused and at a loss when Jason suggested that they have dinner together the following week.

Fran knew that the time had come to confront her own biases, her own internalized oppression. Having grown up in a nondisabled environment, having been groomed to succeed and blend in, she had rarely associated with people with disabilities. Only in the past year had she begun to critically explore her past reluctance to have anything to do with the disabled world. She became aware that she herself held some stereotypical views about disability. That's when she contacted the independent living movement and became involved in some of its causes and activities.

Fran has met some wonderful people through the ILM. The work there has enriched her life immensely. In the friendship she was nurturing with Lesley, a woman with multiple sclerosis, she found herself able to talk about things that she has not shared even with Cathy. Lesley is happily married to Joe, a nondisabled man, and is the mother of a 3-year-old girl. However, she'd had some disheartening experiences in the past as she attempted to form intimate relationships. Fran shared some of her own experiences, including issues she'd had in the past with body image and sexuality. She told Lesley about a doctor who recommended that she consider tubal ligation as a permanent method of birth control. Despite the assertive way in which Fran handled this incident, she felt depressed and disempowered in the aftermath. It took her some time to shake these unpleasant feelings.

Being with Lesley and hearing about her husband and child was an affirming experience for Fran. It restored her faith that she, too, could have this in her life. More important, Fran was beginning to critically evaluate her past yearnings for a nondisabled partner. Perceiving a partner with a disability with disdain is a form of self-devaluation. For the first time, Fran feels free to form a relationship with a loving man—disabled or not. She doesn't have to prove herself to anybody. And right now, there is nothing she wants more than to confirm that dinner date with Jason.

ROWS FOR WELLNESS

Exercise 14: On Disability

By now, you should be very familiar with ROWS exercises. We are going to examine now some of the risks, opportunities, weaknesses, and strengths in Fran's case (see Form 14.1). After that, we ask you to do an exercise yourself (see Form 14.2).

You may not have a disability yourself, but you may know somebody who has, or you may be closely associated with a person with a disability. If you have a disability or a physical impairment, consider what your personal ROWS are. If you are closely related to a person with a disability, complete the exercise from your own point of view as a friend or relative of a person with a disability. How does the disability affect you? If you neither have a disability nor know somebody who has, try to complete the ROWS as if you had a disability. Imagining yourself in such a situation can increase your awareness about some of the challenges people with disabilities face.

As in previous chapters, the question now is what you can do about your ROWS. You can reinforce strengths, or you can fight risks and weaknesses. It's always best to try to do both.

We saw in the ROWS exercise some of the factors affecting Fran's life and your own life. You're familiar by now with the Wellness Readiness Check. We want to help you devise a wellness promotion plan that suits your unique situation. But first, let's have a look at how Fran would go about promoting wellness in the face of her own disability (see Form 14.3).

Now it's your turn to do your own Wellness Readiness Check. Simply transfer the ROWS from the previous exercise to Form 14.4 and put a checkmark below the option that suits your situation best.

Form 14.1   ROWS Exercise 14: Fran's Case

Risks	Mom and Dad ignoring my sexuality
	People who want to help too much
	Others seeing me as either needy and dependent or as a superstar
	Doctor's disablist assumptions
Opportunities	Timothy's growing awareness
	Friends—old and new
	Disability rights movement
	Relationship with Jason
Weaknesses	Internalized oppression
	Feeling like I have to prove myself
	Downplaying impact of disability
	Not confronting certain people
Strengths	Smarts and abilities
	Increased self-confidence
	Ability to change
	Feeling sexual and attractive

Form 14.2 ROWS Exercise 14: On Disability

Risks	
Opportunities	
Weaknesses	
Strengths	

Form 14.3   Wellness Readiness Check 14: Challenges in Fran's Case

ROWS	1 I never thought about doing something about it.	2 I'm thinking about doing something about it.	3 I'm prepared to do something about it.	4 I'm doing something about it.	5 I've been doing something about it for some time.
Risks					
Mom and Dad ignoring my sexuality	X				
People who want to help too much					X
Others seeing me as either needy and dependent or as a superstar		X			
Doctor's disablist assumptions				X	
Opportunities					
Timothy's growing awareness				X	
Friends— old and new					X
Disability rights movement				X	
Relationship with Jason			X		
Weaknesses					
Internalized oppression			X		
Feeling like I have to prove myself			X		

(continued)

Form 14.3   (*Continued*)

ROWS	1 I never thought about doing something about it.	2 I'm thinking about doing something about it.	3 I'm prepared to do something about it.	4 I'm doing something about it.	5 I've been doing something about it for some time.
Downplaying impact of disability					
Not con-fronting certain people		X			
Strengths					
Smarts and abilities					X
Increased self-confidence				X	
Ability to change		X			
Feeling sexual and attractive			X		

Form 14.4   Wellness Readiness Check 14: Your Situation

ROWS	1 I never thought about doing something about it.	2 I'm thinking about doing something about it.	3 I'm prepared to do something about it.	4 I'm doing something about it.	5 I've been doing something about it for some time.
Risks					
Opportunities					
Weaknesses					
Strengths					

15

Injustice

THAT'S NOT FAIR!

Sound familiar? It's easy to think about ourselves when it comes to injustice. Our antennae pick up acts of unfairness against us with ease. However, they're not as sharp when it comes to injustice against others. For multiple psychological and evolutionary reasons, we're on guard most of the time. Deeds of injustice, small or large, damage our dignity.

What about lack of fairness toward others? How sensitive are we to deprivation or dismissal of other people's needs? We venture to say that there is a big gap between our sensitivity to injustices committed against us and our sensitivity to injustices against others. How wide the gap is depends, as noted in previous chapters, on the level of critical consciousness, critical experiences, and critical actions. It is true that we can learn to be more conscious of injustice, but it is also true that in the drama of survival and dominance in which we all participate, our attention is drawn to ourselves most of the time. Rather than pretend that we are all virtuous beings most of the time, we take it as a given that our own interests usually come first. This is not to deny the existence of self-sacrificing people who are willing to give up their lives for others or for a cause, but they are the exceptions that prove the rule.

In this chapter, we discuss the impact of injustice on ourselves, others, and entire communities under the rubrics *thinking about yourself*, *thinking about others*, and *thinking about us*, respectively. These three categories allow us to pay attention to our own issues as well as to others' well-being.

THINKING ABOUT YOURSELF

It turns out that unfairness is not only morally wrong but also dangerous to your health. Lack of fairness can even shorten your life. That is the conclusion from a longitudinal study of 5,726 men and 2,572 women from the British Civil Service working in London. The study examined the effects of unfairness on coronary disease and overall health functioning in the Whitehall II study, mentioned earlier in the book (de Vogli, Ferie, Chandola, Kivimäki, & Marmot, 2006). When Roberto de Vogli, the chief investigator, told me (Isaac) at a conference in Padua, Italy, that unfair treatment can increase your risk of heart disease, I was not surprised, but it was not until I read the paper that I realized the magnitude of the impact. By following up participants for an average of 7 years, the research team was able to ascertain that reports of being treated unfairly predicted lower levels of physical and psychological health and higher levels of heart disease. The study produced three main conclusions:

This study demonstrated that unfairness has an independent impact on coronary events. The risk of incident coronary events among participants who strongly or moderately agree that they were often treated unfairly was 55% higher compared to those who reported low levels of unfair treatment, controlling for age, gender, employment grade, traditional coronary risk factors, and other psychosocial characteristics. Unfairness was also related to poor physical and mental functioning at follow up controlling for baseline factors including health functioning. (de Volgi et al., 2006)

The authors can only speculate about the precise mechanisms linking unfair treatment to disease, yet they reason that an assault on one's dignity increases physiological mechanisms associated with stress and malfunction. Feelings of inferiority induce biological reactions inimical to well-being. As the authors note:

Humiliation due to unfair treatment can also produce important mental health effects. On the one hand, violations of dignity may induce feelings of being de-valued or increase insecurity and anxiety. On the other hand, the response to perceived humiliation may be anger and hostility, often employed as a "face-saving strategy" to defend the loss of dignity. These emotional reactions have also been found to influence stress, and coronary heart disease. (de Vogli et al., 2006)

If you were one of the unlucky participants in this study who experienced a high degree of unfairness, needless to say, your physical and mental health would suffer considerably. It is not unlikely that in your personal life you experience a certain amount of unfairness in your relationships at work or in your family. You might have intuitively known that this is not good for you, but now we have research to support your hunches. Not only does unfairness not feel right, it harms your physical and mental well-being. What to do?

Critical consciousness, critical experiences, and critical action, shown earlier to benefit community health, can help you to overcome the ill effects of oppressive relationships. Granted, not all relationships can be easily changed—you may be unable to confront your boss without risking the loss of your job—but critical reflection and strategizing may help you in significant ways. If you happen to be overpowered by somebody, it helps to know it and to name it. Many people internalize pejorative images projected onto them by others in positions of authority—bosses, teachers, parents, older siblings, spouses, professionals of all sorts. Understanding the power dynamics operating in the relationship can help you ascertain its oppressive nature. Once you realize it's not your fault, you need to strategize how to change the unhealthy dynamics. Easier said than done, you say. We couldn't agree more. It is possible that some of the strategies presented in this book, such as ROWS exercises, may help you. But it is also very possible that you may need help from a trusted friend, sibling, or even a professional helper.

If relationships are complicated and hard to alter, social conditions of injustice are even more difficult to alter. It is possible that you may find some ideas in this book helpful, but joining with others to challenge oppressive norms and practices is more likely to help you than trying to be a lone hero or revolutionary.

Injustice comes in all forms and shapes. Recognizing it in your personal life is the first step in overcoming it. Some people may be able to overcome it by themselves; others will need to rely more on others. There is no single way to resolve injustice. Solutions are as varied as the people who seek them. Many have been known to fight effectively against personal and social injustice, as the examples of Martin Luther King and Gandhi demonstrate.

So far, we have been talking in this chapter about you as the recipient of injustice. But most of us inhabit multiple identities. Though it may be comforting to think that we're only the recipients of injustice, chances are that many of us are also perpetrators of such.

THINKING ABOUT OTHERS

Freud brought to sharp relief the dark side of our personalities. Of course, our behavior is influenced by the environment, but we ignore our own aggressive tendencies at our own peril. Some social conditions inhibit, and others encourage them, but in any case, we all possess the capacity to oppress and inflict pain. Above and beyond the moral imperative to consider the well-being of others, thinking about others is as much a survival mechanism as anything else. Oppressing others or just letting them be oppressed affects your own well-being. Oppression and injustice, inflicted by you or others, breed contempt, anger, and aggression on the part of the aggrieved population. Just look around and see what people think of oppressive colonial forces, in the present and in the past.

To really think about others and their experience of injustice, we think that you must be able to see yourself as capable of oppressing. We all have internal demons we need to confront. We are not concerned here with the question of origins—personality deficiencies, ill parenting, collective unconscious, or capitalism, it's always an interaction—but rather with the question of our potential to hurt others. We believe that within ourselves is the capacity to ignore suffering, if not inflict it directly. Just remember how the world ignored the plight of the Jews during World War II or how the military tortured young activists in Argentina in the late 1970s, to mention only two examples that are close to home. The new film *Imagining Argentina*, released in 2005, portrays in detail the despicable techniques used by the military to squelch opposition to the dictatorial regime. From historical accounts, the film is quite accurate.

To think about others and their experience of injustice we also need to feel secure ourselves. To feel secure, we need to surround ourselves with others who can, in turn, think about our well-being and our struggles with injustice. We've come to a seeming paradox: To think about others we need others who think about us, and for others to think about us, we need to think about them and to embrace their insecurities. This paradoxical situation requires that we position ourselves as both agents and recipients of justice and well-being. If we define ourselves solely as beneficiaries of justice or victims of injustice, we fail to contribute our share to reciprocal nurturing and caring relationships. If we regard ourselves exclusively as contributors to the well-being of others, we neglect the emotional nourishment that is required to both nurture ourselves and provide to others, thereby diminishing our capacity to behave caringly and ethically in the long run. Self-abnegating individuals are only superficially so; sooner or later, the lack of personal care catches up with us, exacting a toll on our resources and our ability to care for ourselves or others. So, we better think of ourselves and others. Without the links of reciprocity in action. Without the links of reciprocity in promoting justice for ourselves or others, neither we nor others can benefit from fairness, health, or well-being.

The reciprocal web of wellness woven between two individuals or groups is always located in a wider network. Our own experiences and vicissitudes with respect to justice are situated in a larger context that engulfs all of us in society.

THINKING ABOUT US

Martin Buber (1971) developed the "I-Thou" concept to signify the interdependence of human beings who engage in mutual caring and reciprocal recognition. The I-Thou relationship supersedes the solitary "I" and the separate "Thou." Thinking about "us" supersedes thinking about "me" and thinking about "you" in fragmented ways. It is only when we see our own justice and injustice linked to your justice and injustice that we can move forward in creating collective fairness.

For many reasons having to do with ideology and self-serving beliefs, a great many people conceive of their own well-being in complete isolation. As Margaret Thatcher was fond of saying, there is no such thing as community; there are only individuals and families. For her, society was an aggregate of atomized individuals who interacted only to advance their own private well-being; any collective good stemming from interactions was fortuitous only. She failed to see how cooperation makes thing happen.

Conceiving our collective fate as interdependent is a necessary but not a sufficient condition for the promotion of justice in the community. In addition to feelings of solidarity, camaraderie, and support, we need principles to help us allocate burdens and resources in a fair manner. In Chapter 3, we introduced criteria for the just distribution of goods in society. In the hope of clarifying what it means to think about us in the context of justice, in this section we expand the discussion started in Chapter 3.

WHAT IS FAIR AND WHAT IS JUST

The classic conception of justice is *To each his or her due* (D. Miller, 1978, 1999). That much we saw in Chapter 3. Although useful, this definition begs four key questions. First, who or what is *each*? Second, how do we decide what is his, her, their, or its *due*? Third, *who* or *what* will be responsible for the distribution? Will it be parents, employers, the state, or a combination thereof? And fourth, how do we decide what is due *from* each person or entity? For a definition to be useful, it has to be precise. For a definition of justice to be precise, we need to answer these four questions.

First Question: Who or What Is *Each*?

The *each* in *To each his or her due* has been traditionally conceptualized as an individual. This is a valid but insufficient answer, for the *each* can also be a family, a group, a community, or even society as a whole. Families are entitled to certain benefits and resources, such as child care, health insurance, special education, privacy, and other privileges. Families are units that have been defined operationally and socially as separate entities. Communities are also deserving of special dispensation, such as affirmative action, Medicare, and discounts for seniors. The nation, as strange as it may sound, is also deserving of protections and justice. A democratically elected government should be defended against the military, an oligarchy, or a foreign power from being taken over. Similarly, governments need to get paid for services they provide; when individuals or corporations evade taxes, they are not giving their due (J. Bakan, 2004). Some people end up paying for services and subsidizing those who violate the law. It is possible, therefore, to expand the definition of *each* to families, communities, and the nation.

In this chapter, we will see that families and communities are legitimate recipients of common resources.

Second Question: How Do We Decide What Is *Due* a Person, Family, or Group?

How do we determine the right amount of reward for a person? How do we figure out a fair allocation of resources to a family or community? As noted in Chapter 3, some moral philosophers argue that needs and work are the main criteria (Facione et al., 1978), and others include rights in the distribution formula (D. Miller, 1999). Assuming we accept these three criteria; the question becomes when to apply each, and which one should take precedence. These authors agree that the answer depends on the context. Depending on the circumstances, they claim, it may be fair to use one criterion over another. They argue that it is "reasonable to suggest that persons are strictly equal as persons. This means they all have some very basic human needs. . . . On this criterion people are equally deserving of having these needs met" (Facione et al, 1978, p. 186). A corollary of this premise is that I should distribute a limited resource, first, among those whose basic needs have not been met yet. Once I've accomplished this, I can proceed to distribute the rest on another basis, such as work or merit.

The principle of work refers to time, ability, effort, and skills invested in a particular task. This criterion implies differential reward based on effort, talent, or both. Following Facione et al. (1978), the criterion for distribution should be determined by the particular circumstances. When jobs are plentiful and wages allow a decent living, the criterion of work makes sense. When jobs are scarce or wages insufficient, the criterion of need must be invoked.

D. Miller (1999) adds rights to the criteria of needs and work. People are owed certain privileges by virtue of citizenship: the right to vote, to be protected, and to hold office, among others. In some countries, the right to health care is fiercely defended by the public (Navarro, 2004; Navarro & Muntaner, 2004). Rights are different from needs in that they derive from civic or communal membership as opposed to biological, psychological, or social sources (Ife, 2001).

Whereas needs and rights present no obvious intellectual problems, the criterion of work deserves to be broken down further. Facione and colleagues (1978) invoke ability, opportunity, and effort, but they don't make them explicit. In our view, these three components deserve separate consideration, for we can have ability but no opportunity, and we can have ability and opportunity but no effort. Therefore, we suggest substituting ability, opportunity, and effort for work.

Finally, there is another criterion often implicit but rarely explicit in distribution formulas: power. Feminist (Hill Collins, 1993; Nussbaum, 1999), critical (Bronner, 2002; Peters, Lankshear, & Olssen, 2003), and develop-ment (Clark, 2002; Sen, 1999b) philosophers contend that power differen-tials must be taken into account when allocating resources and obligations. This is a valid argument, for a person might have abilities and willingness to exert considerable effort, but due to lack of power, she is deprived of oppor-tunities. Such is the case in gender and racial discrimination (Hill Collins, 1998; Nussbaum, 1999).

In summary, we propose six criteria for distribution of resources and ob-ligations: *needs, ability, effort, rights, opportunity,* and *power.* Each one of these criteria derives legitimacy from a different source:

- Needs from biological, psychological, and social sources
- Ability from level of development
- Effort from agency and volitional properties
- Rights from civic membership
- Opportunities from structural conditions and circumstances
- Power from political configurations of interests and domination

Whereas the first three criteria refer to person-centered considerations, the remaining three refer to extra-individual or societal conditions. It would be wrong to concentrate only on person-centered criteria to the exclusion of environmental influences, such as opportunities and power differentials. It would be equally wrong to consider some but not all of these criteria. For it is easy to see how a person may possess skills but no opportunities, rights but no power, and effort but little ability. As a result, all the criteria must be consulted before rendering a judgment of distribution. Other things being equal, it is possible that the person with the least amount of power deserves the greatest share of resources, a notion in line with Rawls's (1972) formula for equality and compensation. These are the criteria for people who seek a just society without large resource gaps (Lakoff, 1996).

Third Question: *Who* or *What* Is Responsible for Distributing Resources and Obligations?

We have answered so far the first two questions regarding the original def-inition of justice: Who or what is the *each* in *To each his or her due* and how should we decide what is *due*? The third question is Who or what is the en-tity responsible for distributing resources, burdens, pains, and gains? This question complements the first. Instead of *to,* we now say *from* each his, her, their, or its due. Who or what is the *each* in this case? In my view, the *each* in this case can be the same as the each in *To each his or her due:* indi-viduals, families, communities, or governments. These four entities are re-sponsible for dispensing justice in different forums: individuals in relationships, families among their members, communities among groups, and governments among their constituencies (Nelson & Prilleltensky, 2005).

Fourth Question: How Do We Decide What Is *Due* from a Person, Family, Group, or Institution?

The only question remaining is what constitutes the *due* in *From each his, her, or their due?*

We suggest that the criteria of needs, ability, and opportunity expressed for the receiver of justice apply also to the provider of it. These three criteria vary, however. These are duties (instead of rights), obligation (instead of effort), and privilege (instead of power). Persons or entities entrusted with allocating resources ought to do so in light of their own needs, abilities, and opportunities, and in accord with their civic duties, moral obligations, and degree of privilege (Nussbaum, 1999). The more privilege there is, the higher the obligation. These six criteria are interdependent. A person may have an opportunity to contribute to the well-being of others, and she may even have a civic duty to do so, but if her own needs are not satisfied, her ability to deliver justice will be diminished.

WORKING DEFINITION

Having answered the four key questions of justice, we are now in a position to formulate a working definition. Justice consists of two complementary statements:

1. To each (individual, family, community, or government) according to his or her or its needs, ability, effort, opportunities, rights, and power.
2. From each (individual, family, community, or government) according to his or her or its needs, ability, obligation, duties, opportunity, and privilege.

As suggested earlier by Facione and colleagues (1978), the context should determine what criterion or criteria must be preferred in each case. In social conditions of inequality, we must accord preference to needs over ability in the first statement of justice. Under conditions of relative equality, where the gap between classes is not very pronounced, it is possible to favor effort over needs. In a context of plenty of opportunities for everyone, it is possible that ability and effort will be the preferred choice.

Equivalent contextual considerations apply to the second statement of justice. Governments with abilities and resources to satisfy the public's needs for proper nutrition and health care, for instance, have a duty to do so. This consideration must supersede the government's putative need for more tax cuts or concessions to the wealthy. Similarly, a person with privilege and opportunity can be expected to contribute more than a person with fewer opportunities and power.

Justice, then, requires multiple and complementary considerations, deriving from sources within and outside of the person. Societal conditions create opportunities, duties, rights, and power structures that impinge on what is just. And what is fair and just is an integral part of well-being (Nelson & Prilleltensky, 2005). We consider next the nexus between justice and family and community well-being.

JUSTICE AS A DETERMINANT OF FAMILY WELL-BEING

Family well-being is a positive state of affairs in which individuals within the family, as well as the family unit as a whole, are able to fulfill their needs and aspirations. To do so, family members and family units have to benefit from the following values: caring and protection of health, self-determination, education and personal development, collaboration and democratic participation, respect for diversity, supportive community structures, and social justice (1. Prilleltensky, Nelson, et al., 2001).

If we adapt the general definition of justice presented earlier, we can formulate justice in the family context as follows:

- To each family member and to each family unit according to his or her or its needs, ability, effort, opportunities, rights, and power.
- From each family member and each family unit according to his or her or its needs, ability, obligation, duties, opportunity, and privilege.

Let's start with the first statement. For justice to take place within the family, we have to take into account members' needs, ability, effort, opportunity, rights, and power. It follows that parents will do their best to meet children's needs, that they will expect behaviors in accordance with the children's level of abilities, that they will recognize effort, provide opportunities for development, respect their children's rights, and not abuse their own power. The same applies to relationships between spouses. Relationships among siblings show the interdependence of justice criteria: A sister cannot be expected to understand her brother's needs until she has reached a certain developmental level herself.

Just treatment among family members will determine, to a large degree, the level of well-being enjoyed by individuals within the unit, for well-being is predicated on the fulfillment of certain needs. And need, as you may recall, is a key criterion of justice. Indeed, the very first criterion of justice is To each according to his or her needs. The provision of needs, as a defining feature of well-being, is premised on the enactment of values: caring and protection of health, education and personal development, self-determination, and the other principles stated earlier.

Justice in the family means providing members with basic necessities such as food and shelter, enacting collaborative and caring relationships that respect diversity, expressing caring and concern, and acknowledging power differentials. This is the part that deals with the first statement of justice: To each his or her due. Children and partners are entitled, by virtue of membership in the human community, to justice (D. Miller, 1999).

But the persons doing the giving within the family, usually the adults, are themselves subject to just or unjust relationships with the outside world. This brings us to the second statement of justice: From each according to his or her needs, abilities, duties, opportunity, obligation, and privilege. Parents themselves may be deprived of opportunities to fulfill their own needs or to promote their own abilities. Many teens who are poor and single parents have too few of their own needs met to provide for the psychological development of their children. Families without health insurance struggle to provide optimal developmental conditions for their children.

If parents are the *each* in the second statement of justice, we must take into account their own needs, abilities, duties, opportunities, obligations, and privilege in their overall capacity to be agents of justice for their children, their partner, and their own parents. Some parents and families are the subject of discrimination, as in the case of gay parents, whereas others benefit from tax cuts that exacerbate their privilege without corresponding duties to the common good. Due to family wealth, some children can afford the greatest private education, whereas others can attend only an underresourced public school. In neither case did the children do anything to deserve their lot, but their fate is dramatically different. Due to their contrasting educational experience, one child goes on to get a job with health care, and the other doesn't. The gap in their well-being will continue to expand and will likely be passed on to their children. The conclusion we arrive at is that *justice within the family is contingent on justice outside the family*, and that *family well-being is contingent on community well-being*.

JUSTICE AS A DETERMINANT OF COMMUNITY WELL-BEING

The definition of family well-being can be expanded to community: Community well-being is a positive state of affairs in which individuals within the community, as well as the community as a whole, are able to fulfill their needs and aspirations. To fulfill their needs and aspirations, community members and the community as a whole benefit from the following values: caring and protection of health, self-determination, education and personal development, collaboration and democratic participation, respect for diversity, supportive community structures, and social justice (S. James & Prilleltensky, 2002; Nelson & Prilleltensky, 2005).

For entire communities to prosper there must be a minimal level of need satisfaction. For certain needs to be satisfied, they have to be enshrined in rights. The need for safety, freedom, liberty, and the pursuit of happiness are publicly acknowledged and defended by the state; health, in contrast, is not, at least in the United States. For vast sectors of the population, health, a constituent element of well-being, is not protected by the government in the form of universal health care (Hofrichter, 2003).

To be sure, what constitutes a right is a matter of debate. But if we regard health as a fundamental aspect of well-being, and if rights are a fundamental criterion of justice, shouldn't we make health care a right, not a privilege (Farmer, 2003)? Some countries have chosen to regard health as a right and have established national mechanisms to ensure that everyone, regardless of economic means, has access to health care (Navarro, 2004; Navarro & Muntaner, 2004).

Health is but one example of many showing that family well-being is partly determined by dynamics operating outside the family itself. The ability of parents to fulfill their children's needs is contingent on their own level of development; exposure to opportunities; and satisfaction of needs and rights, effort, and level of power. Many of these requisites depend on how resources are distributed in society, which brings us back to the contextual considerations of justice.

Recall: When people have adequate opportunities in life, their developmental needs have been met, and when there are jobs available for the skills they have, it is reasonable to reward them based on effort. But when these conditions have not been met due to factors outside of people's control, then we need to accord preference to the criterion of need. If we regard lack of health care as a condition outside of people's control, as millions of families in the United States know all too well, then we must provide health care based on need, and not on ability to secure a job with health benefits.

Children whose parents do not treat them fairly suffer. Their suffering is intrinsically undesirable and extrinsically deleterious to community well-being. This suffering will not be altered until people claim their rights and assume their responsibilities.

JUSTICE, RIGHTS, AND RESPONSIBILITIES

Families have rights and responsibilities. Individual family members and families as a whole have the right to expect just treatment, by each other and by entities outside the family. Similarly, individuals within families and families as a whole have the responsibility to treat each other and to treat others outside the family fairly. The same dictum applies to communities, where members deserve justice and have an obligation to pursue it, both within and outside of their own collectives.

The Right to Justice

Families and communities are entitled to justice. D. Miller (1999) has cogently argued that rights must be a criterion for justice. Citizens, qua citizens, deserve protections and entitlements. Some countries pass legislation making the possession of automatic weapons a right. Others pass legislation enshrining the right to health care. What constitutes a right is a matter of choice. Other countries have chosen to make health care a right of all citizens; the United States hasn't. To enjoy the right to health care, and the right to justice, families and communities must take responsibility and take action.

The Responsibility of Justice

Families and communities have the obligation to pursue justice. Justice cannot exist without the agency of citizens. As defined, the fair and equitable distribution of resources and burdens depends on the key word *each*: *To each* his or her due, and *from each* his or her due. To the extent that each of us has some abilities, opportunities, power, and privilege, each one of us can be an agent of justice. To not accept this responsibility would be an act of injustice.

As agents of justice, those with more privilege and abilities have a higher obligation to pursue it than those with fewer powers, opportunities, and abilities. But all of us, to varying degrees, possess abilities and obligations to pursue justice. We need to structure opportunities for such efforts to take place, and we need to rely on efforts to structure such opportunities.

ROWS FOR WELLNESS

Exercise 15: Justice—Thinking about Me, Others, and Us

Based on the preceding discussion, you might reflect on how justice and injustice manifest themselves in thinking about yourself, thinking about others, and thinking about us. You can identify ROWS that either promote or inhibit justice and foster or block injustice (see Form 15.1).

Now transfer the ROWS to Form 15.2. If most of your ROWS are under the first three columns, consider some action. If some of your ROWS belong in columns 4 or 5, it means you are already taking some action.

Form 15.1 ROWS Exercise 15: Justice—Thinking about Me, Others, and Us

Risks that can either prevent justice or promote injustice	
Thinking about me	
Thinking about others	
Thinking about us	
Opportunities that can enhance justice or prevent injustice	
Thinking about me	
Thinking about others	
Thinking about us	
Weaknesses that make justice less likely and injustice more likely	
Thinking about me	
Thinking about others	
Thinking about us	
Strengths that make justice more likely and injustice less likely	
Thinking about me	
Thinking about others	
Thinking about us	

Form 15.2   Wellness Readiness Check 15: Justice—Thinking about Me, Others, and Us

ROWS	1 I never thought about doing something about it.	2 I'm thinking about doing something about it.	3 I'm prepared to do something about it.	4 I'm doing something about it.	5 I've been doing something about it for some time.
Risks					
Thinking about me					
Thinking about others					
Thinking about us					
Opportunities					
Thinking about me					
Thinking about others					
Thinking about us					
Weaknesses					
Thinking about me					
Thinking about others					
Thinking about us					
Strengths					
Thinking about me					
Thinking about others					
Thinking about us					

16

Arrogance, Complacency, and Blinders

Disability and injustice are serious challenges to well-being, but so are arrogance and complacency. We can recognize these properties in ourselves and others. Overconfidence can lead to mistakes and dogmatism; complacency can lead to more of the same. To promote well-being, two obvious implications emerge: Do something, and do it humbly.

What to do? We hope the preceding chapters gave you an idea of how to foster well-being in your personal life, your workplace, and your community. To help you understand what well-being is, we distinguished in Chapter 1 among signs, sites, sources, and strategies of well-being. In Chapter 2, we introduced SPEC, an acronym that stands for the promotion of strengths, prevention, empowerment, and changing conditions. Chapter 3 discussed the balance required among values for personal, organizational, and community wellness, and Chapter 4 introduced the I VALUE IT set of strategies to engage in action. Throughout these four chapters, we emphasized the weblike quality of various aspects of well-being. Personal, organizational, and community well-being are closely linked, as are the values that support them. Chapters 5 through 13 discussed how these factors enable well-being in our personal, organizational, and collective lives.

The webness of it all tells us that we cannot promote personal, organizational, or community well-being in isolation. Because they are inextricably intertwined, sustainable changes must involve systemic transformations (Capra, 2003). But, as you probably know, starting on all fronts at once can be daunting. Where to begin? Is it better to start with some changes in your organization or in your family life? Should you attend to community issues first? You have to think globally to attend to the webness of well-being, but you have to decide where your efforts will be invested locally. An awful threat we must repel is paralysis by analysis: the inability to act because it's all so complicated. Action has a built-in quality of momentum. Once you tackle a relatively small issue and you feel empowered to do something, you gain confidence in your ability to tackle larger, more complex dilemmas (Kotter & Cohen, 2002). The whole purpose of the ROWS exercises we've been suggesting throughout the book is to get you to take small steps to engage in some action that is personally meaningful to you.

Your action orientation can range from paralytic on one end to agentic on the other. Remember Hem and Haw in Chapter 7? Agentic simply means that you see yourself as an agent of change. The more agentic you are, the greater the chance that you will take some risks. Without a measure of agency it's hard to imagine change at the personal, organizational, or collective level.

Sure enough, some people are more inclined to action than others, but your level of agency is not immutable. The important thing to do is to start small, with something you feel comfortable with, and ask for help along the way. You can always adjust your action to a nonthreatening level. If you become so anxious that the thought of engaging in action completely paralyzes you, you've gone overboard. If that's the case, you might have to modulate the first step so the fear of engaging in it doesn't cause you to freeze.

What about arrogance? Your reaction to a process of change can range anywhere from totally optimistic to hopelessly pessimistic. You can be so maniacal and dogmatic that nothing can stop you, or you can be so despondent that nothing can lift you. If you're unequivocally confident about your point of view, you might run over other people. Modesty is a good antidote, especially when it allows other voices to be heard. A modicum of pessimism is a good tonic for overconfident leaders. Antonio Gramsci, the Italian intellectual who spent years in jail for opposing fascism, is said to have espoused optimism of the heart and pessimism of the mind. It is true that families, organizations, and societies are hard to change, said the mind; but it is also true that positive transformations have and do occur, said the heart. Look at the women's movement, the end of slavery, protection for workers, rights for homosexuals. Look at your own life and you may find plenty of instances when you overcame seemingly insurmountable challenges. Haw eventually found cheese.

Try to figure out where you fit in Figure 16.1. Are you more inclined to pessimism or optimism? Are you predisposed to action or inaction? Use this diagram as a diagnostic for yourself and those close to you. Each quadrant in the picture contains a phrase capturing a typical attitude and stance: drive, difficulty, despair, and delusion. In our view, a healthy spot is somewhere on the righthand side between optimism of the heart and pessimism of the mind. This is not to dampen your enthusiasm, but to remind you that a dosage of pessimism can exercise your brain and analytic skills. Too much confidence can cloud your judgment. Let's explore a little more each position in the picture.

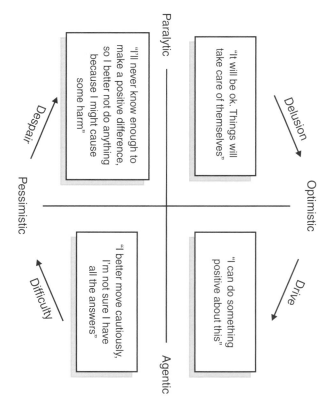

Figure 16.1 Taking Action: Drive, Difficulty, Despair, and Delusion.

DRIVE

This quadrant represents an optimistic action orientation. In working with groups especially, it's important to have such a person, somebody who can infuse hope in the team's ability to achieve its goals. If you're not such a type, you may want to recruit somebody like that or you may want to learn how to be more like that. If you recognize that this is not you, you can do something about it, unless, of course, you're too paralyzed or pessimistic, as Hem was.

The drive stance has the advantages of engaging in action and taking some risks, as Haw did, hoping things will turn out okay. After all, hope is a key ingredient in change processes. Some cheerleading is necessary. However, this posture has some disadvantages. Too much confidence can lead to arrogance, and too much optimism can obviate obstacles along the way. Jumping to action without a good plan is an all too common disease, particularly for managers who are impatient with processes of change and press for quick fixes. Understanding that a good process is a good outcome in itself can mitigate the rush to immediate action. Drive cannot be a substitute for planning.

Drive is a tonic for change, a vitamin for transformation, but like all stimulants, too much of it can be dangerous. At an extreme, the optimist undermines challenges and the hyperagent of change acts without a plan or exit strategy. It's good to be mindful of the risks and benefits of the drive position.

DIFFICULTY

The intersection of the agentic and the pessimistic is the definition of a challenge. People want to act, but they understand the difficulties involved and ponder the use of it all. The merits of this position lie in analyzing realistically the barriers and likelihood of success. Too much pessimism can lead to depression, needless to say, but too little of it can avert realistic appraisal of the situation.

The closer you get to the pessimistic end, the harder it gets to act, because doubt is cast on the nature and meaning of the enterprise. There goes Hem again. An optimal position must be found to maximize the merits of an objective analysis with the advantage of moving forward.

Although this quadrant can mitigate false hopes, it can nevertheless foster arrogance. The armchair revolutionary who casts aspersions on anything the foot soldiers do can be as arrogant as the general who sends the troops to the front without an exit strategy. The optimistic arrogant says, "Don't worry, it'll be okay." The pessimistic arrogant says, "Don't bother, it'll never work." It is theoretically possible that here and there they'll be right, but while they elevate their pomposity they mislead and demoralize others along the way.

DESPAIR

This is a tough spot to be in. If you or your teammates are in it, you need to find a way to get out of it as soon as possible. The combination of pessimism and paralysis is deadly. It can induce depression, lower morale, and affect your overall well-being. No matter what the issue is—a bad marriage or a toxic workplace—lack of hope and inability to act are bad for your mental health.

You may be lucky enough never to be in despair, but it is your responsibility to see who might be. Moreover, it is our collective duty to see what we ourselves might be doing to keep people in such a rotten place. Recall the VIP triangle reviewed in Chapter 8: It stands for values, interest, and power. Often, these factors constellate to oppress those whose views we dislike and whose values we reject. Are our interests and our power involved in creating despair for others in our family or community? Chances are, most of us will summarily dismiss such a possibility, but close inspection of our actions may reveal that we're not as enlightened as we thought we were. Unless we encounter our demons, we can't tame them.

If you happen to be the one in despair, remember that it's very hard to get out of these situations by yourself. Somebody needs to throw you a life jacket. Choose somebody you trust to walk with you in your personal journey of recovery and emancipation. If you happen to be the one inflicting the despair, you will need to gather the courage to admit it and to begin the process of restitution, unless, of course, you choose not to see your role in it, or you have huge blinders.

We can never underestimate the strength of habituation in paralysis. Some people take it for granted that this is their lot in life; others are just too afraid to fail. Acting in the world requires a degree of risk taking that many people prefer to avoid. Too much exposure can bring attention to shortcomings; the fear of failure is just too big. For people like that, emotional support is crucial. If you have students, clients, or relatives like that, you know that holding and containing them is vital. Only gradually can they let go of their fears.

DELUSION

"It will be okay. Things will take care of themselves!" The mix of optimism and paralysis can blind you to the need for change. This stance supports the status quo: "Things are not that bad after all." This is not a negative statement when things are truly good for everybody. However, when injustice and suffering prevail, this amounts to an apology for the status quo.

It is very possible that for some people, things are truly wonderful; Nirvana has arrived. There is nothing wrong with being happy and not wanting to change anything in your life. The problem is that you don't live alone, and your actions forever affect others. It is reasonable to want to relax in comfort when things are peachy for you. But blindly projecting your comfort to others is rather irrational. Things might be okay for you, but not for others who are affected by your behavior, leadership style, parenting, or business practices. If you work with people like that, you may want to wake them up from their slumber. The trouble is, some people don't want to wake up.

BLINDERS

"There are none so blind as those who will not see," goes the old saying. Blinders prevent us from seeing the need for change in ourselves and others. It's hard to promote any kind of well-being when we're wearing blinders. We've identified five common blinders: emotional, polarizing, acquired, situational, and selfish (I. Prilleltensky & Fox, in press).

Emotional Blinders

Some people are so preoccupied with their own emotional issues that it's hard for them to see a way out of the rut they're in, let alone consider others' needs. Feeling despondent can cloud your judgment or your ability to see options. In a sense, it may even seem unfair to expect people who are dealing with their own unresolved issues to help others. The paradox is that if they could help others, they would feel better about themselves. But to get to that point they need help. They need help to help others so that they may help themselves.

In a failed attempt in a community project, we tried in vain to ask people who were emotionally drained to help others. We thought that helping others would lift them from their own powerlessness. What we seriously underestimated was their total lack of energy and mental space. In cases like this, we recommend working with people on their personal and relational well-being until they feel a little stronger to help others. The importance of helping others for one's own well-being cannot be emphasized enough. Part of our dignity relies on being a productive member of society, and helping others fulfills just that role and expectation. Seeing yourself as contributing to others builds your own self-esteem and places you in a network of meaning that cannot be arrived at in isolation.

By being an inclusive host of this person's emotional pain, by listening to her unique narrative, by identifying her strengths and assets, you can help her create a vision for a better future for her and others. But emotional blinders are not the sole province of depressed or despondent people; we all have them from time to time. Being aware of this possibility is a salutary defense against our own excessive pessimistic or paralytic tendencies.

Polarizing Blinders

"You're either with us or against us." In this age of polarizing discourse, this is a common refrain. Demagogues use it all the time to curtail debate and dialogue about serious issues. This indictment is used to demonize those whose views you oppose. Due to emotional insecurity, political interests, or plain limited cognitive abilities, some people invoke this blinder. Complex personal, organizational, and social problems defy black-and-white solutions. Many shades of gray exist, perhaps even more than many people are comfortable with, but our inability to live with uncertainty should not cloud complexities.

The tendency to frame issues in black and white pits one aspect of well-being against another. Thus, libertarians pit the well-being of the individual against the well-being of the community, and right-wing fundamentalists pit the well-being of the community against the well-being of the individual. The former oppose most limitations on personal freedom, and the latter oppose many expressions of it.

Polarizers, if we may so call them, cannot hold the tension that exists among alternative points of view. They want to run away from ambiguity and fail to appreciate the process of discovery involved in creating lasting solutions to problems of well-being. At best, they limit productive debate. At worst, they ridicule others with opposing views. Although sources of polarization are variegated, the outcomes are uniformly bad: dogmatism, demagoguery, and demonizing. Beware of polarizers in your midst, and most of all, beware of your own polarizing tendencies.

Acquired Blinders

"When all you have is a hammer, everything looks like a nail." An acquired blinder is one you've gained through socialization or education. If you happen to have acquired few tools for problem solving, most of your solutions will resemble the limited set of tools you have. When I (Isaac) was dealing with my own grieving process due to my parents' death, I often heard the injunction "Get over it." Men are not supposed to cry. What most people around me knew at the time was to suppress, repress, and deny pain; had they known a little more about psychological processes, they might have been more helpful.

When we encounter a challenge to our personal or organizational well-being, most of us frame it in terms of what we know. It is an automatic process. When I encounter a community problem such as school dropout, I look for the social roots of the problem. I've been trained to look for the metaphorical pump handle described in Chapter 2. When psychoanalysts are presented with a clinical scenario, they invoke certain unconscious dynamics. There is nothing wrong with starting to analyze a problem from the perspective of your specialized lenses. The problem lies in blocking other perspectives. When such blockage occurs, you get closer and closer to arrogance.

Situational Blinders

Sometimes you just can't see an alternative because of your historical, geographical, and cultural location. If you haven't been exposed to other ways of being, or if you have never left your hometown, it's hard to conceive of solutions that don't reproduce what you already know. Coming into contact with other cultures is a way of learning about how other people solve problems. To beat a dead horse, in the United States people cannot easily comprehend how a universal, government-sponsored health plan can work. People invoke all kinds of erroneous assumptions about lack of productivity and the like. People who have not experienced another health care system think that theirs is in fact the only possible one. What's really irritating about this is the ethnocentric attitude that if it's made in the United States, it has got to be the best.

Selfish Blinders

Of all the blinders, this may be the most obvious one: You don't want to see other people's struggles because it's against your self-interest. You rationalize, distort, intellectualize, and undermine other people's problems so you don't have to question your own assumptions or your own behavior. You may even benefit from other people's suffering, but you find ways to rationalize it to yourself. Your wife does most of the housework while you play golf, but it's okay because you work hard at the office during the week. Your children are afraid of you, but it's okay because they have to learn to respect authority. Your subordinates at work feel alienated from you, but it's okay because if you get too close to them they'll take advantage of you. And on and on.

In a real comedy of the absurd, these days the Tennessee legislature convened a special session to deal with ethics in government and the role of lobbyists. While legislators discussed the negative influence of special interest groups, a few lobbyists made campaign contributions to a few lawmakers. Some legislators saw nothing wrong in lobbyists paying for tickets to expensive sports events.

William J. Bennett, former drug czar under President George H. W. Bush, wrote several tomes on virtues and morality. While he was making a fortune on speaking tours, he was also doing some incognito casino tours. For all his moralizing against excessive behaviors of any kind, Bennett had conveniently left out the vice of gambling. Records show he lost hundreds of thousands of dollars in various casinos throughout the country. Apparently, the egotistical blinder was such that he could not, or did not want to see the contradictions between his preaching and his gambling (Green, 2003).

CONCLUSION

The reasons for arrogance and complacency are many and varied: too much confidence and private interest to protect account for the former; too much fear and perfectionistic tendencies for the latter. Either proclivity is unhealthy.

The opposite of arrogance is humility. The converse of complacency is action. Humility makes sure that your self-determination does not override the self-determination of others. Action ensures that unacceptable states of affairs, in your life or in the lives of others, do not continue. Lots of personal and social baggage interferes with our ability to act humbly. We live and breathe a culture that adulates Number One, that infuses competition into everything we do, and that despises losers. Macho cultures exalt winners and show little compassion for the rest. In this climate, being humble goes against the grain. God forbid you should be Number Two.

Similar indoctrination works against social change. We have been taught since a young age that this is the best possible world, and even if we wanted to change it for the better, we couldn't. This breeds a combination of surplus powerlessness and acquiescence to authority (Lerner, 1991; McQuaig, 1998). Supporting text for the status quo abounds, while alternative discourses for families, organizations, and communities are scarce. Blinders of various kinds also reinforce the status quo. Either in the form of personal interests or emotional preoccupation, blinders can stop us from promoting well-being, ours and others'.

We hope to have shown in this book some avenues for transformation in your personal, organizational, and community life. The search for well-being is unique for each of us. We don't know how it will turn out for you, but from ourselves and others, we know that meaning is created along the way.

ROWS FOR WELLNESS

Exercise 16: Overcoming Arrogance, Complacency, and Blinders

In this, your last ROWS exercise, we ask you to consider arrogance, complacency, and blinders. If you start by exploring these in yourself, you may be helpful to others who need to do some work themselves. Using the ROWS, try to identify some of the blinders and expressions of arrogance and complacency discussed in this chapter (see Form 16.1). What are some sources of complacency that might prevent you from looking after your own well-being or the well-being of your organization? What are some of the blinders that might stop you from working to enhance community well-being? Are there any blinders (or a tinge of arrogance) that might even stop you from doing this exercise? Go ahead and try to place some of these thoughts under Risks, Opportunities, Weaknesses, and Strengths. Answer the question, What ROWS stop me or help me to overcome blinders, complacency, and arrogance?

Now transfer the ROWS to Form 16.2 to create an inventory of actions.

Form 16.1   ROWS Exercise 16: Overcoming Arrogance, Complacency, and Blinders

Risks					Opportunities				Weaknesses				Strengths			

Form 16.2   Wellness Readiness Check 16: Overcoming Arrogance, Complacency, and Blinders

ROWS	1 I never thought about doing something about it.	2 I'm thinking about doing something about it.	3 I'm prepared to do something about it.	4 I'm doing something about it.	5 I've been doing something about it for some time.
Risks					
Opportunities					
Weaknesses					
Strengths					

17

Conclusions

In this last chapter we attempt a number of integrating conclusions. They cut across various parts of the book, and bring together common threads. We hope you find them useful.

FIRST CONCLUSION: CONNECT THE DOTS

It is only when we see how our own personal well-being is connected to the well-being of organizations and communities around us that we will invest in transformative efforts on the three fronts: personal, organizational, and communal.

For as long as your woes are internalized as personal failures and the struggles of your clients are construed as innate deficiencies, there will never be sufficient motivation to alter the environmental circumstances that assail individuals and families alike. A holistic understanding of well-being, whereby the trials and tribulations of the one are the trials and tribulations of the many, precedes transformative action. Blinders notwithstanding, our fates are interwoven in webs of wellness and webs of sorrow. The illusion that if you lived in a gated community you would be protected from the misery of others can only be upheld at the cost of blindness, indifference, and arrogance. No matter how much others want to personalize and individualize social problems, that tendency should be resisted at all cost. As the research reviewed in this book shows, our physical and emotional health is closely tied to our places of employment and the communities where we live. The systems we interact with influence our well-being as much as we influence them. By connecting the dots, we might be able to devise strategies that address the personal, the organizational, and the communal at once.

SECOND CONCLUSION: FOSTER A CRITICAL ATTITUDE

It is only when we institutionalize critical consciousness, critical experiences, and critical actions that we have a chance of making a difference in the long run.

It is very possible to have fleeting moments of critical consciousness and powerful experiences that bring together for us the unity of personal, organizational, and communal wellness. It is even possible for us to engage in temporary critical actions that challenge the status quo. The trick is to make these critical moments last. In the absence of enabling structures that meet regularly, that are built into the routines of the organization, and that are given sufficient space and recognition, we fall into the stop-start phenomenon. Every organization has people invested in changing things for the better and improving everyone's well-being, but habituation can kill motivation. What we need is counterhabituation, a process whereby we institutionalize ways of challenging the institution. This sounds paradoxical: No boss will allow workers the time to conspire to create industrial unrest. But it is paradoxical only if the boss is invested in protecting the status quo and preventing positive change. Healthy and learning organizations devote time to collective growth and professional development. The hidden and not-so-hidden costs of attrition and sabotaging more than justify the time, and the structure, to enable workers to find ways of serving themselves and their communities better.

A critical culture ought to be created to allow each worker to feel that her voice really counts and that her experiences can teach the rest of us something meaningful and useful. We ought to capture those nuggets and make them visible. It doesn't matter what you call it: learning teams, quality circles, communities of practice, or professional development groups—each organization, especially workplaces, must institutionalize spaces and times where workers can come together, learn from each other, and challenge each other.

THIRD CONCLUSION: DEMOCRATIZE WELL-BEING

It is only when we take control of health and well-being away from professionals that we have a chance of empowering the population.

Dependence on professionals and experts to promote well-being breeds only that: dependence. Transfer of skills from professionals to the lay public, as well as recognition of assets in community members, are essential components of empowerment. Remember the A in I VALUE IT? It stands for asset seeker. The more we encourage community members to take control of their destiny, and the more we accompany them in their journey—supporting, not directing them—the greater the chance that communal well-being will stick. Professionals come and go, but community members stay. As Len Syme, the Berkeley epidemiologist, is fond of saying, health professionals have messages; community members have lives.

The Better Beginnings Better Futures project in Canada has lasted so long (and it's still going strong) because communities took over. From the moment it was created, the steering committee had a majority of community members who owned the project (Nelson et al., 2005). For as long as communities are following expert prescription as opposed to their own path, sustainability is completely dependent on external advice. Just as community members need to be empowered to take charge, professionals need to be disempowered and let go. This is not to cancel the contributions professionals can make, but to elevate the contributions community members can have. The more we exercise the I VALUE IT system, the more space we create for community members to exercise their voice and choice.

FOURTH CONCLUSION: CREATE A SAFE ENVIRONMENT

It is only when we create a safe environment for taking risks that we can activate the agency part within ourselves and overcome paralyzing barriers and tendencies.

Action takes practice. The more you fail, the more you learn. But to take action and to take risks, you need a safety net that will catch you when you fail. It is hard to activate agency when you risk ridicule or ostracism. Such is the pressure to conform that otherwise bright people are afraid to step up. We have to allow and even encourage dissent and diversity. It may not be pleasant, but it sure beats dogmatism and monochrome solutions.

The more an organization accepts uniqueness, the better the chances of innovating. It is a matter of pushing the envelope on what's acceptable. You may push yourself a little, or you may foster a climate of respect for others to take risks. Either way, you're activating your own agency and that of others.

FIFTH CONCLUSION: LINK PRIVATE ILLS WITH PUBLIC ORIGINS

It is only when community members make the connection between their private ills and their public origins that they can be angry enough to make a difference in the institutions that dominate their lives.

For as long as the public believes that it is their fault that they are unemployed and uninsured, they will look only internally for solutions. When the connections are made between corporate welfare and social welfare, a critical experience is ignited that might just trigger critical consciousness. While many large corporations enjoy millions of dollars in tax breaks, the poorest in the nation go without health insurance. If you happen to be poor and without health insurance, knowing that public taxes are spent on subsidizing multibillion-dollar corporations instead of ensuring your access to health care, you may be justifiably irritated, to say the least (J. Bakan, 2004). The more transparent we can make those connections, the more we learn about the institutions that dominate our lives. The angrier we become about injustice, the greater the chance that we'll do something about it. Make it your business to tell your clients how the world can be different. The combination of critical consciousness with critical experiences has the potential to lead to critical action. Moreover, don't let anybody tell you that telling your clients about corporate welfare is politicizing the therapeutic encounter, because not telling them is equally political.

SIXTH CONCLUSION: TREAT DIGNITY AS SACRED

In whatever organizational or communal action you become involved, always consider the personal well-being of the actors involved sacred.

No matter how just or noble the cause might be, there is never justification for treating your peers, subordinates, students, clients, or community members as if they were means to an end. Over the years, we have encountered plenty of self-appointed defenders of justice and well-being who diminished other people on their way to grandiosity. None of what we prescribed in this book justifies the diminution of anybody's dignity or worth.

SEVENTH CONCLUSION: CHOOSE YOUR OWN PATH

There are multiple paths to well-being, and you create meaning by discovering your unique path.

We offer in this book a frame for personal, organizational, and communal well-being, but you may find it constraining or limited, even somewhat dogmatic. We have our own limitations, our own blinders. Of one thing we're sure, though: There is no one way to create meaning and foster well-being. Our formulations are heavily determined by our own experiences. We do hope, however, that whatever your path is, you'll take it.

EIGHTH CONCLUSION: LINK
THE PERSONAL AND THE POLITICAL

Well-being is as much physical and psychological as political. By concentrating only on one or the other you risk diminishing the overall well-being of yourself, your family, your organization, and your community.

Interpersonal dynamics affect well-being as much as political forces do. The role of personal and institutional power tends to be undermined in discussions about well-being. However, the role of power in injustice, disability, and arrogance cannot be doubted. In every interpersonal interaction, there is power: power to share or power to arrogate, power with or power over.

NINTH CONCLUSION:
BEWARE OF SYSTEMS

Organizations and communities can be sources of well-being, but they can also be sources of oppression.

We may have romanticized the wellness-enhancing properties of groups, teams, or communities. They can be brutal toward dissenting members; social capital can be used for good or ill. Which is precisely why changing them is so crucial. For some people, isolation is much better than being subjected to group pressure or humiliation. Some kids suffer greatly in schools because of bullying and exclusion.

TENTH CONCLUSION:
THINK OF OTHERS

Well-being is a resource, and it needs to be distributed fairly and justly. At some point, your own well-being may come at the expense of somebody else's.

We may also have created the impression that well-being is an endless resource, that the more you have, the more you can give to others. Synergy is a wonderful thing, and when your well-being and mine synergize, that's terrific. But we can think of many instances when my personal well-being might diminish, or be diminished, by yours. For all the techniques and tools that we suggested in this book, nothing replaces the fact that some people have more well-being than others do, and it behooves the privileged to share it.

CHANGE NOT FOR CHANGE'S SAKE—
CHANGE FOR WELL-BEING

Whatever change you embark on, make sure it's a change for well-being. Fads come and go. Change fatigue is ubiquitous. Every new CEO wants a new strategic plan, and every new manager implements yet another set of procedures. Workers are savvy about the difference between change for change's sake and change for well-being. The same goes for community members who are tired of hearing promises before elections. When you start the journey, make sure you board the ship of well-being, and bon voyage.

References

Addleson, M. (2000). What is good organization? Learning organizations, community and the rhetoric of the bottom line. *European Journal of Work and Organizational Psychology, 9*(2), 233–253.

Ainsworth, M., Blehar, M., Waters, E., & Wall, S. (1978). *Patterns of attachment: A psychological study of the strange situation.* Hillsdale, NJ: Erlbaum.

Albee, G. W. (1990). The futility of psychotherapy. *Journal of Mind and Behavior, 11*(3/4), 369–384.

Albee, G. W. (1996). Revolutions and counterrevolutions in prevention. *American Psychologist, 51,* 1130–1133.

Albee, G. W. (1998). No more rock scrubbing. *Journal of Community and Applied Social Psychology, 8,* 373–375.

Albee, G. W., & Gullotta, T. P. (Eds.). (1997). *Primary prevention works.* London: Sage.

Albee, G. W., & Perry, M. J. (1995). Change course without rocking the boat [Review of the book Reducing risks for mental disorders: Frontiers for preventive intervention research]. *Contemporary Psychology, 40,* 843–846.

Albom, M. (1997). *Tuesdays with Morrie.* New York: Broadway Books.

Alexander, D. (2002). *Visions of development.* Northampton, MA: Edward Elgar.

Allahar, A., & Cote, J. (1998). *Richer and poorer: The structure of inequality in Canada.* Toronto, Ontario, Canada: Lorimer.

Argyris, C. (1993). *On organizational learning.* Cambridge, MA: Blackwell.

Aristide, J. B. (2000). *Eyes of the heart: Seeking a path for the poor in the Age of globalization.* Monroe, ME: Common Courage Press.

Austin, M. (Ed.). (2004). *Changing welfare services: Case studies of local welfare reform programs.* New York: Haworth Social Work Practice Press.

Australian Institute of Health and Welfare. (1998). *National health priorities areas: Mental health.* Canberra, Australia: Author.

Bakan, D. (1966). *The duality of human existence: An essay on psychology and religion.* Chicago: Rand McNally.

Bakan, J. (2004). *The corporation: The pathological pursuit of profit and power.* New York: Free Press.

Baker, W. (2005). *America's crisis of values: Reality and perception.* Princeton, NJ: Princeton University Press.

Bales, S., & Gilliam, F. (2004). *Communications for social good.* New York: The Foundation Center.

Bandura, A. (1977). Self-efficacy: Toward a unifying theory of behavioral change. *Psychological Review, 84,* 191–215.

Bandura, A. (Ed.). (1995). *Self-efficacy in changing societies*. New York: Cambridge University Press.

Barker, D. J. (1998). *Mothers, babies and disease in later life* (2nd ed.). Edinburgh, Scotland: Churchill Livingstone.

Barnes, C., Mercer, M., & Shakespeare, T. (1999). *Exploring disability: A sociological introduction*. Cambridge, England: Polity Press.

Batson, C., Ahmad, N., Lishner, D., & Tsang, J. (2002). Empathy and altruism. In C. Snyder & S. Lopez (Eds.), *Handbook of positive psychology* (pp. 485–498). New York: Oxford University Press.

Baumeister, R., & Leary, M. (1995). The need to belong: Desire for interpersonal attachments as a fundamental human motivation. *Psychological Bulletin, 117,* 497–529.

Beck, A. (1976). *Cognitive therapy and the emotional disorders*. New York: International Universities Press.

Becker, T. E. (1998). Integrity in organizations: Beyond honesty and conscientiousness. *Academy of Management Review, 23,* 154–161.

Beckman, H., & Frankl, R. M. (1983). The effects of physician's behavior on the collection of data. *Annals of Internal Medicine, 101,* 692–696.

Berkman, L. (1995). The role of social relationships in health promotion. *Psychosomatic Research, 57,* 245–254.

Berscheid, E. (2004). The greening of relationship science. In H. Reis & C. Rusbult (Eds.), *Close relationships* (pp. 25–34). New York: Psychology Press.

Beutler, L. E. (2000). Empirically based decision making in clinical practice. *Prevention and Treatment, 3*(Article 27). Available from http://journals.apa.org /prevention/volume3/pre0030027a.html.

Bion, W. (1961). *Experience in groups*. New York: Basic Books.

Blakeley, G. (2002). Social capital. In G. Blakeley & V. Bryson (Eds.), *Contemporary political concepts: A critical introduction* (pp. 198–213). London: Pluto Press.

Bolman, L., & Deal, T. (2003). *Reframing organizations*. San Francisco: Jossey Bass.

Boonstra, J. J., & Bennebroek Gravenhorst, K. M. (1998). Power dynamics and organizational change: A comparison of perspectives. *European Journal of Work and Organizational Psychology, 7*(2), 97–120.

Bosma, H., Peter, R., Siegrist, J., & Marmot, M. (1998). Two alternative job stress models and the risk of coronary heart disease. *American Journal of Public Health, 88,* 68–74.

Bowlby, J. (1982). *Attachment and loss: Vol. 1. Attachment* (2nd ed.). New York: Basic Books.

Bradbury, T. N., & Fincham, F. D. (1990). Attributions in marriage: Review and critique. *Psychological Bulletin, 107,* 3–33.

Bradshaw, P. (1998). Power as dynamic tension and its implications for radical organizational change. *European Journal of Work and Organizational Psychology, 7*(2), 121–143.

Bridges, W. (2003). *Managing transitions: Making the most of change*. Cambridge, MA: DaCapo Press.

Bridges, W. (2004). *Transitions: Making sense of life's changes* (2nd ed.). Cambridge, MA: DaCapo Press.

Brisenden, S. (1998). Independent living and the medical model of disability. In T. Shakespeare (Ed.), *The disability reader: Social science perspectives* (pp. 20–27). London: Cassell.

Bronner, S. (2002). *Of critical theory and its theorists*. New York: Routledge.

Brooks, D. (2005, September 11). The best laid plan: Too bad it flopped. *New York Times*. Retrieved September 11, 2005, from http://www.nytimes.com/2005 /09/11/opinion/11brooks.html?th&emc=th.

Brumback, G. B. (1991). Institutionalizing ethics in government. *Public Personnel Management, 20,* 353–364.

Bruner, E., Juneja, M., & Marmot, M. (1998). Abdominal obesity and disease are linked to social position. *British Medical Journal, 316,* 308.

Bruton, H. (2001). *On the search for well-being.* Ann Arbor: University of Michigan Press.

Buber, M. (1971). *I and thou.* New York: Free Press.

Burke, W. (2002). *Organization change: Theory and practice.* London: Sage.

Campaign 2000. (2004). *One million too many: Implementing solutions to end child poverty in Canada.* Retrieved January 23, 2005, from http://www .campaign2000.ca/rc/rc04/rc04NationalReportCard.pdf.

Canadian Mental Health Association, Centre for Addiction and Mental Health, Ontario Federation of Community Mental Health and Addiction Programs, and Ontario Peer Development Initiative. (2005). *Consumer/survivor initiatives: Impact, outcomes and effectiveness.* Toronto, Ontario, Canada: Author.

Cantor, N., & Sanderson, C. A. (1999). Life task participation and well-being: The importance of taking part in daily life. In D. Kahneman, E. Diener, & N. Schwarz (Eds.), *Well-being: The foundations of hedonic psychology* (pp. 230–243). New York: Russell Sage Foundation.

Capra, F. (1996). *The web of life: A new scientific understanding of living systems.* New York: Anchor.

Capra, F. (2003). *The hidden connections: Integrating the biological, cognitive, and social dimensions of life into a science of sustainability.* New York: Doubleday.

Carson, T. (2000). *Value and the good life.* Notre Dame, IN: University of Notre Dame Press.

Carver, C. S., & Scheier, M. F. (2002). Optimism. In C. R. Snyder & S. J. Lopez (Eds.), *Handbook of positive psychology* (pp. 231–243). New York: Oxford University Press.

Cashmore, J. (2001). Family, early development and the life course: Common risk and protective factors in pathways to prevention. In R. Eckersley, J. Dixon, & B. Douglas (Eds.), *The social origins of health and well-being* (pp. 216–224). New York: Cambridge University Press.

Chisholm, J. (2000). *Benefit-cost analysis and crime prevention* (Trends and Issues in Crime and Criminal Justice: No. 147). Canberra, Australia: Australian Institute of Criminology.

Chowdhury, S. (Ed.). (2003). *Organization 21C.* Upper Saddle River, NJ: Prentice-Hall.

City of Milwaukee Health Department. (2005). *2003 Infant mortality disparity fact sheet.* Retrieved September 7, 2005, from http://www.city.milwaukee.gov /display/displayFile.asp?docid=313&filename=/Groups/healthAuthors/MCH /PDFs/2003_fimr_fact_sheet2.pdf.

Clark, D. (2002). *Visions of development: A study of human values.* Northampton, MA: Edward Elgar.

Cohen, D. (2005). *The heart of change field guide.* Boston: Harvard Business School.

Cohen, S. (2004). Social relationships and health. *American Psychologist, 59,* 676–684.

Commonwealth Department of Health and Aged Care. (2000). *Promotion, prevention and early intervention for mental health.* Canberra, Australian Capital Territory: Author.

Community Mental Health Project. (1998). Companions on a journey: The work of the Dulwich Centre Community Mental Health Project. In C. White & D. Denborough (Eds.), *Introducing narrative therapy.* Adelaide, Australia: Dulwich Centre Publications.

Community Tool Box. (2006). *Identification of best practices.* Retrieved February 4, 2006, from http://ctb.ku.edu/tools/bp/en/IdentificationTable.jsp.

Conlon, D., Meyer, C., & Nowakowski, J. (2005). How does organizational justice affect performance, withdrawal, and counterproductive behavior. In J. Greenberg & J. Colquitt (Eds.), *Handbook of organizational justice* (pp. 309–327). Mahwah, NJ: Erlbaum.

Conyne, R., & Cook, E. (Eds.). (2004). *Ecological counseling: An innovative approach to conceptualizing person-environment interaction.* Alexandria, VA: American Counseling Association.

Cowen, E. L. (1991). In pursuit of wellness. *American Psychologist, 46,* 404–408.

Crabtree, S. (2005, January 13). Engagement keeps the doctor away. *Gallup Management Journal.* Retrieved January 21, 2006, from http://gmj.gallup.com /content/default.asp?ci=14500.

Crow, L. (1996). Including all of our lives: Renewing the social model of disability. In J. Morris (Ed.), *Encounters with strangers: Feminism and disability* (pp. 206–226). London: Women's Press.

Davis, C., Martin, G., Kosky, R., & O'Hanlon, A. (2000). *Early intervention in the mental health of young people: A literature review.* Adelaide, South Australia: Australian Early Intervention Network for Mental Health in Young People.

Della Porta, D., & Diani, M. (1999). *Social movements: An introduction.* Oxford, England: Blackwell.

De Vita, C. J., & Fleming, C. (Eds.). (2001). *Building capacity in non-profit organizations.* Washington, DC: Urban Institute.

de Vogli, R., Ferrie, J., Chandola, T., Kivimäki, M., & Marmot, M. (2006). *Unfairness and health: Evidence from the Whitehall II study.* Manuscript submitted for publication.

Diemer, M., Kauffman, A., Koening, N., Trahan, E., & Hsieh, C. (in press). Challenging racism, sexism, and social injustice: Support for Urban Adolescents' Critical Consciousness Development. *Cultural Diversity and Ethnic Minority Psychology.*

Diener, E., & Lucas, R. E. (1999). Personality and subjective well-being. In D. Kahneman, E. Diener, & N. Schwarz (Eds.), *Well-being: The foundations of hedonic psychology* (pp. 213–229). New York: Russell Sage Foundation.

Dimock, H. (1992). *Intervention and empowerment: Helping organizations to change.* Concord, Ontario, Canada: Captus Press.

DiTomaso, N., & Hooijberg, R. (1996). Diversity and the demands of leadership. *Leadership Quarterly, 7*(2), 163–187.

Dobbin, M. (1998). *The myth of the good corporate citizen: Democracy under the rule of big business.* Toronto, Ontario, Canada: Stoddart.

Doherty, W. (1995). *Soul searching: Why psychotherapy must promote social responsibility.* New York: Basic Books.

Dokecki, P. (2004). *The clergy sexual abuse crisis: Reform and renewal in the Catholic community.* Washington, DC: Georgetown University Press.

Doyle, C. (2003). *Work and organizational psychology.* New York: Psychology Press.

Durlak, J. A. (1997). *Successful prevention programs for children and adolescents.* New York: Plenum Press.

Durrant, J., & Jansen, S. (in press). Law reform, corporal punishment and child abuse: The case of Sweden. *International Review of Victimology.*

Durrant, J., & Olsen, G. (1997). Parenting and public policy: Contextualizing the Swedish corporal punishment ban. *Journal of Social Welfare and Family Law, 19*(4), 443–461.

Durrant, J., Rose-Krasnor, L., & Broberg, A. (2003). Physical punishment and maternal beliefs in Sweden and Canada. *Journal of Comparative Family Studies, 34,* 586–604.

Dwyer, D. (2000). *Interpersonal relationships.* London: Routledge.

Eckersley, R. (2000). The mixed blessing of material progress: Diminishing returns in the pursuit of progress. *Journal of Happiness Studies, 1,* 267–292.

Eckersley, R. (2001). Culture, health, and well-being. In R. Eckersley, J. Dixon, & B. Douglas (Eds.), *The social origins of health and well-being* (pp. 51–70). New York: Cambridge University Press.

Eckersley, R. (2005). *Well and good: Morality, meaning and happiness.* Melbourne, Australia: Text Publishing.

Eckersley, R., Dixon, J., & Douglas, B. (Eds.). (2002). *The social origins of health and well-being.* New York: Cambridge University Press.

Edgerton, R. (1992). *Sick societies: Challenging the myth of primitive harmony.* New York: Free Press.

Ellis, A. (1982). The essence of rational emotive therapy. In D. Goleman & K. R. Speeth (Eds.), *The essential psychotherapies* (pp. 157–170). New York: New American Library.

Elsdon, R. (2003). *Affiliation in the workplace: Value creation in the new organization.* New York: Springer.

Emmons, R. A. (2003). Personal goals, life meaning, and virtue: Wellsprings of a positive life. In C. L. M. Keyes & J. Haidt (Eds.), *Flourishing: Positive psychology and the life well-lived* (pp. 105–128). Washington, DC: American Psychological Association.

Evans, G. (2003). The built environment and mental health. *Journal of Urban Health, 80,* 536–555.

Evans, G., & Kantrowitz, E. (2002). Socioeconomic status and health: The potential role of environmental risk exposure. *Annual Review of Public Health, 23,* 303–331.

Evans, S., Hanlin, C., & Prilleltensky, I. (in press). Blending ameliorative and transformative approaches in human service organizations: A case study. *Journal of Community Psychology.*

Facione, P. A., Scherer, D., & Attig, T. (1978). *Values and society: An introduction to ethics and social philosophy*. Englewood Cliffs, NJ: Prentice-Hall.

Farmer, P. (2003). *Pathologies of power: Health, human rights, and the new war on the poor*. Berkeley: University of California Press.

Fawzy, F. I., Fawzy, N. W., Hyun, C. S., Elashoff, R., Guthrie, D., Fahey, J. L., et al. (1993). Malignant melanoma: Effects of an early structured psychiatric intervention, coping, and affective state on recurrence and survival 6 years later. *Archives of General Psychiatry, 50*, 681–689.

Feikema, B. (2005). Human service agencies and public policy advocacy: A call to civic engagement. *Alliance for Children and Youth*. Retrieved September 10, 2005, from http://www.alliance1.org./publications/enews/eNewsFiles /Civic%20Engagement%20Paper%20-%20Alliance%20-%2006062105.doc.

Feuerstein, M.-T. (1997). *Poverty and health: Reaping a richer harvest*. London: Macmillan.

Feyer, A., & Broom, D. (2001). Work and health: The impact of structural workforce changes and the work environment. In R. Eckersley, J. Dixon, & B. Douglas (Eds.), *The social origins of health and well-being* (pp. 178–188). New York: Cambridge University Press.

Fields, S. (2004). The fat of the land: Do agricultural subsidies foster poor health. *Environmental Health Perspectives, 112*, A820–A823.

Fincham, F. (2004). Attribution processes in distressed and non-distressed couples: Responsibility for marital problems. In H. Reis & C. Rusbult (Eds.), *Close relationships* (pp. 427–434). New York: Psychology Press.

Fisher, A., Sonn, C., & Bishop, B. (Eds.). (2002). *Psychological sense of community: Research, applications, and implications*. New York: Kluwer/Plenum Press.

Fixsen, D. L., Naoon, S. F., Blase, K. A., Friedman, R. M., & Wallace, F. (2005). *Implementation research: A synthesis of the literature* (FMHI Publication #231). Tampa: University of South Florida, Louis de la Parte Florida Mental Health Institute, National Implementation Research Network.

Flyvbjerg, B. (1998). *Rationality and power: Democracy in practice*. Chicago: University of Chicago Press.

Flyvbjerg, B. (2001). *Making social science matter: Why social inquiry fails and how it can succeed again*. New York: Cambridge University Press.

Forsyth, D. (1999). *Group dynamics* (3rd ed.). New York: Brooks/Cole.

Forsyth, D. (2006). *Group dynamics* (4th ed.). New York: Brooks/Cole.

Fox, D., & Prilleltensky, I. (Eds.). (1997). *Critical psychology: An introduction*. London: Sage.

Franke, R., & Chasin, B. (2000). Is the Kerala model sustainable? Lessons from the past, prospects for the future. In G. Parayil (Ed.), *Kerala: The development experience* (pp. 16–39). New York: Zed Books.

Frankl, V. (1962). *Man's search for meaning*. New York: Simon & Schuster.

Freire, P. (1972). *Pedagogy of the oppressed*. New York: Herder and Herder.

Freire, P. (1973). *Education for critical consciousness*. New York: Seabury Press.

French, S., Story, M., & Jeffery, R. (2001). Environmental influences on eating and physical activity. *Annual Review of Public Health, 22*, 309–335.

Freud, S. (1949). *An outline of psychoanalysis* (J. Strachey, Trans.). New York: Norton.

Frey, B., & Stutzer, A. (2002). *Happiness and economics.* Princeton, NJ: Princeton University Press.

Friedman, V. J. (2001). The individual as agent of organizational learning. In M. Dierkes, A. B. Antal, J. Child, & I. Nonaka (Eds.), *Handbook of organizational learning and knowledge* (pp. 398–414). New York: Oxford University Press.

Fromm, E. (1965). *Escape from freedom.* New York: Avon Books.

Fryer, D. (1998). Editor's preface: Special issue on unemployment. *Journal of Community and Applied Social Psychology, 8,* 75–88.

Gallup. (2006). *Gallup study: Feeling good matters in the workplace.* Retrieved February 4, 2006, from http://gmj.gallup.com/content/default.as?ki=20770.

Ganster, D. C., Fox, M. L., & Dwyer, D. J. (2001). Explaining employees' health care costs: A prospective examination of stressful job demands, personal control, and physiological reactivity. *Journal of Applied Psychology, 86,* 954–964.

Gardner, H. (2004). *Changing minds: The art and science of changing our own and other people's minds.* Boston: Harvard Business School Press.

Giddens, A. (1994). *Beyond left and right: The future of radical politics.* Stanford, CA: Stanford University Press.

Glover, M., Dudgeon, P., & Huygens, I. (2005). Colonization and racism. In G. Nelson & I. Prilleltensky (Eds.), *Community psychology: In pursuit of liberation and well-being* (pp. 330–347). New York: Pagrave.

Goldston, S. E. (1991). A survey of prevention activities in state mental health authorities. *Professional Psychology: Research and Practice, 22,* 315–321.

Goleman, D. (1994). *Emotional intelligence.* New York: Bantam.

Goleman, D. (1998). *Working with emotional intelligence.* New York: Bantam.

Goleman, D., Boyatzis, R., & McKee, A. (2002). *Primal leadership: Learning to lead with emotional intelligence.* Cambridge, MA: Harvard Business School.

Gore, A. (1993). *Creating a government that works better and costs less: Report of the National performance review.* Washington, DC: U.S. Government Printing Office.

Gottman, J. (1999). *The seven principles for making marriage work.* New York: Three Rivers Press.

Green, J. (2003, June). The bookie of virtues: William J. Bennett has made millions lecturing people on morality: And blown it on gambling. *Washington Monthly.* Retrieved January 17, 2006, from http://www.washingtonmonthly.com/features/2003/0306.green.html.

Greenwood, P. (2006). *Changing lives: Delinquency prevention as crime-control policy.* Chicago: University of Chicago Press.

Griffith, B. (2004). The structure and development of internal working models: An integrated framework for understanding clients and promoting wellness. *Journal of Humanistic Counseling, Education, and Development, 43,* 163–177.

Gurr, J., Mailloux, L., Kinnon, D., & Doerge, S. (1996). *Breaking the links between poverty and violence against women.* Ottawa, Ontario, Canada: Ministry of Supply and Services Canada.

Hager, M. (2001). Explaining demise among nonprofit organizations. *Nonprofit and Voluntary Sector Quarterly, 30,* 795–797.

Hahn, A. (1994). *The politics of caring: Human services at the local level.* Boulder, CO: Westview.

Hall, J., Juhila, K., Parton, N., & Poso, T. (Eds.). (2003). *Constructing clienthood in social work and human services: Identity, interactions, and practices*. New York: Jessica Kingsley.

Halpern, D. (1995). *Mental health and the built environment*. London: Taylor & Francis.

Halpern, D. F. (2005). Psychology at the intersection of work and family: Recommendations for employers, working families, and policymakers. *American Psychologist, 60*(5), 397–409.

Harter, J., Schmidt, F., & Keyes, C. (2003). Well-being in the workplace and its relationship to business outcomes: A review of the Gallup Studies. In C. Keyes & J. Haidt (Eds.), *Flourishing: Positive psychology and the life well-lived* (pp. 205–224). Washington, DC: American Psychological Association.

Hayes, J. (2002). *Interpersonal skills at work*. London: Routledge.

Hazan, C., & Shaver, P. (1987). Romantic love conceptualized as an attachment process. *Journal of Personality and Social Psychology, 52*, 511–524.

Hazan, C., & Shaver, P. (2004). Attachment as an organizational framework for research on close relationships. In H. Reis & C. Rusbult (Eds.), *Close relationships* (pp. 153–174). New York: Psychology Press.

Hill Collins, P. (1998). *Fighting words: Black women and the search for justice*. Minneapolis: University of Minnesota Press.

Hill Collins, P. (1993). Black feminist thought in the matrix of domination. In C. Lemert (Ed.), *Social theory: The multicultural and classic readings* (pp. 615–626). San Francisco: Westview.

Hofrichter, R. (Ed.). (2003). *Health and social justice*. San Francisco: Jossey Bass.

Hook, D. (Ed.). (2004). *Critical psychology*. Lansdowne, South Africa: University of Cape Town Press.

Hopey, D., McFeatters, A., & Bull, J. (2002, July 30). State U.S. launch investigations into Quecreek mine accident. *Post-Gazette*. Retrieved January 23, 2005, from http://www.post-gazette.com/localnews/20020730investigations0730p1.asp.

Hornstein, H. (2003). Framing: It's either us or them. In S. Chowdhury (Ed.), *Organization 21C* (pp. 213–224). Upper Saddle River, NJ: Prentice-Hall.

Hsu, S. (2005, September 9). Leaders lacking disaster experience: Brain drain at agency cited. *Washington Post*. Retrieved September 11, 2005, from http://www.washingtonpost.com/wp-dyn/content/article/2005/09/08/AR2005090802165.html.

Huygens, I. (2004, July). *Scholar in a social movement: Recording the collective praxis of social change workers*. Paper presented at the 9th Biennial Australia-Aotearoa Community Psychology Conference Community Narratives and Praxis: Sharing Stories of Social Action and Change, Tauranga, New Zealand.

Huygens, I., & Humphries, M. (2004, November). *Cumulative theorising across the country*. Paper presented at the 7th Biannual Australia-New Zealand Third Sector Research Conference, Brisbane, Australia.

Ife, J. (2001). *Human rights and social work: Towards rights-based practice*. Cambridge, England: Cambridge University Press.

Ife, J. (2002). *Community development: Community-based alternatives in an age of globalization* (2nd ed.). Frenchs Forest, Australia: Pearson.

An important direction for mental health promotion, prevention, and early intervention. (2000, November 29). Retrieved from http://www.ausienet.com/noticeboard/ausei2000.php.

Institute of Medicine. (2002). *Care without coverage: Too little, too late.* Washington, DC: National Academy Press.

Interfaith Social Assistance Reform Coalition. (1998). *Our neighbours' voices: Will we listen.* Toronto, Ontario, Canada: James Lorimer.

Ivey, A., & Ivey, M. (2003). *Intentional interviewing and counseling: Facilitating client development in a multicultural society.* Pacific Grove, CA: Brooks/Cole.

James, E. (2001). Coverage under old age security programs and protection for the uninsured. In N. Lustig (Ed.), *Shielding the poor: Social protection in the developing world* (pp. 149–174). Washington, DC: Brookings Institution Press/Inter-American Development Bank.

James, S., & Prilleltensky, I. (2002). Cultural diversity and mental health: Towards integrative practice. *Clinical Psychology Review, 22,* 1133–1154.

Janvry, A., & Sadoulet, E. (2001). Has aggregate income growth been effective in reducing poverty and inequality in Latin America. In N. Lustig (Ed.), *Shielding the poor: Social protection in the developing world* (pp. 21–39). Washington, DC: Brookings Institution Press/Inter-American Development Bank.

Janzen, R., Nelson, G., Trainor, J., & Ochocka, J. (in press). A longitudinal study of mental health consumer/survivor initiatives: Pt. IV. Benefits beyond the self? A quantitative and qualitative study of system-level activities and impacts. *Journal of Community Psychology.*

Johnson, D., & Johnson, F. (2000). *Joining together: Group theory and group skills.* London: Allyn & Bacon.

Johnson, S. (1999). *Who moved my cheese?* New York: Putnam.

Kagan, J., Snidman, N., & Arcus, D. M. (1992). Initial reactions to unfamiliarity. *Current Directions in Psychological Science, 1,* 171–174.

Kahneman, D., Diener, E., & Schwarz, N. (Eds.). (1999). *Well-being: The foundations of hedonic psychology.* New York: Russell Sage Foundation.

Kane, R. (1994). *Through the moral maze: Searching for absolute values in a pluralistic world.* New York: Paragon.

Kane, R. (1998). Dimensions of value and the aims of social inquiry. *American Behavioral Scientist, 41,* 578–597.

Kanungo, R., & Mendonca, M. (1996). *Ethical dimensions of leadership.* London: Sage.

Kaplan, R. M. (2000). Two pathways to prevention. *American Psychologist, 55,* 382–396.

Kawachi, I., & Kennedy, B. (1999). Social capital and self-rated health: A contextual analysis. *American Journal of Public Health, 89,* 1187–1194.

Keating, D., & Hertzman, C. (Eds.). (1999). *Developmental health and the wealth of nations.* New York: Guilford Press.

Kekes, J. (1993). *The morality of pluralism.* Princeton, NJ: Princeton University Press.

Kerruish, A. (1995). Basic human values: The ethos for methodology. *Journal of Community and Applied Social Psychology, 5,* 121–143.

Kershaw, K. (2005). *Multidisciplinary rehabilitation in prisons: A values, interests, and power analysis.* Unpublished doctoral dissertation, Victoria University, Melbourne, Australia.

Kets de Vries, M. F., & Florent-Treacy, E. (2003). Global leadership from A to Z. In S. Chowdhury (Ed.), *Organization 21C* (pp. 19–33). Upper Saddle River, NJ: Prentice-Hall.

Kids Count. (2005). *Kids Count state level data online: Tennessee.* Retrieved August 8, 2005, from Kids Count, http://www.aecf.org/kidscount/sld /profile_results.jsp?r=44&d=1.

Kohn, A. (1986). *No contest: The case against competition.* Boston: Houghton Mifflin.

Korten, D. (1995). *When corporations rule the world.* San Francisco: Berrett-Koehler/Kumarian Press.

Kotter, J., & Cohen, D. (2002). *The heart of change.* Boston: Harvard Business School.

Krueger, J., & Killham, E. (2005, December 8). At work, feeling good matters. *Gallup Management Journal.* Retrieved January 21, 2006, from http://gmj .gallup.com/content/default.asp?ci=20311.

Lakoff, G. (1996). *Moral politics: What conservatives know that liberals don't.* Chicago: University of Chicago Press.

Laurenceau, J. P., Barrett, L., & Pietromanaco, P. (2004). Intimacy as an interpersonal process: The importance of self-disclosure, partner disclosure, and perceived partner responsiveness in interpersonal exchanges. In H. Reis & C. Rusbult (Eds.), *Close relationships* (pp. 199–212). New York: Psychology Press.

Layard, R. (2005). *Happiness: Lessons from a new science.* New York: Penguin.

Lemme, B. (2006). *Development in adulthood* (4th ed.). New York: Pearson.

Lerner, M. (1991). *Surplus powerlessness.* London: Humanities Press International.

Lerner, M. (1996). *The politics of meaning.* New York: Addison-Wesley.

Levine, M. (1998). *Prevention and community.* *American Journal of Community Psychology, 26,* 189–206.

Levy, L. (2000). Self-help groups. In J. Rappaport & E. Seidman (Eds.), *Handbook of community psychology* (pp. 591–613). New York: Kluwer Academic/Plenum Press.

Lewis, H. (1990). *A question of values: Six ways we make the personal choices that shape our lives.* New York: Harper & Row.

Lewis, J. A., Lewis, D. M., Daniels, J. A., & D'Andrea, M. J. (2003). *Community counseling: Empowerment strategies for a diverse society* (3rd ed.). Pacific Grove, CA: Brooks/Cole.

Loeb, P. (1999). *Soul of a citizen: Living with conviction in a cynical time.* New York: St. Martin's Griffin.

Loewy, E. (1993). *Freedom and community: The ethics of interdependence.* Albany: State University of New York Press.

Lupton, D. (1994). *Toward the development of critical health communication praxis.* *Health Communication, 61,* 55–67.

Lustig, N. (2001). Introduction. In N. Lustig (Ed.), *Shielding the poor: Social protection in the developing world* (pp. 1–20). Washington, DC: Brookings Institution Press/Inter-American Development Bank.

MacFarlane, S., Racelis, M., & Muli-Musiime, F. (2000). Public health in developing countries. *Lancet, 356,* 841–847.

MacLeod, J., & Nelson, G. (2000). Programs for the promotion of family wellness and the prevention of child maltreatment: A meta-analytic review. *Child Abuse and Neglect, 24,* 1127–1149.

Maddux, J. E. (2002). Self-efficacy: The power of believing you can. In C. R. Snyder & S. J. Lopez (Eds.), *Handbook of positive psychology* (pp. 277–287). New York: Oxford University Press.

Magnani, E. (2003). *El cambio silencioso: Empresas y fábricas recuperadas por los trabajadores en la Argentina* [The quiet change: Businesses and factories recovered by Argentinian workers]. Buenos Aires, Argentina, South America: Prometeo.

Marmot, M. (1999). Introduction. In M. Marmot & R. Wilkinson (Eds.), *Social determinants of health* (pp. 1–16). New York: Oxford University Press.

Marmot, M. (2004). *The status syndrome: How social standing affects our health and longevity.* New York: Times Books.

Marmot, M., & Feeney, A. (1996). Work and health: Implications for individuals and society. In D. Blane, E. Bruner, & R. Wilkinson (Eds.), *Health and social organization* (pp. 235–254). London: Routledge.

Marmot, M., & Wilkinson, R. (Eds.). (1999). *Social determinants of health.* New York: Oxford University Press.

Maslow, A. (1965). *Eupsychian management.* Homewood, IL: Irwin Dorsey.

Maton, K. I., & Salem, D. A. (1995). Organizational characteristics of empowering community settings: A multiple case study approach. *American Journal of Community Psychology, 23,* 631–656.

Maxwell, S., & Kenway, P. (2000). *New thinking on poverty in England: Any lessons for the South?* London: Overseas Development Institute.

May, J. (2001). An elusive consensus: Definitions, measurement and analysis of poverty. In United Nations Development Programme (Ed.), *Choices for the poor* (pp. 23–54). New York: United Nations.

Mayer, J. P., & Davidson, W. S. II. (2000). Dissemination of innovation as social change. In J. Rappaport & E. Seidman (Eds.), *Handbook of community psychology* (pp. 421–438). New York: Kluwer Academic/Plenum Press.

Mayton, D. M., Ball-Rokeach, S. J., & Loges, W. E. (1994). Human values and social issues: An introduction. *Journal of Social Issues, 50*(4), 1–8.

McCain, M. N., & Mustard, J. F. (1999). *Early years study.* Toronto, Ontario, Canada: Ontario Children's Secretariat.

McCrae, R., & Costa, P. (1990). *Personality in adulthood.* New York: Guilford Press.

McGregor, D. (1960). *The human side of enterprise.* New York: McGraw-Hill.

McKnight, J. (1987, May). *Building community through prevention.* Paper presented at the Ontario Prevention Congress, Kitchener, Ontario, Canada.

McQuaig, L. (1998). *The cult of impotence: Selling the myth of powerlessness in the global economy.* Toronto, Ontario, Canada: Viking.

McWhirter, E. H. (1994). *Counseling for empowerment.* Alexandria, VA: American Counseling Association.

Menzies Lyth, I. (1988). *Containing anxiety in institutions.* London: Free Association Books.

Menzies Lyth, I. (1989). *Dynamics of the social.* London: Free Association Books.

Mikulincer, M. (1994). *Human learned helplessness.* New York: Plenum Press.

Mikulincer, M. (2004). Attachment working models and the sense of trust: An exploration of interaction goals and affect regulation. In H. Reis & C. Rusbult (Eds.), *Close relationships* (pp. 175–191). New York: Psychology Press.

Mill, J. S. (2001). *Utilitarianism.* Indianapolis, IN: Hackett Publishing.

Miller, D. (1978). *Social justice.* Oxford: Clarendon.

Miller, D. (1999). *Principles of social justice.* Cambridge, MA: Harvard University Press.

Miller, S., Hubble, M., & Duncan, B. (Eds.). (1996). *Handbook of solution-focused brief therapy.* San Francisco: Jossey Bass.

Morris, J. (1991). *Pride against prejudice.* London: Women's Press.

Morris, J. (1992). Personal and political: A feminist perspective on researching physical disability. *Disability, Handicap, and Society, 7*(2), 157–166.

Morris, J. (1993). *Independent lives? Community care and disabled people.* London: Macmillan.

Morris, J. (1996). Introduction. In J. Morris (Ed.), *Encounters with strangers: Feminism and disability* (pp. 1–16). London: Women's Press.

Morris, J. (2001). Impairment and disability: Constructing an ethics of care that promotes human rights. *Hypatia, 16*(4), 1–16.

Morsillo, J., & Prilleltensky, I. (in press). Social action with youth: Interventions, evaluation, and psychopolitical validity. *Journal of Community Psychology.*

Mullaly, B. (2002). *Challenging oppression: A critical social work approach.* Toronto, Ontario, Canada: Oxford.

Murry, S., Holmes, J., & Griffin, D. (2004). The benefits of positive illusions: Idealization and the construction of satisfaction in close relationships. In H. Reis & C. Rusbult (Eds.), *Close relationships* (pp. 317–338). New York: Psychology Press.

Mustakova-Possardt, E. (2003). *Critical consciousness: A study of morality in global, historical context.* London: Praeger.

Myers, D. G. (1993). *The pursuit of happiness: Discovering the pathway to fulfillment, well-being, and enduring personal joy.* New York: Avon Books.

Nakamura, J., & Csikszentmihalyi, M. (2003). The construction of meaning through vital engagement. In C. L. M. Keyes & J. Haidt (Eds.), *Flourishing: Positive psychology and the life well-lived* (pp. 83–104). Washington, DC: American Psychological Association.

Narayan, D., Chambers, R., Shah, M., & Petesch, P. (1999). *Global synthesis: Consultations with the poor.* Washington, DC: World Bank, Poverty Group. Available from www.worldbank.org/poverty/voices/synthes.pdf.

Narayan, D., Chambers, R., Shah, M., & Petesch, P. (2000). *Voices of the poor: Crying out for change.* New York: Oxford University Press.

Narayan, D., Patel, R., Schafft, K., Rademacher, A., & Koch-Schulte, S. (2000). *Voices of the poor: Can anyone hear us?* New York: Oxford University Press.

Navarro, V. (Ed.). (2000). *The political economy of social inequalities: Consequences for health and quality of life.* Amityville, NY: Baywood.

Navarro, V. (Ed.). (2004). *The political and social contexts of health.* Amityville, NY: Baywood.

Navarro, V., & Muntaner, C. (Eds.). (2004). *Political and economic determinants of health and well-being: Controversies and developments.* Amityville, NY: Baywood.

Nelson, G., Lord, J., & Ochocka, J. (2001). *Shifting the paradigm in community mental health: Towards empowerment and community.* Toronto, Ontario, Canada: University of Toronto Press.

Nelson, G., Ochocka, J., Janzen, R., & Trainor, J. (in press). A longitudinal study of mental health consumer/survivor initiatives: Pt. II. A quantitative study of impacts of participation on new members. *Journal of Community Psychology.*

Nelson, G., Pancer, S. M., Hayward, K., & Peters, R. (2005). *Partnerships for prevention: The story of the Highfield Community enrichment project*. Toronto, Ontario, Canada: University of Toronto Press.

Nelson, G., & Prilleltensky, I. (Eds.). (2005). *Community psychology: In pursuit of liberation and well-being*. New York: Palgrave.

Nelson, G., Prilleltensky, I., Laurendeau, M. C., & Powell, B. (1996). A survey of prevention activities in mental health in the Canadian provinces and territories. *Canadian Psychology, 37*(3), 161–172.

Nelson, G., Prilleltensky, I., & MacGillivary, H. (2001). Building value-based partnerships: Toward solidarity with oppressed groups. *American Journal of Community Psychology, 29*, 649–677.

Nelson, G., Prilleltensky, I., & Peters, R. (1999). Mental health promotion and the prevention of mental health problems. In W. Marshall & P. Firestone (Eds.), *Abnormal psychology perspectives* (pp. 461–478). Scarborough, Ontario, Canada: Prentice-Hall.

Nelson, G., Westhues, A., & MacLeod, J. (2003). A meta-analysis of longitudinal research on preschool prevention programs for children. *Prevention and Treatment, 6*(1), 31 (Article A). Retrieved February 22, 2006, from http://content.apa.org/journals/pre/6/1/31.

Nussbaum, M. (1999). *Sex and social justice*. Oxford: Oxford University Press.

Ochocka, J., Nelson, G., Janzen, R., & Trainor, J. (in press). A longitudinal study of mental health consumer/survivor initiatives: Pt. III. A qualitative study of impacts of participation on new members. *Journal of Community Psychology*.

Olds, D., Kitzman, H., Cole, R., Robinson, J., Sidora, K., Luckey, D., et al. (2004). Effects of nurse home-visiting on maternal life course and child development: Age 6 follow-up results of a randomized trial. *Pediatrics, 114*, 1550–1559.

Olds, D., Robinson, J., Pettitt, L., Luckey, D., Homberg, J., Ng, R., et al. (2004). Effects of home visits by paraprofessionals and by nurses: Age 4 follow-up results of a randomized trial. *Pediatrics, 114*, 1560–1568.

Oliver, M. (1996). A sociology of disability or a disabled sociology. In L. Barton (Ed.), *Disability and society: Emerging issues and insights* (pp. 18–42). Essex, England: Addison Wesley Longman Ltd.

Ornish, D. (1998). *Love and survival: The scientific basis for the healing power of intimacy*. New York: HarperCollins.

Pancer, M., Pratt, M., Hunsberger, B., & Alisat, S. (in press). Community and political involvement in adolescence: What distinguishes the activists from the uninvolved? *Journal of Community Psychology*.

Pancer, S. M. (1997). Program evaluation. In S. W. Sadawa & D. R. McCreary (Eds.), *Applied social psychology* (pp. 47–53). Englewood Cliffs, NJ: Prentice-Hall.

Parenti, M. (2005, September 3). How the free market killed New Orleans. *Z Magazine*. Retrieved September 9, 2005, from http://www.zmag.org/sustainers/content/2005-09/03parenti.cfm.

Pargament, K. I., & Mahoney, A. (2002). Spirituality: Discovering and conserving the sacred. In C. R. Snyder & S. J. Lopez (Eds.), *Handbook of positive psychology* (pp. 646–659). New York: Oxford University Press.

Paterson, L. E., & Welfel, E. R. (2000). *The counselling process* (5th ed.). Belmont, CA: Brooks/Cole.

Patton, M. Q. (1997). *Utilization-focused evaluation: The new century text* (3rd ed.). Thousand Oaks, CA: Sage.

Patton, M. Q. (2002). *Qualitative research and evaluation methods* (3rd ed.). Thousand Oaks, CA: Sage.

Perkins, D., Bess, K., Cooper, D., Jones, D., Armstead, T., & Speer, P. (in press). Community organizational learning: Case studies illustrating a three dimensional model of levels and orders of change. *Journal of Community Psychology.*

Peters, M., Lankshear, C., & Olssen, M. (Eds.). (2003). *Critical theory and the human condition: Founders and praxis.* New York: Peter Lang.

Peterson, C., & Chang, E. C. (2003). Optimism and flourishing. In C. L. M. Keyes & J. Haidt (Eds.), *Flourishing: Positive psychology and the life well-lived* (pp. 55–79). Washington, DC: American Psychological Association.

Peterson, C., & Steen, T. A. (2002). Optimistic explanatory style. In C. R. Snyder & S. J. Lopez (Eds.), *Handbook of positive psychology* (pp. 244–256). New York: Oxford University Press.

Piliavin, J. (2003). Doing well by doing good: Benefits for the benefactor. In C. L. M. Keyes & J. Haidt (Eds.), *Flourishing: Positive psychology and the life well-lived* (pp. 227–247). Washington, DC: American Psychological Association.

Pittman, K. (1995, March/April). Changing the odds. *Youth Today, 4*(2), 46.

Prilleltensky, I. (1994). *The morals and politics of psychology: Psychological discourse and the status quo.* Albany: State University of New York Press.

Prilleltensky, I. (1997). Values, assumptions, and practices: Assessing the moral implications of psychological discourse and action. *American Psychologist, 52*(5), 517–535.

Prilleltensky, I. (2000). Value-based leadership in organizations. *Ethics and Behavior, 10*(2), 139–158.

Prilleltensky, I. (2003, December 17). States, including Tennessee, don't do enough to prevent abuse. *Tennessean.* Retrieved January 23, 2005, from http://tennessean.com/opinion/nashville-eye/archives/04/01/4421306.shtml?Element_ID =4421306.

Prilleltensky, I. (in press). The role of power in wellness, oppression, and liberation: The promise of psychopolitical validity. *Journal of Community Psychology.*

Prilleltensky, I., & Fox, D. (in press). Psychopolitical literacy for wellness and justice. *Journal of Community Psychology.*

Prilleltensky, I., & Gonick, L. (1996). Politics change, oppression remains: On the psychology and politics of oppression. *Political Psychology, 17,* 127–147.

Prilleltensky, I., Martell, E., Valenzuela, E., & Hernandez, P. (2001). A value-based approach to smoking prevention with immigrants from Latin America: Philosophy and program description. *Revista de Psicologia, 102,* 81–100.

Prilleltensky, I., & Nelson, G. (2002). *Doing psychology critically: Making a difference in diverse settings.* New York: Palgrave.

Prilleltensky, I., Nelson, G., & Peirson, L. (Eds.). (2001). *Promoting family wellness and preventing child maltreatment: Fundamentals for thinking and action.* Toronto, Ontario, Canada: University of Toronto Press.

Prilleltensky, I., Nelson, G., & Sanchez, L. A. (2000). Value-based smoking prevention program with Latin American Youth: Program evaluation. *Journal of Ethnic and Cultural Diversity in Social Work, 9*(1/2), 97–117.

Prilleltensky, I., Walsh-Bowers, R., & Rossiter, A. (1999). Clinicians' lived experience of ethics: Values and challenges in helping children. *Journal of Educational and Psychological Consultation, 10*(4), 315–342.

Prilleltensky, O. (2004). *Motherhood and disability: Children and choices.* New York: Palgrave Macmillan.

Prochaska, J., & Norcross, J. C. (1998). *Systems of psychotherapy: A transtheoretical analysis* (4th ed.). Pacific Grove, CA: Brooks/Cole.

Prochaska, J., Norcross, J., & DiClemente, C. (1994). *Changing for good.* New York: Avon Books.

Putnam, R. (2000). *Bowling alone: The collapse and revival of American community.* New York: Simon & Schuster.

Putnam, R. (2001). Social capital: Measurement and consequences. *Isuma: Canadian Journal of Policy Research, 2,* 41–51.

Putnam, R., & Feldstein, L. (2003). *Better together: Restoring the American Community.* New York: Simon & Schuster.

Racino, J. A. (1991). Organizations in community living: Supporting people with disabilities. *Journal of Mental Health Administration, 18,* 51–59.

Ralston Saul, J. (2001). *On equilibrium.* New York: Penguin.

Rawls, J. (1972). *A theory of justice.* New York: Oxford University Press.

Razavi, S. (1999). Seeing poverty through a gender lens. *International Social Science Journal, 51,* 473–482.

Reinhardt, U. E., Hussey, P. S., & Anderson, G. F. (2004). U.S. health care spending in an international context. *Health Affairs, 23,* 10–25.

Reis, H., & Rusbult, C. (Eds.). (2004). *Close relationships.* New York: Psychology Press.

Reissman, F. (1965). The "helper-therapy" principle. *Social Work, 10,* 27–32.

Richardson, J., Sheldon, D., Krailo, M., & Levine, A. (1990). The effect of compliance with treatment on survival among patients with hematologic malignancies. *Journal of Clinical Oncology, 18,* 356–364.

Robertson, A., Brunner, E., & Sheiham, A. (1999). Food is a political issue. In M. Marmot & R. Wilkinson (Eds.), *Social determinants of health* (pp. 179–210). New York: Oxford University Press.

Robertson, N., & Masters-Awatere, B. (in press). Community psychology in Aotearoa, New Zealand: Me tiro whakamuri a kia hangai whakamua. In S. Reich, M. Riemer, I. Prilleltensky, & M. Montero (Eds.), *The history and theories of community psychology: International perspectives.* New York: Kluwer Press.

Rogers, C. (1961). *On becoming a person: A therapist's view of psychotherapy.* Boston: Houghton Mifflin.

Romanow, R. (2002). *Building on values: The future of health care in Canada.* Ottawa, Ontario, Canada: Commission on the Future of Health Care in Canada.

Rossiter, A., Prilleltensky, I., & Walsh-Bowers, R. (2000). Postmodern professional ethics. In A. Rossiter, B. Fawcett, B. Featherstone, & J. Fook (Eds.), *Postmodern and feminist perspectives in social work practice* (pp. 83–103). London: Routledge.

Ryff, C. D., & Singer, B. (2003). Flourishing under fire: Resilience as a prototype of challenged thriving. In C. L. M. Keyes & J. Haidt (Eds.), *Flourishing: Positive psychology and the life well-lived* (pp. 15–36). Washington, DC: American Psychological Association.

Sachs, J. (2005, July 26). The best countries in the world. *Newsweek* (International ed.). Retrieved August 31, 2005, from http://www.msnbc.msn.com/id /5456853/site/newsweek.

Saelens, B., Sallis, J., & Frank, L. (2003). Environmental correlates of walking and cycling: Findings from the transportation, urban design, and planning literatures. *Annals of Behavioral Medicine, 25*(2), 80–91.

Sallins, J., Frank, L., Saelens, B., & Kraft, M. (2004). Active transportation and physical activity: Opportunities for collaboration on transportation and public health research. *Transportation Research Part A, 38,* 249–268.

Schein, E. H. (1992). *Organizational culture and leadership.* San Francisco: Jossey-Bass.

Schulman, M. (2002). How we become moral: The sources of moral motivation. In C. Snyder & S. Lopez (Eds.), *Handbook of positive psychology* (pp. 499–512). New York: Oxford University Press.

Schwartz, B. (2004). *The paradox of choice: Why more is less.* New York: Ecco Press.

Schwartz, S. H. (1994). Are there universal aspects in the structure and contents of human values? *Journal of Social Issues, 50*(4), 19–46.

Schwarz, N., & Strack, F. (1999). Reports of subjective well-being: Judgmental processes and their methodological implications. In D. Kahneman, E. Diener, & N. Schwarz (Eds.), *Well-being: The foundations of hedonic psychology* (pp. 61–84). New York: Russell Sage Foundation.

Seligman, M. E. P. (2002). *Authentic happiness.* New York: Free Press.

Sen, A. (1999a). *Beyond the crisis: Development strategies in Asia.* Singapore, Southeast Asia: Institute of Southeast Asian Studies.

Sen, A. (1999b). *Development as freedom.* New York: Anchor Books.

Sen, A. (2001, December). *Culture and development.* Paper presented at the meeting of the World Bank Tokyo. Retrieved June 10, 2002, from www.worldbank .org/wbi/B-SPAN/sen_tokyo.pdf.

Senge, P. (1990). *The fifth discipline: The art and the practice of the learning organization.* New York: Doubleday.

Senge, P., Ross, R., Smith, B., Roberts, C., & Kleiner, A. (1994). *The fifth discipline fieldbook.* New York: Doubleday.

Senge, P., Scharmer, C. O., Jaworski, J., & Flowers, B. S. (2004). *Presence: Human purpose and the field of the future.* Cambridge, MA: Society for Organizational Learning.

Shafritz, J., Ott, J., & Jang, Y. S. (Eds.). (2005). *Classics of organization theory* (6th ed.). Belmont, CA: Thomson Wadsworth.

Shakespeare, T. (1996). Power and prejudice: Issues of gender, sexuality, and disability. In L. Barton (Ed.), *Disability and society: Emerging issues and insights* (pp. 191–214). New York: Longman.

Shaw, M., Dorling, D., & Smith, G. D. (1999). Poverty, social exclusion, and minorities. In M. Marmot & R. Wilkinson (Eds.), *Social determinants of health* (pp. 211–239). New York: Oxford University Press.

Shinn, M., & Toohey, S. M. (2003). Community contexts of human welfare. *Annual Review of Psychology, 54,* 427–459.

Shonkoff, J., & Phillips, D. (Eds.). (2000). *From neurons to neighborhoods: The science of early childhood development.* Washington, DC: National Academy Press.

Sidgwick, H. (1922). *The methods of ethics* (7th ed.). London: Macmillan.

Singer, P. (1993). *Practical ethics* (2nd ed.). New York: Cambridge University Press.

Smedley, B. D., & Syme, S. L. (Eds.). (2000). *Promoting health: Intervention strategies from social and behavioral research.* Washington, DC: National Academy Press.

Smith, S. (2005). *Ending global poverty: A guide to what works.* New York: Palgrave Macmillan.

Snyder, C., & Lopez, S. (Eds.). (2002). *Handbook of positive psychology.* New York: Oxford University Press.

Speer, P., & Hughey, J. (1995). Community organizing: An ecological route to empowerment and power. *American Journal of Community Psychology, 23,* 729–748.

Speer, P., Hughey, J., Gensheimer, L., & Adams-Leavitt, W. (1995). Organizing for power: A comparative case study. *Journal of Community Psychology, 23,* 57–73.

Spiegel, D., Bloom, J. R., & Kraemer, H. C. (1989). Effect of psychosocial treatment on survival of patients with metastatic breast cancer. *Lancet, 2,* 888–891.

Sternberg, R. (2004). A triangular theory of love. In H. Reis & C. Rusbult (Eds.), *Close relationships* (pp. 213–227). New York: Psychology Press.

Stokols, D. (2000). The social ecological paradigm of wellness promotion. In M. Jamner & D. Stokols (Eds.), *Promoting human wellness* (pp. 21–37). Los Angeles: University of California Press.

Stout, L. (1996). *Bridging the class divide and other lessons for grassroots organizing.* Boston: Beacon Press.

Subramanian, S., Belli, P., & Kawachi, I. (2002). The macroeconomic determinants of health. *Annual Review of Public Health, 23,* 287–302.

Summers, J. (1989). *Soho: A history of London's most colorful neighborhood.* London: Bloomsbury.

Syme, S. L. (1996). To prevent disease: The need for a new approach. In D. Blaine, E. Brunner, & R. G. Wilkinson (Eds.), *Health and social organization* (pp. 21–31). London: Routledge.

Tarrow, S. (1998). *Power in movement: Social movements and contentions politics.* New York: Cambridge University Press.

Taylor, C. (1992). *Multiculturalism and "the politics of recognition."* Princeton, NJ: Princeton University Press.

Thomas, A., & Chess, S. (1977). *Temperament and development.* New York: Brunner/Mazel.

Todd, J., & Bohart, A. C. (1999). *Foundations of clinical and counseling psychology* (3rd ed.). New York: Longman.

Tomison, A. (1997). *Overcoming structural barriers to the prevention of child abuse and neglect: A discussion paper.* Sydney, Australia: New South Wales Child Protection Council.

Totikidis, V., & Prilleltensky, I. (2006). Engaging community in a cycle of praxis: Multicultural perspectives on personal, relational, and collective wellness. *Community, Work, and Family, 9,* 47–67.

Tushman, M., & O'Reilly, C. (2002). *Winning through innovation: A practical guide to leading organizational change and renewal.* Boston: Harvard Business School.

Ungar, M. (Ed.). (2005). *Handbook for working with children and youth: Pathways to resilience across cultures and contexts*. London: Sage.

UNICEF Innocenti Research Centre. (2000, June). *A league table of child poverty in rich nations: Report card No. 1*. Florence, Italy: Author.

UNICEF. (2001). *The state of the world's children 2002*. New York: Author.

U.S. Department of Health and Human Services. (2003). *Child maltreatment 2003*. Retrieved February 22, 2006, from http://www.acf.hhs.gov/programs/cb/pubs/cm03/chaptertwo.htm.

VandeHei, J., & Baker, P. (2005, September 2), Critics say Bush undercut New Orleans flood control. *Washington Post*. Retrieved September 9, 2005, from http://www.washingtonpost.com/wp-dyn/content/article/2005/09/01/AR2005090102261.html.

Waldegrave, C., Tamasese, K., Tuhaka, F., & Campbell, W. (2003). *Just therapy: A journey—A collection of papers from the Just Therapy Team, New Zealand*. Adelaide, Australia: Dulwich Centre.

Warr, P. (1999). Well-being in the workplace. In D. Kahneman, E. Diener, & N. Schwarz (Eds.), *Well-being: The foundations of hedonic psychology* (pp. 392–411). New York: Russell Sage Foundation.

Watkins, K., & Marsick, V. J. (1993). *Sculpting the learning organization*. San Francisco: Jossey-Bass.

Watzlawick, P., Weakland, J. H., & Fisch, R. (1974). *Change: Principles of problem formation and problem resolution*. New York: Norton.

Weisbrot, M. (1999). *Globalization: A primer*. Washington, DC: Center for Economic and Policy Research. Retrieved September 11, 2005, from http://www.cepr.net/publications/global_primer.htm.

Weisinger, H. (1998). *Emotional intelligence at work*. San Francisco: Jossey-Bass.

West, C. (1983). Ask me no questions: An analysis of queries and replies in physician-patient dialogues. In S. Fisher & A. Todd (Eds.), *The social organization of doctor-patient communication* (pp. 75–106). Norwood, NJ: Ablex.

Wilkinson, R. G. (1996). *Unhealthy societies: The afflictions of inequality*. London: Routledge.

Wilkinson, R. G. (2005). *The impact of inequality: How to make sick societies healthier*. New York: New Press.

Wilkinson, R. G., & Marmot, M. (Eds.). (2003). *Social determinants of health: The solid facts*. Copenhagen, Denmark: World Health Organization.

Wineman, S. (1984). *The politics of human services*. Montreal, Quebec, Canada: Black Rose Books.

Wissner, S. (2005, August 7). Not everyone critical of cuts to TennCare. *Tennessean*, p. A1–A2.

Wolfe, A. (1998). *One nation, after all*. New York: Viking.

Wright, R., & Cummins, N. (Eds.). (2005). *Destructive trends in mental health: The well-intentioned path to harm*. New York: Routledge.

Wrzesniewski, A., Rozin, P., & Bennett, D. (2003). Working, playing, and eating: Making the most of most moments. In C. L. M. Keyes & J. Haidt (Eds.), *Flourishing: Positive psychology and the life well-lived* (pp. 184–204). Washington, DC: American Psychological Association.

Author Index

Subject Index